HISTORICAL ENGLISH

AND

DERIVATION

HISTORICAL ENGLISH

AND

DERIVATION

BY

J. C. NESFIELD

GYAN

Published by

Gyan Publishing House
5, Ansari Road
Daryaganj, New Delhi-110002
Phone: 011-47034999, 9811692060
E-mail: books@gyanbooks.com

Distribution Network
gyanbooks.com
India, USA, Canada, UK, Australia

ISBN: 978-93-6208-189-6 (HB)
First Published, 1898

2nd Impression 2024

Printed at: Gyan Press, Delhi.

HISTORICAL ENGLISH AND DERIVATION
Author: J. C. NESFIELD

HISTORICAL ENGLISH

AND

DERIVATION

BY

J. C. NESFIELD, M.A.

LATE DIRECTOR OF PUBLIC INSTRUCTION, NORTH-WESTERN PROVINCES
AND OUDH, INDIA
AUTHOR OF 'ENGLISH GRAMMAR, PAST AND PRESENT'

MACMILLAN & CO., LIMITED
ST. MARTIN'S STREET, LONDON
NEW YORK: THE MACMILLAN COMPANY
1898

CONTENTS

CHAPTER I.—HISTORICAL OUTLINE.

SECTION 1.—ENGLISH AND COGNATE LANGUAGES.

1. Languages first spoken in Britain.—The English language was not native to Britain. It was preceded by Celtic, and to some extent by Latin, before the occupation of the island by English settlers from the Continent.

Celtic.—The language spoken by the ancient Britons was a form of Celtic, similar to what was spoken by kindred tribes in Wales and Cornwall. The English, when they came, paid no attention to this Celtic speech, though they picked up a few words accidentally; but after their conversion to Christianity they adopted the same forms of the Roman letters as those used by the conquered Britons.

Latin.—So long as Britain was a Roman province, Latin was the language of the camps and of the ruling class, and during the last two centuries of the Roman occupation it was the language of the Church also. In the neighbourhood of the forts and monasteries, wherever Roman influence was dominant, a popular form of Latin was already springing up. Had it been left to run its course, it would in time have overspread the island, as it did Gaul and Spain and other continental provinces of the Roman empire. But three events occurred, that rendered this impossible and gave an exceptional character to the future language of Britain: (1) in A.D. 409 the Romans withdrew every garrison from the island and never again returned to it; (2) the heathen Picts and Scots from North Britain overran the provinces which the Romans had left, and destroyed every trace of Roman culture that came in their way; (3) forty years later a new race of heathen, still more formidable, poured into

Britain by way of the North Sea and the Channel, in a series of invasions that spread over at least 100 years, and made their own language the current speech of the best part of the island.

2. Introduction of English.—The new language thus violently thrust into Britain was English, a member of the **Teutonic** group of languages, very different from those that preceded it, and yet, as will be presently shown, remotely cognate.

The invaders came from the low-lying lands about the estuaries and lower courses of the Rhine, the Weser, and the Elbe, and some way up the western coast of Denmark. From the year 449, and for about 100 years in succession, they poured into the island in large flat-bottomed boats, many of which were driven with fifty oars at least, and were capacious enough to carry women and children besides the rowers. A tribe called Angles settled in the country north of the Humber, and as far north as the Highlands of Scotland; Frisians for the most part in the country between the Humber and the Thames; and Saxons in the country south of the Thames. The only territory that remained to the Celtic-speaking natives was the Scotch Highlands, Strathclyde (the land south of the Firth of Clyde), Cumbria or Cumberland (the land of the Cymry or Welsh), Wales proper, and Cornwall.

3. The Aryan family of Languages.—Thus far we have referred to three separate classes of language,—the Celtic, the Latin, and the Teutonic. These, though quite distinct, are found on closer inspection to possess certain points in common sufficiently marked to show that they belong, with others still to be named, to one large family called the Aryan,[1] which is subdivided as follows:—

A. *The Asiatic or East-Aryan Group.*

(*a*) **Sanskrit**, and the neo-Sanskrit languages of India, such as Bengali, Hindi, Punjábi, etc.
(*b*) **Zend**, or old Persian; modern Persian.
(*c*) **Armenian**, ancient and modern.

B. *The European or West-Aryan Group.*

(*d*) **Greek**, ancient and modern.
(*e*) **Romanic**, including Latin and the neo-Latin languages,—Italian,

---

[1] Other, but less suitable, names are Indo-European and Indo-Germanic. *Indo-* is too narrow for A, the Asiatic group; and *Germanic* is too narrow for B, the European. "Indo-Germanic," however, has now become the most usual name through the influence of German scholars.

French, Provençal, Spanish, Portuguese; Romansch of the Engadine, and Roumanian of Eastern Europe.

(*f*) **Lettic**: Old Prussian (dead); Lithuanian, still spoken in Eastern Prussia; and Livonian.

(*g*) **Slavonic**: Old Russian; modern Russian; Polish; Bohemian; Bulgarian; Servian.

(*h*) **Celtic**: Welsh or Cymric; Cornish (dead, but not extinct); Gaelic (Highland Scotch); Erse or Irish; Manx (in the Isle of Man); Breton (of Brittany in France).

(*i*) **Teutonic**:[1] Low German (including English); High German.

Note 1.—There are two points of distinction between Teutonic and the other Aryan languages: (1) the Teutonic languages have shifted certain consonantal sounds of the Dental, Labial, and Guttural series in the manner described in § 269, and no other Aryan language has done the same. (2) No Aryan language except the Teutonic has formed a Past tense by a dental suffix, *d* or *t* (the Weak conjugation).[2]

Note 2.—From the above sketch the student can see what languages are spoken in the British Isles at the present day, viz. English in the whole of England itself, and (in its Scotch dialectal form) in the lower half of Scotland; Cymric or Welsh in Wales; Gaelic in the Highlands of Scotland; Erse in some parts of Ireland; and Manx in the Isle of Man. The four last named are all Celtic.

Note 3.—**Cognate, Derived.**—The student can also understand from the above sketch the difference between cognate words and derived words. Words are *cognate* to one another when they have some root that is found in other languages of the same family: thus we have Gothic *fadar* (father), Anglo-Sax. *fæder*, Icelandic *fathir*, Dutch *vader*, Swed. *fader*, Germ. *vater*. All these are cognate within the Teutonic family. Looking to a still wider group, the Aryan, we find *pater* in Latin, *pater* in Greek, *pidar* in Persian, and *pitar* in Sanskrit. These, therefore, are all cognate words with the Teutonic ones. At the bottom of all of them we find a common root *pa*, to feed or protect, and a common suffix *-ter*, which denotes agent. They are all collateral, co-equal, co-radical, or cognate. We cannot say that any one is *derived* from any other.

Derived words are on an entirely different footing, and are of two main varieties. (*a*) Those derived from some internal source, as *tell* from *tale* by vowel-mutation, § 77; *timely* from A.S. *tima* (time), to which the A.S. suffix *-lic* (ly) has been added. (*b*) Those derived from some external or foreign source, as *manual*, from Lat. *manu-s* (hand), to which the Latin suffix *-alis* (al) has been added.

---

[1] The name *Teutonic* is borrowed from Lat. *Teutonicus*. A tribe which the Romans called *Teutoni* invaded Italy in ancient times. The Modern German name is *Deutsch*, which we have Anglicised to *Dutch*. In North America immigrants from any part of Germany are still called *Dutchmen*.

[2] But the *past participial* suffix *-d*, as in "love-*d*," is identical with that of Lat. "ama-*tus*," and is found in many other Aryan languages. This Aryan suffix is called *-to* in Skeat's *Princ. Eng. Etym.* series i. § 253, ed. 1892. It has no connection with the Teutonic suffix *-d* (A.S. *-de*), with which the Past tenses of Weak verbs are formed.

4. The Teutonic Languages classified.—These are classified under two main headings,—the Low German and the High German.

A. *Low German.*

I. **Gothic** or **South-eastern**: the oldest of the extant Teutonic languages, and the most perfect in its inflexional forms: the language or dialect once spoken by the Goths on the lower Danube. The chief work extant in Gothic is a translation of parts of the Bible made in A.D. 350, while the Roman Empire still existed, by Wulfila (better known as Ulphilas), bishop and missionary of the Goths.

II. **Scandian** or **North-eastern**: represented (1) on the *Continent* by the languages of Denmark, Norway, and Sweden, the native homes of the Norse; (2) in *Britain* by the Anglian or *early* Scandian dialect imported by the Angles, who, in the fifth century A.D., colonised the country north of the Humber up to the Highlands of Scotland; (3) in *Britain* again by the Danish or *later* Scandian imported by the Danes, who in the ninth and tenth centuries overspread Northumbria, besides settling in many parts of the eastern side of England to the south of the Humber; (4) in *Iceland*, where the earliest forms of Scandian have been better preserved than elsewhere through the secure and isolated position of that remote island.

III. **Frisio-Saxon** or **Western**: covering the area now known as Holland and Belgium, situated along the lower courses and estuaries of the Elbe, the Weser, and the Rhine.

(*a*) *Saxon:* represented (1) on the *Continent* by Old Saxon, preserved in the "Heliand" (Healer or Saviour), a poem of the ninth century; (2) in *Britain*, by the Wessex dialect, generally known as Anglo-Saxon, that is, the Saxon dialect of the South of England as distinct from the Saxon of the Continent: it has an older and much more abundant literature than its continental sister.

(*b*) *Friesic:* represented (1) on the *Continent* by Old Friesic, of which nothing is now extant earlier than the thirteenth century, though the forms of the language even at this late date are often very archaic; (2) in *Britain* (as has been inferred), by the Old Mercian dialect (so-called from the kingdom of Mercia), spoken between the Humber and the Thames, of which a few much earlier specimens are extant. Of all the languages of the Continent modern Frisian is most like modern English.

(*c*) *Dutch:* the language of Holland; and closely allied to it, the *Flemish* of Flanders and the dialect of Bremen. These are not represented by any dialect in Great Britain, but are near akin to Saxon and Friesic.

Note.—Another Low German dialect is the Pomeranian, spoken along the southern coast of the Baltic. Even Old Lombardic was Low German, and in its oldest form very like Anglo-Saxon.

B. *High German.*

German.—High German as distinct from Low German is represented solely by what is known as "German,"—the language of Luther, and the official and literary language of the German Empire. It is called High, because it first appeared in the interior and higher parts of Germany. In many districts of Germany, where High German has become the language of the educated classes, Low German is still spoken by the masses. On the difference between Low German and High, see *Note* 1 to § 5.

5. Low German origin of English.—*All* the conquerors of Britain, including (*a*) the Angles, Frisians, and Saxons of the first invasions, (*b*) the Danes and Norse of the later invasions (*c*) the Danes or Normans of the last invasion, were of the Low German stock. Not one of them ever spoke High German. All except the last helped to form the Teutonic portion of the English tongue. The last would have done the same; but it happened that before coming to England they had lived for five or six generations on the north-west coast of France, where they forgot their mother tongue, and became French in speech, though not in blood: hence they contributed very largely towards the Romanic element, which is now numerically greater than the Teutonic, though the words are in less frequent use.

Low German is much more ancient than High. High German was Low German once, and did not begin to exist as a separate branch of the Teutonic languages till after the beginning of the eighth century. But on the Continent of Europe it has now become the more important of the two, and has for several centuries been gaining on its northern rival.

If Low German has lost ground on the Continent of Europe, it has been more than compensated by the great importance of English and its extension to new countries and continents,—America, Australia, India, and South Africa.

Note 1.—The shifting of consonants from the Low German to the High is dealt with in § 269, under the heading of **Grimm's Law**. It is there shown that Low German,—the class to which English belongs,—holds an intermediate place between the Aryan or Classical languages (Sanskrit, Latin, Greek, etc.) on the one side, and High German, its modern offshoot, on the other. The notion (not unfrequently expressed) that English is derived from German is putting the cart before the horse, and is in direct opposition to Grimm's Law. We have borrowed only about twenty-four words from German, and of these less than a quarter are in common use: the most common are ***swindler***, ***plunder***, ***meerschaum***, ***poodle***, ***waltz***.

Note 2.—From what has been said in § 4, English is a *mixed* Low German language, mainly based on the Frisian, Mercian, or Midland speech, but at the same time much indebted to the Scandian dialect of the North and the Saxon dialect of the South.

6. Origin of the names "English" and "England."—It was among the Angles of Northumbria, especially in York, its capital, that a high standard of literary culture first sprang up in Great Britain; for though Kent became Christian a little earlier and started schools of its own, the small size of the kingdom, and its disastrous wars with Mercia and Wessex, appear to have checked its intellectual growth.

In York, as elsewhere, Latin, or *Læden*, as the Angles called it, was the language of the learned. But books began to be written in the vernacular also; and this vernacular was called *Ænglisc* (or English),—that is, the language of the Angles. Our first poet, Cædmon, the cowherd of Whitby, wrote his poems in *Ænglisc;* and before his death the Venerable Bede translated the Gospel of St. John into the same language.

From the example thus set "English" came to be a general name for all the Teutonic dialects of Britain as distinct from Latin. Even the Wessex or Saxon dialect, in spite of its marked differences from the Anglian and the reputation it received from the hands of Alfred the Great, was often called *Ænglisc* by Alfred himself.

In political as well as literary pre-eminence the Anglian kingdom of Northumbria was the first to come to the front. The first Bretwalda was an Anglian king. Hence the island as a whole was called Ængla-land or England, and the people English.

7. Periods in the Growth of English.—The name "English," taken in its widest sense, denotes the language used by the English people from their first settlement in Britain up to the present time, in whatever parts of the world they may have settled since. It has been growing for the last 1400 years, and is now so unlike its earliest forms, that most persons would probably find it harder to learn Anglo-Saxon than to learn French. Yet we must call Anglo-Saxon a form of English, unless we are prepared to deny the name of Englishman to Alfred the Great; for that was the language that he wrote and spoke. Moreover, there are many words that have never altered their form within the historical period, such as *corn*, *lamb*, *nest*, *ram*, *wind*, *hand*, *spell*, *under*, *his*, *him*, *word*, *in*, *bill* (axe), *twist*, *bed*, *gold*, *can*, *blind*, *storm*, *is*, which were so spelt in the seventh century.

The growth of English has been subdivided into three main periods, to each of which approximate dates have been assigned,[1]

[1] Sweet's *Short Historical English Grammar*, p. 1, ed. 1892.

—approximate, because changes in language cannot be other than gradual and continuous :—

I. Old English ; from A.D. 450 to about 1200.
II. Middle English ; from A.D. 1200 to about 1500.
III. Modern English ; from A.D. 1500 to the present time.

Old Eng. has been called the period of *full* endings, Mid. Eng. of *levelled* endings, and Mod. Eng. of *lost* endings.

OLD.	leorn-*ian*,	món-*a*,	sun-*ne*,	sun-*u*,	stán-*as*.
MID.	lern-*en*,	mon-*e*,	sun-*ne*,	sun-*e*,	ston-*es*.
MOD.	learn,	moon,	sun,	son,	stones.

By *levelled* endings is meant that the vowels *a*, *o*, *u* are all changed or levelled to *e*. By *lost* endings is meant that only a very few of them have remained, and these few have mostly become non-syllabic. Thus *stán-as* (two syllables) has become *stones* (one syllable), and *luf-o-de* or *luf-o-den* (three syllables) has become *loved* (one syllable). In *stones* the *e* is written, not so much for the preservation of the vowel in the levelled suffix *-es*, as because the retention of the *e* was found convenient for giving length to the vowel going before.

SECTION 2.—OLD ENGLISH.

8. Dialects of Old English.—The name "Old English" is simply a general name for the three main dialects which came into literary use in our island, and of which the extant specimens are sufficient to show their respective characteristics.

(1) The **Northumbrian** dialect, spoken north of the Humber, and imported by *Anglian* tribes, who came from what is now called the Duchy of Schleswig ; it was afterwards reinforced, but modified, by the language of the *Danes*, a fresh batch of invaders of the same stock as the Angles, viz. Scandinavian. Most of its early literature is lost.

Note.—One of the marked peculiarities of this dialect is the retention of its original gutturals. Thus Northerners to this day say *kirk, brig, rig,* while Midlanders and Southerners say *church, bridge, ridge ;* and the lower classes in Northumberland and Scotland never drop the letter *h* at the beginning of a word. This letter, however, is dropped in Lancashire and Yorkshire, where the Northern dialect has been less perfectly preserved.

(2) The **Mercian** dialect, probably to a large extent of *Frisian* origin, spoken between the Humber and the Thames. On the Continent the Frisians were overlapped by Saxons on the west

and by Angles on the north and east; in England they were overlapped by Angles on the north and by Saxons on the south. This dialect in its most ancient form was more akin to Saxon than to Anglian, though there may have been from the first some northern elements as well as southern in this somewhat mixed dialect. Mercian is the great ancestor of modern standard English, and to this extent is of more importance than either of the other two. Unfortunately, however, most of its early literature is lost.[1]

(3) The **Wessex** dialect, spoken south of the Thames, and imported by *Saxon* tribes, who crossed the Channel from the lower courses of the Rhine and Weser. This was the mother-tongue of Alfred the Great; and an abundant literature has survived. In the *Old* period of English, but not in the Middle, this dialect holds the most prominent place. It had ceased to be used for literary purposes before the Modern period commenced.

Note.—There was a fourth dialect of less importance,—the Kentish, very similar to the Wessex dialect,—that is, of a distinctly Southern character,[2] neither Mercian nor Northumbrian.

9. **Frisian Origin of Mercian.**—This point does not rest upon the direct testimony of ancient records, but partly upon the evidence of language, and partly upon the general probabilities of the case.

(*a*) Procopius,[3] an historian of the sixth century A.D., says that in his time Britain was inhabited by three tribes,—Angles, Frisians, and Britons; so that he evidently included Saxons among Frisians. On the other hand, Bede (A.D. 673-735) says that Angles were sprung from Frisians. Frisians, then, were the intermediate tribe, and formed a large contingent of the first

---

[1] It was called *Mercian*, rather than Frisian, from the old kingdom of Mercia which the Frisians founded in England. The name "Mercia" gradually overspread a much larger area than that of the original kingdom. It was derived from the *marches* or borders by which this inland kingdom was surrounded on all sides.

[2] This point is enforced by the author of the article on "English Language" in *Encyclopædia Britannica*. According to Bede, who wrote in Latin, the kingdom of Kent was founded by a tribe called *Geātas*. These have been rashly identified with the Jutes of Jutland, a sub-tribe of Anglians. But the Kentish dialect was not at all Anglian in character. Hence we must suppose either that the identification is wrong, or, if right, that the Anglian dialect in Kent was afterwards so thickly overlaid with Saxon as to have been submerged and lost.

[3] *De Bello Gothico*, iv. 20.

invaders,[1] by whom the foundations of English were laid in this island.

(*b*) "In England, Mercia lies between the Anglian (north of the Humber) and the Saxon (south of the Thames). Abroad, Friesland lies between Scandinavia and Holland. It was only natural that in crossing the sea the Scandinavians (then known as Anglĕs) should make for the north of England, the Saxons (from the coast of Holland) should go southward, while groups of Frisians or East Saxons would make for Essex" (Skeat).[2]

(*c*) The Old Friesic of the Continent resembled the Mercian of England more nearly than it did either the Saxon or the Anglian, as is shown by the extant remains.[3] "At the present day," says another writer, "the most English dialects of the Continent are those of the North Frisian islands of Amrom and Sylt on the west coast of Schleswig."[4] This is corroborative testimony to the fact that the kingdom of Mercia was founded by Frisians, whose dialect (called Mercian after the name of their kingdom) was the forerunner of our Midland dialect, and through this of modern standard English. There is a well-known couplet, every word of which is said to be both Friesic (of the Continent) and English:—

Good butter and good cheese
Is good English and good Fries.

(*d*) Trevisa, a Cornishman who lived in A.D. 1387, says:—"Englishmen *from the beginning* had three manners of speech, Southern, Northern, and Middle speech, as they came of *three manners of people* of Germany."[5] The Southern speech, we know, came from Saxons; the Northern from Angles; the Midland, as we infer, came from Frisians. Evidently there was a long-standing tradition concerning some specific tribe, which gave to the Midland dialect "from the beginning" its specific characteristics of speech. It is certain that by the founders of the "*Middle* speech" he could not have meant the Geātas of Bede, who lived in *Kent*, and whose speech like his own was *Southern*.

---

[1] Freeman, in *Old English History*, pp. 37-39, admits his inability to say how the kingdom of Mercia was founded. To say, as he does, that it was "probably" founded by Angles is mere guessing, and opposed to the testimony of language.

[2] Letter to the Academy, of 14th March 1896.

[3] Examples are given in the Letter to the Academy by Professor Skeat.

[4] *Ency. Brit.*: article on "English Language."

[5] Quoted from Trevisa's *Polychronicon*, in Skeat's *Princ. Eng. Etym.* series i. p. 31, ed. 1892.

Note.—Some basis for the fact alleged by Trevisa, that "the Middle" or Mercian speech was founded by a distinct "manner of people from the beginning," may be found in the letter that Canute, the Danish King of England (1016-1035), wrote to his subjects from Rome, in which he prescribes that "the *West Saxons*, the *Mercians*, and the *Danes* are all to keep their own customs."[1] Amongst Danes he evidently included their near kinsmen, the Angles, who with the Danes occupied East Anglia and Northumbria; by the West Saxons he evidently meant the Saxons who lived to the south of the Thames and founded the kingdom of Wessex; by the Mercians he must have meant a people who were *neither Saxons nor Anglo-Danes.* We can best fill up this gap by the hypothesis that they were Frisians, whose tribal name, however, was superseded by that of the great kingdom (Mercia) which they founded.

10. Anglo-Saxon not convertible with Old English.—Anglo-Saxon is merely another name for the Wessex dialect, and might conveniently be considered to mean *the Saxon of England* as distinct from *the Saxon of the Continent.*[2] The term is often used, however, as if it were convertible with Old English. But this is a mistake. The Wessex dialect is merely a third part of Old English, and not the whole of it. There are instances in which it fails to give any clue to the origin of modern English words. For example, the Mod. Eng. "*are*" is not derived from A.S. or Wessex "*sindon*," but from the Mercian "*arun*," which was itself borrowed from the Northumbrian dialect.

It is worth noticing, too, that the oldest extant specimen of English is in this Northumbrian dialect, and consists of some lines taken from the original Cædmon (see § 6), and preserved in a fly-leaf of the Cambridge MS. of Bede's *Church History.*

The Wessex or A.S. dialect owes its importance to three causes:—(1) The unification of England under Egbert and his successors, whose capital, Winchester, in the kingdom of Wessex, became the capital of England; (2) the influence and example of Alfred the Great, whose books were written in the Wessex dialect; (3) the preservation of a large part of the Wessex literature, while most of the Mercian and Northumbrian literature

---

[1] Freeman's *Old English History*, p. 244.

[2] The name, unless it is so interpreted, is unsuitable and misleading, because it would tend to confound the Anglian dialect with the Saxon. It was first applied to the Wessex dialect by scholars in the sixteenth century, who wished to revive the study of the language used by Alfred the Great. As Alfred the Great called himself *Anglo-Saxonum rex*,—that is, "king of the Angles and Saxons," they called his language *Anglo-Saxon* also; but no such name was ever given to it by Alfred himself or by any other ancient writer.

has been lost. For the earliest forms of most of our English words we have nothing but Anglo-Saxon to go to.

11. Periods of Anglo-Saxon.—The Anglo-Saxon literature has been so well preserved, that it is possible to subdivide it into periods:[1]—

	A.D. A.D.
Early A.S. (the language of Alfred) . .	700– 900
Late A.S. (the language of Ælfric) . . .	900–1100
Transitional period (the language of Layamon)[2]	1100–1200

Alfred the Great, born in 849, superintended the translation into Saxon of the *History of the World* by Orosius, the *Church History* by Bede, the *Consolations of Philosophy* by Boethius, and the *Pastorals* of St. Gregory (all written in Latin). He also superintended the compilation of the early portions of the *Old English Chronicle*.

Ælfric, abbot of Ensham, Oxon, wrote a collection of *Homilies*, the *Lives of the Saints*, and the *Colloquium*, or conversation in Latin with interlinear Saxon.[3] In the Late A.S. the inflexions were not so perfectly preserved as in the Early.

Layamon, a monk who lived near the Severn, wrote a very lengthy poem of some 56,000 lines, called *Brut*, on the kings of Britain, which was not completed till the year 1205 A.D.

12. Old and Modern English compared.—Old English is distinguished from Modern by two chief characteristics.

(*a*) It was in the main a *Synthetical* language,—that is, it had a large number of inflexions which Modern English has discarded. "Synthesis" (a word borrowed from Greek) means "adding on." A language is said to be in the Synthetical stage when it expresses the grammatical relations of words by adding some flexional suffix to the stems of Nouns, Adjectives, Pronouns, and Verbs. A language that discards such endings as much as possible, and in their place makes a freer use of prepositions and other auxiliary words, is said to be in the *Analytical* stage. This is the character of Modern English.

(*b*) It was in the main a *pure* language,—that is, it contained very few words that were not of Teutonic origin; whereas Mod. Eng. is extremely composite, much more than half its vocabulary being non-Teutonic. Layamon's *Brut*, though it was written a century and a half after the Norman Conquest, and contains some 56,000 lines, has scarcely 150 French words in it. The number of Latin words admitted before this date

---

[1] Sweet's *Short Historical English Grammar*, p. 1.

[2] Many call this Transitional period by the name of *Early English*, and connect the two preceding ones under the common name *Old English*.

[3] Earle's *Anglo-Saxon Literature*, pp. 217-222.

amounted to less than 200; and the number of Celtic borrowings did not come to 15.

To show the difference between Old and Modern English, we may compare Genesis ix. 1, as translated by Ælfric, who wrote late in the tenth century, with the authorised translation published in 1611:—

(1) God blets-*o-de* Noe and his sun-*a*, and cwæth hem tó:
(*God blessed Noah and his sons, and quoth them to:*
Weax-*ath* and bé-*oth* gemenigfil-*de* and á-fyll-*ath* th-*á*
Wax (ye) *and be* (ye) *manifolded and fill* (ye) *the*
eorth-*an*.
earth.)

(2) God bless-ed Noah and his son-s, and said unto them, Be fruitful and multiply, and replenish the earth.

Observe that in (1) every word (barring the Hebrew name *Noe*) is Teutonic; whereas in (2) there are two Romanic words, *multiply* and *replenish*, and one Hybrid or mixed word, *fruitful*. Observe also that in (1) the verbs, adjectives, and nouns have inflexions, which Modern English has discarded.

SECTION 3.—MIDDLE ENGLISH.

(*Approximate dates*, A.D. 1200-1500.)

13. **Character of Middle English.**—In its Middle period English went through three kinds of change:—

(*a*) The Mercian dialect, or Midland, as we should now call it, became eventually predominant in the place of the Wessex or Southern, which up to the Norman Conquest and for two centuries afterwards had held the first place.

(*b*) Many of the vowel sounds were changed; those of the old inflexions that were not lost were "levelled" (§ 7); the lost inflexions were replaced by a freer use of form-words,—prepositions and auxiliary verbs; many Strong verbs were replaced by Weak ones.

(*c*) A very great addition was made to the vocabulary. A large number of French words, which for about 200 years had been used only by the clergy and the upper classes and in the law courts, filtrated at last into the native speech, where much of it became permanently fixed as part of our English vocabulary. The absorption of all this French facilitated the introduction of fresh relays of Latin, which throughout the Middle Ages continued to be the language of the learned and of the Church.

14. **Dialects of Middle English.**—The three main dialects were the same as in the Old period; but instead of

calling them Northumbrian, Mercian, and Wessex (or Anglo-Saxon), it is now more appropriate to call them Northern, Midland, and Southern.

One good test for distinguishing the three dialects is the ending of the Present Plural Indicative. The Northern had *-es*, as sing-*es* (we, you, or they sing); the Southern had *-eth*, as sing-*eth* (we, you, or they sing); the Midland had *-en* or *-e*, as sing-*en* or sing-*e* (we, you, or they sing). Another flexional test lies in the form of the Pres. Part.; the Northern had *-and*, the Midland *-ende*, the Southern *-inde*, the last of which was eventually changed to *-ing*, and superseded the other two.

Another characteristic point of difference between the three dialects is that the Northern was the most tenacious of the old *sounds* and the Southern of the old *inflexions*. The Northern, for example, stuck, and still sticks, to the old guttural *k* or *g*, which in the Southern became *ch* or *j*, as in *church*, *bridge*, for the earlier *kirk*, *brig*. The Midland followed the South in discarding some of the earlier consonantal sounds, and the North in discarding the earlier inflexions.

15. Literary decline of the Southern Dialect.—The Southern dialect lost, through the Norman Conquest, though not till some time after, the political and literary supremacy that it had enjoyed under kings of its own race; and Winchester, the old capital of England, fell into the second rank. The last book of any importance written in the Southern dialect was Trevisa's translation of the *Polychronicon*, made in A.D. 1387 (alluded to in § 9).

As a *spoken* language the Southern dialect is not even now extinct among the peasantry. The rustic dialect that may still be heard in the south of England is the modernised descendant of King Alfred's "Wessex." A few years ago an attempt was made to revive it in the *Dorsetshire Poems* by William Barnes.

16. The Northern Dialect.—The Danish Conquest, which north of the Humber was more complete than anywhere to the south of it excepting in East Anglia, did much to unsettle the inflexions of this dialect, just as the Norman Conquest did those of the other two dialects later on. In and before the twelfth century the final *-n* of the Infinitive was dropping off; the *-eth* of the third person Singular was assuming its modern form *-es*; the final *-e* at the end of nouns (which was syllabic in the

Midland dialect) was becoming mute or disappearing. In fact, by the thirteenth century the Northern dialect had become almost as flexionless as Modern English.

A few more peculiarities of the Northern dialect may here be mentioned, in addition to those given in § 8 (1), *Note* :—

(1) It very rarely employed the suffix *-n* or *-en* for forming the Plurals of nouns, whereas in the Southern this was the commonest form of all. The Northern had only about four such Plurals—*eghen* (eyes), *hosen*, *oxen*, and *schoon* (shoes).

(2) On the other hand, it preserved with great care the final *-en* of the Past Part. of Strong verbs: thus *broke* for *broken*, though common in the Midland dialect, is hardly ever found in the Northern.

(3) It employed only the suffix *-s* (as in Modern English) for forming the Genitive Singular of nouns of any gender, whereas the Southern dialect kept up for a long time the use of the suffix *-e* for forming the Genitive of Feminine nouns.

(4) It formed the Pres. Part. in *-and*, while the Midland formed it in *-ende*, and the Southern in *-inde* (see § 14).

(5) It never used the prefix *ge* (softened down to *i* or *y* in the Middle English period) for forming the Past Participle of verbs, whereas the Southern dialect long continued to use it, as in *y-broke* or *y-broken*.

(6) The Northern dialect used the preposition *at* before the Gerundial Infinitive, while the Southern used *to*. Our noun *a-do* (=at do) is a relic of this.

On those peculiarities of the Northern dialect which have been traced to Danish influence, see § 18.

What is called the Lowland Scotch is the best living representative of the Northern dialect; and the poems of Burns, written not much more than 100 years ago, are its best literary specimen in modern times. The same dialect, but in a less marked form, is still spoken in the northern counties of England. Not many years since it was reproduced as a literary curiosity in Tennyson's "Northern Farmer"; and still more recently by Mary Beaumont in *Joan Seaton*, a story of Yorkshire dales, written in the North Riding dialect.

A line of Scotch poets, commencing with James I. (of Scotland), A.D. 1394-1437, and ending with Sir David Lyndsay, who died in A.D. 1555, was largely influenced by our great Midland poet, Chaucer (§ 17), from whom they borrowed not only their metres, but many peculiarities of phraseology and style, and even of grammar; see *Note* to § 28.

17. The Midland Dialect.—What is now the language of the British Empire is not the descendant of the language of Alfred the Great nor of that of Bede the Northumbrian, but of the Mercian or Midland dialect spoken between the Humber and the Thames. The predominance of this dialect was determined by several causes:—

(*a*) London, the city of ships floating on its broad river, was marked out by nature to be the capital of England. However cultivated Winchester or York might be, the literary life of the nation would eventually centre round the capital. "It is a curious reflection," says Professor Skeat, "that if London had been built on the south side of the river, the speech of the British Empire and of the greater part of North America would probably have been very different from what it is."[1] The Midland or London dialect was the language of the supreme law-courts and of the political and commercial activity of the nation. The last two chapters of the *Old English Chronicle*, which was commenced by King Alfred in his own (the Wessex) dialect, were written up to A.D. 1154 at Peterborough, within the Midland area, and in the Midland dialect. In this dialect was issued, in the reign of Henry III. (A.D. 1258), a proclamation for summoning a parliament from all the counties of England—the first occasion since the Conquest on which English was officially used in preference to French. This was the language in which Wycliff wrote his translation of the Bible, and in which Chaucer, himself a Londoner, raised English poetry to a height of excellence that has hardly been surpassed since. The Universities of Oxford and Cambridge lay within the Midland area. All dialects met in towns like Oxford, Cambridge, and London; and hence the Midland dialect has borrowed from both the others. Thus the phrase "they are" is of Northern origin; the phrase "he hath" is of Southern. The Midland adopted both.

(*b*) Apart from the advantages of its position and the great influence exercised by the writings of Chaucer and Wycliff, the

[1] *Princ. Eng. Etym.* series i. p. 29, ed. 1892. Opinions differ as to what was the dialect *first* spoken in London. Mr. Oliphant (see *Standard English*) thinks that it was originally a form of Saxon or Southern dialect; and that the East Midland dialect, after taking hold of Oxford and Cambridge, crept down to the south, conquering all the dialects on its way, and finally seized on London, where it absorbed and superseded the original Saxon. This opinion appears to be based on the hypothesis that London, being situated in Middle-*sex*, must have had at first a *Saxon* dialect. But it has been shown in § 9 that the *East Saxons* and *Middle Saxons* may have been a tribe of Frisians, speaking a Mercian or Midland dialect from the first.

Midland dialect possessed certain linguistic peculiarities sufficient to suggest the probability of its ultimate ascendancy. (1) It contained fewer Scandian or Danish words than the Northern, but more than the Southern. (2) Its grammar, though more complex than that of the Northern, was less complex than that of the Southern. (3) It received a much larger number of French words than the Northern; and no dialect that aimed at becoming the national standard for speaking and writing could dispense with French, which for more than 200 years had been the language of the court and the government. (4) Being the intermediate dialect, it was intelligible to Northerners and Southerners alike, when these were often not intelligible to each other. "The Mercians," says Trevisa, A.D. 1387, "who are men of the Middle of England, being as it were partners with the extremities, better understand the side-languages, Northern and Southern, than Northern and Southern understand each other."

(*c*) Near the close of the Middle period, the Mercian or Midland dialect was the only one patronised by the printing presses,—the new appliance which Caxton introduced into England in 1477. Henceforth any Englishman who thought he could write something worth reading wrote it in the Midland dialect, which had now become the literary language of the nation and was destined to become that of the empire.

Note 1.—The Midland dialect exhibited two sub-dialects, the Eastern and the Western. It is from the former rather than the latter that Mod. Eng. has chiefly sprung. The Eastern sub-dialect borrowed freely from the Northern Dialect spoken in East Anglia and eventually superseded it there, and its area included the important cities of Oxford, Cambridge, and London.

Note 2.—The stages of the Midland dialect have been roughly subdivided into three periods as follows:[1]—

	A.D.
Early: (Orm's *Ormulum*)	1200–1300
Late: (Robert of Brunne, Mandeville, Wycliff, Chaucer, who died in 1400) . . .	1300–1400
Transitional period: (Malory, Caxton) . .	1400–1500

Compare the three periods of Old English in § 11, and the three periods of English as a whole in § 7.

18. Danish Influence.—The Danes, as the student is aware (§ 4, II.), were of the same stock as the Angles,—Scandinavian, not Frisian or Saxon. But they settled in

[1] Sweet's *Short Historical English Grammar*, p. 1, ed. 1892. The influence of Caxton on Mod. Eng. has hardly been sufficiently recognised.

England about 500 years later than their Anglian kinsmen, and they came from a different part of Scandinavia,[1]—both of which facts would tend to account for some variation of dialect. Thus when Danes settled as they did in great force in East Anglia, and in still greater force north of the Humber, the Angles, in their intercourse with Danes, lost some of the inflexions of their own dialect. Since the stems of the words were the same on either side, the men of one tribe could make themselves better understood by those of the other if they dropped their inflexions than if they retained them. Thus out of the Anglian *sun-u* and the Danish *sun-r* the more simple word *son-e* (now pronounced as *sun*) was formed. The same kind of process is now going forward in the United States, where German immigrants, settled among English-speaking people, find it convenient to strip their German words of their inflexions, so as to adapt them more easily to English speech. This accounts for the early date at which the Northern dialect of English became almost flexionless; see § 16. After about 1250 A.D., the Midland dialect, which in its original Frisian or Mercian form was more like the Saxon spoken south of the Thames, borrowed more from the Northern than from the Southern. The Danish conquests of Mercia and East Anglia must have materially helped to assimilate the Midland to the Northern speech. The following are examples of Northern influence :—

Same.—In the Northern and Midland this took the place of the Southern *thilke*.

Are.—In the Northern and Midland this took the place of the Southern *sindon*.

They, their, them.—All these came from the Northern dialect, and were adopted by the Midland, in preference to *hi, heora, hem*, the old Plurals of *he*.

Till.—This Prep. is of Scandian origin, and was borrowed by the Midland dialect from the Northern.

Note.—The words *that, ours, yours*, and *she* have also been ascribed to Northern influence. But the first three are Anglo-Saxon,

---

[1] The first and earliest batch of Scandians, known in history as Angles, came from that part of the peninsula of Denmark that is nearest the Elbe.

The second batch, known in history as Danes, came from regions lying further north,—that is, from Jutland, the islands of Denmark, and South Sweden.

A third and last batch, less known in history, came from Norway, and colonised the Orkneys, the Western Islands, the Isle of Man, and parts of Lancashire, Cumberland, and Ireland.

and *scǽ* (the earliest form of *she*) is found in the later chapters of the *Saxon Chronicle*, written in Peterborough in the Midland dialect; see below §§ 121, 130, 131.

As to the effect of the Danish Conquest on our vocabulary, the two languages, the Scandian and the Saxon, were so much alike at bottom, that they melted imperceptibly into one:—

House is A.S., but *husband* is Scand.; *drop* (Trans.) is A.S., but *drip* (Intrans.) is Scand.; *shoot* is A.S., but *scud* and *scuttle* are Scand.; *blow* (with *blossom*) is A.S., but *bloom* is Scand.; *sit* is A.S., but *seat* is Scand.; *woe* is A.S., but *wail* is Scand.; *bite* is A.S., but *bait* (its Causal form) is Scand.; *ride* is A.S., but *raid* is Scand., and yet *road* (another noun-form) is A.S.; *true* is A.S., but *trust* and *tryst* are Scand., while *truth* (another noun-form) is A.S.; *weigh* is A.S., but *wag* is Scand., and yet *wain* is A.S.; *rise* is A.S., but *raise* (a Causal form) is Scand.; *knee* is A.S., but *kneel* is Scand.; *gird* and *girdle* are A.S., but *girth* is Scand.; *slay* is A.S., but *slaughter* is Scand.; *strike* (in the sense of "go") is A.S., but *streak* is Scand.; *gleam* is A.S., but *glimmer* is Scandian.

It sometimes happens that we get the *sound* of a word from Southern, and its *sense* from Northern. Thus "dream" is phonetically from A.S. *dréam* (Mid. Eng. *dreem*), which in A.S. did not signify "dream," but "joy," "happiness." But the Norse word *draumr* meant "dream" and nothing else.

19. The Norman Conquest.—The Norman Conquest, the greatest event in our political history, was likewise the greatest in the history of our language. For a long time the two languages, French and English, kept almost entirely apart, like a couple of rivers flowing side by side in parallel streams within the same banks. "The way in which the French-speaking Dane was so long kept apart, by the mere accident of language, from his English cousin, is one of the most curious facts in history" (Skeat). The English of A.D. 1200 is almost as free from French words as that of 1050.

It was not till after 1300 that French words began to be incorporated in large numbers. But by this time English had made itself the daily speech of the upper classes, as it always had been of the lower, while French was going more and more out of daily use. The incorporation was very complete. Such words as *grace*, *peace*, *fame*, *beef*, *ease* (all of French origin) appear now to be as much a part of our original language as *kindness*, *rest*, *shame*, *ox*, *care*, all of which are native words that were in common use in the time of Alfred the Great.

Though English had some sounds unknown to French and *vice versâ*, yet most of the vowels and consonants common to both were at that time pronounced in the same way; and this made the fusion of the two languages all the more easy and complete.

20. Struggle between French and English.—English, in spite of the degradation that it received from the Norman Conquest, never ceased to be used as a literary language. Books continued to be written in English as before, and the stream of literature never ran dry. In the Monastery of Peterborough the *Old English Chronicle* (commenced in about 879 under the direction of Alfred the Great) was written up by two successive hands to the death of Stephen in 1154. "Within two generations after the Conquest, faithful pens were at work transliterating the old *Homilies* of Ælfric into the neglected idiom of his posterity" (*Ency. Brit.*). The huge poem of 56,000 lines, known as Layamon's *Brut*, was not completed before the year 1205.

In 1204 the loss of Normandy, by separating England from France, broke the connection between the French and the Anglo-Norman aristocracies. In 1215 a combination of English and Norman barons forced King John to sign the Magna Charta. In 1258 English was officially used for the first time since the Conquest, in the celebrated proclamation issued in the name of Henry III. for summoning a parliament of *barons* from all parts of England; which shows that French had ceased to be the only language spoken and read by the Anglo-Norman nobles. In 1349, three years after the victory at Crecy, it was ruled that Latin should be no longer taught in England through the medium of French. In 1362 it was ruled that all pleadings in the law courts should be conducted in English, for the reason (as stated in the preamble to the Act), "that French has become much unknown in the realm." We may safely say that by the year 1400 French was not much spoken in England. A vast English literature had sprung up in the interim, which was as popular in the halls of nobles as in the humbler dwellings of knights and burgesses.

21. French Influence on English Grammar.—The only influence of French on English grammar was to accelerate the change from Synthetical to Analytical; in fact, it did for the Midland and Southern dialects what the Danish language had already done for the Northern. We say *accelerate* designedly; for the change would have come in any case, though possibly neither so rapidly nor so completely as it did, without the help of French. Symptoms of the change had shown themselves clearly enough before French influence had begun to work, and even to some extent before the Conquest. In Layamon's *Brut*, which shows no signs of French influence and contains *very few* words of French origin, the "levelled" inflexions of the Middle period begin to be seen side by side with the full inflexions of Old English. The growing tendency of English was to strengthen the accent on the *first* syllable, so that the last syllable, containing the inflexion, was slurred over or lightly sounded. Thus, forms like *nam-a* (name), *sun-u* (son), became *nam-e*, *sun-e*. In the same way all unaccented vowels in the final syllable excepting *i* were "levelled" or assimilated to *e*, so that *-an*, *-as*, *-ath*, *-on*, *-od* became *-en*, *-es*, *-eth*, *-en*, and *-ed*. Adjectives of French origin seldom took English inflexions, which helped English adjectives to discard theirs.

Note.—For some time past there has been a traditional tendency to ascribe our plural suffix *-es* partly, if not principally, to French influence, in supersession of the A.S. *-an*. Even this, however, cannot now be conceded. "It is quite true that the *as* was originally only the plural of *one* declension of *Masc.* nouns, and that the A.S. suffix *-an* was originally rather more common. But the extension of *-as* (which became *-es*) to some of the other declensions set in rather early, say before 1100, at any rate before French had produced any effect on our language. We have now abundant evidence to show (and Prof. Napier has shown it) that the plural in *-es* was overwhelmingly common by 1200. It was pre-eminently common in the Midland dialect, as seen in the later chapters of the *Saxon Chronicle*, that were written in Peterborough up to the death of Stephen. It had nothing whatever to do with French, as we were all taught to believe. Very likely French influence drove the nail home; but it did not put the nail in its place, nor give the initial blows" (Skeat). See also Sweet's *English Grammar*, § 989.

22. Teutonic Preponderance in English Grammar.—The grammatical structure of our language was as strictly Teutonic by the close of the Middle period as it had been before the Conquest, notwithstanding the shock that it had received in the interim. The Teutonic elements are noted below:—

(*a*) *Grammatical forms*:—

(1) Noun-inflexions; the possessive *-'s*, plural in *-en*, plural in *-s*.

(2) All pronoun-inflexions.

(3) All verb-inflexions; the personal endings *-st*, *-th*, and *-s*; tense endings *-d* and *-t*; participial endings *-en* and *-ing*; gerundial ending *-ing*.

(4) Adjective suffixes *-er* and *-est* marking degrees of comparison; and the auxiliary words *more* and *most* used for the same purpose.

(5) All the suffixes used for forming adverbs, and many of those used for forming verbs.

(*b*) *Grammatical words*:—

(1) All nouns forming the Plural by vowel-change.

(2) Almost all nouns having the same form for the Plural as for the Singular.

(3) All the pronouns,—Personal, Demonstrative, Relative, and Interrogative.

(4) All the Demonstrative adjectives,—*the*, *this*, *that*, *other*, *such*, etc.

(5) All the Numerals except *second*, *dozen*, *million*, *billion*, *trillion*.

(6) All the Distributive adjectives.

(7) All adjectives of irregular comparison.

(8) All Strong verbs (except *strive* and possibly one or two more).

(9) All Weak verbs, excepting *catch*, that have different vowels in the Pres. and Past tenses.

(10) All Auxiliary verbs.

(11) All Defective and Anomalous verbs.

(12) The old Causative verbs, viz. those formed by vowel-change.

(13) Almost all the prepositions.

(14) Almost all the conjunctions.

(15) Most of the adverbs of Time and Place.

(16) All pronominal adverbs.

It is easy to make sentences on ordinary subjects without using a single word of French or Latin origin. But it is very difficult to make the shortest English sentence out of French or Latin words, and wherever such words are used, they are forced to submit to all the duties and liabilities of English ones.

23. French Influence on the English Vocabulary.—The Norman Conquest established in England a foreign court, a foreign aristocracy, and a foreign hierarchy. The French language, in its Norman dialect, became for a time the only polite medium of intercourse. The native tongue, at first despised as the language of a subject race, was left for a time to the use of boors and serfs. Words denoting the commonest and most familiar objects,[1] such as the elements, the seasons, divisions of

---

[1] But it is possible to underrate the influence of French in furnishing names even for common and familiar objects. Elements: *air* is French. Seasons: *autumn* is Latin. Divisions of time: *hour*, *minute*, *second* are French. Natural scenery: *valley*, *mountain*, *gravel*, *river*, *torrent*, *fountain* are French. Kinship: *uncle*, *aunt*, *nephew*, *niece* are French; and *grandfather*, *grandmother* are half French. Parts of a house: *brick*, *lintel*, *storey*, *attic*, *ceiling*, *tile*, etc., are French; and *door-post* is half French. Food: *beef*, *mutton*, *veal*, *venison*, etc., are French. Clothing: *gown*, *coat*, *chemise*, *trousers*, etc., are French. Agricultural implements: *hatchet*, *hoe*, *coulter* are French. Agricultural processes: "*turn* the *soil*," *manure*, *fruit*, *herb*, *vegetable*, *cole*, *cauli-flower*, *cabbage*, *grain*, *granary*, *stable*, *car* are French. Trees and plants: *damson*, *chestnut*, *almond*, *laurel*, *bay*, *mustard*, etc., are French. Colours: *blue*, *violet*, *lake*, *crimson*, *carmine*, *mauve* are French.

time, natural scenery, soils and metals, the closest kinds of kinship, parts of a house, food and clothing, agricultural implements and processes, trees and plants, quadrupeds, birds, water animals, insects, parts of the body, actions and postures, etc., are to this day, in a large number of instances (though not by any means exclusively), of Teutonic origin.

A few generations after the Conquest, when English began to be used for general literature in the place of French, most of the terms at hand to express ideas above those of daily life were to be found in the French of the privileged and learned classes, who, for the past two centuries, had had the chief control of art, science, and law. Hence each successive literary effort of the reviving English tongue shows a large adoption of French words to supply the place of the forgotten native ones. Thus in general literature we have *ancestors* for *fore-elders*, *beauty* for *fair-hood*, *caution* for *fore-wit*, *conscience* for *in-wit*, *library* for *book-hoard*, *obstructive* for *hindersome*, *remorse* for *ayen-bite* (= again-bite), etc. (For examples of borrowings in Law, Government, Feudalism, etc., see below in § 43.)

Another effect of French on the English vocabulary was to give it a dualistic or *bilingual* character. Thus nouns or adjectives often go in pairs; as *foe*, *enemy*; *hostile*, *inimical*; *home*, *domicile*; *homely*, *domestic*; *unlikely*, *improbable*; *bold*, *courageous*, etc. Sometimes a Romanic adjective is given to a Teutonic noun; as *bovine*, *ox*; *oval*, *egg*; *human*, *man*, etc. Verbs, too, often go in pairs; as *cast out*, *eject*; *be*, *exist*; *buy back*, *redeem*, etc.

At one time there seems to have been a habit of using words in pairs, one Teutonic and the other Romanic. Thus, at the beginning of the Prayer-book we have "*acknowledge* and *confess*"; "*sins* and *wickedness*"; "not *dissemble* nor *cloke*"; "*humble*, *lowly*"; "*assemble* and *meet together*"; "*pray* and *beseech*." All these pairs of words mean the same thing; and in each pair one is Teutonic and the other Romanic.

24. Other Results of French Influence.—To French influence combined with Latin we owe certain other effects besides those already named:—

(*a*) *Word-building.*—We owe to this influence a very large number of prefixes and suffixes, many of which are still in living use for forming new words. Our Romanic suffixes are even more numerous than our Teutonic ones. The French fem. suffix *-ess* superseded the Teutonic *-ster*. We have also many hybrid words, in which Teutonic and Romanic elements are compounded; as *cott-age* (from A.S. *cote*, "hut," + *age*, Fr. suffix). Our language thus gained in wealth as much as it lost in purity.

(*b*) *Spelling.*—The chief, perhaps the only, harm that French did to our language was to disturb the phonetic spelling that it possessed in its earliest form. (Some account of this will be found in §§ 81, 82.) It is to French that we owe the unnecessary compound *qu* (the function of which was served equally well by our own *cw* in A.S.), the sibilant sound of *c* before the vowels *e* and *i*, the sound of *g* as *j* before the same vowels, and the use of the letter *i* as a consonant to denote the sound now expressed by *j*. Thus almost all words containing a *j* are of French or other foreign origin.

Section 4.—Modern English.

25. Commencement of the Modern Period.—The period of Modern English begins somewhere about A.D. 1500, or a little later. The commencement of this period was preceded or accompanied by several great events, which, in other countries besides England, mark the commencement of Modern as distinct from Medieval history. The art of printing was introduced into England in 1477 by Caxton, who learnt it from the Dutch. Columbus discovered the West Indies in 1492, which led to the discovery of the American continent soon after. Vasco de Gama rounded the Cape of Good Hope in 1497, which brought Southern Asia in touch for the first time with the western nations of Europe. The Renaissance or Revival of Learning opened up new fields of research; and in 1497 Erasmus, the Dutchman, one of the foremost champions of the new learning, visited England, and took up his residence here for a time. Greek began to be studied for the first time in the English Universities. Luther had just begun to lecture in Germany, when Henry VII., the first of our Tudor kings, died on 21st April A.D. 1509.

26. Characteristics of Modern English.—The Modern form of English is distinguished from those that preceded it by two main characteristics:—

(*a*) Our language has now become almost entirely *analytical;* as analytical, in fact, as it is ever likely to be, and more analytical than any other modern language in Europe. All the Old English and Middle English inflexions, excepting the few that still remain, have disappeared. Final *e*, which in the Middle period was syllabic, has either disappeared or is retained to give length to the preceding vowel. The plural and genitive suffixes of nouns have ceased to be syllabic, except when the preceding consonant happens to be of such a kind as to compel the sounding of the final *-es*. Ben Johnson, the dramatist, who wrote a treatise on English grammar, lamented the loss of the plural suffix *-en* in verbs (see § 14, where it is shown that *-en* was the Plural inflexion of the Midland dialect). But the lamentation was in vain; for the suffix had gone beyond recovery. The fact that this suffix, together with the suffix *e* (levelled from *a*, *o*, *u*, see § 7), disappeared *after* Anglo-French had ceased to operate, shows that the tendency to discard inflexions was inherent in the language itself, and was merely accelerated, not produced, by foreign influences.[1]

(*b*) The Modern period is marked by a large number of new borrowings, and these from a great variety of sources. The study of Greek, introduced into England with the revival of learning, led to the influx of a considerable number of Greek words, in addition to such as had been previously borrowed through the medium of Latin. "Surrey, Wiat, and others introduced a knowledge of Italian literature, which soon had a great effect, especially on the drama. Several Italian words came in through this and other influences, either directly or through the medium of French. The discoveries of Columbus and the opening up of the New World brought us into contact with Spanish, and many names of things obtained from the West Indies came to us in a Spanish form. The English victories in India, beginning with the battle of Plassy in 1757, made us acquainted with numerous East Indian words; and English maritime adventure has brought us words from nearly all parts of the world. During the resistance of the Netherlands to Spain, in the time of Elizabeth, English borrowed several words from Dutch: it was not uncommon for English volunteers to go over to Holland to

---

[1] Two proofs have now been given that French influence on English grammar even *indirectly* was really very little,—much less than it has been represented:—(1) In the *Note* to § 21, it has been shown that the plural inflexion *-es* (traditionally ascribed to a large extent to French influence) had begun to take possession of English nouns and oust other plural inflexions *before* French influence had begun to work. In fact, it was our English *-es* that compelled French nouns to change their *-s* into *-es*, so as to bring them into conformity with our own (see below, § 108, *Note* 1). (2) In § 26 it has been shown that the inflexions of Middle English did not begin to drop off until *after* French influence had ceased to operate.

aid in the repulse of the Spaniards. English has also borrowed, chiefly in very recent times, from German, and even from remote continental languages, including Russian, and even Turkish and Hungarian. In fact, there are few languages from which we have failed to borrow words either directly or indirectly. It often requires a little patience to discover from what foreign language a word has been borrowed, and at what period. It is some help to remember that most of the words taken from remote and somewhat unlikely sources have been borrowed during the Modern period, *i.e.* since 1500" (Skeat).

27. Subdivisions of the Modern Period.—The Modern period can be subdivided into three stages or periods :—

I. Tudor English, from about 1500 to 1625, the date of the death of James I. Speaking roughly, its literature may be called that of the sixteenth century, though it goes some twenty-five years beyond it.

II. The English of the remainder of the seventeenth century, which comes to an end with Dryden, who died in A.D. 1700. The language of Milton abounds in Latinisms and other idioms, which are not now admissible. The age of Dryden is marked by a large number of borrowings from Modern French, a good deal of which is not even yet fully assimilated. It is also marked by the thorough establishment for the first time of "*its*" as the Possessive form of "*it.*"

III. The remaining period up to the present day. One main difference between the two centuries represented by I. and II. on the one hand, and the two which have succeeded it on the other, is that "the former is the period of experiment and comparative licence both in the importation of new words and in the formation of idioms and grammatical constructions. The latter period, on the other hand, is marked by selection and organisation" (Sweet). The grammar of Shakspeare is in some points so unlike that of the present day that it has been found necessary for a modern scholar (Dr. Abbott) to publish a "Shakspearian Grammar" explaining its peculiarities. The forms and inflexions used by Shakspeare and his contemporaries are, however, strictly modern.

Another marked difference consists in the great change in the vowel-sounds which took place in the sixteenth and seventeenth centuries. This change, however, has been completely disguised by the absence of a corresponding change in the spelling (see Chapter iv.). If one of Shakspeare's plays were now acted with the pronunciation that was current in his own day, it would be difficult, if not impossible, for the audience to understand it.

28. Decay of Dialects.—In Old and Middle English we were forced to recognise three distinct literary dialects,—the Anglian, the Mercian, and the Wessex in the Old period, answering to the Northern, the Midland, and the Southern in the Middle period.

In Modern English, owing to the complete ascendancy of the Midland dialect, which before the close of the Middle period had left no rivals in the field, we recognise only one language, viz. that of Modern English literature.

Provincial dialects still exist in different parts of England. We may still hear *housen* for *houses* in Wiltshire and Dorsetshire, *brig* for *bridge* in some parts of Yorkshire. But such dialects are no longer literary, or are revived merely as literary curiosities, as in Barnes's *Dorsetshire Poems*, or Tennyson's "Northern Farmer" in imitation of the Lincolnshire dialect.

The only English dialect that survived for some time longer in literary form was what we now call Lowland Scotch, though this is really nothing but a modern form of the old Northern dialect (see § 16). Burns's poetry is mostly written in this dialect, and is its best modern representative.

Note.—From 1422 to 1555 there were three Scotch poets who wrote under the influence of our great Midland poet Chaucer, and under this influence introduced some of the peculiarities of the Midland dialect into their own Northern. James I. (of Scotland) was a prisoner in England for nineteen years. Here he wrote his great poem the *King's Quair* (the quire or book of the king), in close imitation of Chaucer, whose seven-lined stanza has been called the "Rime Royal" after the use made of it by the Scotch king. When the king returned to his own country, his example was followed by Henryson (1480-1508), who wrote a poem called *Testament of Cresseid*, intended to be a continuation of Chaucer's *Troilus*. (It was followed, but to a less degree, by Dunbar, 1465-1529, and by Gavin Douglas, 1474-1522.) Lastly, Sir David Lyndsay (1490-1555), wrote a poem called the *Dreme* in the manner of our old English poet. All these poems contain some Chaucerisms, which influenced not only the phraseology, but the grammar of the Northern dialect.

CHAPTER II.—BORROWINGS.

SECTION 1.—CELTIC.

29. Fewness of Celtic borrowings.—The Celtic borrowings were *very few*, much fewer than has been supposed. Those Britons who were not killed or ousted by the invading English were so completely conquered, that they had every motive for acquiring the new speech and forgetting their own. We are not even sure whether the bulk of them still spoke Celtic; for many had come to speak a rustic kind of Latin, as in Gaul.

Most of the words supposed to have been borrowed by English from Celtic, and still quoted as Celtic in some books, are now known to have been borrowed the other way.[1] The following are a few examples of these mistaken etymologies:[2]—

Balderdash (origin doubtful, certainly not Celtic).
Barrow (A.S. *beorg*, hill).
Bill (A.S. *bill*, axe).
Chine (Fr. *échine*, backbone).
Cower (Sc. *kúr-a*, to doze).
Crimp (Du. *krimp-en*).
Crisp (A.S. *crisp*; Lat. *crisp-us*, curled).
Cudgel (A.S. *cycgel*).
Dainty (O. Fr. *daintie*; Lat. *dignitat-em*).
Filly (Sc. *fylja*, female foal).
Flaw (Sc. *flag-a*, a crack).
Fleam (Fr. *flamme*; Gr. *phlebotomia*, blood-letting).
Frieze (Fr. *frize*, called after Friesland).
Fudge (Low Germ. *futsch*).
Funnel (Breton *founil*; Lat. *infundibul-um*).

30. Geographical Names of Celtic origin:—

Avon (river).—There are said to be fourteen rivers in Great Britain bearing the name of *Avon*.

Exe, Esk, Axe, Ux (river).—In Scotland there are said to be eight rivers called *Esk*. In England we have *Ex*-eter, *Ax*-minster, *Ux*-bridge, and the river *Ouse*, a softened form of *Usk*.

Aber (mouth of a river): *Aber*-deen, *Aber*-ystwith, *Aber*-gavenny, *Ber*-wick (for *Aber*-wick).

Car, Caer (castle): *Car*-lisle, *Car*-diff, *Caer*-narvon, *Caer*-marthen.

Llan (sacred enclosure): *Llan*-daff, *Lam*-peter (in Wales).

Combe (hollow in a hill-side): Addis-*combe*, Ilfra-*combe*, Wy-*combe*.

Lin (pool): *Lin*-ton, *Lin*-dale.

Strath (broad valley): *Strath*-clyde, *Strath*-mere.

Pen, Ben (mountain): *Pen*-rith, *Pen*-zance, *Ben*-Nevis, *Ben*-Lomond, *Pen*-dragon; cf. *Pen*-nine range.

Inch (island): *Inch*-cape.

31. Names of Objects.—Examples are given below:[3]—

(1) Before the Conquest:—*brock* (a badger), *crock* (hence *crockery*), *dun* (brown), *taper* (?) (a small wax candle). (Number of words very small.)

---

[1] This has been proved by Professor Rhys.

[2] Tested by Skeat's *Concise Etymological Dictionary*.

[3] Selected from Skeat's *Princ. Eng. Etym.* series i. chap. xxii. ed. 1892. Since the date of this publication the author, as he informs me, has seen reason to exclude many of the words that he then believed to be Celtic. Some of those given under (2) are still very doubtful. Further research tends to reduce more and more the number of words once supposed to be Celtic; and we must now exclude the following words, all of

(2) After the Conquest, from about 1250 A.D. :—*bald*, *bog* (quagmire), *brag*, *brat*, *bump*, *clock* (orig. a bell), *crag* (rock), *cub* (whelp), *curd* (of milk), *nook*, *plod*, *rub*, *skip*, *prop* (support), *ribbon*. (Many of these, however, are doubtful : see footnote 3 in p. 27.)

(3) From Welsh :—*cam* (crooked, *Shaks.*), *cromlech* (stone monument), *Druid*, *flannel*, *gag* (stop the mouth), *gull* (sea-bird), *hassock* (footstool), *hawk* (clear the throat), *lag* (slack, backward), *toss* (to throw), *bard* (poet).

(4) From Scotch :—*cairn*, *clan*, *claymore* (kind of sword), *galloway* (small horse), *gillie* (a boy, page), *pibroch* (martial tune), *plaid*, *reel* (Highland dance), *whiskey*.

(5) From Irish :—*brogue* (wooden shoe), *colleen* (a little girl), *fun*, *mug* (cup), *shamrock* (a trefoil), *shanty* (small mean dwelling), *tory* (a hostile pursuer, first used in a political sense in 1680).

Section 2.—Danish or Later Scandian.

32. Danish borrowings.—Danish words were used in current speech long before 1250; but it was not till about 1250 or later that many of them were brought into literary use. In those days not one Saxon or Dane in a thousand could read or write, and hence changes were thoroughly established in popular speech long before they showed themselves in writing. The Danish verb "call" appears, however, in the *Battle of Maldon*, an A.S. poem written in A.D. 993. The verb "cast" appears in a Homily written in 1230. These are among the earliest examples of Danish borrowings of *verbs*.

Danish words have a tendency to resist palatalisation,—that is, the conversion of the gutturals *k* or *g* to the corresponding palatals *ch*, *j*, or *y*.[1] Many of our words beginning with *sk*, such as *skill*, *skin*, are Danish. The suffix *-sk*, as in *bu-sk* (prepare oneself), *ba-sk* (orig. to bathe oneself) is exclusively Danish, and is still used in Icelandic.

(1) Nouns of Danish origin :—*tarn* (pool), *stag*, *hustings*, *bark* (of tree), *brink*, *beck* (brook), *bulk* (size), *cleft*, *cur*, *egg*, *fell* (hill),

---

which were supposed to have come from that source :—*cart*, *cradle*, *down* (hill), *merry*, *put*, *slough*, *babe* (imitative), *basket* (Fr.), *boast*, *brisk*, *cabin* (Fr.), *dudgeon*, *lad*, *lass*, *loop*.

[1] The reason usually given for this resistance to palatalisation is that the Danes, being a Northern people and living in a cold climate, did not open their mouths wider than they could help in talking, and were consequently fond of guttural or throat sounds. We are informed, however, by Mr. Skeat that palatalisation is not in any way barred by a fondness for gutturals or a habit of keeping the mouth closed, but is due to the insertion (after *k* or *g*) of the vowel *i* and is extremely common in Swedish,—a Northern language.

fellow (*félági*, partner), *geysir*, *harbour*, *husband*, *kid*, *leg*, *raft*, *reindeer*, *sister*, *skirt*, *sky*, *slaughter*, *trust*, *tryst*, *window*, *wing*.

(2) Verbs of Danish origin:—*bait*, *bask*, *busk*, *call*, *cast*, *dash*, *die*, *drip*, *droop*, *gasp*, *glint*, *glimmer*, *irk* (hence *irk-some*), *are* (Third plur. of *am*), *bark*, *raise*, *rouse*, *rush*, *skim*, *smelt*, *smile*, *take*, *thrive*, *wag*, *wail*, *whirl*, *rive*, *thrive*, etc.

(3) Adjectives and adverbs:—*both*, *bound* (for some journey), *harsh*, *ill*, *irksome*, *loose*, *same*, *scant*, *sleek*, *sly*, *their* (Poss. Pronoun), *tight*, *ugly*, *weak*, etc.[1]

(4) *Patronymics.*—The A.S. suffix for forming patronymics is *-ing*, as *Hard-ing*, *Mann-ing*, etc. The Scandian or Danish suffix is *-son*, as *Ander-son*, *Eric-son*, *Collin-son*, *Swain-son*, *Robert-son*, *David-son*, *Thom-son*, etc.

(5) Prepositions:—*till*, *fro* (a doublet of A.S. *from* or *fram*), *a* for *on* in *aloft*, etc.

(6) Pronouns: *they*, *them*, *their*.

33. Geographical Names.—Scandian names of places are, as we should expect, mostly to be found in the Lowlands of Scotland, the northern counties of England, and Lincolnshire, in all of which the Danes settled in great force.

Beck (brook): *Beck*-ford, Hol-*beck*, Ber-*beck*, Wans-*beck* (Woden's beck).

By (town).—There are said to be about 600 towns or villages in Britain called after this word; of these about 200 are in Lincolnshire, 150 in Yorkshire, and only *one* to the south of the Thames:—

Grims-*by*, Whit-*by*, Apple-*by*, Nase-*by*, Sower-*by*, Soul-*by*, etc.

Dal (dale): Avon-*dale*, Scars-*dale*, Lons-*dale*, Danes-*dale*, etc.

Fell (hill): Scaw-*fell*, Wilber-*fell*, Sna-*fell*.

Force, foss (waterfall): *Foss*-dyke, *Foss*-way, Scale-*force*, Stockgill-*force*, *Foss*-bury.

Frith, forth (estuary, cf. Lat. *port*-us): *Frith* of *Forth*.

Note.—There is also an A.S. word *ford*, which means a river-crossing. Hence Ox-*ford*, Twi-*ford*, etc.

Gate (road, way): Rei-*gate*, Sand-*gate*, Belsay-*gate*, etc.

Gill (ravine, chasm): Orms-*gill*, Cars-*gill*, Esk-*gill*, etc.

Holm (river-flat, or islet): *Holm*-forth, Lang-*holm*; cf. Stock-*holm* in Sweden. Dun-*holm* (turned by Normans to *Dur-eme*, now spelt as *Dur-ham*).

Kirk (church): *Kir*(*k*)-by, *Kirk*-wall, Sel-*kirk*, etc.; cf. Dun-*kirk* in France.

Scar (detached rock): *Scar*-borough, *Scars*-dale, etc.

Skip (ship): *Skip*-ton, *Skip*-with.

Suther (south): *Suther*-land, *Sodor* and Man.

Thorp (village): Bishop-*thorp*, Stain-*drop*.

Thwaite (place; cf. A.S. *stede*, stead): Cross-*thwaite*.

Wich, wick (creek or bay; cf. *Vik*-ing, man from the creek or bay, as Saxons called the Danes): Ips-*wich*, Green-*wich*, Sand-*wich*, *Wick*-low, etc.

[1] Compiled from Skeat's *Princ. Eng. Etym.* series i. chap. xxiii.

Note.—There is also an A.S. *wic*, a town or village. Hence the Norse word can be applied only to places on the sea or navigable rivers, and we cannot always be sure even of them.

It has been usual to add to this list names ending in *ness*, as *Sheer-ness*, and names ending in *ey* or *ea*, as *Jers-ey*, *Angles-ea*; but these endings are no test at all; for *ness* is also A.S., and appears in Beowulf, while Scandian *ey* is merely another form of A.S. *íg*, island. Thus Shepp-*ey* is A.S. Scép-*íg*.

Section 3.—Dutch.

34. Two sets of Dutch borrowings.—(*a*) In the time of Edward III. a large number of Dutch weavers were induced to settle in England, especially in Norfolk, Suffolk, Essex, and Kent. The dialects that they brought with them (Old Frisian and Old Dutch) had much in common with that brought by Frisians and Saxons many centuries before. (*b*) In the reign of Elizabeth, English soldiers, who went out to Holland as volunteers to assist the Dutch against the Duke of Parma, brought home a good many Dutch words with them. After the fall of Antwerp, about a third of its merchants and manufacturers settled on the banks of the Thames, and Dutch sailors at the same time brought some new nautical terms.[1]

(*a*) *First borrowings*:—

(1) Words connected with weaving or the sale of woven goods:—*Botch* (to repair, patch), *brake* (machine for breaking hemp), *curl* (crimple), *lash* (to join a piece and make a seam), *spool* (a reel to wind yarn on), *tuck*, *groat*, *hawker*, *huckster*, *lack* (orig. blemish).

(2) Other words in common use:—*cough*, *mud*, *muddle*, *nag*, *fop*, *loll*, *luck*, *rabble*, *scoff*, *scold*, *slot* (bolt), *slender*, *slight*, *sprout*, *tub*, *tug*, *wiseacre* (Dutch *wijs-segger*, a wise sayer, a sooth-sayer).

(*b*) *Second borrowings*:—

(1) Naval words:[2]—*deck* (of a ship), *freebooter* (pirate or sea-robber), *hoise* or *hoist*, *hold* (of a ship), *hoy* (a small vessel), *hull* (of a ship), *skipper* (mariner), *yacht*, *boom* (pole), *cruise*, *sloop*.

(2) Trade words:—*cope* (orig. to bargain with; cf. *cheap*), *dollar*, *gilder*, *hogshead* (Dutch *oxhoofd*), *holland* (Dutch linen), *ravel* (to unweave or entangle).

(3) Words picked up by volunteers, etc.:—*boor* (Dutch peasant), *burgomaster* (lit. town-master), *canakin*, *frolic*, *fumble*, *glib* (smooth, voluble), *jeer*, *leaguer* (a camp; cf. be-*leaguer*, *lair*, *lie*), *loiter*, *land-*

[1] Skeat's *Princ. Eng. Etym.* series i. chap. xxiv.

[2] It must not be supposed, however, that *all* or even the majority of our naval terms are from Dutch. Others are Romanic, Scandian, or Anglo-Saxon. Romanic: *anchor*, *vessel*, *navy*, *navigate*, *flotilla*, *careen*, *gally*, *hulk*, *prow*, *port*, *mariner*, *poop*, *mizzen*-(mast). Scandian: *lee*, *harbour*, *raft*. Anglo-Saxon: *ship*, *oar*, *seaman*, *sail*, *mast*, *steer*, *stern*, *helm*, *keel*, *fleet*, *yard*.

scape, *manakin*, *mop*, *mope*, *rover*, *ruffle*, *sniff*, *sutler*, *toy*, *trick*, *slope*, *fop*, *waggon*, etc.

(4) A few words connected with painting,[1] such as *easel*, *landscape*, *lay-figure* (Dutch *lee*-man, a jointed model of the human body that may be put up in any attitude).

Note 1.—Some very recent Dutch borrowings have come to us from the Boers in South Africa :—*laager* (a camp), *kraal* (a collection of huts within a stockade), *trek* or *treck* (to migrate with waggons drawn by oxen).

Note 2.—The diminutive suffix *-kin*, as in *bump-kin*, *mana-kin*, *manni-kin*, is usually Dutch, in which it had the form of *-ken*. The suffix *scape* occurring in *landscape* is from Dutch *schap* (shape).

SECTION 4.—LATIN.

35. Latin borrowings distinct from French.—Since French is little else than a modern form of Latin, it has been usual to put the Latin and French borrowings together, and to arrange them in the following periods :—

First Period, A.D. 43-410 :—borrowings traced to the Roman occupation of Britain or picked up on the Continent : *all Latin*.

Second Period, A.D. 596-1066 :—words borrowed during and after the conversion of our ancestors to Christianity : *all Latin*.

Third Period, A.D. 1066-1480 :—words borrowed on and after the Norman Conquest till the accession of Henry VII., the commencement of Modern History : *all French*.

Fourth Period, from A.D. 1480 :—words borrowed during and after the great intellectual movement known as the Renaissance or Revival of Learning : *all Latin*.

The arrangement is faulty, because shoals of Latin borrowings came in within the third period, and shoals of French ones within the fourth. Moreover, there was a special class of French borrowings in the time of Charles II., of which no account is taken in the above arrangement. It is now known, too, that *some* French words occur in late A.S. texts *before* 1066 ; as *turn*, A.S. *tyrn-an*, from Old Fr. *torn-er*; *proud*, A.S. *prūd*, from Old Fr. *prud* (of which our word *prude* is the Fem.); for other examples see *Note*, § 41.

The plan followed in this book is to keep the French and the Latin borrowings apart, and to subdivide each aggregate into separate periods of its own.[2] We shall take the Latin borrowings first, as the earliest of these were fixed in English, even before the French language had begun to exist.

---

[1] On art terms borrowed from Italian see § 50, (1), (*a*).

[2] The arrangement observed in this book is in accordance with that shown in Professor Skeat's *Principles of English Etymology*, series i. and ii.

The first two periods in the new arrangement tally, as will now be shown, with the first two in the old.

36. I. First Period: pre-Christian, up to A.D. 596.—Some of the borrowings belonging to this list may have been picked up on the Continent by the English before they came over to Britain; but some could easily have been learnt in Britain itself from the conquered natives. These borrowings are about ten in number, and almost all of them bear testimony to the Roman occupation:—

Caster, Chester: A.S. *ceaster*, Lat. *castrum*, camp or fortified place; seen only in geographical names:—*Chester*, *Caster*, *Caistor*, *Chester*-field, Lan-*caster*, Don-*caster*, Dor-*chester*, Man-*chester*, Win-*chester*, Ex-*eter* (for Ex-*cester*), Lei-*cester*, etc.

Coln: Lat. *colonia*, military settlement; seen only in geographical names:—Lin-*coln*, *Colne*, *Col*-chester.

Mile: A.S. *míl*, Lat. *mille* (*passuum*), a thousand paces.

Pine (verb): A.S. *pín*, Lat. *pœn-a*: cf. Eng. *pain*, *pun*-ish-ment.

Pool: A.S. *pól*, Welsh *pwll*, Lat. *padul*-is, a marsh: cf. Hartle-*pool*, Liver-*pool*.

Port: A.S. *port*, Lat. *port*-us, a harbour; cf. *Por*-chester, *Ports*-mouth, *Port*-land, Devon-*port*, New-*port*, etc.

Street: A.S. *strǽt*, Mercian *strét*, Lat. *strāta* (*via*), a paved road; cf. *Strat*-ton (town with paved street), *Streat*-ham (South London), *Strat*-ford, *Strad*-brook, etc.

Wall: A.S. *weall*, Mercian *wall*, Lat. *uall*-um, a rampart; borrowed at a time when the Lat. *v* (written *u* in old MSS.) was pronounced as *w*; cf. *Wall*-bury, *Wal*-ton, etc.

Wick, wich: A.S. *wíc*, Lat. *uic*-us, a town or village; seen only in geographical names: *Wick*-ham, *Wig*-ton, etc.

Wine: A.S. *wín*, Lat. *uin*-um.

37. II. Second Period: pre-Norman, A.D. 597-1066.—In A.D. 597 St. Augustine with a band of forty monks landed in Kent to teach Roman Christianity to the heathen English. Their conversion brought England for the first time into connection with the Continent, and especially with Rome and Italy, and this connection brought commerce, with new words and ideas. The number of Latin borrowings during this period, however, amounts to less than 200. English was thus still an almost pure language, and showed little inclination to admit strangers (for we can hardly include Danish words under such a name) until some 200 years after the Norman Conquest, when it began to borrow on a very large scale. The following examples are given in their modern spellings:—

(1) Church terms of Latin origin:—*altar*, *candle*, *chalice*, *cowl*, *creed*, *cup*, *disciple*, *font*, *mass* (sacrificial rite), *nun*, *shrine*, *shrive*, etc.

Church terms of Greek or Hebrew origin borrowed through Latin :—*alms*, *angel*, *anthem*, *amen*, *apostle*, *bishop*, *canon*, *Christ*, *church*, *clerk*, *deacon*, *devil*, *martyr*, *minster*, *monk*, *paschal*, *pope*, *priest*, *psalm*, *school*, *stole*, etc.

(2) Trade words, articles of commerce, etc. :—*beet* (beetroot), *box* (chest), *cap*, *cheese*, *fan*, *fork*, *kettle*, *linen*, *mat*, *mint*, *mul*-(berry), *pease* (Lat. *pis*-um, from which a false singular *pea* has been formed), *pear*, *penny*, *poppy*, *pound*, *sock*, *spend* (Lat. *dis-pend*-ere), *ton*, *tun*, etc.

(3) Miscellaneous :—*ass*, *belt*, *box* (tree), *castle*, *chalk*, *coulter* (of a plough), *fever*, *fiddle*, *fennel*, *hemp*, *kiln* (Lat. *culina*), *kitchen* (Lat. *coquina*), *lake*, *lobster*, *mill*, *mount-ain*, *noon* (Lat. *nona hora*, the ninth hour), *pan*, *pillow*, *pine* (tree), *pipe*, *pit*, *pole*, *post*, *prime*, *punt*, *shambles*, *sickle*, *sole* (of foot), *tile* (Lat. *tegul*-a), *tunic*, *turtle*-(dove), *verse*, *dish* (A.S. *disc*, Lat. *disc*-us), etc.

38. III. **Third Period : pre-Classical or pre-Renaissance, A.D. 1066-1485.**—The Norman Conquest, which took place in 1066, and was the means of making about half our vocabulary French two or three centuries later, gave a great impetus to the study of Latin, from which French itself is mainly derived. When we had already borrowed from French such words as *charity*, *quality*, *quantity*, it was easy to take the Latin word *pugnacitas* and change it to *pugnacity*, although it had not been preceded by a French form *pugnacité*. It is even asserted by the great French lexicographer that the French word *pugnacité* was borrowed from the English *pugnacity*.[1]

It must be remembered, too, that during the Middle Ages, as Craik observes, "Latin was the language of all the learned professions, of law and physic as well as of divinity in all their grades. It was in Latin that the teachers in the Universities (many of whom in England were foreigners) delivered their prelections in all the sciences." The Latin borrowings during this period are much more numerous than those of the pre-Norman period.

In England one of the main sources of supply was the Vulgate Version of the Bible,—that is, the current Latin text. It was from a MS. copy of this text that Wycliff (A.D. 1324-1384) prepared his English translation of the Bible. The Vulgate was constantly quoted in the old Homilies, and it was usual to accompany the quotation with comments in English.

Words borrowed direct from Latin, as the following examples show, are more like the original Latin than the early French borrowings (A.D. 1066 to about 1350).

[1] Skeat's *Princ. Eng. Etym.* series ii. p. 150, chap. viii.

Ab-brevi-ate (Latin *brevis;* cf. Fr. *abridge*). *Ab-negat-ion* (Lat. *neg-*, *negat-;* cf. Fr. "de-*ny*"). *Ac-quiesce* (Lat. *-quiesc-ere;* cf. Fr. *ac-quit*). *Ac-quire* (Lat. *quær-ere;* cf. Fr. "con-*quer*"). *Ad-judic-ate* (Lat. *judic-*, *judicat-;* cf. Fr. "ad-*judge*"). *Ag-grav-ate* (Lat. *grav-*, *gravat-;* cf. Fr. "ag-*grieve*"). *Al-levi-ate* (Lat. *levis*, light; cf. Fr. "re-*lieve*"). *Ap-preci-ate* (Lat. *pretium*, price; cf. Fr. "ap-*praise*"). *Ap-prehend* (Lat. *prehend-;* cf. Fr. "*ap-prise*"). *Ap-proxim-ate* (Lat. *proximus;* cf. Fr. "*ap-proach*," from Lat. *prope*, near). *Dis-simul-ate* (Lat. *simul-*, *simulat-*, to pretend; cf. Fr. "*dis-semble*"). *Bene-diction* (cf. Fr. *benison*). *Male-diction* (cf. Fr. *malison*). *Cad-ence* (cf. Fr. *chance*), etc.

One of the borrowings of this period, *autumn*, has superseded *harvest*, which in A.S. denoted the season (of autumn), and is now made to denote the fruits of the season.

The great difference between the Latin borrowings of Period II. and those of Period III. is that the former were adapted to Saxon models, and the latter to French ones.

39. IV. Fourth Period, from A.D. 1480.—The tendency to Latinise our speech received a new and very powerful impulse from the Renaissance or Revival of *classical* learning, Greek and Latin. In the preceding period the Latin borrowings were from ecclesiastical, legal, and other medieval books. The new period was marked by the study of the poets, orators, historians, etc., whose writings make up the classical literature of ancient Greece and Rome. Latin words began to pour in by shoals, and threatened to swamp our native speech. Fortunately, however, another movement, the Reformation, set in very soon after,—a movement that in England, as elsewhere in Europe, was essentially Teutonic, and found its strength in the native element of our language and character. Hence if a large number of Latin words were borrowed at this time, an equally large number were rejected as superfluous or awkward in the next generation.

The Latin borrowings of this period, like those of the preceding, are *book*-words,—that is, they have kept their Latin shape in all but the last syllable, or have discarded the last Latin syllable altogether, as in *advent*, Lat. *advent-us.*

A writer in Queen Elizabeth's time condemns such innovations as the following, though all but the last three have held their ground:—*audacious*, *compatible*, *egregious*, *despicable*, *destruction*, *homicide*, *obsequious*, *ponderous*, *portentous*, *prodigious*, *attemptat*, *facundity*, *implete.*

Among the rejected words the following will serve as examples:—*torve*, *tetric*, *cecity*, *fastide*, *trutinate*, *immanity*, *scelestick*, *pervicacy*, *stramineous, lepid, sufflaminate, facinorous, immorigerous, stultiloquy, mulierosity, coaxation, ludibundness*,[1] etc.

It has been estimated that the total number of words which we have borrowed immediately from Latin, and not through the medium of French, is considerably above 2400.[2] This estimate includes only such words as are fairly common, and only main or primary words. If the rejected words and derivatives were included, the number would be very much greater.

It is a noticeable fact that many of the words associated with the higher culture are of Latin origin, such as *evolve, evolution, operate, cultivate, demonstrate, horticulture, inductive, educate*, etc.

Latin borrowings did not cease with the Renaissance. Whenever new words are wanted to express something new in art or science, we still borrow from Latin, and sometimes from Greek. In fact, Latin is a language from which we have borrowed at all times, from the fifth century onwards.

40. Formation of English Verbs from Latin ones.—English verbs have been formed out of Latin ones either (*a*) from the stem of the Present Infinitive, or (*b*) from the stem of the Past Participle. The fact that so many *verbs* have been borrowed from Latin shows the thoroughness with which the borrowings of the Third and Fourth Periods were blended with English; for in our Latin borrowings of the two earlier periods we cannot find more than four verbs, all the rest being nouns or adjectives.

(*a*) *Abs-cond* (abscond-ere); *co-erce* (coerc-ere); *con-temn* (contemn-ere); *im-bue* (imbu-ere); *in-stil* (instill-are); *lave* (lav-are); *e-mend* (emend-are, Fr. form *a-mend*); *scan*(*d*) (scand-ere), etc.

(*b*) *Ab-use* (abus-um); *an-nex* (annex-um); *credit* (credit-um); *fix* (fix-um); *e-dit* (edit-um); *act* (act-um); *re-lapse* (re-laps-um); *promise* (promiss-um); *sug-gest* (suggest-um); *sub-stitute* (substitut-um), etc.

Section 5.—French.

41. Three sets of French borrowings.—There are *three* different sets of French borrowings, as against the four of Latin.

I. "Words of **Anglo-French** origin, that came into the language before 1350, and belong to the good old stock, being of equal value and use with the words of native origin." It was the Norman Conquest in 1066 that set this stream flowing in

[1] Trench's *English Past and Present*, ed. 1877, pp. 102-110.

[2] Skeat's *Princ. Eng. Etym.* series ii. p. 250.

force, and led to the formation, in England itself, of a separate Anglo-French dialect.

II. "Words of **Central** (or Parisian) French origin, imported chiefly between 1350 and 1660, the date of the accession of Charles II."

III. "**Late French** words (of Parisian origin), introduced into the language since 1660 or thereabouts. They are on the whole of far less value than those in the two former classes" (Skeat).[1]

Note.—It has been asserted by very high authorities that there was a set of French borrowings which *preceded* the Norman Conquest (see article by Kluge in *Englische Studien*, vol. xxi. p. 334):—*bat*, *capon*, *castle*, *cat* (North Fr.), *catchpoll* (in late A.S. *cæcepol*), *false*, *mantle*, *market*, *proud*, *pride*, *purse*, *rock*, *sot*, *targe*, *trail*, *turn*. All these appear in late A.S., and are traceable to a French origin.

42. Popular and Learned.—The former belong chiefly to Class I., the latter (to a large extent) to Classes II. and III.

(*a*) "Popular" French words are such as grew up orally in ancient Gaul from the intercourse of Roman soldiers and settlers with the Gauls or *people* of the province; and hence they are called *popular*—lingua Romana popularis—lip-Latin, and not book-Latin. Such words are a good deal changed from the original Latin speech. Thus *c* or *k* at the beginning of a word often becomes *ch;* as in *cantare*, *chant;* *camera*, *chamber;* *caput*, *chief.* *C* or *g* in the middle of a word is often left out; as in *decanus*, *dean;* *inimicus*, *enemy;* *securus*, *sure;* *regula*, *rule;* *fact-um*, *feat;* *pericul-um*, *peril.* *B* sometimes disappears between vowels; as in *describe*, *descry;* *subitaneus*, *sudden.* *P* sometimes disappears before *t;* as in *conception*, *conceit;* *compute*, *count.* *D* or *t* often vanishes; as in *radic-em*, *race;* *native*, *naive;* *catena*, *chain;* *amictus*, *amice;* *conduct*, *conduit;* *præda*, *prey;* *radius*, *ray;* *pallid*, *pale;* *medianus*, *mean;* *dilate*, *delay;* *fata*, *fay;* *rotundus*, *round*, etc. *V* between two vowels disappears; as *civit-atem*, *cit-y.* *Ll* between vowels becomes vocalised or disappears; as *bellitas*, *beauty;* *colloc-are*, *couch.* *Di* before a vowel becomes *g* or *ch* or *j;* as *prædic-are*, *preach;* *diurnata*, *journey;* (as)*sedi-um*, *siege.* *Ti* undergoes a similar change; as *viatic-um*, *voyage;* *silvatic-us*, *savage.* *Bi*, *pi*, *vi* before a vowel tend to become *ge* or *ch;* as *rabi-es*, *rage;* *appropi-are*, *approach;* *diluvium*, *deluge.* *B* or *p* becomes *v* or *f;* as *ab-ante*, *van;* *ripa-r-ius*, *river;* *prob-are*, *prove.* Words thus derived make up the

[1] *Princ. Eng. Etym.* series ii. chap. ix.

bulk of the vocabulary of Old French, of which our own Anglo-French dialect was a peculiar offshoot.

(*b*) "Learned" French words are such as were borrowed by French writers from the study of Latin books, and not from lip-Latin. They are merely Latin words slightly altered and put into a French dress. Central or Parisian French enriched itself with a large stock of such words. Our French borrowings of the Second Period, that is, from A.D. 1350 to about 1660, are chiefly words of this class; and we cannot always separate them from words that we borrowed direct from Latin and refashioned in the same way as if we had taken them from French (see § 38). Thus *fierce* is a word of "popular" French origin (Lat. *ferocem*). But *ferocity* (Lat. *ferocitas*) is from learned or literary French, *ferocité*.

43. I. Anglo-French borrowings, up to about A.D. 1350. —These are called Anglo-French, as distinct from those of every other French dialect, because this dialect was *developed in England independently of foreign influence.* At the time of the Conqueror, and for a short time afterwards, it coincided with the French of Normandy, one of the northern dialects of Old French. But being cut off from contact with France by the English Channel, and at the same time in constant contact with English, it was developed in this island in a manner peculiarly its own, until by the time of Edward III. it had become quite distinct from every form of continental French. This dialect did not die out in England, till it had produced an abundant literature and given a bilingual character to our own English speech.

One great mark of the thoroughness with which Anglo-French and Early English were blended into one homogeneous whole is the fact that we borrowed French *verbs* in large numbers, and without hesitation; whereas in our borrowings from Late French we admitted scarcely anything but nouns and adjectives.

Our Anglo-French words are on the whole quite as necessary to our language as our Anglo-Saxon ones. The word *hour*, for example, is indispensable, because A.S. *tíd* (= tide), which also meant "hour," is now used to denote the ebb and flow of the sea. Again, *second* is indispensable as the ordinal for "two," because A.S. *óðer* (= other, lit. "second") has become useful in other ways. Cf. Lat. *autumn* and A.S. *harvest* in § 38.

Examples of Anglo-French borrowings: (on the general character of such borrowings, see § 23):—

(*a*) Titles, offices, etc. :—*duke, marquis, baron, constable, count, lieutenant, mayor, prince, viscount, emperor, vicar, dean, canon, chancellor*, etc.

(*b*) Feudalism and war, etc. :—*aid, cavalry, banner, battle, captain, fealty, lance, realm, armour, arms, fief, escutcheon, homage, vassal, serjeant, serf, trumpet*, etc.

(*c*) Law : *attorney, barrister, damages, felony, larceny, fine, judge, jury, justice, estate, fee, plea, plead, plaintiff, defendant, assize, prison, suit, summons*, etc.

(*d*) Government : *people, parliament, crown, reign, treaty, council, cabinet, court, minister*, etc.

(*e*) Church : *friar, relic, tonsure, ceremony, baptism, Bible, prayer, preach, lesson, cloister, penance, homily, sermon*, etc.

(*f*) Hunting : *course, covert, falcon, leveret, quarry, rabbit, venison* (hunted flesh), *catch, chase*.

(*g*) Cookery : *beef, veal, pork, mutton, pullet, boil, roast, broil, salmon, sausage*, etc.

(*h*) Abstract terms : *sense, honour, glory, fame, colour, dignity, chivalry, piety, art, science, nature*, etc.

(*i*) Relationship : *aunt, cousin, spouse, parent, uncle, nephew, niece*.

Note.—Most terms expressing very close relationship are, however, Teutonic; such as *son, daughter, father, mother*. Hybrids like *grandfather, grandmother* help to show how completely the two languages were blended.

44. II. **Central French borrowings,** from A.D. 1350 to about 1660.—By the middle of the fourteenth century, when English was the only language spoken, and Anglo-French had almost ceased to affect our vocabulary, we had begun to borrow from continental French, not, as before, from the French of Normandy, but from Central or Parisian French, which by this time had become the standard language of France as it still is.

As has been stated already in § 42, many of the French borrowings of this period were from literary French, that is, the French derived from book-Latin, and not that derived, as old French was, from lip-Latin.

Specimens of Central French borrowings found in Chaucer :—

Cadence (Lat. *cadentia*, Anglo-French *chance*), *poetry, advertence, agony, annex, ascendant, casual, complexion, composition, conservative, cordial, duration, existence, fructify, oracle, persuasion, reprehend, triumph, urn, volume, vulgar*,[1] etc.

Specimens in Lydgate, fifteenth century :—*adulation, ambiguity, artificer, combine, condign, chronicle, deception, decoction, demure, dissent, doublet, encourage, fraudulent, hospitality, immutable, inclination, influence, inspection*, etc.

The French borrowings of this period were not all book-

[1] Skeat's *Princ. Eng. Etym.* series ii. p. 153.

words. Some were names of products imported into England through France by way of Calais. The following examples are given in their modern English spelling:—

Sugar, almonds, spicery, vermilion, figs, raisins, saffron, ivory, pepper, ginger, liquorice, sulphur, incense, pæony, anise, dates, chestnuts, olive oil, rice, turpentine, cotton, canvas, fustian, etc.

The writings of Chaucer contain a great many French words, some of which were of Anglo-French origin, and others of Central or literary French. But it would be a mistake to suppose that Chaucer *introduced* them. Before Chaucer wrote, the English language had been deeply interpenetrated by an admixture of French. "He merely employed with great skill and with plastic effect a language that was common to himself and his contemporaries" (Skeat).

45. III. **Late French borrowings**, from A.D. 1660.—By this time the French language had entered fully upon its Modern period, and was a good deal changed from the Old French to which our Norman or Anglo-French dialect belonged, and with which it agreed in the main in pronunciation and accent.

The borrowings of this period differ from those that preceded it in three respects at least—(1) They contain scarcely any *verbs*, which shows that Modern French is to Modern English an exotic, and not a true graft; (2) they have in many instances retained the Modern French system of accentuating the last syllable, whereas the older borrowings followed the English method of throwing the accent back on the first; cf. *cap'-tain* (Old French), *cam-paign'* (Modern French); (3) they have in many instances preserved the Modern French method of pronouncing vowels and consonants; compare for example *rage* (Old French) with *rouge* (= ro͞ozh, Modern French). Old French, on the contrary, was pronounced in nearly the same way as English was at the time of its incorporation (see above, § 19).

Besides individual words, a large number of Modern French *phrases* (such as *à propos*, for example) became current in England at this time, and many of them are still in vogue, though we could do quite as well without them.

An affected preference for everything French came into fashion with Charles II., whose vicious reign of twenty-five years corrupted the language no less than the morals of his country. The poet Dryden (1631-1700), from a desire to please the court, fell in with the prevailing fashion, as when he needlessly substituted the French *fraicheur* for the English *freshness*:—

Hither in summer evenings you repair
To taste the *fraicheur* of the purer air.

The tide receded a little with the accession of William III., but the study of French still continued in fashion.

46. Pronunciation of Late French words.—Some borrowings belonging to this class have become thoroughly naturalised in sound and accent; as *foliage*, *brilliant*, *antechamber*, *console*, *corset*, *deference*, *detach*, *diversion*, etc. (Fr. *mêlée* (a hand-to-hand conflict) has been lately naturalised as *mellay* in Tennyson's *Princess*.) Others are still French, though current in English speech.

A sounded as ȧ: po-mȧde, vȧse, gal-lȧnt, spȧ, chȧ-grin.

At sounded as ȧ: éclat (=é-clȧ).

E sounded as ā: fête (fāte), écarté, soirée, levée, parterre.

Et sounded as ā: ball-et (băllā), val-et, cro-quet, etc.

En sounded as ŏn: en-core (=ŏn-core), en-nui, ren-dez-vous.

I sounded as ē: ré-gime, po-lice, suite, gla-cis, fa-tigue, clique, pique, in-trigue, ma-chine, qui-nine, etc.

Ou sounded as ōō: group, bou-quet, soup, tour, route, rou-é, etc.

Au sounded as ō: mauve (=mōv), haut-boy, au revoir.

Eau sounded as ō: beau, plat-eau, bur-eau, portmant-eau.

Ieu sounded as ū: lieu, purlieu.

Oi sounded as *war*: pat-ois, soi-rée, reser-voir, mem-oir.

Eur: liqu-eur, haut-eur, douc-eur. (In grand-*eur* and amat-*eur* the French sound has been lost.)

On (nasal): coup-on, cray-on, chign-on.

Ch sounded as *sh*: chaise, ma-chine, chan-de-lier, cham-ois.

Ge, j sounded as *zh*: ré-gime, gendarme, mi-rage (=rȧzh), rouge (=rōōzh), ju-jube.

Qu, que sounded as *k*: bou-quet, cro-quet, brusque, marque, qua-drille, co-quette, grot-esque, etc.

S, t (silent): corps, a-propos, pat-ois, trait, de-pot.

Note.—When a foreign word is adopted whole, without any change of spelling, as *addendum* (Lat.), *prestige* (Fr.), *analysis* (Gr.), *bazaar* (Persian), we forget that it is foreign, *provided it accepts an English pronunciation*. Such a word may be said to be "acclimatised." (On the doubtful word *prestige*, see § 47.)

47. Accentuation of Late French words.—In the following examples, all of which are Late French borrowings, the accent is thrown on the last syllable of dissyllables, in accordance with French usage, and in trisyllables there is rather a strong accent on the last syllable besides one on the first:—

Dissyllables: a-droit′, bru-nette′, ca-det′, ca-jole′, cam-paign′, ca-price′, ca-ress′, (cf. older borrowing *lar′*-gess), fes-toon′, gri-mace′, gui-tar′, har-angue′, in-trigue′, gro-tesque′, etc.

Trisyllables: baga-telle', debau-chee', confid-ant', incomm-ode', reprim-and', refug-ee', volunt-eer', palis-ade', barric-ade', arab-esque', etc.

Wavering words: Among the borrowings from Late French some are quite naturalised, some are still French, others are wavering. For example, some pronounce *prestige* as *pres'-tidge*, as if it were thoroughly Anglicised. Others still sound it as *pres-tizh'*, as if it were still thoroughly French.

Section 6.—Greek.

48. Continuity of Greek borrowings.—Greek shares with Latin, though to a much smaller degree, the distinction of having been a continuous source of supply from the fifth century down to the present day.

All Greek borrowings up to the Revival of Greek learning (which for England may be dated from A.D. 1540) reached us at second or third hand through Latin or French.

Since 1540 some Greek words have been borrowed direct from Greek, and are especially so borrowed at the present day, when new words are wanted for some new fact or object in art or science. Others have been borrowed through Latin or French, as before, or through Italian, Spanish, Arabic, Portuguese, or Dutch.

The form of the word borrowed seldom gives any clue as to the date of the borrowing. For instance, *hypnotism*, *theosophy*, *photograph*, *telephone*, etc. (all of Greek origin), were coined lately in England. If they had been borrowed through French many centuries ago, the form of the words would have been just what they are now. But the form of "pro-*gramme*" shows that it came through French; cf. "tele-*gram*," coined in England.

49. Specimens of Greek borrowings:—

(*a*) Out of the Latin borrowings (rather less than 200) of the Second Period (§ 37), at least one-third were Greek before they became Latin:—

Alms (A.S. *ælmesse*, Gr. *eleëmos-yne*); anthem (A.S. *antefn*, Gr. *anti-phona*); angel (Gr. *angel-os*); apostle (Gr. *apostol-os*); bishop (A.S. *biscop*, Gr. *episcop-os*); chest (Gr. *kist-e*); Christ (Gr. *Christ-os*); church or kirk (A.S. *cyric-e*, Gr. *kuriak-a*); clerk (Gr. *cleric-os*); devil (A.S. *déofol*, Gr. *diabol-os*); dish (A.S. *disc*, Gr. *disc-os*); imp (A.S. *imp*, Gr. *emphut-os*).

Note.—Words like *antiphona* and *kuriaka* were Gr. Neuter Plurals, out of which Late Latin Fem. singulars were formed.

(*b*) Greek borrowings that have come through French, having first passed into Latin:—

Blame (Fr. *blasm-er*, Lat. *blasphem-are*, Gr. *blasphem-ein*); currants (Fr. *raisins de Corinthe*, Gr. *Corinth-os*); dropsy (Fr. *hy-dropisie*, Gr. *hydropisis*); fancy (Fr. *fantasie*, Gr. *phantasia*); frenzy (Fr. *frenaisie*, Gr. *phrenesis*); govern (Fr. *govern-er*, Gr. *kubern-ān*); graft (Fr. *graffe*, Gr. *graph-ein*); ink (Fr. *enque*, Gr. *en-caust-on*); place (Fr. *place*, Gr. *plat-eia*); slander (Fr. *esclandre*, Gr. *scandal-on*); surgeon (Fr. *chirurgien*, Gr. *cheir-urg-eon*); palsy (Fr. *paralysie*, Gr. *para-lysis*); al-chemy (Arab. article *al*: Gr. *chemeia*, mingling).

(*c*) Greek borrowings coined from Greek direct:—

Analysis, hydrophobia, monopolist, telephone, anthology, demology, zoo-logy, tele-gram, epi-dem-ic, epi-lepsy, epicure, utopia, æsthetic, cosmetic, cosmo-polite, etc.

(*d*) Hybrids:—

Con-trive (Lat. prefix *con-*; Old Fr. *trov-er*, to find; Gr. *trop-os*, a turn, revolving); re-trieve (Lat. prefix *re-*, base the same as the preceding); in-toxic-ate (Lat. prefix *in-*, Gr. stem *toxic-on*, poison, Lat. suffix *-ate*), etc.

Verbs of Greek origin are rare. But a very large number of verbs have been formed with the Greek suffix *-ize* or *-ise*, which can be freely attached to stems of any origin whatever.[1]

SECTION 7.—MODERN BORROWINGS: MISCELLANEOUS.

50. Modern borrowings.—Under this heading we include the various sources not already named, from which new words came into English within the modern period of our language,—that is, after A.D. 1500.

(1) *Italian.*—The Renaissance or Revival of Learning, which originated in Italy, led to a study of Italian literature. Dante, Tasso, Ariosto, and Petrarch were all translated into English. The poems of Surrey, Wyatt, Spenser, and Milton all show an intimate acquaintance with Italian. In the reigns of the Tudors Italian was as necessary to every courtier as French was in the time of Charles II. The Ottava Rima, Blank Verse, and the Sonnet all came from Italy. The scenes of seven of Shakspeare's plays are laid in Italy. The tide receded with the establishment of the Commonwealth, and was entirely thrown back by the overwhelming taste for French, that set in with the accession of Charles II. But the borrowings were rather numerous, while the fashion lasted.[2]

One word, and possibly two more, came from Italy at a very

---

[1] The spelling *-ise* is French; but this was altered to *-ize* by pedants, who knew Greek, but forgot that *-ise* came to us through Fr. *-iser*.

[2] Skeat's *Princ. Eng. Etym.* series ii. p. 315.

early period. *Pilgrim* occurs in Layamon's *Brut*, spelt as *pilegrim*, from Italian *pellegrino*. Another word is *roam*, probably derived from *Rome*, to which pilgrimages were made by Englishmen from the time of Alfred the Great to that of Chaucer's *Wife of Bath*. *Ducat*, a Venetian word, occurs in Chaucer.

(*a*) Direct from Italian :—

Balcony (It. *balcone*, a stage); bandit (It. *bandito*, outlawed); canto; comply (It. *complire*, Lat. *complere*); contraband (Lat. *contra*, against, *bannum*, a decree); ditto (a thing already said, from Lat. *dictum*, said); duel; duet; monkey (It. *monicchio*); gusto (Lat. *gust-us*, taste); fresco (of the same root as *fresh*); milliner (a dealer in *Milan* goods); isolate (It. *isolato*, detached); imbroglio; grotto; portico; quota; rebuff, etc.

Note.—We are indebted to Italian for many of our terms in music, poetry, and painting :—

Music :—concert, sonata, spinet, fugue, breve, duet, contralto, opera, piano, prima donna, quartet, quintet, solo, soprano, trio, canzonet, tremolo, falsetto, etc.

Poetry :—canto, sonnet, stanza, improvise, octava rima.

Painting :—miniature, profile, vista, model, palette, pastel, mezzotinto, amber, etc. (On painting terms derived from Dutch, see § 34.)

(*b*) Through French :—

Alert (It. *all' erta*, on the watch); arcade; artisan; bank-rupt (It. *banco*, *rotto*, afterwards changed to Lat. *rupta*); brusque (It. *brusco*); bust (It. *busto*); caprice (It. *capriccio*, a whim); canteen (It. *cantina*, a cellar); cartoon (It. *cartone*, Lat. *charta*); cavalcade (It. *cavalcata*, a troop of horsemen); cascade (It. *cascata*, a waterfall), etc.

(2) *Spanish.*—Our borrowings from Spain were not due to a study of Spanish literature, but to our commercial and political relations with Spain, and to the descriptions of the country and her colonies furnished by English travellers.[1] Spanish borrowings are almost as numerous as Italian. The *al-* prefixed to some Spanish nouns is the Arabic article, *al*.

(*a*) Direct from Spanish :—

Alligator (*al ligarto*, a lizard); armada (armed fleet); booby (*bobo*, a blockhead); buffalo; canoe (West Indian); cargo; cigar; armadillo (the little armed one, an animal); cork (*corcho*, Lat. *corticem*, bark); domino; don; filibuster (Sp. *filibuster*; corruption of Dutch *vrijbuiter*, Eng. freebooter); peccadillo (dim. of *pecado*, a sin), etc.

(*b*) Through French :—

Bizarre; calenture; cask (Fr. *casque*, Ital. *casco*); castanets (of the same root as *chestnut*); escalade; garble; parade (*parada*, a show); risk (*risco*, a steep rock), etc.

---

[1] Skeat's *Princ. Eng. Etym.* series ii. p. 339.

(3) *Portuguese.*—About four dozen words :—

Albatross, albino, apricot, caste (Indian trade-guild), corvette (small frigate), firm (mercantile association), lingo (language), marmalade, molasses, parasol, tank (cf. Lat. *stagnum*, a pool of standing water), fetish (Lat. *factitius*, artificial).

(4) *German:* that is, the High German (see § 4, B). Only about twenty-four all told; and all of these are scientific and technical terms, except the following :—

Landau (a kind of carriage), meerschaum, mesmerise, plunder, poodle, swindler, waltz, zinc, carouse (through Fr. *carous*, Germ. *gar-aus*, lit. "quite out," a bumper drunk right off).

(5) *Russian* or *Slavonic:* rather fewer than the German :—

Knout, mammoth, argosy, mazurka (Polish dance), sable (an animal), rouble, polka, slave, steppe, vampire, czar.

(6) *Persian :*—

Bazaar, bezique (a game), caravan, divan, orange (*P. naring*), check or cheque, chess, dervish, exchequer, hazard, jackal, jasmine, jujube (through French), lemon, lilac, etc.

(7) *Sanskrit :*—

Banyan (a kind of tree), camphor, chintz, crimson, ginger, hemp, indigo, jungle, loot (to plunder), etc.

(8) *Hindustáni* (Northern India); for Southern, see (13) :—

Bangle (a ring bracelet), chutny (a kind of pickle), dacoit (highway robber), topee (a sunshade for the head).

(9) *Hebrew :*—

Balsam (cf. older form *balm*, through French), alphabet (through Greek), amen, bedlam (mad-house, corruption of *Bethlehem*), cinnamon, cherub, cider (through French), maudlin (corruption of *Magdalene*), jubilee, jockey (corruption of *jackey*, dim. of *Jack*, Hebrew *Jac-ob*), hallelujah (*halelú jáh*, praise ye God), seraph (coined from the plural *seraphim*), shekel, etc.

(10) *Syriac :*—

Abbess, abbot, abbey (all from *abba*, father), damask (from *Damascus*), damson (a Damascene plum), muslin (from the town *Mosul*), mammon (riches), Messiah (anointed), etc.

(11) *Arabic:* rather numerous; some have come from the Levantine trade through Greek or Italian; others by way of Spain, in which country the Arab-speaking Moors were dominant for about 700 years; others more indirectly by way of France.

Admiral (spelt by Milton as *ammiral;* Arab. *amir*, prince, with suffix *-al*, which may have arisen in various ways: see *New Eng. Dict.*), alcove (a recess), algebra, Arabesque, arsenal, artichoke, assassin, caliph, caraway (seed), cipher, coffee, cotton, garbage, garble, nadir, zenith, etc.

(12) *Turkish* :—

Bey (provincial governor), horde, bosh (nonsense), ottoman (from *Ottoman*, founder of the Turkish empire), yataghan (a dagger-like sword), janizary, horde, and a few more.

(13) *Dravidian* (Southern India) :—

Teak (a kind of timber), bandicoot, mungoose, curry, cheroot, cooly (labourer), mango (kind of fruit), tope (mango-orchard), pariah (out-caste), and a few more.

(14) *Malay* :—

Bamboo, caddy (small tea-chest), cockatoo, gong, mangrove, ourang-outang, paddy (rice), rattan (cane), sago, upas (a (fabled) poisonous tree), amuck (as in the phrase "to run amuck." Dryden treats the *a* as an article, and uses the phrase "to run *an* Indian muck." The noun *mucker* for *muck* is well fixed in colloquial speech).

(15) *Chinese* :—

China (in the sense of porcelain), tea (Ch. *tsa*, *chá*; the last, though not used in England, is universally used in India, where it became current through the Portuguese), nankeen (a kind of cloth, from *Nankin*).

(16) *Thibetan* :—

Lama (Buddhist high priest at Llassa), yak (Thib. ox).

(17) *Australian* :—

Boomerang, kangaroo, paramatta (so called from the place).

(18) *Polynesian* :—

Taboo (a prohibition), tattoo.

(19) *Egyptian* :—

Behemoth, sack (hence dim. *satchel*, and *sack-cloth*), gum, gypsy, ibis, oäsis, paper (*papyrus*).

(20) *North African* :—

Barb (a horse), morocco (from the country), fez (Moorish cap).

(21) *West African* :—

Canary, chimpanzee, guinea, gorilla, yam (sweet potato).

(22) *North American* :—

Caucus (perhaps, one who pushes on ; now, a preliminary meeting for a political purpose), moose, skunk, squaw, tobacco, tomahawk, totem (ancestral symbol), wigwam (Indian hut), opossum, raccoon.

(23) *Mexican* :—

Cocoa (orig. *cacao*), chocolate, copal, jalap, tomato.

(24) *Peruvian* :—

Alpaca, coca (whence cocaine), condor, guano, llama, pampa (a wide grassy plain in South America : cf. *prairie* in North America, and *steppe* in Russia), jerked beef (corruption of *charqui*, raw meat cut up into strips and dried in the sun), puma.

CHAPTER III.—SOUNDS AND SYMBOLS.

(Compiled chiefly from chaps. v. xvi. xviii. of Skeat's *Princ. Eng. Etym.* series i.)

SECTION 1.—ALPHABET, PRESENT AND PAST.

51. Modern English Alphabet.—A letter is a visible symbol intended to represent an articulate sound. The English alphabet now consists of 26 letters, each of which has two forms, the large or capital and the small:—

A, a	E, e	I, i	M, m	Q, q	U, u	X, x
B, b	F, f	J, j	N, n	R, r	V, v	Y, y
C, c	G, g	K, k	O, o	S, s	W, w	Z, z
D, d	H, h	L, l	P, p	T, t		

Capitals are used for the first letter of a sentence following a full stop or a note of interrogation; for proper names; for the names of days and months; for the name of the Deity; for the pronoun "I"; for the first letter of every line of poetry; for titles of honour or office; for the first letters of a quoted speech or sentence; for the interjection "O."

Note.—The order of our letters is based on that of the Greek and Latin alphabets.

52. Anglo-Saxon Alphabet.—The Angles, Frisians, and Saxons, who colonised Britain, brought with them from the Continent their national Runic alphabet, which was founded on Latin as there used.

On their conversion to Christianity they adopted the Latin alphabet in its *British* form, which they learnt from the conquered Celts. To this they afterwards added from their own runes three new symbols—(1) þ (= th, called *thorn*); (2) ð (= th, called *eth*, which is merely a *d* crossed); (3) ƿ (= w, called *wén*); also the vowel æ (= the short sound of *a* in *cat*). (To avoid the risk of ƿ being confused with þ or *p*, editors of A.S. MSS. now use *w* for ƿ).

The A.S. alphabet had no *j*, *q*, or *v*. These were afterwards borrowed from French. *k* and *z* were rarely used.

Note 1.—The name *Runes* was originally given to the letters or characters belonging to the written language of the ancient Norse, but it is often applied to the letters used by any of the ancient nations of Northern Europe, whether Norse or any other branch of Teutons. The oldest runic alphabet had sixteen letters only; the later had many more, up to twenty-four at least. The word *rune* means mystery, in allusion to the fact that the knowledge of runes was confined to a very select few, and these few chiefly wizards or sorcerers.

Note 2.—The symbol *j* is merely a late variant of *i*, and arose from the practice of writing the *i* with a tail, as in i, ij. This explains why the *j* is still always written with a dot.

Note 3.—The symbol *v* is merely another form of *u*, and was used either as a vowel or a consonant. The letter *w* is merely a double *v*, though it is called a double *u*. The Anglo-French scribes substituted *w* for the Runic ƿ.

Note 4.—The A.S. symbol *æ* is now entirely extinct. It must not be confounded with the Romanic *æ* and *œ*, which are sounded as *ē*, or with the Greek *æ*, as in *archæology*, where *æ* is meant to represent the Greek *ai*. The symbols *æ* and *œ* ought not to be used at all. It is much better to write *medieval* than *mediæval*, *phenomenon* than *phænomenon*, as we already write *ether*, *Egypt*, etc. (See Skeat's *Student's Pastime*, p. 223.)

53. Values of Anglo-Saxon Letters.—The consonants *b*, *d*, *k*, *l*, *m*, *n*, *p*, *t* had their present values. *C* was originally sounded as *k* in *all* positions, and of the two was much more commonly used: in later A.S. it became *ch* before *e* and *i*; thus A.S. *cin* gradually became *chin*. Until *qu* was brought into use by Anglo-French scribes, *cw* was used for expressing the sound of *kw* (or *qu*). Similarly *g* had originally the guttural sound of *g* in *go* before *e* and *i*; it never had the *j* sound that it can now have before these two vowels, but it sometimes had the sound of consonantal *y*, as in A.S. *gé*, sounded as *yea*, and now spelt and sounded as *ye* (pronoun). Initial *h* had the same sound that it now has, but medial and final *h* were sounded as guttural *ch*, as in the Scotch *loch* (cf. *Loch* Lomond). *S* did duty for *s* and *z*. The A.S. *z* was sounded as *ts* or *dz*, not as modern *z*. *F* did duty for *f* and *v*, and was sounded as *v* between two vowels, as in *seofon* = seven; cf. Romanic *nephew* = nevew. The letters þ and ð were used promiscuously either for the sound of *th* in "this" or for that of *th* in "thin." The letter *y* was invariably a vowel, never a consonant; and it had the sound of German *ü*, which afterwards became confused and finally identified with our own *i*. The sound of *y* consonant was denoted by *ge* or *gi*, as already shown.

The short vowels *a*, *e*, *i*, *o*, *u*, and the long or accented vowels *á*, *é*, *í*, *ó*, *ú* had the same sounds as in modern Italian. The diphthong *æ*, the most characteristic sound in Old English, had the sound of *a* in *cat*, as was stated in § 52. In the accented form *ǽ* expressed the corresponding *long* sound, and had something like the sound of *a* in *Mary*, or like that of the bleat of a sheep in *baa*.

Note.—In A.S. the *a* (unaccented) was more open than the *a* in *cat*; it was more like the *a* in Ger. *mann* (man).

Section 2.—Consonants.

54. Vowels and Consonants.—Those letters or symbols that are used to express the *open* sounds of a language are called vowels. In producing such sounds the emission of the breath, though it is modified by the organs of speech, is not interrupted or stopped by actual contact between any of these organs.

Consonants, on the other hand, are the symbols used to express the *closer* sounds of a language. Such sounds are produced by the contact of one organ of speech with another, whereby the stream of breath is wholly or partially stopped.[1]

An organ of speech is any part of our bodily structure which helps us to utter articulate sounds.

The chief organs are the tongue, the throat, the palate, the teeth, and the lips. By means of these organs the breath is modified as it passes through the larynx. The science that deals with speech-sounds is called *Phonetics* (from Greek *phon-e*, sound or voice).

55. Classification of Consonants.—Consonants can be classified according to the organ chiefly used in sounding them :—

(1) **Gutturals** (Lat. *guttur*, throat): formed by raising the *back* of the tongue against the soft palate.

(2) **Palatals** (Lat. *palatum*, palate): formed by raising the *front* of the tongue towards the *hard* palate or palate proper.

(3) **Dentals** (Lat. *dent-es*, teeth): formed by bringing the *point* of the tongue towards the teeth or upper gums.

(4) **Labials** (Lat. *labium*, lip): formed by closing the lips.

(5) **Glottal** (Gr. *glottis*, mouth of windpipe): the name given to the open throat-sound expressed by the letter *h*.

Consonantal sounds have been also subdivided into—I. **Stops** or **Mutes**, viz. Gutturals *k*, *g*; Dentals *t*, *d*; and Labials *p*, *b*; in forming which the breath is entirely stopped for a time, until it is released again with an explosion. II. **Continuants** or **Spirants**, viz. Palatals *ch*, *j*; Dentals *th*(in), *th*(is); Labials *f*, *v*, and *wh*, *w*; Sibilants *s*, *z*, and *sh*, *zh*; and the letters *h* and *y*; in forming all which the breath is not stopped, but only squeezed, so that the sound can be kept up by merely con-

---

[1] This definition, however, does not apply to the exceptional letter *h*, which is a mere breath.

tinuing the breath. III. **Liquids** or flowing letters, viz. *l*, *m*, *n*, *ng*, *r*, which are "intermediate between the Stops on the one hand and the Continuants on the other; for they partially obstruct the breath-passage, not closing it entirely like the Stops, nor leaving a free channel for it through the mouth, like the Continuants" (Miss Soames).[1]

A third subdivision is into **Voiced** and **Voiceless**, of which an explanation will be found in § 57.

The tabular statement given in p. 50 shows how our consonantal sounds, twenty-five in number, are classified with reference to the three principles of subdivision just named. These twenty-five sounds, excepting the two marked with an asterisk, are simple: *ch* and *j* are compound.[2]

On account of their hissing sound, *s*, *z*, *sh*, and *zh* are called **Sibilants** (Lat. *sibilant-es*).

W and *y* are called semi-vowels, because they are used sometimes as vowels and sometimes as consonants; cf. *we*, f-*ew*; *ye*-t, th-*ey*.

56. How the Sounds are formed.—The reader should test the accuracy of the following remarks by noting the movements of his own organs of speech in sounding each consonant:[3]—

Stops: The six stops are classified according to the place where the breath is stopped. "In the back-stops **k** and **g** (gutturals), it is stopped by the back of the tongue touching the soft palate; in the point-stops **t** and **d** (dentals), it is stopped by

---

[1] *Introduction to the Study of Phonetics*, p. 35.

[2] The palatal sounds represented by *ch* and *j* have been analysed by phoneticians into *t* + *sh* and *d* + *zh* respectively, and are called by Dr. Murray (*New English Dictionary*) "consonantal diphthongs." In Sanskrit, however, they are regarded as simple sounds, and are both represented by single consonants, which are named *tálabya*, that is, "palatal."

Owing to the insufficiency of our alphabet we use *digraphs* to represent the sounds of *ng*, *th*, *wh*, *sh*, and *zh*. To represent the voiced sound of *th* (viz. that of *th* in "this") a sixth digraph, *dh*, is sometimes added. These six sounds are all as simple as if they were expressed by a single letter, and not by a digraph or combination of two letters.

The sound of *zh* occurs in such words as *azure*, *leisure*, *elision*, etc.

The sound of *wh* is seldom heard except in the North of England and in Scotland. Thus *while* is usually pronounced the same as *wile*.

No mention in the table (p. 50) is made of *c*, *q*, and *x*, because *c* has the sound of either *s* or *k*; *q* has the sound of *k* in *qu* = kw; and *x* has the sound of *ks* in *ex-tra* or of *gz* in *exert*.

[3] The account given in the text is based on the description given by Miss Laura Soames in *Introduction to the Study of Phonetics*, pp. 30-39.

		(1) Guttural.	(2) Palatal.		(3) Dental. (a) Dental.	(3) Dental. (b) Inter-dental.	(4) Labial. (a) Labial.	(4) Labial. (b) Labio-dental.	(4) Labial. (c) Labio-guttural.	(5) Glottal.
I. Stops	Voiceless	k	...		t	...	p	...	...	...
	Voiced	g	...		d	...	b	...	...	...
II. Continuants	Voiceless	...	*ch	sh	s	th(in)	...	f	wh	h
	Voiced	...	*j, y	zh	z	th(is)	...	v	w	...
III. Liquids (all voiced)	Nasal	ng	...		n	...	m	...	...	...
	Lingual	...	r		l	...	...	...	...	...

the point of the tongue touching the upper gums; in the lip-stops **p** and **b** (labials), it is stopped by closing the lips" (Soames).

(1) **Gutturals.**—The digraph *ng* is called a nasal in the above table, because, while the back of the tongue is raised against the soft palate, the breath passes up the nose-passage and escapes through the nostrils. A cold in the head, by blocking up the nose-passage, causes the *ng* to be sounded almost as a pure guttural *g*.

(2) **Palatals.**—In sounding *ch* and *j* the front of the tongue *touches* the hard palate, whereas in sounding *y* it comes *near* the hard palate, but does not quite touch it. For the sounding of *y* the tongue is in very much the same position as in sounding *i*; and hence *i* becomes *y* before a vowel, as in *opinion* = opinyon.

Sh and *zh* are the sibilant palatals corresponding to *ch* and *j* respectively; and hence one is sometimes interchanged with the other; as in *chair*, *chaise* (sounded as shaise); *jujube*, sometimes sounded as *zhuzhube* (Fr.).

In sounding *r* the tongue, after almost touching the hard palate, is made to vibrate towards the upper gums. Hence *r* has been called the trilled consonant. Except in the North, however, it is never really heard as a consonant, unless it is followed by a vowel in the same or in the next word; cf. *far-ther* (sounded as *father*), *farr-ier*.

(3) **Dentals.**—In sounding *t* and *d* the point of the tongue, as has been stated already, touches the upper gums. In sounding *s* and *z* it comes very near the roots of the upper teeth, but does not quite touch them.

The sounds of *th*(in) and *th*(is) are called "inter-dental," because in forming these sounds the point of the tongue is placed *between* (Lat. *inter*) the upper and lower teeth.

In sounding *s* and *z* the point of the tongue, as we have already explained, comes very near the roots of the upper teeth. The tongue is therefore in an intermediate position between that used in sounding *t* and *d* and that used in sounding *th*(in) and *th*(is). Thus a foreigner, unable to sound the *th* in *thanks*, will say *sanks*. Similarly *bind-eth* became *bind-es* (voiceless *s*), and eventually *bind-s* (voiced *s* = *z*, through contact with voiced *d*). Eng. *water* became Ger. *wasser*.

In forming the sounds of *n* and *l* the point of the tongue touches the upper gums; but in sounding *n* the breath escapes through the nose-passage, while in sounding *l* it escapes at one side or at both sides of the tongue. Hence *n* is called a nasal dental, and *l* a lateral one. If the nose-passage is blocked by a cold, the *n* is sounded almost as *d*. *N* is sometimes (though rarely) changed to *l*, owing to the tongue being in very nearly the same position: thus *flannel* was originally *flannen; postern* is from Fr. *posterne* or *posterle* (Lat. *post-erula*, a little back gate).

(4) **Labials.**—In sounding *p*, *b*, and *m* the lips are closed against each other, while the tongue is left to rest on the lower jaw. The letter *m* is called a nasal labial, because, as happens in the case of *ng* and *n*, the breath escapes through the nose-passage. If this passage is blocked by a cold, the *m* is sounded almost like *b*.

In sounding *f* and *v* the edges of the upper teeth are pressed against the lower lip, while the tongue rests on the lower jaw. Hence these letters are called "labio-dentals" or lip-dentals.

In sounding *wh* and *w* the lips are rounded with the corners drawn together, while the tongue is almost in the same position as in sounding *g*. Hence these letters are called "labio-gutturals." For the same reason the letters *w* and *g* are liable to be interchanged; as in *ward*, *guard* (Fr. *garde*).

(5) **Glottal.**—"The aspirate *h* is partly an open throat-sound and partly a breath vowel-glide" (Sweet). As a voiceless Continuant it is liable to be interchanged with another voiceless Continuant, *s*; as *hemi*(sphere), *semi*(circle).

57. Voiceless and Voiced Consonants.—In the table of consonants given in § 55, some are said to be Voiceless and others Voiced.[1] Omitting the Liquids (all of which are Voiced) we have among Stops and Continuants nine sets of letters paired off as voiceless or voiced, which may be more conveniently shown as follows:—

Guttural	k	g	Inter-dental	th(in)	th(is)
Palatal	ch	j	Labial	p	b
	sh	zh	Labio-dental	f	v
Dental	t	d	Labio-guttural	wh	w
	s	z			

The distinction between voiceless and voiced can be easily verified by any one who will make the experiment on his own organs. For example, we find it very easy to sound *ka*, so long as the

[1] Other names given for Voiceless are "Surd" and "Whispered"; and for Voiced other names are "Sonant" and "Breathed." These are equally suitable. The names Hard and Soft, Sharp and Flat are also used; but they are not suitable.

k is followed by a vowel; but if we cut off the vowel and try to sound the *k* alone, we cannot produce an audible sound, though we are conscious of a feeling of muscular tension in the tongue. There is no *voice* or audible sound in it; and hence the consonant is said to be voiceless.

On the other hand, if we make a similar experiment with *ga*, we find that even without the assistance of the vowel it is possible to make an audible guggle. This consonant, therefore, is said to be voiced or sonant. The voiced or sonant consonants are midway between vowels and the voiceless consonants.

Since the organs of speech are the same in all races of men alike, the distinction between Voiceless and Voiced holds good in the pronunciation of *all* languages, and not only of English. The following rules are of wide application :—

Rule I.—Voiceless consonants are assimilated in sound to voiceless ones, and voiced to voiced.

(*a*) In monosyllables the first letter usually holds its ground, and the second one gives way to the first; as *dogs* = dogz, *cabs* = cabz, *looked* = lookt.

(*b*) In dissyllables or compound words the first letter usually gives way to the second one; as in *five-teen*, sounded and spelt as *fif-teen*; *cup-board*, sounded, but not spelt, as *cub-board*; *black-guard*, sounded, but not spelt, as *blag-guard*.

Rule II.—A voiceless consonant is often voiced, when it is placed in vocalic company, that is, between two vowels. Thus in *breath* the *th* is voiceless, while in *breathe* it is voiced. Again *rise* is sounded as *rize*, not as *rice*.

Note.—There are, however, exceptions, as in, *dose*, etc. But the voiceless sound of *s* is more commonly spelt as *c*, provided it is at the end of a syllable and followed by *e* or *i*, as in *vice*, *glance*, etc.

Rule III.—When a consonant of one class is *substituted*, as sometimes happens, for a consonant of another class, a voiceless consonant is replaced by a voiceless one, and a voiced by a voiced, as per Rule I. Thus *bat* (winged mammal) was spelt *bakke* in Mid. Eng., where voiceless *t* has been substituted for voiceless *k*.

Rule IV.—When an *intrusive* consonant (that is, one not belonging to the root) is inserted into a word, the intruder is usually of the same class as the consonant going before :—

Num-*b*-er, Lat. *num-er-us*; gen-*d*-er, Lat. *gen-er-is*; thun-*d*-er, A.S. un-or. (Observe that the *m* and *b* are both labials, while the *n* and *d* are both dentals.)

58. Voiced Consonants changed to Vowels.—A voiced

or sonant consonant (which, as we have shown above, is something midway between a voiceless consonant and a vowel) sometimes loses its consonantal force and becomes vocalic,—a change which began to take effect in Anglo-Saxon times.

A good example is furnished by the letter *g*, which is sometimes vocalised, sometimes made silent, and sometimes lost.

(*a*) From *g* to *gh* (silent):—*hnǽg-(an)* becomes *neigh; weg-(an), weigh; síg-(an), sigh.*

(*b*) From *g* to *y* (vocal) or *i*:—*dæg* becomes *day; grǽg* becomes *gray; nægel* becomes *nail; stigel* becomes *stile.*

(*c*) From final *ig* to *y*; *ǽn-ig* becomes *any; hál-ig, holy; cear-ig, chary.* (Here the *g* fell off altogether, leaving *i*, which became *y*.)

(*d*) From *g* to *w* (vocal):—*ág-en* becomes *own* (adj.); *drag-(an), draw; fug-ol, fowl; búg-(an), bow* (verb).

(*e*) From *g* to *ow* (vocal):—*morg-(en)* becomes *morrow; furg, furrow; sorg, sorrow; holg, hollow.*

Note.—The examples in (*a*), (*b*), (*c*), in which the *g* became silent *gh* or *y*, or fell off altogether, are distinguished from those in (*d*) and (*e*) by the quality of the preceding vowel. In (*a*), (*b*), (*c*) the preceding vowel is palatal, viz. *æ*, *e*, or *i* (by "palatal" it is simply meant that they are sounded in the back of the throat); whereas in (*d*) the vowel is not palatal, but pure *a*, *o*, or *u*, and in (*e*) the *g* is preceded by *r* or *l*.

59. Substitution.—See Rule III. in § 57, by which voiceless consonants of one class can be *substituted* for those of another, and voiced for voiced; as when a child learning to speak will say *tat* for *cat*, or *frough* for *through*, or *loo* for *you*.

(1) **k, s** (ce), both voiceless:—*prank, prance; crook, cross;* Lat. *princ*-ipem (in which the *c*=*k*), Eng. *prince.*

(2) **k, t**, both voiceless:—*apricock* (older spelling), *apricot; bakke* (Mid. Eng.), *bat; milt, milk* (cf. *milter*, the male of *spawner*); Lat. *lac-tuca*, Eng. *let-tuce.*

(3) **sk, sh**, both voiceless:—A.S. *scrif*-an, *shrive;* A.S. *scín*-an, *shine;* A.S. *sco, shoe;* A.S. *scǽþ, sheath.*

(4) **k, p**, both voiceless:—Fr. *trompe* (trump or trumpet), Eng. *trunk* (of an elephant, so called from its trumpeting sound); Lat. *locusta* (locust), A.S. *lopust*, Mod. Eng. *lobster;* Lat. *quinque* (five, cf. *quinquennial*), Gr. *penta* (five, cf. *pentagon*); *sect, sept.*

(5) **p, t** (voiceless); **b, d** (voiced):—*apti-tude, attitude* (from Lat. *aptus*, fit); *crypt, grotto; verb, word; barb, beard.*

(6) **th** (as in *this*), **d**, both voiced:—*seethe* (present tense), *sodden* (past participle); *murther* (older spelling), *murder;* A.S. *byrðen*, Mod. Eng. *burden;* A.S. *cúðe*, Mod. Eng. *could* (with intrusive *l*).

(7) **th** (as in *thin*), **h, s**, all voiceless:—*cast-eth, cast-es*, and finally *cast-s; thanks, sanks* (as pronounced by foreigners, who cannot articulate *th*); Gr. *hemi* (half), Lat. *semi; hyper*-critical, *super*-fluous; Gr. *hept-a* (seven, as in *heptarchy*), Lat. *sept-em* (as in *September*, the seventh month).

(8) **m** (labial nasal) goes with **p**, and **n** (dental nasal) with **t** :—A.S. *henep*, Mod. Eng. *hemp* ; A.S. *æmete*, Mod. Eng. *emmet*, or by contraction, *ant* ; *Hants*, *Hampshire*.

(9) **r**, **l** (both voiced) :—*wrap*, *lap* ; Lat. *purpura*, Eng. *purple* ; Fr. *prune*, Eng. *prune* or *plum*.

(10) **b** or **v**, **g** or **j** (all voiced) :—Lat. *rabies*, Fr. *rage* ; *abbreviate*, *abridge* ; *cave*, *cage* ; *servant*, *serjeant* ; *leger-de-main* (Old Fr. *legier de main*, in which *legier* is from Lat. *leuis*, Late Lat. *levis*).

(11) **s**, **r** (*s* is voiced to *z* before it is changed to *r*) :—*are* for *ase* (plural of *is*) ; *were* for *wese* (plural of *was*) ; A.S. *leós-an* (to lose), pp. *lor-en* (for *los-en*), Mod. Eng. *lorn* (lost) ; A.S. *ísen*, Mod. Eng. *iron* ; Old Fr. *vaslet*, hence *varlet*.

> The parching air
> Burns *frore*, and cold performs the effect of fire.
>
> *Par. Lost*, ii. 594, 595.

Here *frore* is the A.S. *fror-en*, for which Mod. Eng. has substituted *frozen*.

(12) **w**, **g** :—A.S. *weard* (Eng. *ward*), Fr. *gard* (Eng. *guard*) ; Old High Ger. *werre* (Eng. *war*), Fr. *guerre*. (*N.B.*—As the French had no *w*, they used *gu* or *g* instead of it. Both are voiced letters.)

60. Assimilation. — See Rule I. (*a*) and (*b*) in § 57. This process may take place either with or without a change of spelling :—

(*a*) Without change of spelling :—*dogs* = *dogz* ; *looked* = *lookt* ; *pressed* = *prest* ; *cup-board* = *cub-board* ; *hast-en* = *hāsen* ; *ad-journ* = *aj-journ* ; *know-ledge* = *knol-ledge* (rhyming with *college*) ; *soft-en* = *soffen* ; *row-lock* = *rul-lock*.

(*b*) With change of spelling :—*hussy* or *hussif* for *house-wife* ; *lissom* for *lithe-some* ; *gossip* for *god-sib* (related in God) ; *gospel* (for *god-spell*) ; *fif-teen* for *five-teen* ; *wimen* (misspelt as *women*) for older form *wim-men*, for *wif-men* ; *Lam-mas* for *hláf-mas* (lit. the loaf-mass) ; *quag-mire* for *quake-mire* ; *an*(*s*)-*swer* for *and-swer*, etc.

In words of Romanic origin assimilation is equally common ; cf. *ac*-cept, *af*-fix, *ag*-grieve, *al*-low, *an*-nounce, *ap*-proach, *ar*-rive, *as*-sent, *at*-tend. All of these words are formed with the prefix *ad*.

61. Metathesis, or the change of place of adjacent consonants :—

(1) **ks**, **sk** :—A.S. *misc*-an, Mod. Eng. *mix* (= *mics*) ; A.S. *acs*-i-an, Mod. Eng. *ask*, or *ax* (vulgar) ; *task* (a duty imposed), *tax* (a payment imposed), etc.

(2) **ps**, **sp** :—A.S. *wæps*, Mod. Eng. *wasp*, or *waps* (provincial) ; Mid. Eng. *claps*-en, Mod. Eng. *clasp* ; A.S. *hæpse*, Mod. Eng. *hasp*.

(3) **r** :—A.S. *brid*, Mod. Eng. *bird* ; A.S. *þridda*, Mod. Eng. *third* ; A.S. *þurh*, Mod. Eng. *through* ; A.S. *cræt*, Mod. Eng. *cart* ; *scarp*, *scrap* ; *granary*, *garner* (Romanic).

62. Initial "h."—The aspirate in French was weak, in Teutonic strong. Hence, in Mid. Eng., which contained many words of French origin, we have *abit* for *habit*, *eir* for *heir*, *ost* for *host*, *ostel* for *hostel*, *onest* for *honest*, *onour* for *honour*, *umble* for *humble*, *our* for *hour*.

There are several words in Mod. Eng. that have lost their initial *h* through the weakness of the French aspirate :—

Able from Lat. *habilis ; arbour* from Mid. Eng. *herbere*, Lat. *herbarium ; ortolan* from Lat. *hortulan*-us (a bird of the garden) ; *ostler* for *hosteler*, due to Lat. *hospitalis ; ordure* from Fr. *ordure*, due to Lat. *horridus*, of which *ordure* is a derivative.

The habit of sounding the *h* in the wrong place or leaving it out is a very old one. Instances of it occur in the *Romance of Havelok* (reign of Edward I.), where we have *is* for *his*, *eþen* for *heþen* (hence), and *herles* for *erles* (earls) ; the fact being that this MS. was (as Prof. Skeat has discovered) written out by a Norman scribe. It arose, as seems probable, from the desire of the lower classes to imitate their French-speaking masters, by whom, as they saw, the letter *h* was not much patronised. "But nature being too strong for them, they were driven to preserve their *h* from destruction by sounding it in words which had no right to it ; and hence the confused result" (Skeat).[1]

The *h* is almost or quite silent in English, unless its syllable is accented. The *h* in *hit* (now spelt as *it*, but not originally so) was lost through lack of emphasis : thus "*hit* rains" became "*it rains*." When the syllable is not accented, we ought to use *an* before the *h*, and not *a* :—

a his'-tory ; *an* his-tor'-i-cal record.
a hos'-tel ; *an* ho-tel'.
a har'-ri-er ; *an* har-angue'.

63. Palatalisation.—In Modern English, Gutturals have shown a tendency to become Palatals, because Palatals can be more easily sounded ; but in the Northern dialect, that is, in Northumbrian and Lowland Scotch, where the Scandinavian element has been predominant from the first (see first note to § 8), palatalisation has been usually resisted.

k or **c** (guttural) > **ch** : (the symbol > means *becomes*) :—

A.S. *cealc* (borrowed from Lat. *calc-em*), Mod. Eng. *chalk ;*[2] A.S. *cierr* (a turn of work), Mod. Eng. *char*-woman ; A.S. *cild*, Mod.

---

[1] *Princ. Eng. Etym.* series i. p. 360. "But," as the author has since informed me, "this explanation is not quite sufficient. It is now observed that many Dutch and Low German dialects have lost *h* altogether. The explanation in the text can only apply to the insertion of the *h* in the wrong place" (Skeat).

[2] Lat. *calc*=*kalk*. A.S. *cealc*=(1) *kialk*, and later (2) *chalk* (with the *l* sounded). The *ce* (=*ki*) is the intermediate link between *k* and *ch*, and in late A.S. it really became *ch*.

Eng. *child;* A.S. *ceós-an*, Mod. Eng. *choose;* A.S. *ceorl*, Mod. Eng. *churl;* A.S. *wicc-a* or *wicc-e*, Mod. Eng. *witch* (still preserving, however, the *k* sound in *wick-ed*, addicted to witchcraft); A.S. *cear-ig*, Mod. Eng. *char-y* (but still preserving the *k* sound in *care*, Merc. *caru*).

Note.—Observe that the change from *k* or *c* to *ch* takes place only when the guttural is followed by *e* or *i*.

Sometimes we have two forms of the same word, one spelt with the Guttural, and the other with the Palatal. Hence the following doublets:—

Bank, bench; dike, ditch; lurk, lurch; mark, march; shriek, screech; seek, be-seech; kirk, church, etc.

g > **y**, and **gg** (written **cg**) > **j**:—

A.S. *brycge*, Mod. Eng. *bridge* (still, however, pronounced as *brig* in parts of Yorkshire); A.S. *geard*, Mod. Eng. *yard;* A.S. *ge-wis*, Mid. Eng. *ywis* (also spelt as *iwis*, and now wrongly written *I wis*, as if there were two words); A.S. *gear-u* (ready), Mod. Eng. *yare;* A.S. *gearn*, Mod. Eng. *yarn;* A.S. *giern*-an, Mod. Eng. *yearn;* A.S. *gild*-an, Mod. Eng. *yield*.

Note.—This change, like the preceding, takes place only when the guttural is followed by *e* or *i*.

Section 3.—Vowels and Diphthongs.

64. Vocalic Sounds in Modern English.—In addition to the twenty-five consonantal sounds shown in tabulated form in p. 50, there are twenty different vocalic sounds in Modern English, making a total of forty-five different sounds, out of which all English words can be articulated, whatever their spelling may be.[1]

The vowel-sounds in present use are shown in tabular form in p. 58. (This, however, does not include certain French sounds that have become current in English, of which some account has been given above in § 46.)

---

[1] There were eighteen vowels and vowel-sounds in Anglo-Saxon:—Seven short (a, æ, e, i, o, u, y), seven accented or long (á, ǽ, é, í, ó, ú, ý), and four diphthongs (ea, eo, éa, éo); *y* gradually took the same sound as *i*. The A.S. *a* was a little more open in sound than our modern *a* in *cat;* more like the *a* in German *mann* (man). The A.S. *æ* (unaccented) was exactly the same in sound as the *a* in *cat*. The A.S. diphthongs need not be considered, as the sounds are obsolete. The system of Mod. Eng. sounds adopted in this book is that described by Professor Skeat in the Note printed (with his permission) in the Appendix, which tallies in essential respects with that given by Miss Laura Soames in pp. 15-23 and in pp. 39-54 of *Introduction to the Study of Phonetics*.

No.	Symbols in Dictionaries.	Examples.	Anglo-Saxon Equivalents.	Symbols by Sweet and Skeat.
1	ă	=*a* in *marry*	æ	æ
2	â	=*a* in *Mary*	ǽ	ae
3	ȧ	=*a* in *path*	á	aa
4	ĕ	=*e* in *let*	e	e
5	ā	=*a* in *late*	é	ei
6	ĭ	=*i* in *fit*	i	i
7	ē	=*ee* in *feet*	í	ii
8	ŏ	=*o* in *dog*	o	o
9	au	=*au* in *fraud*	*nil*	ao
10	*nil*	=*o* in *o-bey*	*nil*	o'
11	ō	=*o* in *note*	ó	ou
12	ŏŏ	=*oo* in *stood*	u	u
13	ōō	=*oo* in *stool*	ú	uu
14	*nil*	=*a* in *China*	*nil*	ə
15	*nil*	=*ur* in *turn*	*nil*	əə
16	ŭ	=*u* in *but*	*nil*	ɐ
17	ī	=*i* in *pine*	*nil*	ai
18	ū	=*u* in *duke*	íw	iuu
19	oi	=*oi* in *moist*	*nil*	oi
20	ou	=*ou* in *mouth*	*nil*	au

Whenever two vowels are bracketed together in the above scheme, this is intended to show that they go together in a pair. In each pair it should be noticed that the second vowel is (*approximately* speaking) a lengthened variety of the other. Length, however, as will be shown in the sequel, is not the only difference in some of them.

No. 1. This is one of the most characteristic sounds in our language. It was expressed in A.S. by *æ;* but as this symbol has become obsolete, it is now expressed by *a*, as in *marry.* Example, A.S. *ræt*, Mod. Eng. *rat* (the same sound).

No. 2. This sound never occurs in Modern English except before the consonant *r*, and even then it is not a pure or unmixed sound, unless the *r* is trilled (*i.e.* followed by a vowel in the same or in the next word), as in *Mary*, *fairest*. If the *r* is untrilled (*i.e.* followed by a consonant, and not by a vowel), the *r* becomes vocalic and takes the sound of *ə* (No. 14), as in *fair* (sounded *faeə*).

No. 3. The short sound that corresponded with this vowel is extinct in Modern English. In A.S. it was expressed by *a* (unaccented), and had the sound of *a* in A.S. *mann* or German *mann* (which is rather more open than the present sound of *a* in *man*). The long sound of *a*, as in *path*, *ask*, was expressed in A.S. by *á* (accented).

No. 4. This is one of the very few sounds (only four all told) that are expressed by the same symbol at the present day as in Anglo-Saxon times. Example, A.S. *nest*, Mod. Eng. *nest* (the same sound).

No. 5. This sound must not be confounded with No. 2; for it is a closer sound than No. 2, *i.e.* we bring the jaws nearer together in sounding it. It pairs (approximately) with No. 4, which is also a close sound, as in *let*, *late*. In A.S. it was expressed by *é* (accented), the sound of which corresponded with the first *a* in *fa-tal*. (In a syllable like *late*, that ends with a consonant, there is, in our present sounding of it, a glide or slight after-sound expressed by *i*, and hence *ei* is the phonetic symbol assigned by phoneticians to No. 5.)

No. 6. This is another of the sounds expressed in Mod. Eng. by the same symbol as in A.S. Example, A.S. *wind*, Mod. Eng. *wind* (the same sound).

No. 7. This, though now expressed by *ee*, is really *ii*, that is, No. 6 doubled or lengthened, but with a difference. The short of *ii* is not the Eng. *i* in *pin*, but the less open Fr. *i* in *fini*. The sound *ii* was expressed in A.S. by *í* (accented), as in *wín* (wine), then sounded as we now sound *ween*.

No. 8. This is the third example of a sound expressed by the same symbol now as in A.S. Example, A.S. *docga*, Eng. *dog*. The sound of this *o* is quite distinct from that of *o* in *o-bey*, No. 10; for in *dog* the *o* is an open sound, and in *o-bey* a close one. If we sound *dog* with a drawl, as some do, it becomes *daug*, just as our word *not* has actually come out of a quicker and shorter pronunciation of *naught*.

No. 9. This is simply No. 8 lengthened, as has been already explained. It was unknown in A.S., and hence there was no symbol equivalent to it. The use of a digraph to express the sound does not make it anything else than a simple or pure sound. It is not diphthongal.

No. 10. This sound is always unaccented. It is never heard in monosyllables. Nor is it ever heard in polysyllabic words, unless it ends the syllable to which it belongs, as in *o-bey*, *mo-lest*, *dit-to*, *fel-low*.[1] (If it is not the last letter in the syllable, it immediately becomes something else. Thus in *ob-stacle* the sound of *o* is No. 8; while in *but-ton* it is identical with ə, No. 14, *but-tən*.) The sound of *o'* is heard more distinctly at the end of a word than at the beginning. At the beginning it is apt to be sounded like No. 14: thus a man will at one moment say *o'bey* and at another *əbey*. But at the end of a word it comes out clearly; for it is considered a vulgarism to say *fellə* for *fello'* (*fellow*).

No. 11. This is a close sound like No. 10, and not an open sound like No. 8. It therefore pairs with No. 10. It does not, however, make a perfect pair with the *o* in *note;* for in this and other syllables that end in a consonant, the sound of *o* is followed by a glide or slight after-sound expressed by *u*, and hence *ou* is the phonetic symbol assigned to it by phoneticians. When the syllable ends in a vowel, and this is the first syllable of a word and accented, as *no'-ble*, *po'-et*, no glide after the *o* is heard.

No. 12. This sound is equivalent to A.S. *u*, as in A.S. *ful*, Mod. Eng. *full* (the same sound); and might be classed with *e*, *i*, and *o* as the fourth example, in which the sound in Mod. Eng. is expressed by the same symbol as in A.S. But excepting in syllables beginning with *p*, *b*, or *f* (as in *pull*, *bull*, *full*), the sound is now usually expressed by *ŏŏ*, as in *stood*. The substitution of the digraph *oo* for A.S. *u* cannot, of course, alter the fact that the sound is single and simple as before.

---

[1] The rule, however, is not quite universal, when this vowel occurs in the final syllable. If a verb like *bellow* is augmented by some grammatical inflexion, as *bellow-s*, *bellow-ed*, the original sound of *o'* is retained, notwithstanding the final consonant. Similarly, if the plural inflexion *-s* or *-es* is added to a noun, the sound of *o'*, which occurred in the final syllable of the singular, is retained in the plural: as *hero*, *hero-es*; *window*, *window-s*.

No. 13. This is No. 12 lengthened, and was expressed in A.S. by *ú*, as in A.S. *rúm*, Mod. Eng. *room* (the same sound).

No. 14. This sound is not represented, so far as we have seen, by any symbol in the current Dictionaries; yet it is one of the commonest sounds in our language. It is called by phoneticians the Obscure, Indefinite, or Neutral vowel, and is symbolised by ə (turned *e*). It is always unaccented. It occurs in almost every variety of spelling, as in the last syllables of *China*, *button*, *sudden*, *humble*, *cupboard*, *tortoise*, *meerschaum*, in the first and last syllables of *America*, *abandon*, and in the middle syllables of *history*, *mystery*, *teachable*. This sound is so natural to human speech, that hesitating speakers use it to fill up gaps in their sentences.

No. 15. This is No. 14 doubled, but long and usually accented. It is never heard except when it is followed by an *untrilled* "*r*" or some equivalent sound, as in *kernel*, *colonel*, *burn*, *bind*, *first*, etc. It was unknown in A.S. (In the word *perturb* it is accented in the second syllable, and unaccented in the first.)

No. 16. This sound is approximately an accented form of No. 14, and is heard in such words as *but*, *one*, *flood*, *touch*, etc. It was unknown in A.S.

No. 17. This sound was not represented by anything similar in A.S. It is compounded of No. 6 preceded by the *a* of German *mann* or A.S. *mann*.

No. 18. This sound is heard in such words as *few*, *Europe*, *you*, etc. The A.S. equivalent was *íw*, as in the words *híw*, hue; *íw*, yew; in which we have made no change in the sound or sense, but only in the spelling. This sound is compounded of No. 6 and No. 13.

No. 19. This sound appears in such words as *moist*, *boy*, etc. It was unknown in A.S. It is compounded of No. 9 and No. 6.

No. 20. This sound is heard in such words as *mouth*, *now*, etc. It was unknown in A.S. It is compounded of No. 3 and No. 12.

Note.—Among the above pairs the most perfect are 1 and 2 (*marry*, *Mary*), 8 and 9 (*dog*, *fraud*), 12 and 13 (*stood*, *stool*), 14 and 15 (*China*, *turn*). But even in these there is some difference of quality, besides that of mere length; for the short vowel in every case is rather more open than the corresponding long one. In the three remaining pairs there are, as we have shown, other slight differences.

65. Classification of Vocalic Sounds.—The main classification is into Simple (*i.e.* pure, unmixed) and Compound (*i.e.* mixed or diphthongal).

The **Simple** sounds, 14 in number, are either Short or Long.

Short (eight)	ă in *marry*.	Long (six)	â in *Mary*.
	ĕ in *let*.		ȧ in *path*.
	ĭ in *fit*.		ē in *feet*.
	ŏ in *dog*.		*au* in *fraud*.
	o' in *o*-bey.		ōō in *stool*.
	ŏŏ in *stood*.		*əə* in *turn*.
	ə in Chin-*a*.		
	ŭ in *but*.		

The **Compound** (or diphthongal) sounds are the following:—

Partly diphthongal (two)	*ā*, made up of A.S. *é*+*i*, as in *late*, *vein*.
	ō, made up of A.S. *ó*+*u*, as in *note*.
Wholly diphthongal (four)	*ī*, made up of *a*+*i*, as in *pine*, *aisle*.
	ū, made up of A.S. *i*+*ú*, as in *duke*.
	oi, made up of *au*+*i*, as in *moist*.
	ou, made up of A.S. *á*+*u*, as in *mouth*.

The two first, viz. *ā* and *ō*, are called *partly* diphthongal, because when they end the syllable, as in *fa*-tal, *no*-ble, they are Simple, corresponding precisely with A.S. *é* and *ó* respectively; but when they are followed by a consonant in the same syllable, as in *late*, *note*, they are compounded with a semi-vowel, which serves as a glide or slight after-sound. In the former the semi-vowel is *i*, as shown above; in the latter *u*.

The four last are on a different footing. They are *wholly* diphthongal. Here the second element is not a mere glide or semi-vowel, but a fully sounded vowel. Otherwise nothing like the compound sounds expressed by *ī*, *ū*, *oi*, *ou* can be produced. The full sounds of both vowels are fused into one, so as to make a third sound distinct from either.

In the compound *ī*, the first vowel is the short *a* of the German *mann*. The long *a* of *path* would give us the vocalic sound heard in *naive*, *aye*, *Isaiah*, *ayah* (Indian maid-servant), which is much more open than the *ī* of *pine*, *aisle*.

In the compound *ū*, the *i*, being placed in contact with A.S. *ú* or Eng. *ōō*, becomes *y*. Hence *u-nit* is sounded as *yoo-nit*.

With the help of an *untrilled* "*r*" (which has the sound of *ə*), five more diphthongs and four triphthongs can be expressed.

Diphthongs:—care, deer, drawer, mower, poor.
Triphthongs:—fire, pure, (de)stroyer, power.

66. Vowel-lengthening by final "e."—The device most commonly used for expressing the sound of a long vowel or diphthong, as distinct from that of a short one, is by adding *e* after a single consonant. How did this device come into existence?

Take the word *stone* as an example. The A.S. and Mercian form was *stán*, and in the Dative case *stán-e*. The corresponding forms in Mid. Eng. were *ston* or *stoon* (Nom.) and *stón-e* (Dat.). Now most of the prepositions in Old and Mid. Eng. were followed by the Dative case, and hence this form of noun was more frequently seen than any other. "As the use of *ston* for *stoon* made the length of the vowel in *ston* uncertain, while in the Dative case there was no such doubt, the use of a suffixed *e* after a single consonant soon came to be associated with the idea of vowel length, and it is now distinctly recognised as the usual way of representing a long sound. It is an extremely poor contrivance; but it came about naturally enough" (Skeat).[1]

In the case of words like *wrote*, *arose*, etc. (which are not nouns, but parts of a verb, and therefore not susceptible of the Dative suffix *-e*), the addition of final *e* for the purpose of vowel-lengthening was due to analogy. In A.S. the past tense of *writ'-an* (to write) was *wrát*, in Mid. Eng. *wroot*. So the word went through the same changes of sound and spelling as *stán*.

67. Shifting of Long Vowel sounds.—The whole of the

---

[1] *Princ. of Eng. Etym.* pp. 32, 33, ed. 1895. Another explanation is given in *Ency. Brit.* under art. "English Language":—"In the thirteenth century the Old Eng. short vowels in an open syllable still retained the short quantity, as *nă-ma*; but by the beginning of the fourteenth century they were lengthened to *nā-me*, a change which has also taken place in all the Teutonic and even in the Romance languages, as in *buō-no* for *bŏ-num*. The lengthening of this penultimate left the final syllable by contrast shortened or weakened, and paved the way for the disappearance of final *e* in the century following, through the stages *nā-me*, *nā-m*, *nām*, the one long syllable *nam*(*e*) being the quantitative equivalent of the two short syllables in *nă-mĕ*; and thus came the idea that mute *e* makes the preceding vowel long, the truth being that the lengthening of the vowel made the *e* mute."

These explanations are not contradictory, but supplementary, both being quite correct. The first (Mr. Skeat's) explains the case of a vowel that was always long. The second takes the case of a vowel that has been made long, but was originally short.

Long Vowel system of Anglo-Saxon sounds fell to pieces, and was replaced in the sixteenth and seventeenth centuries by a new scheme throughout; and even these sounds have since changed (without corresponding changes in symbol) to those current in our present language. (See Skeat's *Princ. Eng. Etym.* chap. v. series i.)

I. A.S. *á* as in *bath*, changed to Mod. Eng. *ō*, as in *both*.
II. A.S. *é* as in *same*, changed to Mod. Eng. *ē*, as in *seem*.
III. A.S. *í* as in *meet*, changed to Mod. Eng. *ī*, as in *mite*.
IV. A.S. *ó* as in *boat*, changed to Mod. Eng. *ōō*, as in *boot*.
V. A.S. *ú* as in *shoot*, changed to Mod. Eng. *ou*, as in *shout*.

The above scheme is interesting for one reason, if for no others,—that it explains how *oo* came to express the sound for which it is now used. One would have thought that *oo* would be intended to express a long *o*, just as *ee* is used to express a long *e*, as in *seem*. This is what *oo* did actually express for some words in Mid. Eng., when the symbol *oo* first came into use, just as *brooch* is still sounded as *brōch*. Since then, however, the sound has shifted to that of *oo* in *boot*, *shoot*, etc. The sound has changed, but the spelling has remained.

Note.—In Mid. Eng. the symbol *oo* had two different sounds—(1) the sound of *oa* in *broad*, Mid. Eng. *brood*; usually denoted by *au*, as in *fraud*; see table in p. 58, No. 9; and (2) the sound of *ō*, as in *hole*, *both*, *coal*; see table in p. 58, No. 11.

The shifting of the *oo* sound implies what is the fact, that there was a general shifting of the long vowel sounds all along the line, such as is shown in the scheme given above. When the A.S. *ú* ceased to express the sound of *oo* as in *shoot*, a new sound was given to it, namely, that expressed by the *ow* in *now* (A.S. *nú*).[1]

68. I. The A.S. "á."—In A.S. (as has been shown in line I. of § 67) this vowel was sounded as the *a* in *bath*, *father*, etc. In Mid. Eng. this was changed to *o* or *oo*, but pronounced as *au*, the *oa* in *broad*. Since the sixteenth century the sound of Mid. Eng. *au* has shifted to that of *ō*, as in *both*, *whole*, *goal*.

A.S. *wá*, Mod. Eng. *woe*; A.S. *cnáw-an*, Mod. Eng. *know*; A.S. *ná*, Mod. Eng. *no*; A.S. *cláð-ian*, Mod. Eng. *clothe*; A.S.

[1] The A.S. *ú* never became *yōō* in sound, but always *ou* or *ow*, as in *nú*, now; *cú*, cow. But the Anglo-French *u* (from Lat. *u*) did become *yōō* in sound. Hence the rule that all words having *ū* pronounced as *yōō*, if correctly spelt, came out of a Latin *u*, usually long; as *pure*, Lat. *pūrus*; *sure*, Lat. *secūrus*. (An exception is *duke*, where the *u* has been lengthened; from Lat. *dŭc-em*.)

ðás, Mod. Eng. *those;* A.S. *gást*, Mod. Eng. *ghost;* A.S. *sáwel*, Mod. Eng. *soul;* A.S. *stán*, Mod. Eng. *stone;* A.S. *hám*, Mod. Eng. *home;* A.S. *tá*, Mod. Eng. *toe;* A.S. *hál*, Mod. Eng. *whole;* A.S. *wrát*, Mod. Eng. (*he*) *wrote;* Scand. *lágr*, Mod. Eng. *low*, etc.

Note.—Here belong nearly all the words written with *oa*, or ending with *oe*.

69. II. **The A.S. "é."**—The sound of A.S. *é*, as has been shown in line II. of § 67, was similar to that of the former element of the *ā* (= *ei*) in *same*, but in Mod. Eng. has shifted to the sound of *ē* in *seem*.

A.S. *hé* (sounded as *hā*), Mod. Eng. *he;* A.S. *ðé*, Mod. Eng. *thee;* A.S. *wé*, Mod. Eng. *we;* A.S. *mé*, Mod. Eng. *me;* A.S. *gé*, Mod. Eng. *ye;* A.S. *hél*, Mod. Eng. *heel;* A.S. *téþ*, Mod. Eng. *teeth;* A.S. *cwén*, Mod. Eng. *queen;* A.S. *tén* (ten), Mod. Eng. *teen* (as in *thirteen*); A.S. *grén-e*, Mod. Eng. *green;* A.S. *sém-an*, Mod. Eng. *seem;* A.S. *bléd-an*, Mod. Eng. *bleed*, etc.

70. III. **The A.S. "í."**—The sound of A.S. *í*, as has been shown in line III. of § 67, was the same as *ē* or *ee* in *meet*, but has shifted in Mod. Eng. to the diphthongal sound of *ī* in *mite*. (In Tudor English it had the sound of *ā* in *fame* or *ei* in *vein*):—

A.S. *bí* (sounded as *bē*), Mod. Eng. *by;* A.S. *mín*, Mod. Eng. *mine;* A.S. *hwíl*, Mod. Eng. *while;* A.S. *wríð-an*, Mod. Eng. *writhe;* A.S. *ís*, Mod. Eng. *ice;* A.S. *rís-an*, Mod. Eng. *rise;* A.S. *líf*, Mod. Eng. *life;* A.S. *wíf*, Mod. Eng. *wife;* A.S. *ðín*, Mod. Eng. *thine;* A.S. *swín*, Mod. Eng. *swine;* A.S. *líc*, Mod. Eng. *like;* A.S. *rím*, Mod. Eng. *rime* (misspelt as *rhyme*); A.S. *twín*, Mod. Eng. *twine*, etc.

Note 1.—The original sound of *í* has survived in a shortened vowel in *women* (pronounced as *wĭm-men*, from A.S. *wíf* compounded with *man*), and in *stirrup* (A.S. *stí-ráp*).

Note 2.—In a large number of Romanic words of late introduction ending in "*i . . . e*," the final syllable is still sounded as if the vowel were *ee*:—*un-ique*, *po-lice*, *clique*, *quin-ine*, etc. (The *ē* sound in "ob-*lige*" has now become archaic.)

> Dreading e'en fools, by flatterers besieged,
> And so obliging that he ne'er ob-*liged*.
>
> Pope, *Prol. Sat.* 208.

71. IV. **The A.S. "ó."**—The sound of A.S. *ó*, as has been shown in line IV. of § 67, was similar to the former element of *ō* in *boat*, but has shifted in Mod. Eng. to the sound of *ōō* in *boot*:—

A.S. *scó*, Mod. Eng. *shoe*; A.S. *dó*, Mod. Eng. *do;* A.S. *tó*, Mod. Eng. *too* and *to;* A.S. *eów*, Mod. Eng. *you;* A.S. *bót*, Mod. Eng. *boot;* A.S. *slóh*, Mod. Eng. *slew;* A.S. *drόg*, Mod. Eng. *drew;* A.S. *mód*,

Mod. Eng. *mood;*[1] Scand. *blóm*, Mod. Eng. *bloom;* A.S. *gós*, Mod. Eng. *goose;* A.S. *tóð*, Mod. Eng. *tooth*, etc.

In the following examples the A.S. *ó* has shifted to the shorter sound "*ŏŏ*," chiefly before *k*, *t*, and *d*:—

A.S. *fót*, Mod. Eng. *fŏŏt;* A.S. *stód*, Mod. Eng. *stŏŏd;* A.S. *gód*, Mod. Eng. *gŏŏd;* A.S. *cóc*, Mod. Eng. *cŏŏk;* A.S. *bóc*, Mod. Eng. *bŏŏk;* A.S. *hóc*, Mod. Eng. *hŏŏk*; A.S. *bósm*, Mod. Eng. *bosom* (sounded as *bŏŏsom*), etc.

In the following examples the vowel sound has been still further shortened and unrounded to *ŭ*:[2]—

A.S. *óðer*, Mod. Eng. *other* (sounded as *ŭther*); A.S. *módor*, Mod. Eng. *mother;* A.S. *glóf*, Mod. Eng. *glove;* A.S. *flód*, Mod. Eng. *flood* (sounded as *flŭd*); A.S. *blód*, Mod. Eng. *blood* (sounded as *blŭd*); A.S. *móste*, Mod. Eng. *must;* A.S. *ge-nóg*, Mod. Eng. *enough*, etc.

Note.—In words of French origin the sound of *ŭ* is sometimes spelt as *o* and sometimes as *ou*. The former usually occurs before or after *m*, *n*, or *v*. The latter at first had the sound of *ou* in *soup* (=*sŏŏp*); *i.e.* it was at first *ú* (long), but has been shortened.

Front, on-ion, doz-en, gov-ern, com-rade, com-bat, etc.
Troub-le, doub-le, scourge, jour-ney, coup-le, etc.

72. V. **The A.S.** "**ú**."—The sound of A.S. *ú*, as has been shown in line V. of § 67, was the same as *ōō*, as in *shoot* or *boot*, but has shifted in Mod. Eng. to the sound of *ou* or *ow*, as in *shout*, *crowd*. In the word *un-couth* (A.S. *un-cúð*) the symbol in the second syllable has preserved its original sound.

A.S. *hú*, Mod. Eng. *how;* A.S. *ðú*, Mod. Eng. *thou;* A.S. *nú*, Mod. Eng. *now;* A.S. *cú*, Mod. Eng. *cow;* A.S. *úr-e*, Mod. Eng. *our;* A.S. *hús*, Mod. Eng. *house;* A.S. *mús*, Mod. Eng. *mouse;* A.S. *dún*, Mod. Eng. *down;* A.S. *tún*, Mod. Eng. *town;* A.S. *út-*, Mod. Eng. *out;* A.S. *ab-út-an*, Mod. Eng. *about*, etc.

73. Two, who, one, etc.—The vowel sounds in these three peculiar words have undergone more than one shifting.

Two, who.—The A.S. forms were *twá*, *hwá*, the vowel in each case being immediately preceded by *w*. The *á*, after passing through the intermediate sound of *au* as in ordinary cases, acquired in due course the sound of *ō* as shown in line I. in § 67. But instead of stopping there it passed into the

[1] We have another word *mood*, which is derived from Lat. *mod-us*, manner or mode. *Mode* is the usual spelling of this word; but in grammar it is spelt *mood*. A.S. *mód* and Latin *mod-us* are not cognate, and in fact have different vowels.

[2] "Rounding" means the lateral compression of the lips, so as to give a narrower passage for the vowel sound. The "unrounding" is the relaxation of this. Cf. *move* with *glove*.

sound of *ōō*, as per line IV. in § 67, owing to the influence of the *w;* and the sound of *ōō* remained, even after the *w* had become silent. (*Twá > twau > twō > twōō > tōō.*)

One.—The history of the sound of this word is still more peculiar. The A.S. form of the word was *án;* in Mid. Eng. it was changed to *oon*, the vowel of which was sounded as *au* in *fraud*, and afterwards as *ō* in *both* or *bone* (see line I. in § 67). In the fifteenth century a parasitic *w* prefixed itself to the vowel, which changed the spelling of *oon* to *woon*. The *woon* was still at first sounded as *wone* (cf. *bone*, *both*). But by the influence of the parasitic *w* the *ō* sound gradually shifted to the *ōō* sound (see line IV.). It was then gradually shortened to *ŏŏ*, and finally unrounded to *ŭ*, so that the word is now sounded as *wŭn*, rhyming with *bŭn*. When the *w*, that caused all this confusion, was discovered to be a parasite, it was discarded, so as to bring the spelling of the word a step nearer to the classical and cognate word *un-us* (Latin). But the pronunciation *wŭn* stuck and still sticks to the altered spelling *one*.

Only, *alone*, *atone*.—In these words, all of which are compounded with *one*, the earlier sound of the vowel, as in *bone*, survived, because in these compounds the syllable "one" was not corrupted by the parasitic *w*.

Anon.—This word was once spelt *an-oon*, being derived from the A.S. phrase *on án* (= "in or on one"). Here then the *á* shifted to *oo*, in accordance with § 68. But the *oo* or *ō* (pronounced as *au*) was gradually shortened to *ŏ*, as we now have it. Cf. *dog*, vulgarly sounded as *daug*.

An (Indef. Article).—This was originally the A.S. *án* (= one). But when *án* came to be used as an Indef. Article, owing to lack of stress the *á* was shortened to *ă*.

74. The "au" sound.—It was stated in § 68 that in Mid. Eng. the intermediate sound between the *á* of A.S. and the *ō* of Mod. Eng. was *au*, as in *fraud*, but that in Mid. Eng. it was spelt as *o* or *oo*. We have still a few words spelt with *o*, *oo*, or *oa*, in which the *au* sound has been retained, especially before *r* or after *cl*, or after *r* preceded by another consonant, as in *wrath*, *broad*:—

A.S. *cláð*, Mod. Eng. *cloth;* A.S. *wráð*, Mod. Eng. *wroth;* A.S. *gár*, Mod. Eng. *gore;* A.S. *ge-ára*, Mod. Eng. *yore;* A.S. *brád*, Mod. Eng. *broad;* A.S. *ár*, Mod. Eng. *oar;* A.S. *bár*, Mod. Eng. *boar;* A.S. *hár*, Mod. Eng. *hoar;* A.S. *sár*, Mod. Eng. *sore;* A.S. *már-a*, Mod. Eng. *more;* A.S. *lár*, lore; A.S. *rár*-ian, roar; A.S. *gán*, gone (sounded as *gaun*), etc.

In some other words spelt with *oo* or *o*, but not similarly derived, the *au* sound is still found :—

Door, floor, loss, lost, frost, cost, soft, off, often, broth, etc.

Note.—In *door* and *floor* the *au* sound is due to the *r*. In *soft*, A.S. *sóft-e*, the ō was shortened to ŏ before *ft*, so as to make *sŏft-e* (which was more easily pronounced), and afterwards (when the word became monosyllabic) it was lengthened out again. In the remaining words the original vowel was ŏ, which was lengthened to *au*, the long sound of the vowel *o* described in No. 9, p. 58.

75. The diphthong "ea."—It was in the Tudor period that the diphthong *ea* first came into use. It was then sounded as ā, like *ea* in *great*. But the ā sound has, with few exceptions, shifted to that of ē, as in *dream*, *beat*, etc. ; cf. line II. in § 67. The change was gradual, and we find considerable variety in English poets up to a recent date :—

Here thou, great Anna, whom three realms obey,
Dost sometimes council take, and sometimes *tea*.—POPE.
The lowing herd winds slowly o'er the *lea*,
And leaves the world to darkness and to me.—GREY.
I am monarch of all I survey,
From the centre all round to the *sea*.—COWPER.
But I beneath a rougher *sea*,
And whelmed in deeper gulfs than he.—COWPER.

Note.—The only words in which the diphthong *ea* has retained the Tudor sound of ā are :—*Steak, bear* (verb), *bear* (noun), *wear, tear* (verb), *break, great, pear, swear,*—nine words in all. In every instance, except that of *steak*, the ā sound has been preserved by the influence of the following *r*, or that of the preceding *br* and *gr*. In *steak* the retention of the ā sound is perhaps due to the strong combination *st*.

76. The diphthong "oa."—This symbol, like the preceding, first came into use in the Tudor period, and had the sound of *au*, as in *broad*, being intended to supply the place of *oo*, which in Mid. Eng. had also the sound of *au* in some words. (See *Note* to § 67.)

We still have some words in which the *au* sound has been retained with the *oa* spelling (see examples in § 74). But there is a much larger number of words in which the *au* sound has shifted to that of ō, and the diphthong *oa* (which, when final, takes the form of *oe*) is very largely used to express this sound in Mod. Eng. spelling :—

Boat (A.S. *bát*) ; *oak* (A.S. *ác*) ; *loan* (A.S. *lán*) ; *road* (A.S. *rád*) ; *oath* (A.S. *áð*) ; *toad* (A.S. *tád*) ; *loaf* (A.S. *hláf*) ; *loath* (A.S. *láð*) ; *roe ; toe ; doe ; foe*, etc.

77. Vowel-mutation.—The modification that a vowel

may receive, through the influence of another vowel occurring in a following suffix, is called Mutation. The first vowel is by this process modified in the direction of the second one. In almost every instance the mutating or modifying vowel is *i*. Thus *Franc-ish* became *Frenc-isc*, afterwards shortened to "French." Here the *a* is modified in the direction of *i*, the result being a new vowel intermediate to the other two.

But the *i* (though usually seen in Gothic, an older language) cannot always be detected in the extant forms of Anglo-Saxon; for it not unfrequently happened that the *i*, after having produced a mutation of the preceding vowel, dropped out of sight and was lost. This is called *concealed mutation*, examples of which are very common in English.

The kinds of examples in which concealed mutation is chiefly seen in Mod. Eng. are:—

(1) In the formation of the plurals of certain nouns, in which the final *-is* is now lost, as *foot, feet*. See below, § 111.

(2) In the formation of Causal verbs; as *set* from *sat*, Past tense of *sit*. Here the mutation is caused by the *i* of the old Infin. ending *-ian*. See below, § 79.

(3) In the formation of the Present tenses of certain Weak verbs; as *sell*, from *sale* (A.S. *sal-ian*). Here the mutation is caused by the *i* in *-ian*, as in (2). See below, § 138.

(4) In the formation of Degrees of Comparison in certain adjectives; as *old, elder, eldest* (A.S. *eald, yldra, yldesta*, through *-ira, -ista*, the more ancient forms of the suffixes *-ra, -esta*). Similarly the *o* in *fore* has been mutated to *y* or *i* in *for-ist, first* (A. S. *fyrst*). ("Older," the other form of the Comparative, is of recent date, and according to the rules of Mod. Eng. grammar has been regularly formed from *old.*)

(5) In the formation of Trans. verbs from nouns or adjectives; as *full, fill; gold, gild; hale, heal; foul, de-file*, etc. The process of change was as follows:—A.S. *ful* (adj.), *full-ian* (Causal verb, "to make full"), *fyll-an*, Mod. Eng. *fill;* A.S. *gold* (noun), *gold-ian* (Causal verb), *gyld-an*, Mod. Eng. *gild;* A.S. *hál* (whole, hale, adj.), *hál-ian* (Causal verb), *hǽl-an*, Mod. Eng. *heal;* A.S. *fúl* (foul, adj.), *fúl-ian* (Causal verb), *fýl-an*, Mod. Eng. (*de*)-*file*. (The forms *full-ian, hál-ian, fúl-ian* are theoretical in A.S., but are actually found in Gothic, where the radical vowels did not undergo mutation.)

(6) In nouns formed by adding certain suffixes; as *fox, vix-en* (in which the *-en* was originally *-in*); *thumb, thimb-le* (A.S. *thým-el*, from *thum-i-la*); *corn, kern-el* (A.S. *cyrn-el*, from *curn-i-la*); *long* (A.S. *lang*), *length* (for *lang-itha*); *strong* (A.S. *strang*), *strength; broad* (A.S. *brád*), *breadth*, etc.

(7) In adjectives by adding the suffix *-ish;* as *Angel* (*Angle*), *English* (*Angel-ish*); *Frank, French* (*Frank-ish*); *Wales, Welsh* (*Wal-ish*).

Note.—Mutation is not confined to words of Teutonic origin. Thus we have *kitchen* from Lat. *coquina* (a cook-room); *kettle* from

Lat. *catillus* (a bowl); *pit* (older form *pyt*) from Lat. *puteus*, *putius* (a well); *mill* (*miln* in Mid. Eng., *mylen* in A.S.) from Lat. *molina* (a grinder); *minster* from *monister* for Lat. *monasterium* (abode of monks).

78. Vowel-gradation.—Gradation must not be confounded with Mutation. It is seen, for example, in verbs of the Strong conjugation. The principal parts of a verb are the present tense, the past tense, and the past participle, as in *sing*, *sang*, *sung*. Here *sing* is in the *i* grade, *sang* in the *a* grade, and *sung* in the *u* grade. But Gradation is by no means confined to the conjugation of Strong verbs; thus we have *bind*, *bond*, *band*. These words are co-radicals,—that is, we cannot say that one is derived from another, and the only safe way to express the primitive root would be by leaving out the vowel and calling it *b*nd*. But derivatives (that is, derived words) may be formed from any grade or special form of the root.

Band, *band-age*, *band-y* (from A.S. *band*, pt. t. of *bind-en*, to bind); *bond*, *bond-age*; *bund-le* (from A.S. *ge-bund-en*, pp. of *bind-en*). *Abode* (from A.S. *abád*, pt. t. of A.S. *abíd-an*, to abide). *Strike* (verb, A.S. *stríc-an*); *streak* (Swed. *strek*, a line), *stroke* (A.S. *strác*, pt. t. of *stríc-an*). *Shov-el* (from A.S. *scof-en*, pp. of *scúf-an*, to shove); *sheaf* (from *sceáf*, pt. t. of *scúf-an*). *Bairn* (from A.S. *bǽr*, pt. t. singular of *ber-an*, to bear), *bier* (from *bǽr-on*, pt. t. plural of *ber-an*), *bur-den*, *birth* (from *bor-en*, pp. of *ber-an*).

Note.—The difference between vowel-gradation and vowel-mutation throws some light upon that between Cognate words and Derived words (see § 3, *Note* 3). Thus if we take the verb *bear* as an example, we find that it is cognate with Gr. *pher-o*, Lat. *fer-o*, Sanskrit *bhar-ámi*, and Goth. *bair-an*, and that in English itself it has three cognate forms, viz. *bear* (Pres.), *bare* (old Past), and *bor-en* or *bor-n* (Past Part.), all based upon the Aryan root *bher*. Each of the cognate forms last named has a vowel grade of its own, but none is derived from any other. On the other hand, *bair-n*, *bar-m*, (wheel)-*barr-ow*, *bier*, *birth*, *berth*, *burden*, are all derived words,—derived from one or other of the graded roots, the vowels of which have in some instances undergone mutation.

79. Gradation and Mutation combined.[1]—Both processes are exemplified in the formation of Causal or Transitive Verbs (Weak) from Intransitive (Strong). (Some, however, of the Intransitives, that were Strong in A.S., have since become Weak.)

Causal verbs were usually formed—(1) from the stem of the *Past* tense of Strong verbs (Gradation); (2) by adding an *i* to the

[1] The German names for Gradation and Mutation are *Ablaut* (off-sound) and *Umlaut* (about-sound) respectively.

stem of this tense, which produced a change in the stem-vowel (Mutation). The *i* is seen in Gothic, but rarely in Old English, in which the *i*, after producing mutation, was dropped.

Intransitive.				Transitive.	
Eng.	A.S.	Past tense by Gradation.	Causal Infinitive.	Infin. by Mutation.	English.
To drink	drinc-an	dranc	dranc-ian	drenc-an	to drench.
To sit	sitt-an	sat	sat-ian	sett-an	to set.
To quail	cwel-an	cwal	cwal-ian	cwell-an	to quell.
To lie	licg-an	lag	lag-ian	lecg-an	to lay.
To rise	ris-an	rás	rás-ian	rǽr-an	to rear.
To blink	blinc-an	blanc	blanc-ian	blenc-an	to blench.
To clink	clinc-an	clanc	clanc-ian	clenc-an	to clench.
Can	cunn-an	can	can-ian	cenn-an	to ken.
To bow	búg-an	béag	béag-ian	býg-an	to bow
To sink	sinc-an	sanc	sanc-ian	senc-an	to sink

The two following verbs, both of Scandian or Old Norse origin, are examples of gradation without mutation, because the Old Norse *ei* is not subject to mutation :—

Eng.	Old Norse.	Past tense by Gradation.	Causal Infinitive.	English.
To rise	ris-a	reis	reis-a	to raise.
To bite	bit-a	beit	beit-a	to bait.

In the three following verbs the Causal forms are from the Present tense, not the Past (mutation without gradation) :—

Eng.	A.S.	Causal Infinitive.	Infin. by Mutation.	Eng.
To fall	fall-an	fall-ian	fell-an	to fell.
To swoop	swáp-an	swáp-ian	swǽp-an	to sweep.
To fare	far-an	far-ian	fer-i-an	to ferry.

Note.—In the verb *ferry*, the final *y* represents the *i* of the Infinitive suffix *-ian*, which was preserved in A.S., and not lost, as in the other examples, because of the preceding *r*, which required that the *i* should be retained.

CHAPTER IV.—SPELLINGS.

SECTION 1.—HISTORY OF ENGLISH SPELLING.

(Compiled from chap. xvi. of Skeat's *Princ. Eng. Etym.* series i.)

80. Phonetic Character of A.S. Alphabet.—An alphabet is said to be strictly phonetic—(1) when every simple sound is represented by a distinct symbol, and (2) no sound is represented by more than one symbol.

Anglo-Saxon spelling was in the main phonetic. Among the consonants the chief defects were the double use of *f* for the sounds of *f* and *v*, the double use of *s* for the sounds of *s* and *z*, and the uncertain uses of þ and ð for the sounds of *th* in *this* or *thin*. Another defect was that the *k* was at first superfluous, as *c* had originally the sound of *k* in *all* positions.

The letter *h* had two distinct sounds, but these were not used at random. Initially *h* was simply an aspirate, as in *hot*. Medially and finally it had a guttural sound like that of *ch* in *Loch Lomond;* cf. A.S. *riht*, sounded as *richt*, which led to Mod. Eng. *right*, in which the guttural, though lost to the ear, is still preserved to the eye.

81. Anglo-French Scribes.—In the thirteenth and fourteenth centuries the English language was respelt according to the Anglo-French method by scribes who were familiar with Anglo-French, but not with Anglo-Saxon.[1] Hence the A.S. forms of the Latin letters were gradually replaced by French ones borrowed from the Continent. The change was not violent, as most of the French forms were nearly the same as those previously in use in Old English. The symbol *æ* (the most characteristic of all the vowels in Old English) and the mark denoting vowel-length were discarded. The letter ƿ was replaced by a French *w* similar to what we still use. The symbol ð had almost disappeared before 1300; but þ, denoting either sound of *th*, lingered on much longer. In the fifteenth century the form of þ was identified with that of *y;* so that in our early printers we find "y^e" for *the* and "y^t" for *that*, used, however, simply to save space, and not to indicate that *the* and *that* were to be sounded like *ye* and *yat*. Thus in Tunbridge Wells there is a street called "Ye Pantiles," a survival of the Caxton method of printing "the."

82. Further Changes in Middle English.—The A.S. *c* (originally sounded as *k* in all positions) was often replaced by *k;* thus the A.S. *cyn* was respelt as *kin;* and *kin* it still remains. On the other hand, the Anglo-French *c* had the sound of *s* before *e* and *i;* and was therefore used with this power in

[1] Though they were ignorant of Anglo-Saxon, they were fond of Mid. Eng., which they learnt, rewrote, studied, and in fact saved. Although in the thirteenth century they spelt English inaccurately, we find that in the fourteenth century many of their mistakes were corrected, as by that time they had acquired the pronunciation of nearly all the sounds except that of *gh*, which perished in the struggle, being dropped by common consent.

words of Anglo-French origin, such as *certain*, *city*. *Cw* was turned into *qu*, as in A.S. *cwic*, Mid. Eng. *quik*, Mod. Eng. *quick*. The vowels *u* and *y*, which in A.S. were vowels only, came to be used as consonants also, the former with the sound of *v*. The vowel *i* or its capital form *I* was made to represent the Anglo-French sound of *j* as in "joy,"—a sound unknown in Anglo-Saxon. The same scribes introduced the new diphthongs *ai* or *ay*, *au* or *aw*, *ei* or *ey*, *eu* or *ew*, *oi* or *oy*, and *ou* or *ow*, together with the consonantal combinations *ch*, *th*, and *sh*. The gutturals *c* and *g* of early A.S. were liable to be followed by a short intrusive *e*, as *ceaf*, *geard*; and this favoured the change in late A.S. of *ceaf* into *chaff*, and of *geard* into *yard*. "Gu" was never followed by a vowel in A.S.: all such words as *guard*, *guise*, *guile*, *guerdon*, *guide* are either new words introduced from French (as is the case with the words named) or new spellings of old words; as *guest* for A.S. *gæst*, and *guild* needlessly substituted for *gild*. *Hw*, which gave and still gives correctly the sound of the first letters in *which* and similar words, was changed to *wh*.

Notwithstanding all these changes, the spelling was still in the main phonetic, though less regularly so than in the A.S. period.

83. Decay of the Phonetic System.—The phonetic system, which characterised the earliest phases of our language, is now a thing of the past: it is lost beyond recovery. Our present spelling is chaotic. The decay of phoneticism may be briefly traced as follows:—

(1) The mixture of French words with English consequent on the Norman Conquest, the disuse of marks to denote the lengthening of vowels, the introduction of new symbols and combinations, and the investing of some of the old symbols with new sounds, weakened, though it did not greatly disturb, the phonetic system. "As the Anglo-French symbols were also Latin letters, many of which retained their Latin sounds, not much harm was done" (Skeat).

(2) As time went on, the sounds changed more rapidly than the symbols did. In about A.D. 1400, the sound of final *e* (already lost in the Northern dialect) was lost in the Midland also. When it remained, as in *base*, it no longer formed a distinct syllable, but denoted that the preceding vowel was long. But even this rule was not regularly applied; for the vowel was still short in *come*, *give*, *have*, *live*, *love*, etc. Consonants at the end of an accented syllable were doubled after a short

vowel, as in *better*. But here again the rule was not consistently acted on; as in *city*, *metal*, etc.[1] The introduction of printing in 1477 (of which "Caxton English" was the first visible result) tended to preserve symbolical forms that were not in keeping with contemporary sounds.

(3) Phonetic spelling was still aimed at even in Caxton English. But a new principle, which worked in the opposite direction, was introduced with the Revival of Learning in the sixteenth century. It was held by the scholars of that day that, whatever the demands of pronunciation might be, the spelling of a vowel ought to be made to represent *to the eye* the forms from which words were derived, especially words derived from Latin and Greek. So it came to pass that, after 1500, English spelling was governed by two conflicting principles, namely, the *phonetic*, which chiefly concerned *popular* words (*i.e.* the oldest and commonest words in popular use); and the *etymological*, which chiefly concerned *learned* words (*i.e.* words derived immediately from Latin or Greek). Thus the Mid. Eng. *vitailles* (provisions), which we borrowed from French, was respelt as *victuals*, because the root of the word could be traced back to Lat. *vict*-us, food. Similarly *dett*, borrowed from French *dette*, was respelt as *debt*; and *dout*, borrowed from French *dout*-er, was respelt as *doubt*, because the former could be traced to Lat. *debit-um*, and the latter to Lat. *dubit-o*. Similarly the Mid. Eng. *sutel* was respelt as *subtle* for the sake of the Lat. *subtilis*, although the *b* had never been admitted into Old French, from which *sutel* was borrowed.

But owing to the faulty scholarship of that age, many of the so-called etymological spellings were wrong. Thus *sythe* and *sent* were respelt as *scythe* and *scent*, because an *sc* was used in the highly classical word "science"; whereas *scythe* is from A.S. *sī e*, and *scent* from Fr. *sent*-ir, or Lat. *sent*-ire. The Middle English *ake* (derived from A.S. *ac-an*, verb) was respelt as *ache* from a supposed connection with Greek *achos*. *Rime* (derived from A.S. *rīm* = number) was respelt as *rhyme* from a supposed connection with Greek *rhuthmos*, from which we get the entirely different word "rhythm." *Stile*, which is really derived from the Lat. *stilus*, was supposed to be derived from the Greek *stulos*, a pillar; and so it was respelt as *style*. The

[1] In point of fact, the final consonant is usually doubled before *e*, but seldom before other vowels: thus we have *pal'-ate*, *met'-al*, *cit'-i-zen*, *prem'-isses*, *mem'-o-ra-ble*, *hon'-our*, *pop'-u-lar*, *mod'-u-late*, etc.

Mid. Eng. *tunge* or *tonge* was respelt as *tongue*, because the absence of *u* after the *g* looked bad by the side of Fr. *langue*, Lat. *lingua*. The Mid. Eng. *iland*, derived from A.S. *íg-land* (= *íg*, an island + *land*, land), was respelt as *island*, the *s* having been inserted, because it was supposed to be derived from French *isle*, Lat. *insula*. Even words of Latin origin were wrongly respelt to make them look like Greek; thus *silvan* (from Lat. *silva*, a forest) was respelt as *sylvan*, because it was supposed to be derived from Gr. *hul-e* or *hyl-e*. The authors of these and such-like innovations, by which our spelling has been ruined, knew something (though not enough) about one portion of our language, viz. that derived from Latin and Greek, but nothing at all about the other, that derived from Anglo-Saxon.

(4) The changes in spelling since 1600 are comparatively trifling; but the changes in pronunciation, especially in the vowel-sounds (see § 67), have been very great. For instance, the symbol *oo*, which ought to express, and did once express the sound ō (as *ee* in *queen* does the modern sound of ē), now has the same sound as the A.S. *ú*, as in "fool." Again, the symbol *ou*, which in Mid. Eng. stood for A.S. *ú*, as in Mod. French, and sometimes even in Mod. Eng., as in "soup," "group," "route," is now usually sounded as in "foul," "sound." Again, the symbol *oa* (introduced in the Tudor period), which once was sounded as *au*, as it still is in *broad*, is now used to express the sound of ō, as in *toad*, *boat*. Again, the symbol *ea*, which in the Tudor period (when it was first introduced) expressed the modern sound of ā (as it still does in *great*), is now chiefly used to express the modern sound of ē, as in *beach*.

84. Summary.—The spelling of Mod. Eng. is, in fact, little better than a chaos. The main causes of confusion were—(*a*) the respelling of English by Anglo-French scribes, which, though it did not greatly disturb the phonetic system at the time, did much to weaken its powers of resistance and expose it to future inroads; (*b*) the adoption of the so-called etymological principle in the sixteenth century by men imperfectly acquainted with the Classical portion of our language and totally ignorant of the Teutonic portion; (*c*) the violent later changes in our vowel sounds, which were not accompanied by any corresponding changes in spelling. We still spell words in much the same way as they were spelt in the days of James I. "Practically we retain a Tudor system of symbols with a Victorian pronunciation" (Skeat).

SECTION 2.—SUMMARY OF ENGLISH SPELLINGS.

85. Summary of Spellings.—In order to give a fairly complete summary of English spellings, we must first enumerate the different sounds, consonantal and vocalic, to be expressed by letters, and then the different letters or combinations of letters that are in actual use for expressing these sounds.

I. *Consonantal Sounds and Spellings.*

From the scheme of consonants given above in p. 50, it will be seen that in English as now used there are altogether twenty-five consonantal sounds, which, taking them as nearly as we can in the order of the alphabet, run as follows:—

1. b 2. d 3. f	4. g 5. h 6. j	7. k 8. l 9. m	10. n 11. p 12. r	13. s 14. t 15. v	16. w 17. y 18. z	19. ch 20. ng 21. th(is)	22. th(in) 23. sh 24. zh 25. wh

Note.—*Qu* (=kw) and *x* (=ks or gz) are not included.

We have now to show the different ways in which each of these sounds can be expressed or spelt:—

1. **b**: *b*ond (initial), e*bb* (final), *bu*oy, cu*pb*oard.

2. **d**: bon*d*, la*dd*er, call*ed*, hor*de*, wou*ld*.

3. **f**: *f*elt, whi*ff*, *ph*legm, lau*gh*, ha*lf*, o*ft*en, sa*pph*ire, lie*u*tenant (where *ieu* = *ef*).

4. **g**: *g*ame, e*gg*, *gh*ost, *gu*ard, ton*gue*.

5. **h**: *h*ot, *wh*o.

6. **j**: *j*ob, *g*ist, Geor*ge*, ju*dge*, sol*di*er, ju*dg*ment, Greenwi*ch*, *g*aol.

7. **k**: *k*ill, *c*all, a*cc*ount, ba*ck*, bis*cu*it, *q*uell, li*qu*or, grotes*que*, *ch*aos, a*che*, wa*lk*, Ba*cch*anal, lou*gh*.

8. **l**: *l*ake, ki*ll*, is*l*and, ais*le*, gaze*lle*, sera*gl*io, Woo*lw*ich, Gui*ld*ford.

9. **m**: *m*end, ha*mm*er, hy*mn*, la*mb*, progra*mme*, phle*gm*, psa*lm*, Ha*mp*den, dra*chm*.

10. **n**: pi*n*, i*nn*, dei*gn*, *kn*ee, *gn*aw, Jo*hn*, Linco*ln*, We*dn*esday, riba*nd*, bor*ne*, A*nne*, coi*gne*.

11. **p**: *p*lace, ha*pp*y, ste*ppe*, Cla*ph*am, hiccou*gh*.

12. **r**: *r*ain, bo*rr*ow, *rh*ythm, *wr*ite, No*rw*ich.

13. **s**: *s*elf, ki*ss*, den*se*, *c*ell, dan*ce*, *sc*ene, coales*ce*, *sch*ism, quart*z*, *sw*ord, ha*st*en, is*th*mus, *ps*alm, creva*sse*.

14. **t**: we*t*, ke*tt*le, gaze*tte*, *Th*ames, look*ed*, *tw*o, de*bt*, indi*ct*, recei*pt*, ya*cht*, cas*te*.

15. **v**: *v*est, ha*ve*, na*vv*y, o*f*, ne*ph*ew, ha*lve*.

16. **w**: *w*ine, *wh*en, s*u*ave, ch*o*ir.

17. **y**: *y*ield, un*i*on, hallelu*j*ah, vi*gn*ette (where *gn* = ny), coti*ll*on, mi*lli*on.

18. **z**: *z*eal, fi*zz*, hi*s*, clean*se*, sci*ss*ors, *X*erxes, fur*ze*, Wedn*es*day, Chi*sw*ick, Win*ds*or, ven*is*on, *cz*ar, bu*si*ness, beau*x*.

19. **ch**: *ch*ur*ch*, ni*che*, la*tch*, na*t*ure, ques*ti*on, righ*te*ous, violin*c*ello.

20. **ng**: thi*ng*, thi*n*k, to*ngue*, ha*nd*kerchief, Birmi*ng*ham.

21. **th**(is): *th*en, soo*the*.

22. **th**(in): brea*th*, Ma*tth*ew.

23. **sh**: *sh*all, A*s*ia, ti*ss*ue, pen*si*on, mousta*che*, fu*chs*ia, mi*ssi*on, fa*shi*on, offi*ci*ate, so*ci*al, o*ce*an, con*sci*ence, *sch*edule, vi*ti*ate, por*ti*on, lun*che*on, *ch*aise.

24. **zh**: sei*z*ure, lei*s*ure, occa*si*on, transi*ti*on, rou*ge*, ré*g*ime, *j*u*j*ube (sometimes sounded as *jujube*).

25. **wh**: *wh*ile, etc. (often sounded as *w*, except in the North).

Total, 180 spellings for 25 sounds.

Silent Consonants.

(1) **b** (after *m*): lam*b*, lim*b*, dum*b*, num*b*, plum*b*, clim*b*, clom*b*, tom*b*, wom*b*, crum*b*, thum*b*, com*b*, bom*b*: (the *b* is excrescent in *crumb*, *limb*, *numb*, and *thumb*; in the rest it is part of the root).

b (before *t*): dou*b*t, de*b*t, de*b*tor.

(2) **ch**: ya*ch*t, dra*ch*m, s*ch*ism.

(3) **g** (before *n* and *m*): *g*nat, *g*naw, *g*nash, *g*narled, *g*neiss, dei*g*n, fei*g*n, rei*g*n, champa*g*ne, campai*g*n, coi*g*ne, impu*g*n, phle*g*m.

(4) **gh** (final): hi*gh*, nei*gh*, wei*gh*, dou*gh*, slou*gh* (mire), plou*gh*, thou*gh*, throu*gh*, bou*gh*.

gh (before *t*): cau*gh*t, hau*gh*ty, frau*gh*t, fou*gh*t, nau*gh*t, thou*gh*t, sou*gh*t, bou*gh*t, tau*gh*t, mi*gh*t, ri*gh*t, etc.

(5) **h**: *h*eir, *h*our, *h*onour, *h*umour (where u = yoo), *h*onest, Jo*h*n.

Note.—*h* is sometimes silent in the middle of a word, as "ex*h*ibitor."

(6) **k** (before *n*): *k*now, *k*nack, *k*nave, *k*nead, *k*nee, *k*nell, *k*night, *k*nit, *k*nob, *k*nock, *k*not, *k*nuckle, *k*nack, *k*nout, *k*noll, *k*nacker, *k*napsack, *k*nife.

(7) **l**: cou*l*d, shou*l*d, wou*l*d; yo*l*k, fo*l*k; wa*l*k, ta*l*k; psa*l*m, pa*l*m; ha*l*f, ca*l*f; Linco*l*n.

(8) **n** (after *m*): autum*n*, hym*n*, condem*n*, dam*n*, colum*n*, lim*n*.

(9) **s**: vi*s*count, pui*s*ne (= puny), i*s*le, i*s*land, ai*s*le.

(10) **t** (after *s* and *f* and before *l* and *n*): has*t*en, lis*t*en, glis*t*en, mois*t*en, this*t*le, whis*t*le, wres*t*le, jos*t*le, of*t*en, sof*t*en.

(11) **w** (before *r*): *w*rap, *w*retch, *w*raith, *w*rath, *w*roth, *w*reath, *w*reck, *w*rite, *w*right, *w*rench, *w*rest, *w*rinkle, *w*riggle, *w*rist, *w*rithe, *w*rong, *w*rought, a*w*ry.

w: s*w*ord, ans*w*er, t*wo*, *w*ho, Kes*w*ick, Chis*w*ick.

Note.—**The letter "r"**: The letter *r* in such words as *dear*, *deer*, *moor*, *rour*, *pour*, is not sounded as a consonant (unless the next word begins with a vowel), but has the sound of the Indefinite vowel ə (described in § 65), so that here it helps to make a diphthong. It is not sounded as a *consonant* except before a word or syllable beginning with a vowel. Compare "*far*, *farr'*-ier"; "*far*, *far'* away"; "*hair*, the *hair'* of a man"; "*boor*," "a *boor*-ish man."

It also helps to form a triphthong or treble vowel-sound, in such words as *fire*, *pure*, *destroyer*, *power*, unless the next word begins with a vowel, in which case the *r*, as before, is sounded as a consonant. See above, § 65.

II. *Vocalic Sounds and Spellings.*

The different vocalic sounds, twenty in number, are shown in p. 58. We have now to give examples of the different ways in which these can be expressed:—

(1) **ă**: m*a*d, pl*ai*d, h*ave*, s*al*mon, thresh.

(2) **â**: M*a*ry, *ai*ry, *ae*rie, b*ea*rer, m*ayo*ralty, *Aa*ron, *ao*rist, th*ere*in.

(3) **å**: p*a*th, *ar*t, h*ear*t, cl*er*k, *au*nt, baz*aar*, p*al*m, hurr*ah*, v*ase* (Fr.), pl*ai*ster, é-cl*at* (Fr.).

(4) **ĕ**: b*e*d, h*ea*d, *a*ny, s*ai*d, s*ay*s, l*eo*pard, l*ei*sure, r*ey*nard, *ate*, fr*ie*nd, Tham*e*s, b*u*ry.

(5) **ā**: f*ate*, t*ai*l, pl*ay*, f*a*-tal, camp*aig*n, str*aigh*t, v*ei*n, th*ey*, r*eig*n, w*eigh*, st*ea*k, f*ê*te (Fr.), cong*é* (Fr.), ball*et* (Fr.), champ*ag*ne (Fr.), dem*es*ne (Fr.), g*ao*l, g*au*ge, *eh*, d*ah*lia, h*alf*penny.

(6) **ĭ**: b*i*t, n*y*mph, pr*e*tty, g*ive*, surf*ei*t, marr*ie*d, coff*ee*, happ*y*, guin*ea*, donk*ey*, w*o*men, b*u*sy, br*ee*ches, s*ieve*.

(7) **ē**: th*eme*, m*e*-teor, qu*ee*n, *ea*ch, f*ie*ld, s*ei*ze,[1] *æ*sthetic, rout*ine*, inval*i*d, qu*ay*, p*eo*ple, C*ai*us, B*eau*champ.

(8) **ŏ**: fr*o*m, w*a*n (after *w* or *qu*), h*ou*gh, y*ach*t, sh*one*, kn*ow*-ledge, l*au*rel.

(9) **au**: h*au*l, l*aw*, l*o*st, t*a*ll, t*al*k, p*our*, *ough*t, br*oa*d, s*ore*, l*or*d, w*ar*, w*a*ter, wr*a*th, V*augh*an, g*one*.

---

[1] The following is a list of all the words in which *ei* has the sound of *ē*:—*conceive*, *deceive*, *receive* (and their derivatives), *ceiling*, *seize*, *either*, *neither*, *plebeian*, *weir*, *weird*, *seignory*, *inveigle*, *Leigh*, *key*. So this spelling is by no means limited to syllables beginning with *c* or *s*, as is often asserted. See for instance Mason's *English Grammar*, p. 14.

(10) o': her-*o*, foll-*ow*, her-*oe*s, foll-*ow*ed, fur-*lough*, de-p*ôt*, Phar-*aoh*.

(11) ō: not*e*, n*o*-ble, b*o*th, t*oa*d, t*oe*, s*ou*l, d*ough*, m*ow*, br*oo*ch, *oh*, m*au*ve (Fr.), b*eau* (Fr.), dep*ôt* (Fr.), à prop*os* (Fr.), y*eo*man, s*ew*, C*ock*-burn.

(12) ŏŏ: h*oo*k, b*u*ll, c*ou*ld, w*o*lf.

(13) ōō: f*oo*l, t*o*mb, sh*oe*, m*ove*, s*ou*p, thr*ough*, tr*u*th, bl*ue*, j*ui*ce, sl*eu*th-hound, sl*ew*, r*u*d*e*, man*œu*vre.

(14) ə: o'-c*ea*n, Sa'-r*ah*, suf'-f*e*r, but'-t*o*n, Eu'-r*o*pe, thor'-*ough*, tor'-t*oise*, fa'-m*ou*s, meer'-sch*au*m, waist'-c*oa*t, cup'-b*oa*rd, pleas'-*ure*, mar'-t*y*r. (All in *unaccented* syllables.)

(15) ŭr: t*ur*n, c*ol*onel, h*er*d, h*ear*d, b*ir*d, bl*urr*ed, *err*ed, st*irr*ed, w*or*d.

(16) ŭ: sh*u*t, bl*oo*d, s*o*n, c*o*m*e*, t*ou*ch.

(17) ī: m*i*n*e*, *i*-dol, tr*y*, l*y*r*e*, s*ig*n, h*igh*, h*eigh*t, d*ie*, r*ye*, *is*land, *ais*le, ch*oi*r, ind*ic*t, *eye*.

(18) ū (=yōō): t*u*n*e*, d*u*-ty, d*ue*, s*ui*t, f*eu*d, n*ew*, l*ieu*, v*iew*, imp*ug*n.

(19) oi: c*oi*l, b*oy*.

(20) ou: l*ou*d, d*ow*n.

Total, 200 spellings for 20 sounds.

Grand total of spellings for consonants and vowels, 380.

Note.—The number of spellings would be still further increased, if we added the five diphthongs and four triphthongs formed with the help of the letter *r*, to which allusion is made in § 65.

86. The same Spelling with different Sounds.

Consonants:—

c: violin*c*ello, *c*at, *c*ity.
ch: *ch*aos, *ch*aise, su*ch*, *ch*oir, dra*ch*m (silent).
j: *J*ew, *j*ujube, hallelu*j*ah.
ge: rou*ge*, villa*ge*.
g: *g*ive, *g*in*g*er.
ti: no*ti*on, ques*ti*on, transi*ti*on.
s: ha*s*, ga*s*.
sc: *sc*ene, *sc*arce.
sch: *sch*eme, *sch*edule.
si: occa*si*on, disper*si*on.
th: *th*in, *th*is, *Th*ames.
x: bo*x*, e*x*ample (=eg*z*ample), chateau*x*, *X*enophon.
ph: nym*ph*, ne*ph*ew.
gh: *gh*ost, lau*gh*, hou*gh*.
qu: li*qu*or, *qu*een.

Vowels :—

a : c*a*t, t*a*ll, p*a*th, m*a*ny, m*a*de, c*a*re, w*a*s, stew*a*rd.

a . . . e : r*a*v*e*, h*a*v*e*, *a*r*e*.

ai : m*ai*d, s*ai*d, pl*ai*d, *ai*sle.

au : *au*nt, h*au*nt, g*au*ge, m*au*ve, meer-sch*au*m.

e : h*e*r, cl*e*rk, b*e*d, pr*e*tty.

e . . . e : w*e*r*e*, h*e*r*e*.

ea : h*ea*r, st*ea*k, h*ea*rt, h*ea*d.

ei : v*ei*n, l*ei*sure, s*ei*ze, surf*ei*t, h*ei*ght.

ey : *ey*e, th*ey*, k*ey*.

ew : n*ew*, s*ew*.

i . . . e : b*i*t*e*, n*i*ch*e*, pol*i*c*e*.

ie : f*ie*ld, d*ie*, s*ie*ve.

o : h*o*t, c*o*ld, w*o*lf, w*o*men, wh*o*m, s*o*n, butt*o*n, l*o*st, her-*o*.

o . . . e : c*o*v*e*, pr*o*v*e*, l*o*v*e*, m*o*r*e*, sh*o*n*e*.

oa : l*oa*d, br*oa*d, cupb*oa*rd.

oe : sh*oe*, t*oe*.

oo : h*oo*k, f*oo*l, br*oo*ch, fl*oo*d, d*oo*r.

ou : p*ou*r, th*ou*gh, thr*ou*gh, y*ou*ng, th*ou*.

ough : r*ough*, hicc*ough*, c*ough*, h*ough*, tr*ough*, b*ough*, th*ough*, thr*ough*.

Note.—The reasons why our vowels came to express so many different sounds are—(1) because the Anglo-French scribes discarded the marks or accents denoting vowel-length in Anglo-Saxon words (see § 81), and their example has been followed ever since; (2) because our vocalic symbols, though sufficient for the simple and pure language for which they were originally intended, are not sufficient for the very composite language that English has since become; (3) because one of the vocalic symbols (æ) used in A.S. has disappeared in modern English, though the sounds that it expressed have remained; (4) because in the sixteenth and seventeenth centuries a general shifting of the vowel-sounds took place, which was very seldom accompanied by a change of spelling (see § 67); (5) because the sounds of certain vowels are affected by the proximity of certain consonants, the presence or absence of an accent, and by syllabic division; in short, the sound of a vowel varies with its surroundings.

For example, the vowel *a*, as shown above, is now used to express at least eight different sounds, viz. those exemplified in *cat, tall, path, many, made, care, was, steward.* (1) The sound of *a* in *cat* was represented in A.S. by the symbol *æ*; as this has become obsolete, *a* is made to do duty for it. (2) The sound of *a* in *tall* is produced by the liquid *l*, which has had the effect of prolonging the vowel and deepening its tone. (3) The sound of *a* in *path* was represented in A.S. by *á*; but as the accent has gone out of use, there is nothing but the simple *a* left to express this sound. (4) The sound of *a* in *many* (A.S. *manig*) may be ascribed to the frequent interchange of *a* and *e* in English; cf. A.S. *thenc-an, thank:* the sound of the *a* in *manig* has changed, but the spelling has remained. (5) The sound of *a* in *made* was represented in A.S. by *é* (very nearly); but as the sound of A.S. *é* has since shifted to that of *ee* in *seem*, the vowel *a* has been made to do duty for it. (6) The sound of *a* in *care* was represented in A.S. by *ǽ* (very nearly); but as this symbol has become obsolete, the vowel *a* followed by *re* has had to take its place. (7) The sound of *a* in *was* (=*wos*) is produced by the rounding of the lips in sounding the *w* that goes before; and in sounding the vowel *o*, the lips are somewhat rounded also. (8) The indefinite or neutral sound of *a* in *steward* arises from the want of accent on the syllable in which it stands.

To take the example of *o*. The short sound in *nŏt* is the same as the short sound in A.S. The long sound in *nō-table* was equally common in A.S., but in A.S. the vowel was accented to express this. The *au* sound of *o* in *cloth* is explained in § 74. The *oo* sound of *o* in *two* is explained in § 73. The *u* sound of *o* in *mother* (=mŭther) is explained in § 71.

CHAPTER V.—ACCENTUATION, SYLLABIC DIVISION.

87. Accent, Emphasis.—When we lay stress upon a *single syllable*, we call it **accent**:[1]—

Sup-ply′, sim′-ply. Re-bel′ (*verb*), reb′-el (*noun*).

When we lay stress upon an *entire word*, we call it **emphasis**:—

Silver and *gold* have I none.
I appeal from Philip *drunk* to Philip *sober*.

Note.—When the mark ′ is placed against the side of a completed syllable, this is intended to show that the *whole syllable* is accented, and not merely the last letter against which the symbol is placed; as *hum′-ble, chil′-dren.*

SECTION 1.—WORDS OF NATIVE OR TEUTONIC ORIGIN.

(Compiled from chap. xxv. of Skeat's *Princ. Eng. Etym.* series i.)

88. Position of the English Accent.—The modern English language delights in throwing the accent as far back as possible, and this in all words, whether of Romanic or Teutonic origin.

89. Medial Long Vowel shortened by Accent.—The

[1] There is, however, another meaning of accent, viz. a mark placed over a vowel to show that the vowel is long. See the seven accented vowels in A.S. described in footnote to § 64, p. 57.

long vowel of an *accented* monosyllable is apt to become shortened, if an *unaccented* syllable is added to it.

The added syllable may be (*a*) a suffix, or (*b*) a word.

(*a*) *An added suffix*:—

Gŏs'-ling (once *goose-ling*) is from *goose*. *Heath'-er* (sounded as *hĕth'er*) is from *heath* (but in *hea'-then* the vowel of the first syllable remains long, the accented syllable being *hea'*-, and not *heath'*-). *Rŭm'-mage* (for *room-age*) is from *room*. *Saus'-age*, sounded as *sŏs'-age*. *Thrŏt'-tle* is from *throat*. *Hăr'-rier* is from *hare*. *Chĭl'-dren* is from *chīld*. *Sŏrr'-y* is from A.S. *sár*, sore. *Dăr'-ling* for *dear-ling*. *Strip'-ling* for *stripe-ling*.

Note.—In *thrŏttle, hărrier, chĭldren* the original short vowels of A.S. *thrŏtu, hăra*, and *cĭld* have been retained by the accent.

The vowel-shortening is conspicuous in forming the past tenses and past participles of some "Weak" verbs.

Thus *lead* (Mid. Eng. *lēd-en*) made the Past tense *lĕd'-de*; hence (after the elision of the final *e* in Mod. Eng.) we have the Past tense in *lĕd-d*, which was finally abbreviated to *lĕd*. From *read* we have *read* (pronounced as *rĕd*); from *hide* we have *hĭd*; from *hear* we have *heard* (pronounced as *hĕrd*); and from *feed* we have *fĕd*. In forming the past participles of such verbs a similar process has been at work.

Vowel-shortening is produced, if the added suffix contains no vowel:—

Thus *wide* gives *wĭdth*; *broad* gives *bread-th* (pronounced as brĕdth); *blithe* gives *blĭss*; *bear* gives *ber-th* and *bir-th*.

(*b*) *An added word*:—

Bŏn'-fire from *bone+fire*. *Break'-fast* (pronounced as *brĕk-fast*) from *break+fast*. *Crăn'-berry* from *crane+berry*. *Hŭs'-band* from *house+band*. *Hŭs'-sif* or *hŭs'-sy* from *house+wife*. *Lăm'-mas* (a name for 1st August or feast of first-fruits) from A.S. *hláf+mæsse* (through spellings *hlăm-mæsse, lăm'-masse*=loaf-mass). *Wĭm'-men* (misspelt as *women*) from *wife-men*. *Fĭf-ty* from *five-ty*. *Mĕr'-maid* from *mere+maid* (=water-maid). *Nŏs'-tril* from *nose+thirl*. *Sher'-iff* from *scír+réfa* (a shire-reeve). *Star'-board* from *steer+board* (Mid. Eng. *stere+bord*, later *ster+bord*). *Tăd'-pole* is from *toad-poll*, a toad which is all head or poll. *Whit'+by* from *white+by*. *Es'-sex* from *East-sex*, *Sŭs'-sex* from *South-sex*, *Sŭf'-folk* from *South-folk*. *Vĭn'-yard* from *vine-yard*. *Fore-head* is sounded as if it rhymed with *horrid*, and *know-ledge* as if it rhymed with *college*. *Shĕp'-herd* is from *sheep+herd*. *Stĭr'-rup* from *sty+rope* (A.S. *stíg+ráp*, where *stíg* means to climb or ascend). *Hŏl'-i-day* from *holy+day*. *Twopence, threepence, fourpence, fivepence* are sounded as if they were spelt *tŭp'-pence, thrĕp'-pence, fŏr'-pence, fĭp'-pence*. *Rowlock* sounded as *rul'-luck* (a corruption of *oar-lock*).

90. Final Long Vowel shortened through want of Accent.

—The vowel in the last syllable of a dissyllabic compound, though originally long, is apt to become shortened, if no accent is thrown upon it.

The *swain* in *boat'-swain*, *cock'-swain*, is often sounded as *s'n* (*bŏs'n*, *cŏx'n*). The *stone* in *brim'-stone*, *grind'-stone* is often sounded as *stŭn* (*brim'-stŭn*, *grīnd'-stŭn*). The *bour* (originally A.S. *búr*) in *neigh'-bour* is sounded as *bŭr*. The *reeve* in *sheriff* (put for *shire-reeve*) is sounded as *rĭf*. The *rŭp* of *stir'-rup* was originally *ráp*, A.S. for *rope*. The *y* of *daisy* was once *eye*, as in *day's-eye* (the eye of day). The *bănd* of *hus'-band* was originally *bōndi* or *búandi*, dweller. The *coat* of *waist'-coat* is sounded as *cŭt*. The *dŏm* of *king'-dom* was originally *dōm*; the *lŏck* of *wed'-lock* was originally *lác*, which by § 68 should have given *loke*. The *rĕd* in *hat'-red* was originally A.S. *rǽden* (mode, condition, state). The *-en* of kitt-*en* was orig. *-oun*, as in Mid. Eng. kit-*oun*. Similarly the *-er* of cat-*er* was orig. *-our*, as in Mid. Eng. cat-*our*. The *day* of *Monday*, *Tuesday*, etc., is sounded as *dў* or *dĭ*. In proper names *town* is reduced to *tŏn*, and *hám* is reduced to *hăm*, as in *Hamp-ton*, *Taun-ton*, etc.; *Nor-ham*, *Totten-ham*, etc.

91. Short Vowel or Syllable in Dissyllables cancelled.
—In dissyllables the vowel of the unaccented syllable, if short, may disappear, and in extreme cases even the whole of the unaccented syllable.

(*a*) *Disappearance of short vowels:—*

Heron is sometimes written *hern; heronery* is always sounded *her'-nery*. The cancelling of the short vowel is very common in the past tense and past participle of "Weak" verbs, such as *loved* or *lov'd*, *looked* or *look't*. Hence we obtain the etymologies of *fond*, *lewd*, *shrewd*. *Fon-d* is for Mid. Eng. *fonn-ed*, acting like a *fonne* or fool. *Lew-d* is for Mid. Eng. *lew-ed*, unlearned, belonging to the laity. *Shrew-d* is for Mid. Eng. *schrew-ed*, wicked, lit. accursed, pp. of *schrew-en*, to accurse. *Fol-d*, occurring in the compound word "sheep-fold," has no connection with the verb "fold," to double together, but comes from A.S. *fald*, also *falod* and *falud*. In the plural and the Possessive suffixes *-es*, the *e* is generally cancelled; thus *day-es* has become *days; mann-es* (Possessive) has become *man's*. Similarly the Mid. Eng. *runn-es* has become *runs*. The A.S. word *ælmesse* (of Greek origin) passed into *almesse* (later *almes*) in Mid. Eng., and finally into *alms* in Mod. Eng. *Luf-o-de* was in three syllables in A.S., *love-de* was in two (sometimes three, *lov-e-de*) syllables in Mid. Eng., and *loved* is in one syllable in Mod. Eng.

(*b*) *Disappearance of whole syllable:—*

Since for *sithence*; *nor* for *nother*; *or* for *other*; *lone* for *alone; drake* for *endrake* (unless the *en* was confounded with *an*, Indef. article); *wanton* for *wan-towen* (*wan* = lacking or not, *towen* = trained or educated); *lark* (bird) for Mid. Eng. *laverk*.

92. Short Middle Syllable in Trisyllables cancelled.—

In trisyllables, of which the first syllable is accented, the short middle syllable sometimes disappears :—

Four-teen-night has become *fortnight* ; *fore'-castle* is often sounded *fō'c'sle*. *Hŏ-lĭn-oak* (that is, the holly-oak) has become *holm-oak* ; *furrow-long* has become *furlong*. *Zoet'-el-aar* (Dutch for "victualler") has become *sutler*. *Glou'-ces-ter* is sounded as *Glos'-ter*, *Dav'-en-try* as *Daintry*. The days of the week have all except Saturday lost a medial short syllable. Thus A.S. *Sunnan-dæg*, *Monan-dæg*, *Tiwes-dæg*, *Wodnes-dæg*, *Thunres-dæg*, *Frige-dæg* have become respectively *Monday*, *Tuesday*, *Wednesday* (sounded as Wens-day), *Thursday*, *Friday*.

93. Emphasis.—When emphasis is thrown or not thrown on a word of one syllable, it sometimes produces doublets—that is, a pair of words derived from the same elements, but differently spelt and having different meanings.

Thus *to* and *too* are distinguished by emphasis, the first being sounded as *tŏŏ* (unemphasised), and the second as *tōō* (emphasised) ; as, "I *too* will go *to* London." Similarly *off* (pronounced as *auf*) is the emphasised form of *of* (pronounced as *ŏv*) ; as, "He fell *off* his horse" ; "The horse was within a mile *of* its stable."

Initial *h*, if the word is emphatic, or if the syllable is accented, is sounded ; otherwise it is weak, so as to be practically silent.

Thus we sound the *h* very clearly if we say, "I saw *her*, but not *him*." But we do not sound it at all in such sentences as, "I saw *her* yesterday. I shall see *him* to-morrow." Similarly, if the first syllable of a word is accented, we are careful to sound the *h* clearly and give the indefinite article the form of *a ;* as "*a* hos'-tel." But if the first syllable is not accented, we do not sound the *h*, and we give the indefinite article the form of *an ;* as "*an* ho-tel'" (see § 62).

To the same cause we must ascribe the loss of *h* in the unemphatic pronoun *it*, which in A.S. was *hit*.

The absence of accent or emphasis sometimes changes or helps to change a voiceless letter into a voiced one.

Thus in the common monosyllables *with*, *thou*, *the*, *they*, etc., the *th* was originally voiceless ; but now through lack of emphasis they are voiced. In plural nouns, and in the third person singular of verbs, the final *-es* in the Mid. Eng. forms was not accented. The *s* (originally voiceless) became voiced even in Mid. Eng., and is sounded as *z* after voiced consonants. Thus *day-es* has become *days*=dayz ; *runn-es* has become *runs*=runz. Similarly in the common unaccented words *is* and *was*, the *s* became voiced quite early, so that *is*=*iz*, and *was*=*waz*.

Section 2.—Words of French or Latin Origin.

(Compiled from chap. v. of Skeat's *Princ. Eng. Etym.* series ii.)

94. French Accent.—In an Anglo-French word the accent fell as a rule on the same syllable as that on which it fell in the corresponding Latin word. Thus the Latin accusative *ra-ti-on'-em* came into Anglo-French in the form of *re-soun'*.

But in English the accent is thrown on the first syllable of a word (§ 88). Hence when the French word *re-soun'* found its way into Middle English, there was a strong tendency to turn it into *re'-son*, and the Mod. Eng. *rea'-son* is the natural result.

In Chaucer's time the accent in this and analogous words was still unsettled; and the poet uses whichever form happens to suit his rhyme or metre best at the time :—

> Til that he knew, by grace and by *re-soun'*.—*Monk's Tale.*
> As fer as *re'-soun* axeth, hardily.—*Clerk's Prologue.*

Similarly in one line he has *hon-our'*, and in another *hon'-our*; in one line he has *for'-tune*, in another *for-tun'-e*.

The words *riches*, *duress*, and *laches* all show a shortening of the final syllable, which in French was *-esse* (accented) and not *-es* (unaccented). Hence these words are now pronounced *rich'-es, du'-rĕss, lach'-es*. The French word *pres-tige'* has with some acquired the English pronunciation of *pres'-tige*. The Italian *bal-co'-ne* is now pronounced in English as *bal'-co-ny*.

95. Accent in Nouns and Verbs.—Nouns are distinguished from the corresponding verbs by the position of the accent, the noun being accented on the first syllable, and the verb on the second; as *ex'-port* (noun), *ex-port'* (verb). Two causes helped to produce this result.

(1) In Old English it was the custom to accent the verb in verb-compounds, as *un-dōn'* (to undo), and the prefix in noun-compounds, as *to'-cyme* (arrival). The same practice was afterwards extended to compounds of Latin or French origin.

(2) When *nouns* were borrowed, they were made to conform in point of accent to nouns of Teutonic origin. Thus the noun *con'-vert* was accented on the same principle as the Teutonic words *fath'-om, moth'-er*. But when *verbs* were borrowed, they came in under different conditions; for they did not come into Middle English as dissyllables, as nouns did, but as trisyllables. Thus the Infinitive mood of the verb *convert* was *con-vert'-en*, while the past tense was *con-vert'-ed*, and the pres. part. *con-vert'-ing*. The accent, being thus thrown on the stem of the verb from the first, was retained as a convenient mode of distinguishing between two parts of speech :—

Ab'-stract (noun), *ab-stract'* (verb); *ac'-cent* (noun), *ac-cent'* (verb); *af'-fix* (noun), *af-fix'* (verb); *com'-mune* (noun), *com-mune'* (verb); *com'-pound* (noun), *com-pound'* (verb), etc.

In words of three syllables, the noun, as before, has the accent on the first syllable, and the verb on the second :—

At'-tri-bute (noun), *at-trib'-ute* (verb) ; *en'-vel-ope* (noun), *en-vel'-op* (verb).

Note.—There is no difference of accent, however, in the noun *ex'-er-cise* and the verb *ex'-er-cise* ; but in the other verbal form *ex-ert'*, not only does the accent fall on the second syllable, but the absence of accent in the first has changed the sound of *x* from *ks* to *gz*.

If the contrast is between an adjective and a verb, the verb, as before, has the accent on the second syllable, and the adjective on the first :—

Ab'-sent (adj.), *ab-sent'* (verb) ; *fre'-quent* (adj.), *fre-quent'* (verb).

But if the question is between an adjective and a noun, the noun takes the accent on the first syllable, and the adjective on the second :[1]—

Com'-pact (noun), *com-pact'* (adj.) ; *in'-stinct, in-stinct' ; in'-val-id, in-val'-id ; pre'-ce-dent, pre-ce'-dent ; min'-ute, mi-nute'.*

Sometimes, however, there is no change of accent to distinguish one part of speech from another :—

Con-tent' (adj. and verb), *con-tents'* (noun). *As-say', con-sent', her'-ald, sup-port', re-spect'* (all nouns and verbs). *Con'-crete, pa'-tient* (adjectives and nouns).

Note.—There is now, however, a tendency to pronounce *contents* (noun) as *con'-tents*, according to the analogy of other English words.

96. Transfer of Accent gradual.—The process of transferring the accent (in words of French or Latin origin) from the last to the first syllable was gradual. It was very unsettled, as we have seen in Chaucer's time ; and was by no means definitely fixed in the Tudor period.

Spenser.—In this poet we have *cap-tive', cru-el', en-vy', for-ést', pre-sage', tres-pass'* ; and *mis-chie'-vous,* which we now pronounce as *mis'-chie-vous,* though in lower life *mis-chie'-vous* is still common.

Shakspeare.—The nouns *con'-verse, rec'-ord, in'-crease, in'-stinct* are given as *con-verse', re-cord', in-stinct'* ; *con'-trary* is given as *con-tra'-ry,* and *ex'-tir-pate* as *ex-tir'-pate.*

Milton.—The following words in Milton all have their accent on the last syllable, where we now have them on the first :—*ad-verse', as-pect', com-rade', con-test'* (noun), *con-trite', e-dict', im-pulse', in-sult'* (noun), *pre-text', pro-cess', pro-duct', pro-strate', sur-face', up-roar'.*

---

[1] Probably the reason why in such adjectives the accent is on the second syllable is that in the adjective the word is nearer to its original use as a past or present participle ; i.e. *compact'-us, instinct'-us, inval'-id-us, ce'-dens, minut'-us.*

The following lines all show some peculiarity of accent, which has since been changed :—

Ne let *mis-chie'-vous* witches with their charms.—SPENSER.
Our wills and fates do so *con-tra'-ry* run.—SHAKSPEARE.
O argument *blas-phe'-mous*, false and proud.—MILTON.
In this great *ac-a-de'-my* of mankind.—BUTLER.
'Twixt that and reason what a nice *bar-rier'*.—POPE.
Com-pens'-a-ting his loss with added hours.—COWPER.
Perishing gloomily,
Spurred by *con-tu'-mely*.—HOOD.

97. Transfer of Accent resisted.—In a few instances the attempts made to throw the accent back were thwarted. Thus Dryden's *ap-os'-to-lic* has not held its ground against *ap-o-stol'-ic;* and in trisyllables the tendency to throw the accent back on the first syllable is not so strong as in dissyllables.

Ab-do'-men, a-cu'-men, ad-mon'-ish, ad-ven'-ture (but *ad'-vent*), fa-nat'-ic (but *lu'-na-tic*), re-mon'-strate (but *dem'-on-strate*), in-ter'-pret, in-ter'-stice (but *in'-ter-val, in'-ter-est*), so-nor'-ous, etc.

When an adjective has a negative prefix attached to it, the original accent is sometimes retained and sometimes thrown back :—

Retained :—doc'-ile, in-doc'-ile ; du'-ly, un-du'-ly ; de'-cent, in-de'-cent ; no'-ble, ig-no'-ble ; hon'-est, dis-hon'-est ; pru'-dent, im-pru'-dent ; mod'-est, im-mod'-est, etc.

Thrown back :—po'-tent, im'-po-tent ; fa'-mous, in'-fa-mous ; fi'-nite, in'-fi-nite ; pi'-ous, im'-pi-ous, etc. (These words are less *felt* to be compounds than those above.)

When a new syllable is added to the end of a dissyllabic word, the accent is sometimes retained and sometimes thrown back :—

Retained :—ad-here', ad-he'-rent ; a-vow', a-vow'-al ; per-use', per-u'-sal ; de-fend', de-fend'-ant ; com-ply', com-pli'-ance, etc.

Thrown back :—de-spair', des'-pe-rate ; pro-vide', prov'-i-dent ; pro-test', prot'-es-tant ; sub-side', sub'-si-dence ; con-fide', con'-fi-dent ; pho'-to-graph, pho-tog'-ra-phy ; in'-cense, frank'-in-cense, etc.

98. Disappearance of Unaccented Syllables.—The force of the English accent is so strong that unaccented syllables run the risk of disappearing altogether. This has been exemplified already in the case of Teutonic words (see §§ 91, 92). It is no less true in the case of Romanic words also, and shows itself—(*a*) in Aphesis, or the loss of an initial *vowel ;* (*b*) in Apheresis, or the loss of a longer initial syllable ; (*c*) in Apocope, or the loss of a final syllable ; and (*d*) in Syncope, or the loss of a medial syllable.

(*a*) Aphesis :—*mend* for *amend; peal* (of bells) for *appeal; pert* (saucy) for Fr. *apert; prentice* for *apprentice; vanguard* for Fr. *avant-garde; bishop* for Lat. *episcopus; scutcheon* for *escutcheon; special* for *especial; sterling* for *Easterling; squire* for *esquire*, etc.

(*b*) Apheresis :—*fray* for *affray; spend* from Lat. *dis-pend-ere; spite* for *despite; sport* from Lat. *dis-port* (Fr. *desport*); *gin* for *engine* (Lat. *ingenium*); *sample* for *en-sample; cheat* for *escheat; spital* for *hospital* (Lat. *hospitale*); *dropsy* for *hydropsy* (Gr. *hydropsis*).

(*c*) Apocope (the most common loss is that of final *e*, one of the marks that distinguish Modern from Middle English) :—*beast* for *best-e; feast* for *fest-e; chivalry* for *chivalry-e; riches* for *riches-se; duress* for *dures-se*.

(*d*) Syncope :—*punch* for *punish; clerk* for *cler-ic; French* for *Frenc-isc* (Frankish); *but-ler* for *bot-il-ler* (one who attends to bottles); *chim-ney* for *chim-e-nee; laun-dress* for *lav-end-er-ess; crown* for *cor-one* (Lat. *corona*); *par-lous* (Shakspeare) for *per-il-ous; part-ner* for *parc-e-nere; ward-robe* for *war-* or *gar-de-robe; dam-sel* for *dam-o-sel; mar-shal* for *mar-es-chal; proxy* for *pro-cur-a-cy; pal-sy* for Mid. Eng. *pal-es-y*, Fr. *par-a-lys-ie* (Gr. *par-a-lys-is*); *sext-on* for *sa-crist-an*.

Section 3.—Syllabic Division.

99. Rule of Syllabic Division.—Syllabic division is ruled by accentuation, and not, as has been sometimes maintained, by etymology. "Word-division has nothing to do with etymology. From a practical point of view *im′-pu-dence* is right, being based on true phonetic principles, *i.e.* on the spoken language. It is only when we take the word to pieces that we discover that it is formed from *im-* (for *in-*), the base *pud*, and the suffix *-ence*. The practice here is one thing, and theory another. The spoken language has *pe-ruse′* at one moment, and *pe-ru′-sal* at another. It rightly regards ease of utterance, and nothing else" (Skeat).[1]

It may be added that syllabic division by etymology is impracticable for two reasons—(1) the component parts of a word are sometimes so mixed together as to be indistinguishable; as *monkey* (2 syll.) from Old Ital. *moniccio* (4 syll.); (2) the etymologies of words can be known only to those few persons who have studied the subject; whereas all men should know how a word ought to be sounded. (Cf. *banqu-et* (little bench), *ban′-quet*.)

La-ment′, lam′-en-ta′-ble ; at′-om, a-tom′-ic ; at′-tri-bute (noun), at-trib′-ute (verb) ; or′-tho-dox, or-thog′-ra-phy ; pro-vide′, prov′-i-dence ; tel′-e-gram, te-leg′-ra-phy ; ex-pect′, ex′-pec-ta′-tion ; me-chan′-ic, mech′-a-nism ; do-min′-ion, dom′-i-nant ; fi′-nite, fin′-ish ; ta′-ble, tab′-let ; nu′-mer-al, num′-ber ; o′-cean, o′-ce-an′-ic, etc.

---

[1] *Student's Pastime*, ed. 1896, pp. 119, 120. The rules for Syllabic Division given in Miss Soames's *Introduction to the Study of Phonetics*, pp. 73, 74, are based upon the same principle.

The terminations *-cial*, *-cious*, *-cean*, *-sion*, *-gion*, *-tion*, *-tial*, *-tious*, since they are sounded as one syllable, should not be divided into two:—

So′-cial, o′-cean, le′-sion, le′-gion, con′-scious, mo′-tion, par′-tial, cap′-tious, fi-nan′-cial.

But in such cases as the following, the initial consonant of any of the above syllables goes with the preceding short vowel, in order to preserve the accent:—

Re-lig′-ion, con-trit′-ion, prec′-ious, con-dit′-ion, o-pin′-ion, on′-ion, ver-mil′-ion, de-cis′-ion.[1]

CHAPTER VI.—ACCIDENCE.

SECTION 1.—THE FORMS OF NOUNS.

Gender.

100. Gender in Old and Modern English.—What we call gender in Mod. Eng. is based not on a difference of words, but on one of sex. Males are said to be Masculine, females Feminine, things without life Neuter,—that is, of neither sex. From a grammatical point of view this is not gender at all.

In Old English, however (as in Lat., Greek, and to this day in Mod. German), the gender of a noun depended on the *forms* that a noun assumed in the course of its declension, not on the sex or absence of sex in the person or thing denoted.

Thus in A.S. *here* (army) was Masc.; *wynn* (joy), Fem.; *wíf* (woman), Neuter; *wíf-man* (another word for woman), Masc.; *mægden* (maiden), Neuter; *sunne* (sun) was Fem.; *móna* (moon) was Masc.

Adjectives had gender as well as nouns; and an adjective took the gender of the noun associated with it.

Gender gradually went out of use, with the general decline of the inflexional system. It was very seldom seen after the beginning of the fourteenth century.

101. Masculine and Feminine endings in Old English.—Three distinct sets of suffixes for expressing gender were once

---

[1] Some of these words cannot be written so as to describe the sound. Thus *religion* is really *re-ligi′-on*, and *contrition* is really *con-triti′-on*. The *gi* represents the *j*, and the *ti* the *sh*. The *g* and *t* are palatalised by the *i*, which then disappears in sound. Precisely as in the case of Umlaut (vowel-mutation, see § 77), so here the spelling represents the stage before palatalisation was completed. In words like *opinion*, *onion*, *union*, *vermilion*, the *i* in the last syllable becomes *y* through contact with the *o* following. The final syllable is therefore *-ion* = *-yon*.

common. In the following examples the grammatical gender tallied with the natural:—

(1) *Masc.* **-a.**	*Fem.* **-e.**
wicc-*a* (sorcerer)	wicc-*e* (sorceress).
widuw-*a* (widower)	widuw-*e* (widow).
han-*a* (cock)	henn-*e* (hen).
(2) *Masc.* **-ere.**	*Fem.* **-estre.**
tæpp-*ere* (bar-man)	tæpp-*estre* (bar-woman).
spinn-*ere* (male spinner)	spinn-*estre* (female spinner).
sang-*ere* (male singer)	sang-*estre* (female singer).
(3) *Masc.*	*Fem.* **-en.**
fox (dog-fox)	fyx-*en* (bitch-fox).
munec (monk)	mynec-*en*-u (nun).
god (a god)	gyd-*en* (a goddess).

All these marks of sex, except a few survivals, are now extinct:—

(1) "Widuw-*e*" has become "widow" by the loss of final "*e*." "Widuw-*a*" (the old Masc.) is now "widow-*er*,"—that is, the masc. suffix *-ere*, now spelt as *-er*, has been tacked on to the stem *widuw*. The suffix *-ere* or *-er* has lost its Masculine force in all but three words, *widow-er*, *murder-er*, *sorcer-er*. The last two have the Fem. forms *murder-ess*, *sorcer-ess*. All other nouns ending in *-er* will stand for either sex; cf. *milter*, *spawner*.

(2) "Spinn-*estre*" is now spelt as "spin-*ster*," but this word does not now denote a female spinner. "Sang-*estre*" has become "song-*ster*," a noun of Common gender, out of which a hybrid Feminine "song-*str-ess*" has been formed by adding the Romanic Fem. suffix *-ess*. With the exception of *spinster*, all nouns ending in *-ster* now stand for either sex, though more commonly for a male than for a female.

(3) "Fyx-*en*" has become "vix-*en*," but this is not now used only for the feminine of "fox." This is the only word in which the fem. suffix *-en* has survived. (The change of *o* in *fox* to *i* in *vixen* is an example of mutation caused by the suffix *-en*, orig. *-in*; see § 77, 6.)

The Teutonic suffixes *-e* and *-en* were ousted in the fourteenth century by the Romanic (French) suffix *-ess*. The suffix *-estre* or *-ster* fought the ground for some time with *-ess*, until eventually hybrids like "songstress" were formed, which showed that the original Feminine force of *-ster* was forgotten. In fact, the final *er* of *ster* was mistaken for the Masculine suffix *-er*, and so *-ess* was added to it to make it Feminine.

102. Romanic Feminine Suffixes.—Four kinds are seen in Mod. Eng.:—

(1) **-ess,** which is added to native as well as foreign words.
(2) **-ine,** as in hero-*ine*, Czar-*ina*, Margrav-*ine*, Landgrav-*ine*.
(3) **-a,** as in donn-*a*, in-fant-*a*, sultan-*a*, signor-*a*.
(4) **-rix,** from Lat. nouns ending in *-or*, as in testat-*or*, testat-*rix*.

The first is from Fr. *-esse*, popular Lat. *-issa*. This is the only one that became naturalised; but even this is not now used as freely as it once was; for no new Feminines (unless perhaps jocosely) are now coined with it. Thus we do not say "doctress," but "lady doctor."

In Wycliff we have:—dawnser-*esse*, neighbor-*esse*, techer-*esse*, cosyn-*esse* (female cousin), servaunt-*esse*, spous-*esse*, etc.

In the Tudor period we have:—waggon-*ess*, hero-*ess*, butler-*ess*, doctr-*ess*, foster-*ess*, champion-*ess*, vassal-*ess*, etc.

103. Feminines in "ess" less regularly formed:—

Abb-ess, Old Fr. ab-*esse*; Late Lat. abbat-*issa*.

Duch-ess, Old Fr. duc-*esse*, duch-*esse*; Lat. dux, duc-is.

Mistr-ess, not formed by adding *-ess* to *master*, but borrowed direct from Old Fr. maister-*esse*, Fem. of "maistre," Lat. magister.

Miss, a contraction of "mistress."

Marchion-ess.—The French word is *marquise*, the regular Fem. of *marquis*. "Marchion-*ess*" is from Late Lat. "marchion-*issa*," the stem of which is "marchion-," prefect of the marches or border.

Murder-ess, formed by adding *-ess* to the noun "murder." *Er* (the old A.S. suffix *-ere*) is added to "murder" to make the Masculine; cf. "widow-*er*."

Sorcer-ess.—The Masc. form is "sorcer-*er*." The stem is Old Fr. *sorc-ier*, Late Lat. *sort-iarius*, in which the suffixes *-ier*, *-arius* denote the agent. When the Fem. "sorcer-*ess*" had been formed, *-er* was substituted for *-ess* to make the Masculine.

Empr-ess, govern-ess, nur-se.—In these three words the suffix is from Latin *-icem*, not *-issa*. "Imperatr-*icem*," "gubernatr-*icem*," "nutr-*icem*," were shortened into French words ending in *-ice*, which in English become *-ess* or *-se*, by analogy with *-ess* from *-issa*.

104. Different words for Masculine and Feminine.—See list of examples below:—

Bachelor, maid.—Old Fr. *bachelor*, Late Lat. *baccalarius*, the origin of which is not known for certain. A.S. *mægd-en* (maid or maiden), in which *-en* is a diminutive suffix.

Boar, sow.—A.S. *bár*, a male pig. A.S. *sugu*, a sow. "Swine" is quite a distinct word, and denotes a pig of either sex. See § 114, *Note* 3.

Boy, girl.—"Boy" is not found in A.S., but in Old Dutch "boef," cognate with Lat. *pup*-us, whence the diminutive form *pup*-illus, "pupil." In Mid. Eng. "boy" meant a menial, as it still does in *pot-boy*, *stable-boy*, *post-boy*, *Capeboy*, etc. In A.S. the word for "boy" was *cnafa*, which in Mod. Eng. has degenerated into *knave*. "Girl" is formed (with diminutive suffix "*l*") from Old Low Germ. *gör*, a child of either sex. In Mid. Eng. we find *cnave-girle* (that is, boy-child) for "boy."

Brother, sister.—A.S. *bróðor*, cognate with Lat. *frater*. Scand. *systir*, cognate with A.S. *seostor*, allied to Lat. *soror* for *sosor*.

Buck, doe.—A.S. *bucc-a*, a male fallow-deer. A.S. *dá*, doe.

Bull, cow.—"Bull" is not found in A.S. except in the diminutive form *bull-uc*, a bull-calf or bullock. "Cow" is from A.S. *cú*, sounded as *cōō*, as it still is in the north of England. In A.S. the name *ox-a* (ox) stood for both. Wycliff has *shee-oxe* for "cow."

Bullock or **steer, heifer.**—A.S. *bull-uc* (not *-uca*), bullock. A.S. *steór*, steer. A.S. *heáh-fore*, heifer. (*Heáh* means high or full-grown; and *fore* is cognate with Greek *por-is*, a cow-calf or young cow.)

Cock, hen.—A.S. *cocc*, of imitative origin; cf. "cuckoo." A.S. *henn-e*, the Fem. counterpart of A.S. *han-a*, a cock. On the Masc. suffix *-a* and the Fem. *-e*, see § 101 (1).

Colt or **foal, filly.**—A.S. *colt*, which meant the young of any animal. In Scand. *kullt* meant "boy." *Foal* is from A.S. *fol-a*, the male young of an animal; on the suffix *-a* see § 101 (1). *Filly* is from Scand. *fyl-ja*, a female foal.

Dog, bitch.—A.S. *docga;* Mid. Eng. *dogge*, dog. A.S. *bicc-e*, bitch. On suffix *-e* see § 101. The *cc* has been palatalised to *tch* (§ 63).

Drake, duck.—No connection between these words. Mid. Eng. *dok-e, duk-e*, a bird that dives (on the Fem. suffix *-e* see § 101). *Drake* is perhaps a contraction for *ened-* or *end-rake*, and the *-en* has been confounded with *an*, the original form of the Indef. article, or lost from want of accent. *Ened* is A.S. for "duck"; but the meaning of *rake* is not known.[1]

Drone, bee.—A.S. *drán*, the hummer. A.S. *beó, bí*, bee.

Earl, countess.—A.S. *eorl*, a man: (its use as a title of rank is of Scand. origin). Old Fr. *cont-esse*, the fem. form of *count*.

Father, mother.—A.S. *fæder;* Scand. *fađir*, cognate with Lat. *pater*, lit. a feeder or supporter. A.S. *móder;* Scand. *mođir*, cognate with Lat. *mater*, which perhaps meant "measurer" or "manager."

Friar or **monk, nun.**—Old Fr. *freire*, a brother, cognate with Lat. *frater*. A.S. *munec*, Lat. *monach*-us, Gr. *monach*-os, one who lives alone. A.S. *nunn-e;* Late Lat. *nunna, nonna*, mother.

Gaffer, gammer.—The first is a contraction of Eng. *grandfather;* the second of Fr. *grand-mère* (grandmother).

Gander, goose.—A.S. *gan-d-ra* (gander), in which the *-ra* is a suffix, and the *d* is excrescent. The stem is *gan-*, cognate with Lat. *an-ser;* Gr. *chēn*. "Goose" is from A.S. *gós*, plur. *gés*, of which the root is *gan* as before. Hence "gander" and "goose" are from the same Teutonic root, *gan*.[2] (The Aryan root is *ghan*.)

Gentleman, lady.—Fr. *gentilhomme;* Eng. gentleman. For the origin of "lady" see "lord" below.

Hart, roe.—A.S. *heort*, hart. A.S. *ráh*, roe.

Horse or **stallion, mare.**—A.S. *hors*, lit. a runner (cf. Eng. *cours-er*). Fr. *estalon*, a stalled horse. A.S. *mere*, Fem. form of A.S. *mearh*, a battle-horse.

Husband, wife.—Scand. *hús-bóndi*, house-occupier; from Pres. Part.

---

[1] Dr. Murray (*New. Eng. Dict.*) declares himself unable to ascertain the meaning of *rake*. It has been said that *rake* means "master" (hence male) and is allied to *ríc* (dominion), as in "bishop-*ric*." "But it cannot go with *ríc*, as the gradation is wrong" (Skeat).

[2] The A.S. *gós* is from the form *gan-s*, in which *s* is only a suffix. *Gans* became *gons* and eventually *gós*, the *n* of *gons* having been lost through the lengthening of the *o*.

of *búa*, to dwell in: (no connection with *bond*, *band*, or *bind*). A.S. *wíf*, a woman; cf. "fish-wife," a fish-woman, one who sells fish.

King, queen.—A.S. *cyn-ing*, "one of noble kin" (*cyn*=kin, tribe). (It has been said that *cyn-ing* means "son of the tribe," but that is not the explanation now given.) A.S. *cwén*, woman. Its meaning as a title of rank is of later origin.

Lad, lass.—It used to be said that *lad* and *lass* were from Welsh *llawd* and *llodes*. But this is now abandoned. No one knows the etymology of either word. Possibly *lad* may mean "one led," Mid. Eng. *lad*, pp. of *led-en*, to lead.

Lord, lady.—A.S. *hláford*=*hláf-weard*, the loaf-keeper; cf. A.S. "stí-weard," stykeeper or steward. A.S. *hláf-dige*, loaf-kneader, hence lady.

Man, woman.—A.S. *mann*, a person of either sex. A.S. *wíf-man*, a female person; plur. A.S. *wíf-men*, late A.S. *wim-men*, the sound of which still attaches to the modern misspelling "women."

Milter, spawner.—"Milter" means a fish with *milt* or *milk;* the old word for soft-roe was *fiske-melk*, fish-milk. "Spawner" means a fish that scatters eggs; Old Fr. *espandre*, to scatter.

Nephew, niece.—Old Fr. *neveu*, Lat. *nepot*-em, grandson or nephew. Old Fr. *niece*, Lat. *neptis*, granddaughter or niece. (The pair of words in A.S. was *nef-a* and *nef-e;* see suffixes *-a* and *-e* in § 101; but "nephew" and "niece" could not have come from these words.)

Papa, mamma.—Fr. *papa*, Lat. *pappas;* due to the infantile repetition of *pa, pa.* "Mamma" should have been spelt *mama*, due to the child's repetition of *ma, ma.*

Ram or **wether, ewe.**—A.S. *ram*, a male sheep. A.S. *weðer* (wether) a yearling; from Aryan *wet*, a year. A.S. *eowu*, a female sheep; cf. Lat. *ov*-is.

Sir, madam or **madame.**—Fr. *sire*, Lat. *senior*, older. Fr. *madame*, Lat. *mea domina*, my lady.

Sire, dam.—Origin as above.

Sloven, slut.—Etymology distinct. Teut. base *slup-*, to slip, with Mid. Eng. suffix *-ein*, Fr. *en*, gives *sloven.* "Slut" is from Mid. Eng. *slutt-e*, an untidy woman; cf. Scand. *slöttr*, a lazy man.

Son, daughter.—A.S. *su-nu*, cognate with Gr. *hui-os* for *sui-os*, son. A.S. *dóhtor*, daughter. (It has been said that "daughter" meant orig. "milkmaid." But this is now disbelieved by the best authorities.)

Stag, hind.—"Stag" has been traced to Scand. *stíg-a*, to mount; hence "stag" would mean lit. the mounter. But this etymology is not now accepted, because the vowel is wrong. A.S. *hind*, the female of stag.

Swain, nymph (used in poetry for "youth" and "damsel").—Scand. *sveinn*, a lad or servant. Lat. *nymph-a*, a nymph.

Tapster, barmaid.—For *tapster* see § 101 (2). Orig. a feminine; but when the final *er* in *-ster* was mistaken for the Masc. suffix *-er*, the compound *bar-maid* was formed to supply the place of a feminine.

Uncle, aunt.—Fr. *oncle*, Lat. *avunculus*, a little grandfather. Old Fr. *ante*, Lat. *amita*, a father's sister.

Wizard, witch.—A.S. *wicc-a* (Masc.), *wicc-e* (Fem.); see suffixes

-*a* and -*e* in § 101. "Witch" is from both forms, and was once of Common gender:—

Your honour is a *witch*.—SCOTT.

"Wizard" = *witt-ish-ard*. Old. Fr. *wisch-ard* or *guisc-art*, sagacious.

Widower, widow; see above, § 101.

Bridegroom, bride.—A.S. *brýd*, a bride. To give this stem a Masc. form, A.S. *guma* (man) was added. Hence A.S. *brýd-guma* bride-groom); but in Mid. Eng. the word *grome* (Mod. Eng. *groom*) was substituted for *guma*.

Note.—A reason can sometimes be shown why words of separate origin should have been selected to note the distinction of sex. (1) The function or position of the male as distinct from that of the female is sometimes denoted by the names that stand for male and female respectively: thus *father* means the supporter, feeder, *mother* the manager; *husband* means house-occupier, *wife* means woman; *king* means one of noble kin, *queen* means woman, and came to denote a king's woman or wife; *lord* means the loaf-keeper, *lady* the loaf-kneader; *milter* means the fish that carries milk or milt, *spawner* the fish that scatters eggs,—that is, the female. (2) The male or female is sometimes denoted by the etymology of the word; thus *boy* meant a male, so *girl*, which originally denoted either sex, was restricted to the female; *dog* (A.S. *docg-a*) meant originally the male, and *bitch* (A.S. *bicc-e*) the female; *earl* meant originally a male, and so the want of a noun to denote the feminine title of rank had to be supplied by a new word, *countess;* as *friar* denoted brother, a new word *nun* (*nunn-e*) was wanted to express the female counterpart; *ewe* (A.S. *eowu*) denoted a female sheep, so *ram* was needed to denote the male; *sir* (from Lat. *senior*) denoted a male, so *madam* or *madame* was needed to denote the female. *Bride* (A.S. *brýd*) denoted a female, so it was necessary to add *groom* (A.S. *guma*) to the word to denote the male, "the bride's man."

Case.

105. Case in Old English.—There were five cases: Nominative, Accusative, Genitive, Dative, Instrumental. "Case" means "falling": the Nom. was considered to be the upright form, from which the others fell to one side, and were thence called "oblique" or slanting.

All the Case-endings except that of the Genitive (which we now call Possessive) have disappeared.

The loss of -*m* and -*e* for the Dative Singular, and of -*um* for the Dative Plural, left the Dative undistinguished from the Accusative, both of which we now call by the common name "Objective." A few Dative forms, however, have survived, as in *whil-om*, *seld-om*, *who-m*, *the-m*, *hi-m*.

The Dative inflexion in -*e* appears in the written form of

many words, as in *ston-e* (§ 66); but is no longer *known* to be a Dative. Similarly a Dative form lies concealed in *meadow* (from A.S. *mǽdw-e*, Dat. of *mǽdu*) and in *shadow* (from A.S. *sceadw-e*, Dat. of *sceadu*). The Dative survives, therefore, etymologically, but not grammatically.

106. Possessive Case-endings.—In Old English there were various declensions, as in Latin and Greek, and for these different declensions there were different Genitive endings—(*a*) for the Singular, (*b*) for the Plural.

(*a*) The ending *-es* was originally limited to (Strong) Singular nouns, and then only to Masculines and Neuters. For (Strong) Feminine nouns, Singular, the Genitive ending was *-e:* (contrast *Lord's-day* with *Lady-day*). Another Genitive ending (Singular) for Masculine and Feminine nouns of the Strong declension was *-an*. The same was also used for Neuter nouns of the Weak declension.

Thus we have *Sun-day* (A.S. *Sunn-an* (Fem.) *dæg*, day of the Sun), *Mon-day* (A.S. *Món-an* (Masc.) *dæg*, day of the Moon), *Tues-day* (A.S. *Tíw-es* (Masc.) *dæg*, day of Tíw, the god of war), *Wednes-day* (A.S. *Wódn-es* (Masc.) *dæg*, day of Woden), *Thurs-day* (A.S. *Þunr-es* (Masc.) *dæg*, day of Thunor, thunder), *Fri-day* (A.S. *Frig-e*, the Genitive of *Frigu*, the goddess of love), *Satur-day* (A.S. *Sæter-dæg*, or *Sætern-dæg*, a compound noun, and therefore not requiring a Genitive suffix to *Sætern*, Saturn).[1]

(*b*) It was not till the fourteenth century that *-es* became the ordinary Genitive ending for the Plural as well as the Singular; and as grammatical gender became extinct at about the same time, no question arose as to whether the same ending could be given to Fem. nouns as to Masc. ones. It was therefore given henceforth to all nouns alike, in both numbers. One of the old plural suffixes was *-ena*, of which there is now one solitary example left, viz. *Wit-ena-gemót*, "the assembly of wise men," the Saxon parliament.

The ending *-es* continued for some time to be a distinct syllable. This occurs, though very rarely, in Shakspeare:—

Larger than the moon-*ës* sphere.—*Midsummer Night's Dream*, ii. 1.
To show his teeth as white as whal-*ës* bone.—*Love's Labour's Lost*, v. 2.

---

[1] There were two forms for "Saturday" in A.S.—(1) *Sætern-dæg*, which is simply a compound word; and (2) *Sæternes dæg*, in which the noun *Sætern* appears with a Genitive suffix *-es*. The latter form fell out of use, because it was longer and less convenient than the compound form *Sætern-dæg*, from which our *Saturday* has come. The noun *Sætern* is, of course, borrowed from Lat. *Saturnus:* whereas every other day of the week has been named after some Teutonic god or goddess.

In the place of *-es* we now always write " *'s* " (apostrophe *s*), in which the apostrophe or comma is intended to denote the elision of *e*. This in Singular nouns. In Plurals we cut out the *-es* altogether, and leave only the apostrophe, as *horses'*, unless the Plural ends in *-n*, as *men's*.

Note.—For the sake of uniformity, and to distinguish the Genitive Singular from the Nom. and Obj. Plural, we write the apostrophe even in nouns, in which there has been no actual elision of *e*, as *stone's*, the original form of which was A.S. *stán-es*, Mid. Eng. *stoon-es*.

107. Substitution of "his" for "s."—The Genitive or Possessive suffix was sometimes spelt as *-is*. As this was sometimes [1] written apart from the noun, it became confounded with *his*, through the uncertainty of initial "*h*" (§ 62).

> Argal *his* brother.—LAYAMAN, A.D. 1200.
> Decius Cæsar *his* tyme.—TREVISA, A.D. 1380.
> For Jesus Christ *his* sake.—*English Prayer-book.*

Note.—It was once supposed that the *his* gave rise to the Possessive suffix *-es* or *'s*. This theory is, of course, ridiculous, for two reasons—(1) the Possessive suffix *s* gave rise to the Genitive pronoun *his*, and not *vice versa*; (2) the same suffix is used with Feminine nouns, as "Jane's bonnet," and with Plural nouns, "men's work." We could never have said "Jane *his* bonnet," or "men *his* work."

Number.

108. Plural endings in Old English.—The chief Plural endings in Anglo-Saxon were *-as*, *-an*, *-a*, *-u*.

(1) A.S. stán-*as*, stones. (3) A.S. hand-*a*, hands.
(2) A.S. steorr-*an*, stars. (4) A.S. lim-*u*, limbs.

Of these the most common was *-an*. Another very common one was *-as*. At first the ending *-as* could be used with nouns of only one declension, and these only of the Masculine gender; but eventually it became the plural ending of almost all English nouns; and even in A.S. it was from the first very common, because the number of nouns of that declension happened to be very large.

The 3rd and 4th died out in the twelfth century. The 1st and 2nd, which remained, took the forms of *-es* and *-en* in Mid. English.

Note 1.—The earlier ending in English was *-es*, not *-s*; as A.S. *cyning-as*, Mid. Eng. *king-es*, Mod. Eng. *king-s*. The rule now is to

[1] It was chiefly used (as in the examples quoted) with *foreign proper names*, which had no real genitive. So *is* was written separately, by way of denoting a genitive; and this *is* became confounded with *his*.

contract *-es*, to *-s*, wherever the pronunciation of the word allows it. In such a word as *stones* (A.S. *stán-as*) the *e* is retained, not for the sake of the *s*, but to give length to the *o*. In French, on the other hand, the plural suffix was at first *-s*, not *-es*, as Anglo-French *flur-s*. But the French *-s* was forced to conform to the Mid. Eng. *-es*, which was syllabic. Thus we have Anglo-French *flur-s*, Mid. Eng. *flour-es*, Mod. Eng. *flower-s*. See *Note* to § 21.

Note 2.—The Plurals in **ics**, as *mathematics*, *physics*, were many of them introduced with the Revival of Learning, in imitation of the Greek plurals, from which our own words were borrowed. In Gower we have *mathem-atic* (Sing.), not *mathem-atics* (Plur.).

109. Plurals in -ies.—It is usually said that nouns, which end in *y* in the Singular, form the Plural in *-ies*. It would be nearer the truth to say that such nouns in forming the Plural have retained the original Singular ending in *-ie* and added *-s* to it :—

Flie (=fly), flies. Citie (=city), cities.

Note.—*Dice* is the modern spelling of Mid. Eng. *dys*, Old Fr. *dez*, the plural of *det*. Out of this plural we have coined a Sing. *die*, the small cube on which the dice are engraved.

110. Plurals in -ves.—The nouns *wife*, *knife*, *life*, *sheaf*, *leaf*, *thief*, *calf*, *self*, *shelf*, *wolf*, *beef* form the Plural in *ves;* while *reef*, *chief*, *roof*, *hoof*, *proof*, *scarf*, *wharf*, *dwarf*, *turf*, *gulf*, *cliff*, *grief*, *safe*, *strife*, *fife* form it in *fs* or *fes*.

(*a*) As regards the first list it should be noted—(1) that the nouns there given are all (except the last, *beef*, *beeves*) of *Teutonic* origin; and (2) the change from *f* to *v* occurs in the Genitive and Dative *Singular*, and all through the Plural in Mid. Eng.

A.S.	Nom. Sing. *hláf*	Gen. Sing. *hláf-es*	Nom. Plur. *hláf-as*
Mid. Eng.	,, ,, *lof*	,, ,, *lov-es*	,, ,, *lov-es*
Mod. Eng.	,, ,, *loaf*	,, ,, *loaf's*	,, ,, *loaves*

Note.—The changing of *f* into *v* is merely an example of the voicing of voiceless consonants, as explained in § 57, Rule II., the voiceless *f* being placed between two vowels. Indeed, the *f* between two vowels was sounded as *v* even in A.S.

(*b*) As regards the second list, it should be noted that the words there given are either of French origin, or they end in *rf* or in *ff*, or the final *f* is preceded by *oo*. Thus in *hoof*, *roof*, *proof*, the *f* is preceded by *oo;* and moreover *proof* is of French origin. *Chief*, *gulf*, *grief*, *safe*, *strife*, *fife* were all French before they became English. The rest all end in *rf* or in *ff*. *Reef* is merely a modern spelling of *riff*.

Note.—The Fr. plural ending was *-s*, and not *-es*, as in Early and Middle English. This may help to explain why the form *-s* is given to nouns of foreign origin, and *-es* to native ones.

Tennyson has *hooves*, and we sometimes, though rarely, hear *wharves*, *dwarves*. *Scarves*, however, is rather more common than *scarfs*.

111. Mutation Plurals,—that is, Plurals formed by a change of the root-vowel. The A.S. forms of these nouns, Singular and Plural, are shown below :—

A.S.		*Mod. Eng.*		*A.S.*		*Mod. Eng.*	
Sing.	*Plural.*	*Sing.*	*Plural.*	*Sing.*	*Plural.*	*Sing.*	*Plural.*
Mann	menn	Man	men	Fót	fét	Foot	feet
Mús	mýs	Mouse	mice	Tóð	téð	Tooth	teeth
Lús	lýs	Louse	lice	Gós	gés	Goose	geese

The *earliest* forms of the above plurals were *mann-is*, *mús-is* (cf. Lat. *mur-es*), *lús-is*, *fót-is* (cf. Lat. *ped-es*, Gr. *pod-es*), *tóð-is* (cf. Lat. *dent-es*), and *gós-is*. The Plural, in fact, was formed by adding the ending *-is*.

The effect of the *i* in the ending *-is* was to change *mann-* into *menn-*, *mús-* into *mýs-*, *lús* into *lýs-*, *fót-* into *fét-*, *tóð-* into *téð-*, and *gós-* into *ges-*; so that after the suffix *-is* had dropped off, as it did even in Anglo-Saxon times, nothing but the mutation of the root-vowel was left as a mark of the Plural.

Note 1.—*Women*, being derived from A.S. *wíf-man*, has the same mutation plural that *man* has. The sound of the vowel in the first syllable is still as if the word were spelt *wimmen*; but the vowel in the singular has been affected by the *w*.

Note 2.—Several other nouns had once a form of Plural marked by a change in the root-vowel. Thus the old plural of *bóc* (book) was *béc*, which superseded a still older plural *bóc-is*, and was itself eventually superseded by the new plural *books*. Similarly *bróc* formed its plural in *bréc* (whence the modern double plural *breeks*). The same process is seen at work in *bræthr*, the Northern plural of *brother*, and in *kŷ*, the plural of *cow* (A.S. *cú*). All these are instances of what in § 77 is called "**Vowel-Mutation**."

112. Plurals in -en or -ne.—If our literary language had remained purely Southern (that is, if our modern standard English had sprung from the Anglo-Saxon, and not from the Midland dialect), its predominant Plural suffix might possibly now be *-en*, and instead of Plurals like *steorr-an* being turned into *stars*, we might have had a borrowed noun like *art* forming its Plural in *art-en*, like *ox*, *ox-en*.

Ox-en is now the only noun left, in literary English, that has formed its Plural regularly in *-en*.[1] The other three words,

[1] The word *bracken* as plural of *brake* was once included in this list. But this has been disproved in the *New English Dictionary*.

children, *brethren*, and *kine*, are Double Plurals, as will be shown in § 113.

Note.—The suffix *-en* died hard. *Hosen* (plural of *hose*) occurs in Old Test., Dan. iii. 21 ; and *shoon* (plural of *shoe*) occurs in Shakspeare. Spenser has *eyen* for *eyes*, and *foen* for *foes*. In a book written about 1420 we find *been* for *bees*, *een* for *eyes*, *fleen* for *flies*, *pesen* for *peas*, and *toon* for *toes ;* and a century later *treen* for *trees*, and *sistren* for *sisters*. In villages in the south of England *housen* is still heard for *houses*, though the A.S. plural was *hús* (unchanged).

113. Double Plurals.—There are at least five words in common use whose Plural is formed with *two* Plural suffixes :—

Child-re-n.—In A.S. there was a declension in which the case-endings of the plural were preceded by an *r*. Thus the Plural of *cild* (child) was *cild-ru.*[1] In Mid. Eng. *cild-ru* became *child-re* or *child-er*, which, when a second Plural suffix was added, became *child-re-n* or *child-er-n :* (*childern* is still heard in villages, and *childer* occurs in Tudor dramatists). Similarly the old plural of *lomb* (lamb) was *lomb-ru*, of *cealf* (calf), *cealf-ru*, and of *ǽg* (egg), *ǽg-ru*. Cf. Calv*er*-ley=calves' lea or field.

Brethre-n.—In A.S. the singular was *bróðor*, hence our Plural *brothers*. In Icel. the Sing. was *bróðir*, which by vowel-mutation gave a plural *bræthr*. This in the fourteenth century became *brethre*, because *r* in Eng. required a vowel after it. To this *-n* was afterwards added, making the double plural *brethr-e-n.*[2]

Kine.—The old plural of *cú* (cow) was *cý* (see *Note* 2 to § 111). This was developed into *kine* by adding *-en* to the plural stem, making *cý-en*, *ký-en*, *kine*. (The A.S. *c* was sounded as *k*.)

Breeks, breeches.—In A.S. the plural of *bróc* (see *Note* 2 to § 111) was *bréc*. By adding *-s* or *-es* we get *breeks* or *breeches*. (In A.S. *c*=*k*, and the *c* of *bréc* was palatalised to *ch*.)

Sixpen-ce-s.—*Pen-ce* is one of the Plurals of *penny.*[3] "Sixpence,"

---

[1] A more complete explanation of the *r* in *children* is as follows :— "The word *cild* was a neuter in *-os*, like Gr. *gen-os*, Lat. *gen-us* (=**gen-os*). The *e-* stem corresponding to the *o-* stem in *-os* was *-es*. This appears in the genitives :—Gr. *gen-es-os* (=*gen-e-os*, the *s* having dropped out), Lat. *gen-es-es*=*gen-er-is*. So Nom. Sing. **cild-os* became **cild-oz*, **cild-o*, *cild*. But the plural was **cild-es-us*, the A.S. neut. plur. suffix *u* being added. This became *cild-er-u*, and then *cildru*" (Skeat).

[2] A more complete explanation of this mutation-plural is as follows :— "The original plur. of *bróðir* was *brǿð(i)r*, in which the *i* dropped out. But only the oldest Icel. MS. used the symbol *ǿ*=*oe*, the umlaut of *o*= A.S. *é*. The *ǿ* came to be confused with *ǽ*, and *ǽ* was wrongly written for it. That is how the *æ* came in. As the Icel. *æ* is always long, the mark denoting length was not written over it. Since this *æ* really meant *œ*, it was, of course, written *é* in English" (Skeat).

[3] *Penny* is from A.S. *pening*, later A.S. *penig*, whence Mid. Eng. *peni*, with Plur. *penies*, or (contracted form) *pens*. Our mod. Plur. *pennies* is from Mid. Eng. *penies*, and *pence* from Mid. Eng. *pens*.

though really a Plural, was regarded as a Singular Collective noun, to which the Plural suffix *-s* was added.

114. Same form for Plural as for Singular.—To this class belong *deer*, *sheep*, *swine*, *yoke*, *score*. In A.S. the nouns *deer*, *sheep*, *swine* were Neuter, and Neuters had the same form for Plural as for Singular, provided the vowel was long either by nature or position.

Note 1.—This class of noun once included many more; such as *folk*, *year*, *head* (Neut. Plur. in A.S., *héafŏd-u*, *héafd-u*), *pound* (enclosure), *horse*, *night* (in A.S. Fem. Plur. *night-a*, where the Fem. suffix *-a* dropped off). A.S. *geŏc* (yoke) was also Neuter; but as the vowel was short, it formed its plural in *geŏc-u*, which by the change of *u* to *e* gives us the Mod. Plur. *yoke*. A.S. *scor-a* (score) was Feminine, not Neuter; and was a Plural already: (as a Sing. it is not found in A.S.). The change of *a* to *e* gives us its Mod. Eng. form *score*, which now stands for both numbers. To this day we say "forty *head* of cattle," "a body of 1000 *horse*," "fort*night*" (a contracted form of "fourteen *night*"), "ten *score*" (not *scores*).

Note 2.—A few nouns such as *salmon* (lit. the leaper or jumper), from Lat. root *sal*, have the same form for Plural as for Singular, by the analogy of Teutonic words. To the same class belong *grouse*, *trout*, *cod*, *heathen*, *brace*, *dozen*, *gross*; these are all modern imitations, and all but *heathen* are of foreign origin. The word *stone* is very peculiar. Its proper plural is *stones* (A.S. *stán-as*). But in the sense of weight, it has the one form *stone* for both numbers.

Note 3.—The student must not yield to the temptation of supposing that *sow*, *swine* make up a pair of words analogous to *cow*, *kine*. "Sow" is from A.S. *sugu*, a female pig; "swine" is from A.S. *swín*, a pig of either sex, the suffix *n* being adjectival and therefore applicable to either gender.

Sing. { *This* foul *swine* (pig) . . . *lies* now
Near to the town of Leicester, as we learn.

SHAK., *Richard III.* v. 3.

Plur. All the *swine* (=pigs) were sows.

TENNYSON'S *Princess.*

Observe, too, that the derivative *swin-ish* shows that *swine* is Singular; for adjective-suffixes like *-ish* and others are added to Singulars, not to Plurals. The genitive singular *swin-es* appears in the name "Swineshead" in Huntingdonshire.

115. Plurals that have become Singulars.—Of this there are several examples:—

Truce.—In A.S. *tréowa* meant a pledge (Singular). In Mid. Eng. this word was respelt as *trew*, and had *trews* as its Plural, which in Mod. Eng. has become *truce* and is regarded as a Singular.

Bodice.—This is simply a respelling of *bodies*, the Plural of *body*.

Baize.—Coarse woollen stuff: an error for *bayes*, an old Fem. Plur. of French *bai*.

Trace.—A respelling of French *traits*, Plural of *trait*, a line. We now say *traces* for the straps by which a vehicle is drawn.

Sledge.—Apparently a respelling of *sleds*, plural of *sled*, the word still used in Canada for "sledge," from Icel. *sleði*.

Small-pox.—Here *pox* is the Plural of *pock*, A.S. *poc*, a pustule.

Chess.—The Norman plural of *check;* the original meaning of which was "king," of Persian origin. The original sense of *check* was "King! mind the king!"

Welkin.—In A.S. the Sing. *wolcen* (cloud) had as its Plural *wolcn-u;* see Plural suffix in § 108 (4). *Wolcn-u* became in Mid. Eng. *wolken* (clouds), which is now spelt as *welkin* and has lost its Plural force.

A **sixpence.**—"Pence" is merely another spelling of *pennies*, the Plural of *penny*. In the compound form of *sixpence* it can be pluralised as *sixpences*, since *sixpence* (the silver coin) is Singular in sense.

116. Singulars which have become Plurals.—There are at least nine such words, and two more about which the student should be on his guard:—

Burials.—Originally a Singular, from A.S. *byrgels*, a tomb; re-spelt in Mid. Eng. as *buriels*. When the *e* was changed to *a* in Mod. Eng., *burials* seemed to be a Plural like *victuals*, *vitals*, *trials*, *removals*, etc.

Riddles.—In A.S. the word was *rǽdelse*, which had as its Plural *rǽddels-an*. Out of *riddles* we have coined a Sing. *riddle*.

Peas.—In A.S. the word was *pisa*, Plur. *pis-an*. When the Plural suffix was lost, the *s* looked like a Plural, and so a Singular *pea* was formed out of the modernised *peas*. We still, however, say *pease*-pudding, not *pea*-pudding.

> The vaunting poets found nought worth *a pease*.
> SPENSER, *Shep. Calendar*.
>
> Not worth two *peas*-en.—SURREY.

Skates.—Dutch *schaats*, Plural *schaats-en*.

Eaves.—A.S. *efese*, Mid. Eng. *evese*, with Plural form *eves-es*. Though *eaves* is now always used as a Plural, no Singular *eave* was coined till very lately by Tennyson, who has given us the compound *eave-drop* for *eaves-drop*.

Alms.—A.S. *ælmesse*, from Gr. *eleëmosyne*, whence the adj. *eleemosynary*. No Singular *alm* has been coined, like "burial," "riddle," "pea," "skate."

> Seeing Peter and John about to go into the temple, he asked *an alms*.—*Acts* iii. 3.

Cherry.—This Singular has been coined from Mid. Eng. *cheris*, Old Fr. *cerise*, Lat. *ceras*-us (a cherry-tree), Gr. *keras*-os. Here, as before, the final *s* of *cheris* was wrongly taken for a Plural suffix.

Minnows.—This could not have arisen from A.S. *myne;* but came orig. from Old Fr. *menuise*, which gave Mid. Eng. *menuse*. The last looked like a Plural, which gave rise to a new Sing. *menu* or *menow*, from which we get our mod. Sing. *minnow*.

Riches.—Fr. *richesse*, richness, wealth; cf. *caress*, *largess*. In Mid. Eng. it was spelt, as in French, *richesse*, and had a plural *richess-es*, like our present word *caress-es*.

Against the *richesses* of this world shall they have misease of poverty.—CHAUCER.
In one hour *is* so great *riches* come to naught.—*Rev.* xviii. 17.
Riches do not consist in having more gold and silver.—LOCKE.

Summons, laches.—These words have both retained their Singular force so far; but the final *s* exposes them to danger. *Laches* is a French word parallel to *riches*, signifying "laxity," to which it is allied in root. *Summons* is from French *semonce*, and not, as has been supposed, from Lat. *sub-* or *sum-moneas*.

Note on the Number of Nouns.

It has been observed that there are instances in English in which (1) a plural sense is found without a plural inflexion; (2) a plural inflexion without a plural sense.

(1) *A plural sense without a plural inflexion*:—

Examples of this are nouns of Multitude, as *cattle*, *poultry*, *vermin*, *people*, *gentry*. Other examples are given in § 114, where the nouns have the same form for the Plural as the Singular, as *sheep*. Other examples are nouns that retain a Singular form in order to denote some specific quantity, as *a twelvemonth*. Other examples are shown in § 116, where the nouns given were originally Singular, but have been mistaken for plurals, and thus acquired a plural sense, as *alms*.

(2) *A plural inflexion without a plural sense*:—

Examples of this are Plural nouns which have acquired a Singular sense, as *news*, *means*, *amends*, *odds*. Other examples are nouns which denote a single science, but have acquired a Plural form in *-ics* in imitation of the Greek plural from which they have been translated, as *physics*. Other examples are those shown in § 115, where the words given were originally Plural, but have been mistaken for Singulars and acquired a Singular sense, as *truce*.

SECTION 2.—THE FORMS OF ADJECTIVES.

117. Loss of Adjective Inflexions.—In Old English adjectives had two different modes of declension—(1) the Weak, when the adjective was preceded by a Demonstrative adjective; (2) the Strong, when it was not so preceded. Gender, number, and case had each its own set of inflexions for both. But with the gradual *levelling* of inflexions, peculiar to the Middle period of English (see § 7), the two declensions merged eventually into one, and most of the inflexions took the form of *-e*, which itself disappeared in Modern English, leaving nothing.

In Chaucer (whose death was in 1400) the Strong declension has usually no inflexion for the Singular, and the Weak has *-e* throughout. Both declensions had *-e* throughout the Plural. This, however, applies only to adjectives of *one* syllable. If the adjective was of more than one syllable, it was generally uninflected in both numbers, more especially if the adjective was of Romanic origin.

Note. 1.—The word *old-en* appears to contain a trace of the obsolete adjective suffix *-an*, which was a common suffix in the Weak declension, Singular and Plural.

Note 2.—In the word *alder-liefest* (dearest of all) Shakspeare has preserved an old genitive Plural form, which in Old English was spelt as *-ra*; A.S. *eal-ra*, Mercian *al-ra*.

With you, mine *alder*-liefest sovereign.—2 *Hen. VI.* i. 128.

Note 3.—The Dative and Instrumental suffix *-um* in the Plural of both declensions has survived in *seld-om*, Old Eng. *seld-um*, at rare (times).

Note 4.—The only flexional forms that have survived and are still in common use are *these* and *those*, both of which were originally plurals of *this*, but are now allotted to *this* and *that* respectively.

118. **Cardinals**: so called from Lat. *cardin-em*, a hinge, because on them the Ordinals were said to hinge or depend. All our Cardinals, except *dozen* and *million*, are of Teutonic origin.

One: A.S. *án* (cf. Lat. *un-us*), from which the Indefinite article *an* or *a* has also come. *Only* is from A.S. *án-lic* (one-like).

Note.—The word *aught* is from A.S. *á*+*wiht*, a thing or particle. From its negative form *naught* we get *not*. (Here *á* stands for *án*.)

Two.—A.S. *twá*, the Fem. and Neut. of *tweyen*, whence *twain*, *be-tween*, *twin*. Cf. Gr. *duo*, Lat. *du-o*, whence *dual*, *duel*. The Fr. cognate is *deux*, and the German *zwei*.

Both.—Lit. "they two." Old Norse, *báðir*. The last syllable (*ðir*) signifies "they." For *bá* compare A.S. *bá*, Lat. am-*bo*, and Gr. am-*pho*.

Three.—A.S. Masc. *þrí*, Fem. and Neut. *þreó*. Our word *three* is pronounced exactly like A.S. *þrí*, but comes from *þréo*.

Four.—A.S. *feówer*; cf. Goth. *fidwor*, Lat. *quatuor*.

Five.—A.S. *fíf*; cf. Germ. *fünf*, Lat. *quinque*.

Six.—A.S. *six*, Lat. *sex*, Gr. *hex*.

Seven.—A.S. *seofon*, Lat. *septem*, Gr. *hepta*.

Eight.—A.S. *eahta*, Lat. *octo*, Gr. *okto*.

Nine.—A.S. *nigon*, Mid. Eng. *nin-e*, where the *e* is a Plural suffix; cf. Lat. *novem*.

Ten.—A.S. *tén*, *teón*, a contraction of A.S. **tehon*, like Goth. *taihun*; cf. Lat. *decem*, Gr. *deka*. Our English numeral has therefore lost a medial guttural. (* denotes that the form is theoretical.)

Eleven.—A.S. *end-lufon*, Goth. *ain-lif*, where *ain* means "one," and *lif* means "over" or "left." So "eleven" means "ten and one over."

Twelve.—A.S. *twelf*, Goth. *twa-lif*=ten and two over.

Dozen.—Old Fr. *dos-aine*, from *dose* (=twelve, Lat. *duodecim*), with suffix *-aine*.

Thirteen—nineteen.—All formed by adding *teen* (A.S. *tin*, sounded as *teen*) to the Cardinals.

Twenty.—A.S. *twen-tig*. Here *twen* is short for *twegen*, two; and *tig*=ten, cognate with Lat. *dec*-em. Thus *-teen* is added to denote addition, and *-tig* to denote multiplication.

Score.—A.S. *scor-a* (Plur.), a long notch cut in a stick called tally.

> Whereas our forefathers had no other books but the *score* and the *tally*, thou hast caused printing to be used.—*Henry VI.* part ii.

Thirty—ninety.—All formed in the same way as "twenty."

Hundred.—A.S. *hund* (cognate with Lat. *cent*-um), and *réd* or *rǽd*, reckoning.

Thousand.—A.S. *þúsend*, Scand. *þúsund*, also written *þús-hund* by a popular and false etymology. The *und* (wrongly written *hund*) does not mean "a hundred." The real sense and origin of ***þúsund*** are not known.

Million.—Fr. *million*, Lat. *million-em:* the root is *mille*.

119. **Ordinals**; from Lat. *ordin-em*, because such numerals show the *order* in which things or persons stand. All but one are of Teutonic origin.

First.—A.S. *fyrst*=fore-est, superlative of *fore*, in which the *o* has become *i* or *y* by the influence of *i* in *-ist*, later *-est*. See § 77 (4).

Second.—Lat. *secundus*, which superseded A.S. *óðer* (other), a comparative form=beyond this, second.

Third, for *thrid*, A.S. *thridda;* cf. Lat. *tertius*.

Fourth, and the remaining ordinals, are formed by adding *th* (A.S. *ta* or *ða*) to the Cardinal.

Multiplicatives, formed by adding either (*a*) Teutonic *fold*, or (*b*) Romanic *-ple* or *-ble :*—

Teutonic: two-*fold*, three-*fold*, etc. (A.S. *feald*).

Romanic: sim-*ple* (one-*fold*), dou-*ble*, tre-*ble*, tri-*ple*, etc. (Lat. *plex*).

Note.—Simple (from Lat. *simplex*) has ousted the Old English word *án-feald*, one-*fold*.

120. **Indefinite Adjectives** of Quantity or Number :—

All.—A.S. *eal* (Sing.), *ealle* (Plur.).

None, no.—A.S. *ne*+*án* (not one). "No" is short for "none."

Many.—Noun or Adj. Noun A.S. *menigu*, adj. A.S. *manig*.

Several.—Old Fr. *several*, Late Lat. *separale*, a thing apart.

Some.—A.S. *sum*.

Enough.—A.S. *ge-nóh* or *ge-nóg*, Mid. Eng. *inóh*, *enógh*.

Few.—A.S. *féa* (Sing.), *feáwe* (Plur.); Mid. Eng. *fewe*.

Sundry.—A.S. *syndrig;* cf. *sundr-ian* (verb), to divide or separate; hence "sunder."

Much.—A.S. *myc-el*; from the first syllable we get *much;* from the entire word we get the obsolescent *mickle*.

Little.—A.S. *lyt*, *lyt-el*. "Little" has no connection with *less*. The base *lut* means to deceive. Hence "little" still sometimes means "base," "mean," "small-minded," "narrow-minded."

Any.—A.S. *ǽnig*, from A.S. *án*, one.

Whole.—The *wh* is no longer sounded, but was substituted for *h* in the sixteenth century. A.S. *hál*, Mid. Eng. *hool*, Mod. Eng. *whole*.

Half.—A.S. *healf*, side. Hence "on my behalf" means "on my side," "in my interests."

121. Demonstrative Adjectives:—

The.—(*a*) Now the Definite article: A.S. *ðe*, used at first as an indeclinable Relative. It next became a Demonstrative adjective, as it now is. (In Old Eng. *se* (Masc.) and *seó* (Fem.) were used as the Def. article before Masc. and Fem. nouns.[1])

(*b*) Before Comparative adjectives or adverbs: A.S. *ðý* or *ðí*, the Instrumental case, Singular; as, "*The* more, *the* merrier."

That.—A.S. *ðæt*, neuter Sing., Nom. and Accus. The suffix *-t* is a mark of the Neut.; cf. *i-t*, *wha-t*; Lat. *i-d*, *qui-d*, *illu-d*, etc. Before the close of the Mid. period "that" could be used with any Sing. noun in any case or gender.

This.—A.S. Masc. *ðes*, Fem. *ðéos*, Neut. *ðis*. Our modern "this" is most like the Neuter.

These, those.—A.S. *ðǽs*, *ðás*; two plural forms of *ðes*. In Mod. Eng., however, *these* has been allotted as the plural of *this*, and *those* of *that*.

Such.—A.S. *swylc*, from *swá* (so) and *lic* (like). Hence the modern phrase "such-like" is pleonastic.

Note.—The obsolescent *thilk* means "the like," from A.S. *þylc*, composed of the instrumental *þí* + *lic*. In the seventeenth century "other-like" was used for "such-like."

Same.—A.S. *same*, used only as an adverb. Its use as an adject. was due to Danish influence. Cf. Lat. *sim*-ul.

Other.—A.S. *óðer*, second, different from the first. The syllable *ðer* is a Comparative suffix; cf. Lat. "al-*ter*." "Other" means "more than this or that," hence "different from this or that."

Yon, yonder.—A.S. *geon* (adj.), distant. *Yonder* was an adverb derived from *yon*, and was used as such. *Yon*, though an adj., has been used adverbially:—

> I and the lad will go *yonder*.—*Old Testament*.
> Him that *yon* soars on golden wing.—MILTON.

An (Indef. article), the unemphatic and weaker form of A.S. *án* (one).

Ilk.—Originally an adjective, from A.S. *ylca*, same. Hence the phrase *of that ilk* means "of that same." It is quite a different word from *thilk*.

---

[1] In Old Eng. *se* (Masc.) and *seó* (Fem.) were used as the Def. article in the Nom. case only: all the other cases were taken from the root found in the Neuter *ðæt*.

122. Distributive Adjectives:—

Each.—A.S. *ǽlc*, for *á-ge-líc*=*á-gi-líc*, where the *i* in *gi* causes mutation; aye-like or ever like.

Every.—From A.S. *ǽfre* (ever) and *ǽlc* (each); in Mid. Eng. *ever-ich*, *ever-ilc*.

Note.—Thus the modern idiomatic distinction in the use of *each* and *every* has no foundation in etymology.

Either . . . n-either.—A.S. *ǽgþer*, a contraction of *ǽ-g-hwæþer*, formed from *á* (ever)+*gi* for *ge* (a prefix)+*hwæþer* (which of two). Here the vowel *á* has been mutated by the *i* in *gi*.

Comparison of Adjectives.

123. Modes of expressing Comparison.—Four different modes, as shown below, have existed in English. Of these the 1st, 3rd, and 4th are synthetic or flexional, and the 2nd is analytical.

(1) **-er, -est**: A.S. -(*i*)*ra* and *-ast*, *-ost*, or *-est*.[1] The *ra* is made up of -(*i*)*r-a*, in which the *r* is the real Comparative suffix, and the *a* is merely the Weak adjectival inflexion. The *r* stands for an original *s*, as seen in the allied languages of the Aryan speech. Cf. our own form "wor-*se*." In the Tudor period the suffixes *-er* and *-est* were attached to adjectives, which cannot now receive them. Thus we find the following:—

Inventivest, honourablest, ancienter, eminentest, eloquenter, learnedest, solemnest, famousest, virtuousest, repiningest, delectablest, movingest, unhopefullest (Shakspeare).

(2) **More, most**: A.S. *mára*, *mǽst*. Used with all adjectives that do not take *-er* and *-est*, and sometimes with those that do. This mode of comparison is first seen in the fourteenth century, and may perhaps have been partly due to French influence. Even in the Tudor period it was freely used with monosyllables:—

Ingratitude *more strong* than traitor's arms.—SHAKSPEARE.

This analytical mode of comparing adjectives is indispensable for adjectives ending with a suffix. If we attached *-er* and *-est* to a suffix, it would seem like comparing the suffix, instead of the quality denoted by the adjective.

---

[1] Philologists have traced these forms still farther back. They say that the original Teutonic suffix for expressing the comparative degree was *-iz* or *-ōz*, which stands for an Aryan or Indo-European *ies*, *iōs*. The *-iōs* appears in Latin as *-ior*, as in dur-*ior*, Gen. dur-iōr-is, the *s* being changed to *r*. The superlative *-est* is said to be compounded of the comparative suffix *-is* (weak form of *ies*), and the superlative suffix *-to*. Both appear in the Greek "meg-*is-tos*," greatest. On the Latin form *-mus*, see (4) in § 123. See Brugmann, *Comp. Gr.* ii. § 135.

(3) **-ter, -ther** (Comparative suffix): cf. Lat. "al-*ter*," "u-*ter*." In English this comparative form is seen in :—

O-*ther*, ei-*ther*, whe-*ther*, af-*ter*, un-*der*, ne-*ther*, fur-*ther*.

Note 1.—"Far-ther" does not strictly belong to this list. The Mid. Eng. *farr-er* was changed to *far-ther* in imitation of "fur-ther," the Comparative of *fore*.

Note 2.—"Other" means "beyond this," from an Aryan root *ana*, signifying "this"; cf. Lat. *al-ter*, Sansk. *an-tar*. See § 121, **Other**. The Comparative origin of *other* comes out very clearly in such a phrase as "other *than* a soldier."

(4) *-ma* (Superlative suffix): cf. Lat. *-mus*, as in *opti-mus*, *postu-mus*, etc. In Old Eng. the *-ma* sometimes stands alone, and sometimes is reinforced by the addition of *-est*, which made the double suffix *-mest*. This has been misspelt in Mod. Eng. as *most* through a confusion with the other "most" described under (2), with which, however, it must not be confounded; for in A.S. the one was spelt *mest*, and the other *mǽst*.

In-*most* (A.S. inne-*ma* or inne-*mest*), ut-*most* (A.S. úte-*ma* or úte-*mest*), hind-*most* (A.S. hinde-*ma* or hinde-*mest*), fore-*most* (A.S. for-*mest*), mid-*most* (A.S. mede-*ma* or mede-*mest*).

Note.—We sometimes have *most* added to nouns; as "top-*most*," "end-*most*," "head-*most*." These words probably mean "most at the top," "most at the end," etc., in which the "most" described under (2) has been confounded with that under (4).

124. Double Comparisons.—The doubling of Comparatives and Superlatives is not now permitted, though it was once common. We now intensify Superlatives with the help of phrases; as "*by far* the best," "the *very* worst," "the lowest *of the low*," etc.

After the *most straitest* sect of our religion I lived a Pharisee.—*Acts* xxvi. 5.
Less gifts and *lesser* gains I weigh them not.—HALL'S *Satyres*.
Let not my *worser* spirit tempt me again.—*King Lear*, iv. 6.
More kinder. More sweeter. More corrupter.—SHAKSPEARE.

The only double Comparatives now used are *lesser*, *nearer*. On the formation of *nearer*, see below, § 126, I.

125. Mixed Comparisons.—In the words *inner-most*, *upper-most*, *utter-most*, *further-most*, *hinder-most*, *nether-most*, we have what looks like the double Superl. suffix *-most* added to Compar. forms *inner-*, *upper-*, *utter-*, *farther-*, *hinder-*, *nether-*. But probably *innermost*, *uttermost*, *nethermost* are merely misspellings of A.S. *inne-mest*, *úte-mest*, *niðe-mest*; and *uppermost*, *furthermost*, *hindermost* must have been formed by analogy, for they are not found in A.S.

In *former* we have the Comp. *-er* added to the Superl. *for-ma*, which was common in A.S.

In *near-est* (= nigh-er-est) we have the Superlative *-est* added to the Comparative *near* (= nigh-er), and in *near-er* we have a double Comparative, as is shown in § 126, I.

126. Irregular Comparisons.—These may be classified under three different headings, as below:—

I. *With change of root-vowel:*—

Old, elder, eldest.—A.S. *eald, yld-ra, yld-est.* (There was originally an "*i*" before the *-ra* and *-st*, which produced a change in the vowel of the positive.) The forms *older, oldest* are more recent. A special meaning is now assigned to each pair of forms.

Nigh, near, next.—A.S. *néah* or *néh*, *neár* (short of *néah-ra* = *nigher*), *néh-st* (which in Mod. Eng. is spelt *next*). The word *near* is therefore a Comparative:—

The *near* in blood, the nearer bloody.—*Macbeth*, ii. 3.
The *nere* to the church, the ferther from God.—HEYWOOD'S *Proverbs*.

Out of the word "near" we have formed a new trio, *near* (Pos.), *near-er* (double Comp.), *near-est* (Superl. added to Comp.). A special meaning is now assigned to *next* and *nearest* respectively.

Late, later, latest.—A.S. *læt, lator, latost.* In the thirteenth century we get *late, lat-re* (hence *latt-er*), and *lat-st* (hence *last*, a contraction of *lat-st, lat-est*; cf. "best," a contraction of "bet-st," "bet-est"). A special meaning is now assigned to each pair of forms.

II. *From obsolete roots:*—

Good, better, best.—*Good* is from A.S. *gód; better* and *best* from obsolete A.S. *bat*, from which we get the verb "batten"; but the noun "boot" (profit) is by gradation. *Best* is a contraction of *bet-st*, which was formed by mutation from *bat-ista;* see § 77 (4).

Bad or **evil, worse, worst.**—*Bad* is from A.S. *bæd-del*, an effeminate man; *evil* from A.S. *yfel*, and *ill* from Scand. *illr. Worse* is from A.S. Comparative form *wyr-sa* (in which the *-sa* or *-se* is not changed into *ra* or *re*, as usual, but retained). *Worst* is from A.S. *wyrr-est.*

Little, less, least.—The positive is from A.S. *lyt, lyt-el.* The Comparative and Superlative are from the root *lǽs* (adv.), which gave *lǽs-sa* (less, the *-sa* not being changed to *-ra*), and *lǽs-st* (least). *Less-er*, the double Comp. form, is a deriv. of *less.*

Much or **mickle, more, most.**—A.S. *mic-el, má-ra, mæ-st.* These are at bottom from the same root, which in A.S. was *mag-* (to be able, hence *might*), in Latin *mag-* (hence *mag-nus, magnitude*, etc.), and in Gr. *meg-* (hence Greek coinages like *meg-a-ther-i-um*). *Much* is from the first syllable of *mic-el. Má-ra* means more in point of size, and in Mod. Eng. is assigned as comparative of *much* or *mickle.*

Many, more, most.—A.S. *manig, má, mǽst.* On *many* see above,

§ 120. *Má* is not a Positive adjective,[1] but a Comparative adverb that was afterwards turned into an adjective, and made to signify "more" in point of number. There is no etymological connection between *many* and the two words that have been assigned to it as Comparative and Superlative.

III. *From adverbial roots of time and place:—*

Far, farther, farthest.—A.S. *feor, fyr-ra, fyrr-est;* the vowel of the Positive was mutated by an *i* which preceded *-ra*, as in *-ira;* see § 77 (4). In Mid. Eng. the forms were *fer, ferr-er, ferr-est.* Hence it is clear that the *th* in "farther, farthest" is intrusive, based on the analogy of "further, furthest." See § 123, *Note* 1.

Fore, former, foremost or **first.**—A.S. *fore: former* (not seen before sixteenth century) was got by adding the Comp. *-er* to the A.S. Superl. *for-ma; foremost* is a double Superl. got by adding *-est* to *for-ma. First* is from A.S. *fyrst* (=for-est, the regular Superl. of *fore*, in which the *o* is changed to *y* by the influence of the *i* in Teutonic *-ist*).

Forth, further, furthest.—These are duplicates or doublets of the preceding. *Forth* is an extension of *fore,* A.S. *forð*, from which the Comp. and Superl. are not formed. (It has been clearly proved that *ther* was a comparative suffix of *fore*, see § 123 (3); and that the Superlative *furth-est* was formed out of the Comparative *fur-ther*, mistaken for *furth-er.*)

Ere, erst, A.S. *ǽr, ǽr-ra, ǽr-est.*—Our mod. *ere* (which is now a conjunction only) was formed from the Positive, though it is nearer in signification to the Comparative. *Erst* is now only an adverb.

Hind, hinder, hindmost or **hindermost.**—*Hind* is from A.S. *hind-an* (adv. backwards, hence *hind*). "Hinder" in A.S. was used as a Positive adverb, and was therefore a different part of speech from our mod. Comparative adjective. Chaucer has *hinderest*, and Wycliff *hindermore. Hindmost* is from A.S. *hinde-ma* (to which *-est* or *-ost* has been added, making *hind-most*).

Neath, nether, nethermost.—*Nether* is from A.S. *ni-ðer*, in which *-ther* is a comparative suffix; see above, § 123 (3). *Nethermost*, which looks like a double Superl. *most* added to the Comparative *nether*, is more probably a corruption of A.S. *niðemest* (=ni-ðe-m-est). Here *ni* (down) is the base, *ðe-m* is the Aryan *ta-ma*, such as we see in "op-*ti-mus*," and *-est* is the usual A.S. Superlative suffix.

Out, outer or **utter, utmost** or **uttermost.**—A.S. *úte* or *útan, útor, úte-ma* or *úte-mest.* In *mest* there are two Superl. suffixes, *-ma* and *-est.* "Utter" and "outer" are now both used as Positives, having

---

[1] The distinction between *mára* and *má* is that the former was an adjective and the latter an adverb in A.S. The *s* (the original sign of the Comparative) has become an *r* in the former word, having been preserved by the following *a*. But it dropped off in the adverb, to which no Nom. inflexion was attached, leaving only *má.* In Gothic these forms were *mai-z-a* (adjective) and *mais* (adverb). The former appears in A.S. as *má-r-a*, and the latter as *má.* The *z* in the one became *r*, and the *s* in the other was lost.

lost their Comparative force. The word *út* had two Comp. forms, *úttor* and *útor*, besides a third *ýter*, which became obsolete. The first has produced the Modern English *utter* by a shortening of the first vowel from *ú* to *u*. The second has produced *outer*, by retaining the long vowel, but changing its sound from *ú* to *ou*, as explained in § 72.

In, inner, inmost or **innermost**. — A.S. *in*, *inne-ra*, *inne-mest*. The last has been contracted to *in-most* or expanded to *inner-most*.

Note.—Adjectives are said to be **defective** in their comparison, when they do not possess all three Degrees of Comparison complete.

To this class belongs *rathe*, *rather*. *Rathe* = early, and is now rarely used :—

Bring the *rathe* primrose that forsaken dies.—MILTON.

Rather has become adverbial. *Rathest* is obsolete.

To the same class belong all those named under II. and III. Under II. we have Positives, viz. *good*, *bad*, *little*, *much*, *many*, which have no comparatives or superlatives of their own ; and Comparatives with Superlatives, viz. *better*, *best*,—*worse*, *worst*,—*less*, *least*,—and *more*, *most*, which have no positives of their own. Under III. we have a list of Comparative and Superlative adjectives to which there is no corresponding *adjective*, but only an adverb, in the Positive degree.

SECTION 3.—THE FORMS OF PRONOUNS.

Forms of Pronouns of the First and Second Persons.

127. First and Second Personal Pronouns declined.—In A.S. there was a dual number of the First and Second Personal Pronouns, which died out before A.D. 1300. The Singular and Plural forms are given below for purposes of reference, not for committal to memory :—

I. *First Person.*

Case.	Singular.		Plural.	
	Old Eng.	Mod. Eng.	Old Eng.	Mod. Eng.
Nom. .	Ic	I	wé	we
Gen. . .	mín	mine, my	úser, úre	our, ours
Dat. . .	mé	me	ús	us
Accus. .	mec, mé	me	úsic, ús	us

II. *Second Person.*

Case.	Singular.		Plural.	
	Old Eng.	Mod. Eng.	Old Eng.	Mod. Eng.
Nom. .	ðú	thou	gé	ye
Gen. . .	ðín	thine, thy	eówer	your, yours
Dat. . .	ðé	thee	eów	you
Accus. .	ðec, ðé	thee	eówic, eów	you

128. Nominative.—The only difference of inflexion between the Old Eng. and Mod. Eng. forms is the *c* at the end of the Nom. Sing. *ic.* This letter has dropped off, as in several parallel instances; cf. *godly* for A.S. *godlíc*, *holy* for A.S. *hálig.*

Ich, in the Southern dialect, is found up to the close of the Middle period :—

Ich am an old man.—AWDELY, A.D. 1565.

Shakspeare puts the following sentences in the mouth of Edgar, who had disguised himself as a Somersetshire peasant and assumed the peasants' dialect :—

Ch'ill (=Ich will=I will) not let go.
Ch'ud (=Ich would=I would) ha' been zwaggered.
Ch'ill (=Ich will=I will) pick your teeth.—*King Lear*, iv. 6.

129. Accusative, Dative.—The *c* of *mec* and *ðec* (Singulars), and the *ic* of *ús-ic* and *eów-ic* (Plurals), have dropped off, like the *c* of *ic* in the Nominative. In other respects the forms in Mod. Eng. are almost the same as those in Old Eng.

The effect of the loss of these endings has been to make the Accus. form coincide with the Dative. These two cases we now call by a single name, Objective.

130. Genitive, Possessive.—The forms of the Genitive or Possessive can be thus accounted for :—

(1) **Mine, thine.**—These are merely modern spellings of *mín* and *thín*, a final *e* having been added to indicate the lengthening of the preceding *i*. The final *n* is or was a Genitive suffix in all the Teutonic languages. In the south of England we still hear *hisn*, *ourn*, *yourn*; see below (3).

My and *thy* are shortened forms of *mín* and *thín*. In the twelfth century the final *n* began to drop off before a consonant, which gave rise to the modern *my* and *thy*. In point of idiom, however, separate uses have been assigned in Mod. Eng to *mine* and *thine* on the one hand and to *my* and *thy* on the other.

Note.—The Reflexive or emphatic *own*, as in "my own," "his own," etc., is from A.S. *ágen*, p.p. of the verb *ág-an*, to possess. It therefore means literally "possessed."

(2) **Our, your.**—These are modern spellings of *úre* and *eówer*. The final *re* is a Genitive suffix (Plural) of adjectives; cf. all-*er*, all-*re*, al-*ra*, the old Genitive plurals of "all."

(3) **Ours, yours.**—A.S. *úres*, *eówres*, both of which contain the Gen. suffix *-es* superadded to the Gen. suffix *-re*. The forms *ours*, *yours* are therefore not due to Northern influence, as has been alleged. In Mid. Eng. we sometimes find *our-en* for *ours*, and *her-en* for *theirs*. In peasant English, in the southern counties, we still hear *hisn*, *hern*, *ourn*, *yourn*, *theirn*, which, like "mine," "thine," "ours," and "yours," are used only when there is no noun expressed after them.

Forms of the Pronoun of the Third Person.

131. The Third Personal Pronoun declined.—The pronoun of the third person, which is also a Demonstrative pronoun, was declined as follows in A.S. The original stem or base of the word is **hi.**

Singular.

Case.	Masculine.		Feminine.		Neuter.	
	Old Eng.	Mod. Eng.	Old Eng.	Mod. Eng.	Old Eng.	Mod. Eng.
Nom. .	hé	he	héo	she	hit	it
Gen. .	his	his	hire	her	his	its
Dat. .	him	him	hire	her	him	it
Accus. .	hine	him	hí	her	hit	it

Plural, all Genders.

Case.	Old Eng.	Mod. Eng.
Nom. . .	hig, hí	they
Gen. . .	hira, heora	their
Dat. . .	hem, heom	them
Accus. . .	hig, hí	them

(1) **He.**—This has come to us unchanged (except in the sound of the vowel and in the loss of accent) from A.S. In Mid. Eng. we find the form *ha*, which in peasant language is now sounded as *a*. This *ha* is an unemphatic form of A.S. *hé;* cf. our use of *thə* for *the*.

> "Rah, tah, tah," would *a* say; "bounce" would *a* say; and away again would *a* go; and again would *a* come.—2 *Hen. IV.* iii. 2, 303.

(2) **His.**—This contains the Genitive suffix *s* attached to the root *hi*, and has come to us unchanged from A.S. The single form *his* does the double work, for which in the other pronouns two possessive forms exist: (*a*) "This is *his* horse"; (*b*) "My horse is better than *his*."

(3) **Him.**—The *m* is the Dative Singular suffix, either Masculine or Neuter, but not Feminine; cf. who-*m*. This Dative form, on account of the greater frequency of the Dative case in Old English, has superseded the accusative *hine*, and now stands for both under the single name "Objective." By Chaucer's time the old Accusative *hi-ne* had wholly disappeared from the *literary* form of the Midland dialect. But it is still used in common talk—"I saw *'un*" (sounded *ən*).

Note.—It is worth noticing that the Dative case in A.S. has contributed much more than any other to the shaping of nouns and pronouns in Mod. Eng. Another example of this is given in § 66.

(4) **She.**—This has replaced *héo*, the feminine form of *hé*, which lasted as late as 1387. *She* has been supposed to be an altered form of A.S. *seó*, the feminine form of the Definite article *se*. See above, § 121, under the word **The.** But it is now believed that *she* has come from the Midland *scǽ*, which occurs in the last chapter but one of the *Saxon Chronicle*, written in the twelfth century at Peterborough, within the area of the Midland dialect.

(5) **Her.**—This word in Mod. Eng. stands—(1) for the Old Eng. Genitive *hire*, which contains a Genitive feminine suffix *-re;* (2) for the Old Eng. Dative *hire*, which contains a Dative feminine suffix *-re;* (3) for the old Accusative form *hí*, which was superseded by the Dative.

(6) **Hers** is a double Possessive form, due to the analogy of *ours* and *yours*, and not (as has been alleged) to Northern influence.

(7) **It.**—The final *t* is a true Neuter suffix, as in *tha-t*, *wha-t*. Cf. Lat. *i-d*, *illu-d*, *quo-d*, etc. Our Modern form *it* stands for—(1) the Old Eng. Nominative *hit*, by the loss of the initial *h;* (2) the Old Eng. Dative *him* (Neuter); and (3) the Old Eng. Accusative *hit*.

(8) **Its.**—This has replaced the Old Eng. Neuter *his*, which lasted into the Tudor period:—

> No comfortable star did lend *his* light.—SHAKSPEARE.
> Put up again thy sword in *his* place.—*Matthew* xxvi. 52.

Along with the use of *his* we find, in the fourteenth century, an uninflected genitive *hit*, which in the Tudor period appears in the unemphatic form of *it*, the *h* having been lost through want of accent.

> The hedge-sparrow fed the cuckoo so long,
> That it had *it* head bit off by *it* young.—*King Lear*, i. 4.

The inflected form *its*, which is now predominant, is used only three times by Milton, A.D. 1608-1674, not once in the version of the Bible printed in 1611, and occurs in only a few passages, in Bacon and Shakspeare. Dryden is the first great authority who is quite familiar with its use.

Note.—*Its* is written without the apostrophe, because it never had one; for no such form as *it-es* ever existed, and hence there was no *e* to be elided.

(9) **They.**—It was in the north of England, and in the thirteenth century, that this word came into use in supersession of *hig, hí*, the Nominative Plural of *hé*. The earliest forms of it were *thei, tha.*

The A.S. forms *hig, hí* were retained in the Southern dialect till near the end of the fourteenth century.

They originally was the Nominative Plural of the Old Norse definite article, and was spelt in Norse as *their.*[1]

(10) **Their,** the Gen. Plur. of the def. art.. Old Norse *þeirra* (cf. A.S. *þára*). These superseded *hira, heora,* the Genitive Plural of *hé*. All these forms contain a Genitive Plural suffix *-ra, -r.* The form **theirs** is formed in the same way as *ours, yours,* and answers the same purpose.

(11) **Them.**—This is a Dative form, containing the Dative Plural suffix *-m*; cf. whil-*om*, seld-*om*. In A.S. the Dative Plural of the def. art. was *ðám;* in Old Norse, *þeim*. The latter replaced (*a*) *hem, heom,* the Dat. Plur. of *hé;* and (*b*) *hig, hí,* the Accus. Plur. of *hé*.

Note 1.—It will be seen from the above that the A.S. or Old Eng. pronoun of the Third Person was formed from a single stem, **hi** (=he); but the Mod. Eng. pronoun of this person contains forms based on three different stems, viz. **hi, sa,** and **tha.** **Hi** is the stem used throughout the Singular, except in the Nom. Fem. *she*, when **sa** is the stem used. **Tha** is the stem used throughout the Plural.

Note 2.—The Old Accus. Plur. *hem* is not extinct. It is seen in the dramatists in the form of *'em.* The apostrophe has been printed under the mistaken notion that *em* is a contraction of *them;* whereas it is simply a survival of *hem,* with loss of initial *h;* cf. *hit, it.* The form *em* (sounded as *əm*) is very common to this day in colloquial English.

Interrogative and Relative Pronouns.

132. Relative Pronoun in A.S.—In A.S. the only kind of Relative was the indeclinable particle *þe* (the), which was usually joined as a suffix to some part of the declinable Demonstrative adjective *sé.*

In Mid. Eng. the Relative in ordinary use was the indeclinable *that.*

133. The Interrogative Pronoun in A.S.—The Interro-

[1] There was a form *þá* in A.S., which became *tho*, and not *they*, and was once common.

gative Pronoun, which in A.S. answered to "who" and "what," was declined in the manner shown below. It was used only as a pronoun proper,—that is, it was not placed before a noun, as in "what man."

Case.	Masculine and Feminine.		Neuter.	
	Old Eng.	Mod. Eng.	Old Eng.	Mod. Eng.
Nom.	hwá	who	hwæt	what
Gen.	hwæs	whose	hwæs	whose
Dat.	hwám, hwǽm	whom	hwǽm	what
Accus.	hwone, hwæne	whom	hwæt	what
Inst.	hwí	why (adv.)	hwí	why (adv.)

(1) **Who.**—A.S. *hwá*, Masc. and Fem. This was used as an Interrogative from the earliest times. As a Relative, though found occasionally in the fourteenth and fifteenth centuries, it did not come into common use before the sixteenth, and then, as now, it was restricted to *personal* antecedents.

"Who" as a Relative is not recognised by Ben Jonson, who in his English Grammar speaks of "one Relative *which*." "Who" and "which," however, were both used in the Tudor period :—

> Our Father, *which* art in heaven.—*New Test.*
> God, *who* at sundry times, etc.—*New Test.*

Both forms of the Relative are found in Shakspeare. Shakspeare even uses *who* where we should now use *which* :—

> A lion *who* glared.—*Julius Cæsar.*
> The winds
> *Who* take the ruffian billows by the tops.—2 *Hen. IV.*

(2) **Whose.**—A.S. *hwæs*, of all genders. The *s* is a true Gen. suffix ; cf. hi-*s*. The "whose" of Mod. Eng. is generally limited to persons,[1] though we sometimes find it applied to things as an equivalent to "*of which*."

> Nebuchadnezzar the king made an image of gold, *whose* height was threescore cubits.—*Dan.* iii. 1.

[1] This limitation may perhaps have arisen from the analogy of *his* and *its*, the former being now limited to persons and the latter to things. Our language has gained nothing but inconvenience by restricting the use of *whose* to persons, and it may be hoped that the older practice of using *whose* for all genders will be some day resumed. It is much easier to say "*whose* height" than "the height *of which*."

Of man's first disobedience and the fruit
Of that forbidden tree, *whose* mortal taste, etc.—*Par. Lost*, i. 2.

(3) **Whom.**—A.S. *hwǽm*, Dative Sing., in which the *m* is a true Dative suffix; cf. the *m* in *hi-m*.

Between the A.S. *hwǽm* and the modern *whom* two differences exist:—(1) *Hwǽm* applied to all genders, whereas *whom*, according to present idiom, applies only to Masc. and Fem., and then only to human beings, not to the lower animals. (2) *Hwǽm* was strictly a Dative, whereas *whom* is used both as a Direct and an Indirect objective, and has superseded the A.S. Accus. *hwæ-ne*, as *him* (Dative) has superseded *hi-ne* (Accus.). The old Accus. *hwæne* or *hwone* became obsolescent in the thirteenth century.

(4) **What.**—A.S. *hwæt*, originally Neuter (like A.S. *tha-t*, and Lat. *illu-d*), and never Masc. or Fem. Its present capacity of being used for all genders and both numbers commenced at the beginning of the thirteenth century, in the Northern dialect.

What woman is this! *What* man is that?

According to present idiom, "*what*" takes the place of "*which*," either (*a*) when no antecedent is expressed, or (*b*) when the antecedent is placed *after* the relative.

The strict observance of this distinction, however, is of recent date, as is clear from the following uses of *what*:—

I fear nothing *what* (=which) can be said against me.—*Timon of Athens*, iv. 2.

That *what* (=which) is extremely proper in one company, may be highly improper in another.—CHESTERFIELD.

Note.—The use of *what* in such a construction as the following has now become a vulgarism:—

A thief is a man *what* steals.

(5) **Whether.**—A.S. *hwæðer*=which of the two, has now become archaic.

God Cupid, or the keeper, I know not *whether*,
Unto my cost and charges brought you thither.
BEAUMONT AND FLETCHER.

The last syllable *-ther* is a Comparative suffix (see § 123, 3); and as the Comparative degree implies a comparison between *two* things or persons, it is from this suffix that the word "whether" acquired the sense of "which of the *two*."

(6) **Which.**—A.S. *hwilc*, short for *hwí-lic*, why-like; *hwí* is the Instrumental case of *whá*, and the origin of adv. *why*.

(7) **As.**—Short for Mid. Eng. *also*; A.S. *eal-swá* (quite so).

SECTION 4.—THE FORMS OF VERBS.

134. Forms of verbs in Old and Modern English.—The parts of a verb can be formed either—(*a*) synthetically, that is, by suffixes or personal endings attached to the tense-stem; or (*b*) analytically, by the use of Auxiliary verbs in company with Participles and Infinitives.

In Old as in Modern English the conjugation of a verb was chiefly analytical; the only tenses formed synthetically were the Present and the Past, and these only in the Active voice. Hence it has been said that there are only two real tenses in English.

Future time could be expressed by the Auxiliaries "shall" or "will," followed by an Infinitive, if it was necessary to use them. But if future time was implied by the context, the Present tense did the work of a Future also; and this, in preference to the other, was the ordinary idiom.

The Perfect and Continuous tenses were then, as now, formed by the use of Auxiliaries in combination with Participles.

Then, as now, there were three Finite moods,—the Indic., the Imper., and the Subjunc.,—besides the non-Finite parts of a verb,—the Infinitive, and the Participle.

The tenses of the Subjunctive were usually formed synthetically in Old Eng., but the Auxiliary "should" is also met with occasionally.

The Passive voice was then, as now, conjugated analytically throughout, though the verb *weorðan* (to become) was rather more commonly used than the verb "to be."[1]

On the whole, then, the structure of a verb in Old Eng. was the same at bottom that it is in Modern. It was far less synthetical than in Latin.

135. Old Conjugation of Strong and Weak Verbs.—For purposes of reference, not for committal to memory, a Strong and a Weak verb are conjugated below in those parts that were formed synthetically in Old Eng.

The exclusion of *all* Plural inflexions from *all* tenses of *all* the Finite moods, and of the Simple and Dative inflexions from the Infinitive mood, is what chiefly distinguishes a Modern from an Old Eng. verb.

All those Plural inflexions which were not *-en* in Old Eng. became *-en* (and sometimes *-e*) in the Midland dialect. It was the loss of this *-en* that Ben Jonson deplored. (See § 26.)

---

[1] Even in Gothic, the oldest of all the Teutonic languages extant, only a few instances of Passive forms due to inflexions had survived. Wright's *Primer of the Gothic Language*, ed. 1892, p. 135.

A. Strong Verb. *Nim-an*, to take.

Present Tense.

Indicative.		Subjunctive.	
Singular.	*Plural.*	*Singular.*	*Plural.*
1. ic nim-*e*	wé nim-*ath*	ic nim-*e*	wé nim-*en*
2. ðú nim-*est*	gé nim-*ath*	ðú nim-*e*	gé nim-*en*
3. hé nim-(*e*)*th*	hí nim-*ath*	hé nim-*e*	hí nim-*en*

Past Tense.

Indicative.		Subjunctive.	
Singular.	*Plural.*	*Singular.*	*Plural.*
1. ic nam	wé nám-*on*	ic nám-*e*	wé nám-*en*
2. ðú nám-*e*	gé nám-*on*	ðú nám-*e*	gé nám-*en*
3. hé nam	hí nám-*on*	hé nám-*e*	hí nám-*en*

Imperative.	
2nd Sing. . .	nim
2nd Plur. . .	nim-*ath*

Infinitive.	
Simple . .	nim-*an*
Dative or *Gerundial*	tó nim-*anne* or -*enne*[1]

Participle.	
Pres. . . .	nim-*ende* or -*inde*[2]
Past or Passive .	num-*en*

[1] The change from -*anne* to -*enne* is an example of vowel-mutation. The original form was -*anni*, the last vowel of which changed the *a* to *e*, and was itself eventually reduced to *e*.

[2] The change from -*ende* (the original form) to -*inde* took place after A.D. 1066. It is an example of the regular change from *en* to *in* as in *henge*, "hinge."

B. Weak Verb. *Hýr-an*, to hear.

Present Tense.

Indicative.		Subjunctive.	
Singular.	*Plural.*	*Singular.*	*Plural.*
1. ic hýr-*e*	wé hýr-*ath*	1. ic hýr-*e*	wé hýr-*en*
2. ðú hýr-*est*	gé hýr-*ath*	2. ðú hýr-*e*	gé hýr-*en*
3. hé hýr-*eth*	hí hýr-*ath*	3. hé hýr-*e*	hí hýr-*en*

Past Tense.

Indicative.		Subjunctive.	
Singular.	*Plural.*	*Singular.*	*Plural.*
1. ic hýr-*de*	wé hýr-*d-on*	1. ic hýr-*de*	wé hýr-*d-en*
2. ðú hýr-*de-st*	gé hýr-*d-on*	2. ðú hýr-*de*	gé hýr-*d-en*
3. hé hýr-*de*	hí hýr-*d-on*	3. hé hýr-*de*	hí hýr-*d-en*

Imperative.	
2nd Sing. . .	hýr
2nd Plur. . .	hýr-*ath*

Infinitive.	
Simple . .	hýr-*an*
Dative or *Gerundial*	tó hýr-*enne* or -*anne*

Participle.	
Pres. . . .	hýr-*ende* or -*inde*
Past or *Passive* .	hýr-*e-d*

136. Strong and Weak Verbs distinguished.—Both classes of verbs are found in Gothic, the oldest of the extant Teutonic languages. There is reason to think, however, that Strong verbs are the older of the two;[1] for few or none of our

[1] The Strong conjugation in the Teutonic languages may be compared with the 3rd conjugation in Latin, which was probably older than the

primitive or root-verbs belong to the Weak class, and examples occur in which the original root has perished and only the derivative remains.

In A.S., whenever a new verb was derived or formed from another, or from a noun, the Derivative verb always assumed the Weak form, and not the Strong. Thus we have the Weak verb *fell* (Causal) from the Strong *fall*, and the Weak verb *love* (A.S. *luf-ian*) from A.S. *lufu*, love (noun). Similarly in Mod. Eng., whenever a verb is formed from a noun or some other word, or is borrowed from some foreign source, it invariably assumes the Weak form.

In Old English the two classes of verbs were distinguished as follows:—

(1) The Past tense in *Strong* verbs was formed by vowel-*gradation* (§ 78); while in *Weak* verbs it was formed by adding the suffix *-de* or *-te* to the stem of the Present tense. (If, as sometimes happens, a vowel-change is seen in some Weak verbs also, this is the result of *Mutation*, not gradation; see § 138, *b*.) (2) In *Strong* verbs the Second Pers. Sing. of the Past tense was expressed by the suffix *-e*, while in *Weak* verbs it was expressed by adding the suffix *-st* to the suffix *-de*. (3) In *Strong* verbs the stem of the Second Pers. Sing. and of all persons in the Plural of the Past tense had not always the same vowel as the stem of the First and Third Persons Singular:[1] (observe the difference of accent in the Past tense of specimen A, § 135). (4) In *Strong* verbs the Past Part. was formed by the suffix *-en*, while in *Weak* verbs it was formed by the suffix *-d*.

In Mod. Eng. these characteristics have been preserved in the main, but with the following modifications:—

No. (1) remains as before, except that the final *e* of the Weak suffix *-de* has disappeared, leaving no distinction in Weak verbs between the form of the Past tense and that of the Past participle.

No. (2) has entirely gone. *All* verbs, whether Weak or Strong, now have *-st* or *-est* as the suffix of the Second Person Singular in the Past tense.

No. (3) has also gone, but not without leaving several traces

---

other three: for in this conjugation the past tense was sometimes formed by reduplication, as sometimes in Gothic and always in Greek, and sometimes by a change of the root-vowel, as in *ag*-o (Pres.), *ēg*-i (Past).

[1] It depends upon the conjugation whether the vowel changes or not. The verbs *fall* and *shake* kept the same vowel throughout the Past tense.

of its former existence. Thus the stem of the Plural *were* (Past tense of the Strong verb *wes-an*, with the *s* changed to *r*) has not the same vowel as that of the Singular *was*. There was once a good deal of uncertainty about the Past tenses of such verbs as *swim*, *begin*, *run*, *drink*, *shrink*, *sink*, *ring*, *sing*, *spring*, all of which now take the stem of the A.S. Past. Sing. *swam*, *began*, *ran*, etc. Yet Byron has the following:—

The isles of Greece, the isles of Greece,
Where burning Sappho loved and *sung*,
Where grew the arts of war and peace,
Where Delos rose and Phœbus *sprung*.

On the other hand, the verbs *spin*, *slink*, *stink*, *sting*, *win*, *fling*, *wring*, *cling*, *string* all now form their Past tenses in *spun*, *slunk*, *stunk*, etc., which was once the stem of the *Plural*, and not that of the Singular.

No. (4) remains as before, except that many of the Strong verbs have lost or half-lost the suffix *-en* that was once universal in the Past Participle.

137. Strong Verbs classified: reduplicated Past.—In Gothic (as in Latin, Greek, and other Aryan languages) Past tenses could be formed by reduplication of the root-syllable. In Gothic such verbs were a special class of the Strong conjugation; such as *hait-an* (to call), *hai-hait*; *ték-an* (to touch), *tai-tók*.[1]

The Strong verbs in Teutonic thus naturally fall into two main divisions—(1) reduplicative verbs; (2) gradation verbs. The first class constituted one single conjugation; the second was distinguished into six sub-classes, the peculiarities of which need not be discussed in this book.[2]

In A.S. examples of reduplication are very few, and these few were far less distinctly preserved than in Gothic. The chief examples are:—

Héht (Gothic *hai-hait*), pt. t. of *hát-an*, to call; which shows reduplication by the repetition of *h*.

---

[1] Gothic uses *ai* with two values, viz. *ĕ* and *ai*. In this case it has the value *ĕ*. Hence the Gothic *hai-*, *tai-* stand for *hĕ-*, *tĕ-*; and exactly correspond to the Latin and Greek reduplicative prefixes "*pe*-pendi," "*te*-tupha."

[2] The seven Strong conjugations have been called after certain typical verbs selected to represent each class. These have been put into a couplet by Professor Skeat as a help to remembering them:—

Drive slowly; wisely *choose*; from *drink* for-*bear*;
Mete justly; *shake* the tree; down *falls* the pear.

Réord (Gothic *rai-róth*), pt. t. of *rǽd-an*, to advise; which shows reduplication by the repetition of *r*.

Léolc (Gothic *lai-laik*), pt. t. of *lác-an*, to skip; which shows reduplication by the repetition of *l*.

Léort (Gothic *lai-lót*) pt. t. of *lǽt-an*, to permit; where an *r* has been substituted for the repeated *l*.

Dréord, pt. t. of *drǽd-an*, to dread, in which the *dr* has been reduplicated as *rd* by metathesis or change of order in the consonants.

More commonly the repeated consonant is lost, and a diphthong is substituted for the root-vowel; as Goth. *fai-fall*, A.S. *féoll*, Eng. *fell;* Goth. *hai-hald*, A.S. *héold*, Eng. *held*.[1]

In Mod. Eng. all traces of reduplication are lost, except in one, and possibly two, examples. The certain example is *hight* (the Past tense of *hát-an*, to call), which in A.S. was spelt *hé-ht*, and in Gothic *hai-hait*, as shown above. The other example that has been alleged is *did*, the Past tense of *do*. But this example is doubtful; for in A.S. the form corresponding to *did* was *dy-de*, apparently a Weak past tense formed with the suffix *-de*.[2] Some, however, believe it to be reduplicated.

138. Weak Verbs classified.—Weak verbs in Old English may be subdivided into two main classes—(*a*) those which had the vowel *o* or *e* between the verb-root and the Past suffix *-de*, as *luf-o-de*, I loved; *styr-e-de*, I stirred; and (*b*) those which had no intervening vowel, as *hýr-de*, I heard.

Class (*a*).—The intervening *o* took the form of *e* in Mid. Eng. The A.S. *luf-o-de* thus became *lov-e-de* (three syllables), or *love-de* (two syllables), which in Mod. Eng. (through the loss of the final *e*) became *loved* (one syllable). Hence the real suffix of Weak verbs of this class is not *ed*, but *d*, the *e* being part of the formative stem of the verb itself.[3]

Class (*b*).—If the final consonant of the root was voiced, the Past suffix was *-de*. But in verbs that ended in *-nd*, *-ld*, and *-rd*,

---

1 Skeat's *Princ. Eng. Etym.* series i. pp. 159, 160.

2 Mr. Sweet in *Short Hist. Eng. Grammar*, ed. 1892, p. 190, § 731, calls *dy-de* a "Weak past." But Brugmann, the German philologist, believes it to be reduplicated. He compares our *do* with the Greek root *thē*, the Ionic imperfect of which was *e-ti-the-a*. This reduplicated form, if we leave out the first and last vowels, gives us a past tense *ti-the*, which is very like A.S. *dy-de*, Old Sax. (of the Continent) *dĕ-da*, and Old High German *tĕ-ta*. The most direct argument for considering it a Strong (redup.) past is that in A.S. itself some texts use *dǽdon* for the plural, whereas if the tense were Weak it would be *dydon*.

3 Skeat's *Student's Pastime*, pp. 175-178. In fact, the verb was a derivative from the noun *luf-u;* and the *o* in *luf-o-de* takes the place of the final *u* in *luf-u*.

t was gradually substituted for *d*, because in such verbs the past tense thus modified could be more rapidly pronounced. Thus we have *send-de, send-e, sent-e, sent.* In the same way we get *build, built* (or older *builded*); *gild, gilt* (or *gilded*); *bend, bent* (or *bended*).

If the final consonant of the root was voiceless, as *f, p, s, t, h* (*h* or *gh*), the Past suffix was not *-de*, but *-te* from the first. Hence in Mid. Eng. we have *slip-te, skip-te, slep-te, met-te, brough-te,* which in Mod. Eng. appear as *slipped, skipped, slept, met, brought.* It is the perversity of English spelling which makes us write *ed* in some cases and *t* in others. The latter is the more phonetic, besides being historically correct.

Verbs with a long root-vowel, as *feed* (A.S. *fédan*), are very apt to incur a shortening of this vowel, when the suffix *-te* or *-de* is added to them. Thus, *leave* (A.S. *lǽf*-an) formed its Past tense originally in *lǽf-de*, and *féd*-an in *féd-de.* But by the rule given in § 89 (*a*) *féd-de* became shortened (through the accent on the first syllable) to *fĕd-de*, and when the final *e* dropped off, the second *d* became superfluous, and so the Past tense took the form of *fĕd.* Similarly *lǽf-te* became *lĕf-t.*

There is a class of Weak verbs which appear to incur a vowel change when *d* or *t* is added for the Past tense. The change of vowel in these verbs is not of the same kind as that in Strong verbs. In Strong verbs the difference of vowel is the result of *Gradation;* in Weak of *Mutation.* In these it is really *the Present that has changed,* not the Past. In the Present the root-vowel is mutated by the influence of *i* in the Infinitive suffix *-ian.* Thus we have *salde* (I sold), Inf. *sell-an*, through an older form *sal-ian*, and hence the Present tense is *sell.* In the same way we get *tell-an* (tell), *teal-de* (told); *bycg-an* (buy), *bóh-te* (bought); *séc-an* (seek), *sóh-te* (sought); *wyrc-an* (work), *worh-te* (wrought); *thenc-an* (think); *thóh-te* (thought).

139. Origin of Suffix "-de."—It was once believed, and is still widely asserted in books,[1] that the suffix *-d* or *-de* is an abridgment of *did*, the supposed reduplicated Past tense of *do;* so that *loved* = *love-did*, *lovedst* = *love-didst.* This theory is now entirely exploded. It was merely a conjecture from the first.

The A.S. suffix *-de* was founded on the form *-da*, which in Gothic, the oldest of the Teutonic languages, was one of the

[1] As, for example, in Mason's *English Grammar*, § 223.

Past suffixes of Weak verbs. We cannot trace the origin of *-de* farther back than this.

In Gothic there were no less than three forms of the suffix of the Past tense of Weak verbs, viz. *-da*, *-ta*, and *-tha*, which in A.S. are represented by *-de*, *-te*, and *-the*.

Gothic	nasi-da (I saved)	A.S. neri-de.
	brah-ta (I brought)	A.S. bróh-te.
	hun-tha (I could)	A.S. cú-ðe.

The theory that the *-de* came from *did* is inadmissible—(1) because there is no evidence for it; (2) because it does not account for such a Past tense as *bróh-te*, nor yet for such a Past as *cú-the*, which appears as "I couth" in Lowland Scotch; (3) because the A.S. *-de* is traced to an older Gothic form *-da*.

140. Interchange of Weak and Strong.—The prevailing tendency in the history of our language has been towards the Weak conjugation in preference to the Strong. This has shown itself in two ways—(*a*) Many Strong verbs have become Weak; and (*b*) Whenever new verbs were or are admitted from foreign sources, or coined from internal ones, they took and take the Weak form. Ben Jonson in his English Grammar calls the Weak class "the common inn to lodge every stranger and foreign guest."[1]

(*a*) The following will serve as examples of Strong verbs which have become Weak:—

Pres.	*Past* (A.S.).	*Pres.*	*Past* (A.S.).
ache	óc (ached)	gnaw	M.E. gnew (gnawed)
burn	bearn (burnt)	laugh	hlóh (laughed)
bring[2]	brang (brought)	melt	mealt (melted)
creep	créap (crept)	sow	seów (sowed)
fare	fór (fared)	suck	seác (sucked)
fold	feóld (folded)	wash	wósc (washed)

[1] There was an obvious reason why all foreign verbs should take the Weak, and not the Strong form. The change of the root-vowel peculiar to the Strong conjugation was not possible in any but Teutonic verbs: it was a purely Teutonic process, of which foreign verbs were incapable, because they were foreign. But it was very easy to add a suffix like *-ed* to a foreign stem, and hence this was the mode of conjugation, to which all foreign imports were compelled to conform. The decay of the Strong conjugation may be partly ascribed to the large influx of foreign verbs, all of which were necessarily Weak. The Weak native verbs, reinforced as they were by the Weak foreign ones, set the fashion, and many of our Strong native verbs yielded to its influence.

[2] In A.S. there were two forms of this verb—(1) a Strong verb, *bring*-an, pt. t. *brang;* and (2) a Weak verb, *breng*-an, pt. t. *bróh-te.* Mod. Eng. retains only the Weak past *brought;* and the two presents *bring* and *breng* have melted into one.

The same tendency is seen in verbs, whose recent Weak form has not yet entirely ousted the older Strong:—

Pres.	*Past.*	*Pres.*	*Past.*
climb	clomb, climbed	cleave	clove, cleft
crow	crew, crowed	thrive	throve, thrived
hang	hung, hanged		

(*b*) There are, however, a few examples of verbs originally Weak, which have become Strong either wholly or in part. Verbs that are partly Strong and partly Weak are called **Strong-Weak** or Mixed:—

Pres.	*Past Tense.*	*Past Part.*	*Pres.*	*Past T.*	*Past Part.*
wear	wore	worn	show	showed	shown, showed
stick	stuck	stuck	rot	rotted	rotten, rotted
dig	dug	dug	stave	stove, staved	staved
hide	hid	hid, hidden			
spit	spat	spat			

Note 1.—The verb *rot* is a peculiar case. It is really Weak. The pp. *rotten* is a remnant of a lost Strong verb, and is far older than the Weak past part. *rotted.*

Note 2.—Two entirely distinct verbs have become confused in *stick.* This verb in the sense of "stab" was always Strong; in Mid. Eng. its forms were Infin. *stek-en,* Past tense *stak,* Past part. *stek-en.* But "stick" in the sense of "adhere" was originally Weak; A.S. *stic-ian,* Past tense *stic-o-de,* Past part. *stic-o-d.*

Note 3.—A similar confusion has occurred in the verb *cleave.* In the sense of "split" this verb was Strong: A.S. *cleóf-an,* pt. t. *cleáf,* pp. *clof-en,* whence we get *cleave, clave, cloven.* In the sense of "stick" "adhere," it was Weak: A.S. *clif-ian* or *cleof-ian,* pt. t. *clif-o-de,* pp. *clif-o-d,* from which we get the forms *cleaved, cleft.*

Note 4.—In the verbs *hide* and *spit,* the change of conjugation from Weak to Strong is more apparent than real; for in A.S. we find Infin. *hýd-an,* Past tense *hýd-de;* and Infin. *spitt-an* or *spǽt-an,* Past tense *spǽt-te;* (the alternative form *spit-te* is not found). In Mod. Eng. the final *-te* or *-de* was discarded, because when the *-e* had disappeared, the *t* or *d* became superfluous after *t* or *d* in the stem of the tense. In the case of *hide* the change of conjugation from Weak to Strong appeared to be so complete, that the Past part. *hid* acquired an alternative form *hidden,* which is an undoubted mark of the Strong conjugation.

(*c*) There are four verbs which in Mod. Eng. follow so closely the analogy of other Weak verbs ending in *d* or *t,* that it is convenient now to class them as Weak. But in A.S. they were Strong.

	Modern English.			*Old English.*		
	Pres.	*Past.*	*Past Part.*	*Pres.*	*Past.*	*Past Part.*
(1)	Burst	burst	burst	berst-e	bærst, burst-on	borst-en
(2)	Let (permit)	let	let	lǽt-e	léort	lǽt-en
(3)	Shed	shed	shed	sceád-e	scéod	scád-en
(4)	Shoot	shot	shot	scéot-e	scéat, scut-on	scot-en

In (1) the Plural of the Past tense has evidently supplied the form of the *Present* tense in Mod. Eng. as well as that of the Past part. In (2) the reduplicated Past *léort* (see § 137) has evidently succumbed to the united influence of the stems of the Present tense and Past part., which were identical; so that *lǽtt* was the usual form even in A.S. In (3) the Present tense and Past part. have both yielded to the influence of the Past tense, whose vowel, however, has been shortened from *éo* or *é* to *e*. In (4) the Past tense in both Sing. and Plur. forms has yielded to the influence of the Past Part., while the Present tense has assumed a form different from both by change of accent from *éo* to *eó*.

Note.—Two entirely distinct verbs have become confused in *let*. In the sense of "hinder," it was always a Weak verb. In the sense of "permit" it was a Strong verb of the reduplicated class (§ 137).

141. Some peculiar Weak Verbs:—

Teach: A.S. *tǽc-an*, *tǽh-te*, *tǽh-t*. In the Pres. the final guttural, *c* or *k*, has been palatalised to *ch*. In the other two forms it has been changed to *gh*.

Catch: from Old Fr. *cach-ier*, conjugated like *lacch-en* (latch), *laughte*, which are now obsolete as verbal forms, though *latch* is still in common use as a noun. The verb *latch* had the same sense as *catch*. This is one of the very few examples of a foreign verb which has undergone a change in its root-vowel as if it were a native one. Cf. *beef*, *beeves*, the only example of a foreign noun in *f* which has formed its plural in *v* after the manner of native nouns; see § 110 (*a*).

Clothe: Northumbrian *clāð*-ian (later *clath*-en), Past tense *clǽð-de*, pp. ge-*clad*-ed. The last has given us the alternative form *clad* for *clothed*.

Make: A.S. *mac-e*, *mac-o-de*, *mac-o-d*. The Past tense and part. lost the *c* or *k* as early as the 13th century. Hence the mod. form *made*.

Flee: A.S. *fleón*, Scand. *flý-ja*. The Past tense *fled* is from Scand. *flý-ði*, a Weak past.

Hang: there are two chief forms of this verb, one Weak and the other Strong. The Weak form is from A.S. *hang-ian*, Past tense *hang-o-de* (=Eng. *hanged*). This in A.S. was Intransitive. The Strong verb has a very peculiar history. In A.S. there was a verb *hón* for *háhan*, pt. t. *héng*, pp. ge-*hang*-en. In Mid. Eng. the corresponding forms were *hing*, *hang*, *hung* (on the analogy of *sing*, *sang*, *sung*). In Mod. Eng. the forms are *hang*, *hung*, *hung*.

Say: A.S. *secg-e*, 3rd Pers. Sing. *seg-eth*, *sæg-de*, *sæg-d*. Here the gutturals have been vocalised into *say*, *said*, *said*. But the form *say* is derived from such parts of the verb as had only one *g*; it cannot be derived from *secg-an* or *secg-e*. Thus *seg-eð* > *sey-eth* > Mod. Eng. *saith*.

Lay: A.S. *lecg-e*, 3rd Pers. Sing. *leg-eth*, *lecg-de*, *lecg-d*. As above.

Buy: A.S. *bycg-e*, 3rd Pers. Sing. *byg-eth*, *bóh-te*, *bóh-t*. Here the guttural *h* (=Mod. Eng. *gh*) has survived in the Past tense and Past Part. The *g* of the stem *byg-* was vocalised, as in *seg-*, *leg-*.

Went: originally the Past tense of *wend*.

Work: A.S. *wyrc-e*, *worh-te*, *worh-t*. The form *wrought* (which is closely allied to *worh-te*) is now less common than the more modern *worked*.

Think: A.S. *ðenc-an*, *ðóh-te*, *ðóh-t*. (This verb must not be confounded with *ðync-an*, to seem, the base of the Impersonal "methinks.")

142. Present Participle.—In early Middle English the suffix was *-ende* (Midland), *-inde* (Southern), *-and* (Northern). In the latter part of the twelfth century the suffix *-inge* (borrowed from the so-called Gerund, to be described in § 148) began to be substituted by Anglo-French scribes for the original suffix *-inde*, and the substitution became established in the Southern and Midland dialects by about 1350,—an unfortunate result, which has been the cause of endless confusion between the Pres. part. and the Gerund.

The Northern suffix *-and* was sometimes used archaically in the Tudor period:—

> Glitter-*and*; trench-*and*.—SPENSER.
> Trill-*and* brooks. A stink-*and* brock (badger).—BEN JONSON.

This Northern form of the Pres. part. was adopted from that part of the *Romaunt of the Rose* which was written in a purely Northern dialect, but was wrongly ascribed to Chaucer, because it was placed among poems of which Chaucer was the real author. Chaucer himself never uses *-and*.

The suffix *-and* held its ground much longer in the Northern dialect than *-ende* or *-inde* did in the Midland or Southern. If only it had spread to these dialects, and ousted the bogus form *-ing*, it would have saved much confusion in English grammar.

143. Past or Passive Participle.—In Old English this participle, as the student is aware, invariably ended in *-en* in Strong verbs, and in *-t* or *-d* in Weak. We give precedence to *-t*, because that was the Aryan form, and *-d* resulted from it.

(*a*) In *Weak* verbs the final *t* or *d* has remained to this day, unless the final consonant of the root happens to be a dental, in which case the addition of the dental suffix is generally superfluous; as *hit* (Present), *hit* (Past part.). The Past part. suffix *-t* or *-d* is identical with that of Lat. "ama-*t*-us"; see footnote 2 to § 3.

(*b*) In *Strong* verbs the suffix *-en* has in many cases been lost; and even when the suffix was gone, the stem of the Past part.

was not always preserved. The prevailing tendency was for the Past tense and Past part. to assume the same form, as we see in such a verb as *swing, swung, swung;* contrast with this such a verb as *smite, smote, smitten.* The assimilation of the Past tense and Past participle was effected in more ways than one. (1) In some verbs the Past part. has taken the form of the Past tense, as *shone* (A.S. *scán*), *held* (A.S. *héold*), *stood* (A.S. *stód*), *awoke* (A.S. *wóc*), *abode* (A.S. *ábád*), which superseded the older Participial forms *scin-en, heald-en, stand-en, wac-en, abid-en.* (2) In other verbs the Past tense Singular has taken the form of the Past tense Plural, as *wound, ground, spun, won, bound, found, wrung, clung, swung,* which superseded the old Past tenses Singular, *wand, grand, span, wan, band, fand, wrang, clang, swang.* In such verbs the Past tense (to take the first example) was—

Singular.	*Plural.*
1st, *wand;* 2nd, *wund-e;* 3rd, *wand.*	*wund-on.*

The Past tense has been levelled all through to the form of the Plural, the stem of which was the same as that of the Second person Singular. (3) But in some verbs the *Plural* forms of the old Past tenses had a different stem-vowel from that of the Past tenses now in use. In such verbs the Past tenses now in use must be ascribed to the influence of the Past participle; as in *shoot, shot, shot* (A.S. *sceót-an, sceát, scot-en*); *steal, stole, stolen* (A.S. *stel-an, stæl* (Sing.), *stǽl-on* (Plur.), *stol-en*); *break, broke, broken* (A.S. *brec-an, bræc* (Sing.), *brǽc-on* (Plur.), *broc-en*); *tear, tore, torn* (A.S. *ter-an, tær* (Sing.), *tǽr-on* (Plur.), *tor-en*).

(*c*) The Past part. of Weak and Strong verbs alike was once very frequently preceded by the suffix *ge*, as *ge-cum-en* (come), *ge-fund-en* (found). In Mid. Eng. this prefix was reduced to *i*, *y*, or *e*, as "*i*-fund-e" (found). In Mod. Eng. only one example remains—"*y*-clept" (called).

> Hail, thou goddess, fair and free,
> In heaven *y*-clept Euphrosyne.—MILTON.

Note.—Milton (we do not know on what authority) adds this prefix to a Present participle in the phrase "star *y*-pointing."

144. Continuous and Perfect Tenses.—In Old English, as in Modern, the Continuous tenses were formed with the Present participle and the Perfect with the Past, each participle being, of course, preceded by the appropriate Auxiliary verb. Thus as Present and Past Continuous tenses we have in A.S. *Hé is gang-ende* (=he is going); *Hé wæs gang-ende* (=he was going).

In forming, however, the *Perfect* tenses there was one difference between the Old and the Mod. constructions. In Old English, if the verb was *Intransitive*, "is" or "was" or "worth" (which was very common) was the Auxiliary verb used; and if the verb was *Transitive*, "has" or "had" was the Auxiliary. But in Mod. Eng. "has" or "had" is used with Intransitive verbs also; and if "is" or "was" is still used at all, it conveys, according to present idiom, rather a different sense.

(*a*) *Intrans.* { Hé *is* ge-cum-en = He is come. (*Sing.*)
Wé *sindon* ge-cum-en-*e* = We are come. (*Plural.*)

The student will observe that in Old Eng. the participle agreed in number and gender with the subject to the verb.

(*b*) *Trans.* { Hé *hæfth* hine ge-fund-enn-e (or ge-fund-en-e).
He has him found = has found him.

Here the student will observe that *hine* in the Accus. case is object to the Trans. verb "has" going before, and that the participle following agrees with it in case, number, and gender.

But in later A.S. the Past participle in this connection became indeclinable; in other words, it ceased to be a participle in the proper sense of the word, and became part of a tense.

Hé hæfth hine ge-fund-*en* = He has found him.

This change in the character of the participle paved the way to "have" taking the place of "be" with *Intransitive* verbs no less than with Transitive ones. When "have" became an Auxiliary verb, *i.e.* one used for forming tenses and moods, and resigned for that purpose its Transitive sense of possession, there was nothing to prevent its being followed by an Intransitive verb as easily as by a Transitive one.

Note.—In three kinds of examples *have* has usurped the place of *be* in the construction of a sentence or phrase:—

(1) When followed by an *Intransitive* Infinitive:—

I *am* to go, or I *have* to go.

(2) In phrases like "I had as lief," "I had rather": for which in older English the phrases were "liefer me *was*," "me *were* better."

(3) In forming the *Perfect* tenses of the Intransitive verbs, as is shown in this paragraph (144).

145. Simple Infinitive.—The history of this Infinitive may be summed up as follows:—

(1) In Old English the Simple Infinitive was a kind of Abstract noun, formed by adding the suffix *-an* or *-ian* to the root of the verb, as *bind-an*, "the act of binding." It was

commonly used as Subject to a verb, or after certain Auxiliaries and after Intrans. verbs of Incomplete Predication.

(2) In Mid. Eng. the *-an* or *-ian* became *-en* or *-ien* (later *-en*), of which many examples are to be found in Spenser, and a few—very few—in other writers of the Tudor period:—

> Come down and learn the little what
> That Thomakin can *sayne*.—SPENSER.
> Henceforth his ghost
> In peace may pass-*en* Lethe Lake.—SPENSER.
> Thinks all is writ he speak-*en* can.—SHAKSPEARE.
> And with a sigh he ceased
> To *tellen* forth the treachery and the trains.—SACKVILLE.
> The soil that erst so seemly was to *seen*.—SACKVILLE.

In Wycliff the Infin. suffix is for the most part *-e;* in Chaucer *-e* and *-en* are both common. Spenser's use of *-en* was archaic (out of date).

(3) When the final *n* had fallen into disuse and the *e* was becoming mute, writers began to distinguish the Infinitive (which otherwise was likely to be confounded with many other parts of the verb) by placing the preposition "to" before it; and this, for want of something better, was borrowed from the Dative (the so-called Gerundial) Infinitive. The *to* before a Simple Infin. began to be seen about the end of the twelfth century.

(4) The use of "to" went on gaining ground from century to century, till at last it succeeded in restricting the Simple or *to*-less form to the few instances that have survived; but for some time, even so late as the Tudor period, there was a good deal of uncertainty as to whether the "to" should be used or not.

> She tells me she'll *wed* the stranger knight,
> Or never more *to view* nor day nor night.—*Pericles*, ii. 5, 7.
> I would no more
> *Endure* this wooden slavery than *to suffer*
> The flesh-fly *blow* my mouth.—*Tempest*, iii. 1, 62.
> You ought not *walk*.—*Julius Cæsar*, i. 1, 3.
> How long within this wood intend you *stay?*
> *Midsummer Night's Dream*, ii. 1, 138.

(5) The *Noun*-character of the Simple Infin., notwithstanding that the prep. "to" was placed before it, was perceived by old writers, who treated it as a kind of compound noun whenever they placed another prep. before it:—

> Without *to make* any noyse.—CAXTON, *Aymon*, 78.
> He was about (= near) *to die* (= death).—*Mod. Eng.*
> He desired nothing except or but *to succeed* (= success).
> —*Mod. Eng.*

The difference between the two Infinitives, in spite of their identity of form, is well shown in the following :—

I want *to eat* something. (*Simple Infin.—object. to* "want.")
I want something *to eat*. (*Gerund. Infin.—attrib. to* "something.")

146. Dative or Gerundial Infinitive :—

(1) What modern grammarians have called the Gerundial Infinitive was, in Old English, merely the Dative case of the Simple Infinitive preceded by the prep. "to"; as *tó cum-enne* (to come), *tó bind-enne* (to bind), which gradually became *to cum-en*, *to bind-en*, and finally *to come*, *to bind*.

(2) When the *-en* itself disappeared, as it did in the Transition period between Mid. and Mod. English, there was no difference *in form* between "to come" as a Simple Infin. and "to come" as a Gerundial Infin. In *function*, however, they were as distinct as before, the one being subject to all the duties and liabilities of a noun, and the other to those of an adjective or adverb.

147. Forms of the Subjunctive Mood.—From specimens A and B given in § 135 it will be seen that there was no distinction between Weak and Strong verbs in regard to Subjunctive endings. In this mood, as in the Indicative, there were only two tenses that were formed by flexional endings, viz. the Present and the Past. In all persons of the Present tense the ending was *-e* in the Singular number, and *-en* in the Plural. The *-e* was at first syllabic: after becoming non-syllabic and mute, it was dropped altogether, since it was no longer necessary. The *-en* died out also, like the *-en* and *-enne* of the Infinitive, and the *-on* of the Past tense Indicative.

In Mod. English, as in Old, there are no endings in the *Present tense* to distinguish the Second and Third persons from the First. Thus we have "if I *see*, if thou *see*, if he *see*." But in the *Past* tense the Second person has acquired the ending *-st* or *-est*, borrowed from the Second person of the Indicative. The truth really is that the Past Subj. is dead, and the Present is dying.

148. History of the Gerund.—In Mod. Eng., if we meet with such sentences as "He was fond of *hunting* foxes," "He was fined for *having lost* his hat," we call "hunting" and "having lost" Gerunds, the one denoting present time, and the other past. This is the accepted name; but it is purely modern, and the form which it denotes has a peculiar history.

(1) The only Gerund in A.S. is what we now call the Gerundial Infinitive; see § 146. It invariably ended in *-ne;* it was invariably a Dative; and was invariably preceded by the preposition *tó* (our modern *to*); as A.S. *tó bind-enne* > Mid. Eng. *tó bind-en* > Mod. Eng. *to bind.* The final *-enne* never took the form of *-inge* or *-ing;* and hence the adoption of the name "Gerund" for the form ending in *-ing* was an encroachment.

(2) The form ending in *-ing* was in A.S. simply a **noun.** It was not part of a verb at all, but a noun pure and simple. The *-ing* or *-ung* (both forms are found in A.S.) was simply a noun-forming suffix, like *-th* in "steal-*th*," or *-r* in "stai-*r*," or *-l* in "aw-*l*," or *-m* in "doo-*m*." It is not correct to call it "a *verbal* noun,"[1] because this name implies that such a word as "bind-*ing*" was part of the conjugation of the verb "bind"; and we are no more entitled to say this than we are to say that "steal-*th*" is part of the verb "steal," or "doo-*m*" a part of the verb "do." The form ending in *-ing* was not a verb or part of a verb, because it was *never* followed by a noun in the *Accusative* case. It was a noun for two reasons—(*a*) it took noun-inflexions, it still takes the plural inflexion *s;* and (*b*) it could be followed by another noun in the *Genitive* case; as,

Búton	sceawunge-*e* (Dat.)	ǽnig-*re* (Gen.)	ár-*e* (Gen.).—Beda, i. 5.
Sine	exhibitione	ullius	misericordiæ (*Latin*).
Without	showing	(of) any	compassion (*English*).

That *ár-e* is Genitive is clear from the adj. *ǽnig-re,* since no adj. has an Accus. ending in *-re.* The prep. "of" was not used in early times, because, as long as the Genitive inflexion lasted, it was not required.

(3) It was during the Middle period of English (the Pres. part. having in the meantime taken the form *-inge* instead of *-inde*), that the confusion began. Since the Pres. part. could be followed (as in fact it often was) by a noun in the Accus. case, the noun in *-ing,* having precisely the same form as the Pres. part., *seemed* (through a confusion of ideas in men's minds) to demand an Accusative also, and this led by degrees to the omission of the preposition "*of.*" Hence in Mid. Eng. we find two constructions—(*a*) with the *of,* (*b*) without it:—

[1] Another reason why the name "verbal noun" is unsuitable, is that the suffix *-ing* is not always attached to verb-stems. In "out-*ing*," "off-*ing*," "inn-*ings*," it is attached to adverbs. In "air-*ing*," "ceil-*ing*," "lin-*ing*," "morn-*ing*," "even-*ing*" (A.S. ǽfen-ung) it is attached to nouns. So the name "*verbal* noun" is inaccurate.

(*a*) Wyse in bying *of* vitaille.—CHAUCER, *Prol.* 569.
(Wise in buying of victuals.)
(*b*) Schavinge oure berdes.—MAUNDEVILLE.
(Shaving our beards.)

In example (*b*) the omission of "*of*" seemed to make "oure berdes" in the Accus. case, and this seemed to make "schavinge" a Gerund, that is, a part of the verb "shave." But in point of fact the construction is merely *elliptical;* for "schavinge" is still a pure noun, with the "of" omitted after it, as it is after "board" in the phrase "on board ship."

(4) In the Modern period a new bogus phrase came in. Since "shaving" was believed to be a Gerund, that is, part of the verb "shave," a past form was coined corresponding to the past participle, just as forms like "shaving" corresponded with the present participle. Thus we have such a sentence as—

He was punished for *having broken* a window.

This past form of the so-called Gerund is never followed by "of," as the present is, because it was late in coming; else it would have been.

"The phrase (*having broken*) is now an accepted one, so that the Grammarians in despair have invented, for words thus used, the term *gerund*, under the impression that to give a thing a vague name is the same thing as clearly explaining it. This term, however, should only be employed for convenience, with the express understanding that it refers to a modern usage, which has arisen from a succession of blunders" (Skeat).[1]

Auxiliary and Defective Verbs.

149. To be.—The conjugation of this verb is made up of parts that are formed from three distinct roots, viz. (1) *es-*, (2) *wes-*, and (3) *béo-*. The first gives the Pres. Indic., the second the Past Indic. and Past Subj., the third the Pres. Subj., the Imper., the Infin., and the Present and Past participles.

Am: A.S. *eam* or *eom*, for a theoretical *es-m*, in which the *m* is supposed to have come from *me* (the First personal pronoun). Cf. Lat. *su-m*, Gr. *es-mi*, Sanskrit *as-mi*.

Art: A.S. *eart*, for theoretical *es-t*, in which *s* has been changed

[1] Skeat's *Princ. Eng. Etym.* series i. p. 260. Sweet accepts this Gerund as an established fact in modern English: "The Mod. Eng. verb is characterised by the development of a gerund" (*Short Hist. Eng. Grammar*, ed. 1892, p. 149). In fact, we cannot now do without the name "gerund," however short its pedigree may be; and we must treat the Gerund as part of the verb, although originally it was simply an abstract noun.

to *r* (as in *was*, *were*), and the *t* is supposed to have come from *thou*, the Second pers. pron. Cf. the suffix in *shal-t*, *wil-t*, *wer-t*.

Is, A.S. *is*, for *es*, *es-t*, in which the *t*, the suffix of the Third pers. Singular, has been lost. Cf. Lat. *es-t*, Gr. *es-ti*, Sanskrit *as-ti*, Germ. *is-t*.

Are, for theoretical *es-on*. This came from the Northern dialect, which substituted *ar-on* for A.S. *sind*, *sind-on*.[1]

Note.—Besides the Pres. Indic. formed with the root *es-*, we once had another form of the tense based on the root *be-*.

	Sing.		*Plur.*	
	A.S.	*Tud. Eng.*	*A.S.*	*Tud. Eng.*
1.	béo	be	béo-th	be or bin (=be-en)
2.	bi-st	be-est	béo-th	be or bin (=be-en)
3.	bi-th	be	béo-th	be or bin (=be-en)

If thou *be-est* he; but O, how fallen! how changed!—Milton.
As fresh as *bin* the flowers in May.—Peele.
We *be* twelve brethren.—*Old Testament.*

Was: A.S. *wæs*, past tense of the verb *wes-an*; of the Strong conjugation, as is proved by the change of root-vowel, and by the absence of any personal ending from the First and Third persons. See specimen A in § 135.

Wast: not established till the fourteenth century. The A.S. form was *wǽr-e*, in which *r* has been substituted for the radical *s* (cf. *art* for *ast*), and *-e* is the correct suffix for the Second pers. Sing. in the Past tense of Strong Verbs. (See specimen A in § 135.) Another form of the Second pers. Sing. was *wert*, formed like *shal-t* and *wil-t*, now obsolete or obsolescent (except in the Subjunctive mood, in which it has been wrongly placed as second person):—

Before the sun, before the heavens thou *wert*.—*Par. Lost.*

Were: A.S. *wǽr-on*, where *r* is again substituted for *s*. The difference of the stem-vowel in *was* and *were* has arisen from the fact that in the older stage of our language the stem-vowel of the Past tense Singular differed in gradation from that of the Past tense Plural. (See again specimen A in § 135.)

Be, Imperative: A.S. *béo* (Sing.), *béo-th* (Plur.). These superseded the alternative A.S. forms *wes* (Sing.), *wes-ath* (Plur.).

Be, Infinitive: A.S. *béo-n*, which superseded the alternative A.S. form *wes-an* in the twelfth century.

Being: The A.S. form of the participle was *wes-ende*, which was superseded by the Mid. Eng. form *be-inde*, later *be-inge*. "Being" is also a verbal noun denoting "existence."

Been: Mid. Eng. *i-beon*, which superseded A.S. *ge-wes-en*.

150. Can, dare, shall, may, wot.—All these verbs were originally Past tenses of Strong verbs, which acquired a

[1] These two words are not so distinct in origin as they look. *Ar-on* (for theoretical *es-on*) and *sind-on* (for theoretical *es-ind-on*) both contain the root *es*. Both, too, have the suffix *-on* (which, however, is usually attached to the plural of *Past* tenses). The *-ind* of *es-ind-on* is another plural suffix; cf. Germ. *sind*, Lat. *sunt*, Sanskrit *sant-i*. For the *-unt* of *s-unt*, cf. Lat. *reg-unt*.

Present signification to compensate them for the loss of their Present tenses. Hence in Old English (as also in Modern) their adopted Present tense is conjugated like the Past of *Strong* verbs, while they have formed new Past tenses according to the *Weak* conjugation. Such verbs have been called **Past-present** (or Preterite-present) verbs.[1] To these we must add *quoth*, which, however, did not form a new Past tense like the rest.

The student will remember (see specimens A and B in § 135) that neither Strong nor Weak verbs have a Third personal suffix in the Past tense, Singular. Hence we have *can, dare, shall, may, wot, quoth* all in the Third person Singular without the suffix *-s*.

In the Second person Singular, however, *can, dare, shall,* and *may* have taken the suffix *-st* or *-t* in lieu of the original Past Suffix *-e*. All other Strong verbs (as is stated in § 136) have done the same. Thus we have *can-st, dar-est, shal-t, may-est.* Similarly in Mid. Eng. the Second person of *wot* was *wos-t*, and in Tud. Eng. *wott-est.* The verb *quoth* has no such form, as it is not used in the Second person.

Note.—The omission of *s* in the Third pers. Sing. occurs in the verb **need**, as "He *need* not go," whenever the Infinitive following is not preceded by *to*. But this peculiarity seems to be due to the analogy of the verbs *can, dare*, etc., as *need* was never anything else than a Present tense, and in every part except the Third pers. Sing. Pres. this verb is regularly conjugated as a Weak verb.

Can: old Past Indic. *cú-ðe*, coul-d, in which a non-radical *l* has crept in from analogy with *should* and *would*. Cf. the old pp. in *un-cúð*, uncouth, lit. unknown. "Con," to study, is a causal of "can." "Cunning" (=knowing) is a verbal noun formed from *cunn*-**an** (to know). The same word is also used as an adjective.

Dare: The root is *dars*.[2] Hence Past tense *dors-te*, durst; which, however, has often a Present meaning. "Dare" in the sense of "challenge" has formed a new Past tense *dared*, which is also used for *durst*, as "He *dared* not go." The Third Sing. Pres. *dare* is regular, as explained above; but *dares* is used whenever the Infin. following is preceded by "to"; as "He *dare* not go"; "He *dares* to go."

Shall: A.S. *sceal* or *scal* in First and Third persons. Past tense *scol-de*, should. In Mod. Eng. "should" very often implies duty; as "you *should* do this." So in Old and Mid. Eng. *sceal* or *scal* sometimes meant "owe." The Second person was *scealt* or *scalt* (shalt).

Hú micel *scealt* ðú ?=How much owest thou ?—*Luke* xvi. 5.

---

[1] These verbs are also called **Strong-Weak**, because they have formed a Weak past tense out of a Strong past tense, the latter having lost its own present form and acquired in place of it a present signification. The name "Strong-Weak" might also be given to Mixed verbs like *beat, beat, beaten*, which are strong in some forms and weak in others: cf. *cleave, clave* or *cleft, cloven* or *cleft.*

[2] In Gothic "I dare" was *ik dars*, which in A.S. appears as *ic dearr*, with *rr* for *rz*, Gothic *rs*. The plural in A.S. was *wé durr-on* for *wé durz-on, durs-on.*

May: A.S. *mæg*, may; cf. A.S. "dæg," day (the *g* having been vocalised, see § 58). Past tense *meah-te* (Weak past), might.

Wot: A.S. *wát*, from which is formed our Present tense *wot*. Past tense *wis-te*, from which we get our Past tense, *wist*; here, as in *mus-t* (§ 152), *s* was substituted for the radical *t*, so as to make a suitable base for the suffix *-te*. *To wit* (=namely) is a Gerundial Infin., A.S. *tó wit-enne*. The Pres. part. appears in "un-witting-ly."

Quoth.—This verb answers to A.S. *cwæth*, Past tense of the verb *cweth-an*, to say, and therefore has no *s* in the Third person Singular. *Quoth* is the only form of the verb that is now used; it denotes either present time or past. But it is never used with a plural subject, and never with any person but the First or Third. Its subject is invariably placed after it.

151. Will.—This verb resembles those described in the previous paragraph, in having no suffix *-s* in the Third pers. Sing., but from a different cause. "Will" was originally not a Past Indic., but a Past Subjunctive, and this mood, as the student will remember from specimens A and B given in § 135, never took a suffix *-s* for the Third person. With the Past Subj. form Pres. Indic. forms were afterwards mixed, and an Infin. *will-an*. A Weak past was formed, *wol-de* (would), in which the *i* of the base was changed to *o* by the influence of *w*. The phrase *willy-nilly* (A.S. *sam hé will-e, sam hé nill-e*) is elliptical for "whether he *will* or not *will*"; since it expresses a doubt, it is naturally in the Subjunctive mood, which recalls the original Subjunctive force of *will*.[1]

Wil-t.—Here the *t* is Second personal suffix as in "shal-t," and is due to analogy. "Would" is from Past Indic. *wol-de* (Weak form).

Won't=will not. Here we have a trace of the Mid. Eng. *wol*, an alternative form of *wil*.

152. Ought, must.—These two verbs are Past-past tenses in form, like *could*, *should*, *would*, *might*, *wist*, but (unlike the verbs just named) they are used in a Present sense, because their Past-present forms are obsolete.

Ought.—The obsolete present *áh* was originally a Past tense in the Strong conjugation, like *can*, *dare*, *shall*, *may*, *wot*, *quoth*. From *áh* was formed the Weak past tense *áh-te*, from which we get *ought* in Mod. Eng. This word occurs in Shakspeare in a past sense as equivalent to "owed":—

You *ought* him a thousand pounds.

Our verb *owe*, "to be in debt," is from A.S. *ág-an*: it had a

[1] It might be supposed that the *y* of *willy* is a survival of the *e* in the A.S. Subjunctive form *will-e*. But the *e* was lost in the thirteenth century. Probably *willy* arose from *will-I*, and was extended to *will he*.

past part. *ág-en*, from which we get our adj. *own*, as in the phrase "his *own*." From this past part. the Weak verb *ágn-ian* was formed in A.S., from which we get our verb *own*, "to possess."

Note.—There is another verb "own," which means "to acknowledge." This is probably also derived from A.S. *ágn-ian*, though it has been doubtfully ascribed to A.S. *unn-an*, to grant. Our modern spelling (perhaps rightly) takes no account of the difference.

Must.—The obsolete present *mót* was originally a Past tense in the Strong conjugation, like the obsolete *áh*. From *mót* was formed the Weak past tense *mós-te*, in which *mós* was substituted for *mót* in order to furnish a suitable base for the suffix *-te*. From the Past-past tense *mós-te* we get our modern word *must*.

The old word *mót* has survived in the obsolescent phrase "so *mote* it be" (so be it, amen), in which *mote* is in the Subjunctive mood of *mót*, used in the sense of wish, as the Subjunctive is still sometimes used.

153. Let.—The verbs *let* in the sense of "hinder" and *let* in the sense of "permit" are quite distinct. The former is A.S. *lett-an*, a Weak verb, derivative of *læt*, late, which had as its Past tense *let-te*, Mod. Eng. *let*. The latter is from A.S. *lǽt-an*, a Strong verb which formed its Past tense in *léort* (Reduplicated, § 137), *léot*, and *lét*, Mod. Eng. *let*. So the two verbs have become confused.

Let (permit) is not a real Auxiliary. But in the forms "*let* me go," "*let* him go," etc., its meaning has been so reduced as to make a periphrastic Imperative in the First and Third persons.

154. Have: A.S. *habb-an*, a Weak verb, which formed its Past tense in *hæf-de*, later *hed-de* or *had-de*, and its Past part. in *ge-hæf-d*, later *i-haf-d*, or *y-had*: (when the final *e* of the Past tense was lost, there was no use in retaining the *d*). In A.S. the Pres. Indic. Singular was *hæbb-e*, *hæf-st*, *hæf-th*. The loss of the radical *f* gives us *hast*, *hath*. The A.S. short vowel "*æ*" has bequeathed a shortening of the "*a*" in "have," nothwithstanding the final *e*. (*Have* is really a misspelling for *hav*.)

155. Do.—This is a Strong verb in the Past part. *ge-dón* (done), and is possibly a Strong verb (of the reduplicated class) in the Past tense also, *dy-de*; see § 137, and footnote. It is Auxiliary only for forming emphatic, negative, and interrogative sentences.

In Mid. Eng. it had the sense of *cause*; as it still has in the almost obsolete phrase "I *do* you to wit" = I cause you to know. It became useful for this purpose, when our language had lost the power of forming Causal verbs, like *raise* from *rise*.

As a pro-verb its use is at least as old as **Chaucer** :—

He slep no more þan *doþ* the nightingale.

156. Worth.—A.S. *weorð-an*, Past tense *wearð*, a Strong verb. In Old English it was the verb usually employed as an Auxiliary for forming tenses in the Passive voice.

Now, it survives only in the Third pers. singular Subjunctive, and only in the phrase "Woe *worth* the day."

Wont.—A.S. *wun-od*, Past part. of A.S. *wun-ian*, to dwell, to be accustomed to (Weak verb). A second participial suffix *-ed* was added, when the origin of *wont* had been forgotten; so that *wonted* = *won-d-ed*, with two participial suffixes. The word *wont* came by degrees to be used as a noun, as well as a participle.

Section 5.—The Forms of Adverbs.

157. Origin of Adverbs.—The origin of adverbs has been thus described in general terms by Whitney :—"Adverbs (the most ancient and necessary class of indeclinable words or particles) are by origin, in the earliest stage of a language as well as in the latest, forms of declension, *cases of substantives, adjectives, or pronouns.* Both the general classes of adverbs, made by means of apparent adverbial suffixes, and the more regular and obscure single words of kindred meaning and office, which we trace in the earliest vocabulary of the family, are of like derivation."

In the account of adverbs given below, the student will find many facts that bear out the above description of their origin.

Adverbs formed by Case-endings of Nouns.

158. Genitive Case-ending.—In Old and Mid. Eng. the suffix *-es* was used for forming adverbs from nouns and adjectives. A few such adverbs have survived; more have become extinct. In Mod. Eng. the prep. "of" has taken the place of the Genitive suffix; as, *of course*, *of necessity*, *of a truth.*

Extinct.—Summer-*es*, winter-*es*, dæi-*es* (by day), niht-*es*, will-*es* (willingly), sóþ-*es* (of sooth, truly), hi-*s* þonk-*es* (of his own accord), other-while-*s*.

Extant.—Need-*s*, el-*se* (A.S. ell-es), sin-*ce*, then-*ce*, hen-*ce*, when-*ce*, on-*ce* (A.S. *án-es*), twi-*ce*, thri-*ce*, sometime-*s*, alway-*s*, sideway-*s*, lengthway-*s*, the while-*s*(t), again-*s*(t), amid-*s*(t), eftsoon-*s* (archaic), longway-*s*, backward-*s*, wondrou-*s* (a corruption of wonder-*s*).

The Genitival adverb was common in Tudor English :—

Anyway-*s* afflicted or distressed.—*Prayer-book.*
He would have tickled you other gate-*s* (in another way or gate than he did).—*Twelfth Night*, v. 1, 198.
Come a little nearer this way-*s*.—*Merry Wives of Windsor*, ii. 1, 50.
'Tis but early day-*s*.—*Troilus and Cressida*, iv. 5, 12.

The Genitival suffix is sometimes attached to a phrase formed with a noun and the prep. *be* (by) or *a* (on).

Be-time-*s*, be-side-*s*, un-a-ware-*s*, now-a-day-*s*, a-night-*s* (colloquial), a-Sunday-*s* (colloquial).

159. Dative Case.—The Dative case-ending in *-um*, Singular or Plural, was used with an adverbial force :—

Extinct.—Micl-*um* (much, Sing., from adj. *micel*), lytl-*um* (a little, Sing., from adj. *lytel*), piece-mǽl-*um* (piece-meal), Plural.
Extant.—Whil-*om* (A.S. hwíl-*um*, at times ; hwíl = while, time), seld-*om* (A.S. seld-*um*, at rare times ; seld = rare). Both Plural.

Note.—At random is from Old French *à randon*, in violent haste.

160. Accusative Case.—This is now called the Adverbial objective. Adverbs were formed from adjectives as well as nouns in this case.

The while (A.S. *þá hwíl-e*), something, somewhat (here *what* is not relative), nothing, nowise, noway, yesterday, day and night, straightway, meantime, meanwhile, midway, halfway, home, north, south, east, west, all, enough (A.S. *genoh*).

Many of the Adverbial accusatives have now a Genitive form ; as in *alway-s*, *side-way-s*, *the while-s(t)*, *sometime-s*, etc.

Note.—Sometime = formerly ; *sometimes* = occasionally.

Nouns and Adjectives preceded by Prepositions.

161. Prepositional Adverbs.—Sometimes the prep. is attached to the word as a prefix ; sometimes it stands apart so as to make an adverbial phrase.

A = *of: a-kin*, *a*-down (A.S. *á-dún-e*, for "of dune," from a hill), *a*-new, *a*-fresh, *a*-thirst, *a*-clock (now written "o'clock" ; cf. Jack o' lantern).
A = *on : a*-bed, *a*-way, *a*-back (also "back"), *a*-gain, *a*-sunder, *a*-foot, *a*-sleep, *a*-live, *a*-head, *a*-breast, etc. Now-*a*-days, un-*a*-wares, *a*-year (= Lat. *per annum*), *an*-on (in one second, immediately).

Note.—"*A*" has been substituted for Fr. *en*, in *a-round*, *a-front* ; and for Fr. *à* in *a-part* (à part) and *a-pace* (à pas).

A=A.S. *an* or *and*, **against**: *a*-long (A.S. *and-lang*, over against in length).

At: *at* large, *at* length, *at* odds, *at* first, *at* all, *at* once, etc.

Be or **by**: *be*-sides, *be*-times, *be*-fore, *be*-yond, *be*-hind, *be*-low, *be*-tween, *by* all means, *by* force, etc.

In, **on**: *in* general, *in* future, *in*deed, *in* two, etc. *On* high, *on* trust, *on* purpose, etc.

Of: *of* kin, *of* late, *of* old, *of* a truth, *of* necessity, etc.

Per, Lat. prep.: *per*chance, *per*force, *per*haps.

To: *to*-day (A.S. *tó dæg-e*), *to*-night (A.S. *tó niht-e*), *to*gether, *to* boot, here-*to*-fore.

Adverbs formed with Suffixes "-ly," "-ling."

162. The Suffix "-ly."—The suffix "-ly" is from A.S. *líc-e*, formed from the adj. *líc* (like). When the final *e* was dropped, *líc-e* was reduced to *líc*, and eventually to *ly*; as *on-ly*, A.S. *án-líc-e*, *án-líc*; Mid. Eng. *oon-li*.

Note.—If the adjective itself ends in *-ly*, as *kind-ly*, *low-ly*, *sick-ly*, etc., the adverb is usually formed by a phrase, as, *in a kindly way*, *with lowliness*, etc.[1]

This is the commonest mode of forming adverbs, and the suffix "-ly" can be as freely attached to Romanic stems as to Teutonic ones. It can also be attached to Participles, as "knowing-*ly*," "learned-*ly*," "mistaken-*ly*"; and to adjectives formed with a suffix added to nouns, as "play-ful-*ly*," "slav-ish-*ly*."

It has been said that the *-e* of A.S. *líc-e* is the Dative case of the Adj. *líc*. But this cannot be; for adjectives in early A.S. had no such Dative form. For the origin of *líc-e* we must go to Gothic *leik-o*; but what the origin of the *o* may be is unknown.[2]

The Suffix "-ling" or "-long": A.S. *-lung-a* or *-ling-a*, in which the *a* was a Genitive plural case-ending; hence this suffix is of the class explained in § 158.

Side-*ling*, side-*long*; head-*long*.
Dark-*ling*, grove-*ling* (flat on the ground).

Note.—The suffix *ling* looks so like the Pres. part., that verbs have been coined from it. "To *grovel*" is now well established. "To *darkle*" is used by Thackeray. "To *sidle* up to a person" is used colloquially.

---

[1] Edgar Allen Poe, however, has *lowlily* to rhyme with *holily*. The first word is adopted for the sake of the rhyme; the second is not open to objection, because *holy* is from A.S. *hálig*. Shakspeare also uses *holily*: "What thou wouldst highly, that wouldst thou *holily*" (*Macbeth*). To avoid the awkwardness of such an adverb as *god-li-ly*, we find the adj. *godly* used as an adverb in New Test.: see *Titus* ii. 12.

[2] Wright's *Gothic Primer*, § 283, p. 124.

163. Loss of Adverbial Suffix.—Another Gothic adverbial form was *-u-ba*, as in *hard-u-ba*, which in A.S. (by the loss of *ba*) appears as *heard-e*. The final *-e* in Anglo-Saxon adverbs eventually dropped off. Hence we have several adverbs in Mod. English, which have the same form as adjectives; cf. A.S. *fæst* (adj.), *fæst-e* (adv.) = fast (adj. and adv.).

He speaks *loud*. He works *hard*. Speak *fair*. Come *quick*.
He talks *fast*. The moon shines *bright*. He sleeps *sound*.
Full many a year. *Right* along the bank.

Hence from a false analogy adjectives, which could not have taken the suffix *-e*, are used adverbially in Tudor English :—

Which the false man does *easy*.—*Macbeth*, ii. 3, 143.
Thou didst it *excellent*.—*Taming of the Shrew*, i. 1, 89.
Grow not *instant* old.—*Hamlet*, i. 5, 94.
'Tis *noble* spoken.—*Antony and Cleopatra*, ii. 2, 99.

Even so late as Sir W. Scott, we have an adjective used to qualify an adverb :—

Notwithstanding the darkness of the place, Julian succeeded *marvellous* quickly in preparing for his journey.—*Peveril of the Peak.*

Pronominal Adverbs.

164. Pronominal Adverbs.—The following table shows how adverbs have been formed from Pronominal and Demonstrative stems :—

Pron. and Dem. stems.	Place where.	Motion to.	Motion from.	Time.	Manner.	Cause.
who	where	whither	whence	when	how	why, what
the	there	thither	thence	then	thus	the
he	here	hither	hence	...	...	...

Where, there, here: A.S. *hwǽr, ðǽr, hér*: "the suffix *r* seems to be due to a Locative case" (Skeat).

Whither, thither, hither: A.S. *hwæder* or *hwider*, *ðider*, and *hider*; cf. Lat. ci-*tra* (on this side of), Sanskrit ta-*tra* (to that side). Originally the suffix may have had a comparative force; see comp. suffix *-ther* in § 123 (3). In this view, the *-ther* in *hither*, etc., would mean "more to this place," "in this direction."

When, then.—In A.S. there were three pronominal adverbs denoting time, *hwonne*, *ðonne*, and *heon-an*. These are very like the Accusative cases of the corresponding pronouns, and are probably of the same origin. From the last we might have had a modern form *hen*, corresponding to *when* and *then*. But the Mid. Eng. *henne* has been superseded by *now*, which is of the same root as *new*.

Whence, thence, hence.—These contain the Genitive suffix *-es*, and answer respectively to A.S. *hwanan*, Mid. Eng. *whenn-es*; A.S. *ðanan*, Mid. Eng. *thenn-es*; A.S. *hinan*, Mid. Eng. *henn-es*. The base is closely allied to the Accusative cases referred to under *when*, *then*.

Why, how.—"Why" answers to A.S. *hwí*, the Instrumental case of *hwá*. "How" answers to A.S. *hú*, which is probably only another form of *hwí*.

Thus answers to A.S. *ðus*, which is probably another spelling of *ðýs*, the Instrumental case of *ðes* = this.

The answers to A.S. *ðý* (Mid. Eng. *the*), the Instrumental case of the Def. art. (or Dem. pron.), used only in such phrases as "*the* more, *the* merrier" = by what degree or on what account more, by that degree or on that account merrier.

What answers to A.S. *hwæt*. In Tudor English this word is sometimes used as an Adverbial Interrogative = why.

What need we any spur but our own cause?—*Julius Cæsar*, ii. 1.

The compound adverb *some-what* (= slightly) is of common occurrence.

165.—Compound Pronominal Adverbs.—The pronominal adverbs shown in § 164 can be compounded (*a*) with prepositions, (*b*) with other adverbs:[1]—

(*a*) *Compounded with prepositions*:—

There: therein, thereto, thereat, therefore, therefrom, therewith, thereout, thereon, thereof, thereby, thereabouts.

Here: herein, hereto, heretofore, hereat, herewith, hereon, hereof, hereby, hereafter.

Where: wherein, whereto, wherefore, whereon.

Hither: hitherto.

(*b*) *Compounded with other adverbs*:—

Where: wherever, wheresoever, whereas.

Hence: henceforth, henceforward.

Thence: thenceforth, thenceforward.

Adverbial Uses of Prepositions.

166. Adverbial Uses of Prepositions.—Most of our prepositions can be used adverbially, and in fact most of them were adverbs originally. The *forms* of prepositions will be shown in the next section. Examples of their adverbial use are given below:—

About.—He is walking *about*. *About* forty were present.

Above.—He lived in the *above*-named house.

---

[1] It is pointed out, however, in Skeat's *Concise Etymological Dict.* that in these compound forms *there* is not the Locative *ðær*, but *ðære*, the Dative Fem. of the definite article; see below, § 174 (*a*).

Aft, after.—Fore and *aft*. He came ten days *after*.
Before.—He walked on *before*.
Behind.—He was left *behind*.
By.—*By* and *by*. They passed *by* on the other side.
Down.—He has gone *down* in the world.
From, fro.—They are walking to and *fro*.
In.—Break *in* the horse. Pull the horse *in*. Give *in* (yield).
Off.—He got *off*. They have set *off* (started).
On.—Go *on* (go forward). Hold *on* (stop). He got *on* well.
Over.—Is there any money *over?* Call *over* (recite) the names.
To, too.—Go *to* (let me expostulate). *To* and fro. That was *too* bad.
Under.—This medicine will bring the fever *under*.
Up.—It is all *up* with us. The time is *up* (exhausted).
Within.—You will find him *within* (in the house).
Without.—He stood *without*.

Compound Adverbs or Adverbial Phrases.

167. Compound Adverbs; Adverbial Phrases.

(*a*) *Compounds of "where" and "how"*:—else-where, some-where, any-where, every-where, no-where, somehow, any-how.

(*b*) *Adverbial phrases*:—maybe (=it may be, perhaps), howbeit (=however that may be), to wit (=namely), to be sure (=certainly), as it were (=if I may say so).

(*c*) *Adverbs in pairs*:—up and down, to and fro, here and there, hither and thither, in and out, backwards and forwards, now and then, off and on, by and by.

Miscellaneous Adverbs.

168. Unclassified List.—There are a few adverbs in common use, which cannot be classified under any of the headings hitherto discussed.

Ago: retrospectively from the present time, short for Mid. Eng. *agon*, A.S. *á-gán*, pp. of the verb *á-gán*, to pass or go away. In Mid. Eng. we have the form "ago" as well as the form "agon."

Ay, aye (1): spelt as *I* in old editions of Shakspeare. Apparently a corruption of *yea*.

Aye (2), (ever): Scand. or Old Norse *ei*, A.S. *á*, *áwa*; Goth. *aiw*, adverb formed from noun *aiws*, an age; cf. Lat. *æv*-um, Gr. *ai*-on; and Gr. adverb *ai*-en=always.

Ever, never: A.S. *æfre*, *næfre*. There is no saying what is the origin of the suffix *re* or *e*. Related to A.S. *áwa*.

Far: A.S. *feor*, Mid. Eng. *fer*; cognate with Gr. *per-an*, beyond.

Fore, forth: A.S. *fore*, allied to "far," beyond. In composition we have *forthwith*, *henceforth*, *forwards*.

Ill, adj., adv., or noun: Scand. *illr*, adj. Not a contracted form of A.S. *yfel* (=evil), adj. or noun, as has been maintained.

Little: A.S. *lytel*, adj. *lytl-um*, adv. (with Dative suffix).

Less: A.S. *læs-sa* (see § 126, II.).

Much: A.S. *mycel* (great); Mid. Eng. *muchel*, *muche*.

Nay, of Sc. origin, *nei*; Mid. Eng. *nay*: the negative of *aye* (2).

No (1): negative adverb, the opposite to "yes." A.S. *ná*, from *ne* (negative particle) and *á*, "ever," = Scand. or Old Norse *ei*: a doublet of *nay*.

No (2): short for *none*, A.S. *nán* (*ne* + *án*, not one). "None" and "no" are both used adverbially, as "*none* the better," "*no* better."

Not: a shortened form of "naught" or "nought," from A.S. *ná*, negative particle, and *wiht*, a whit. Hence "naught" means literally "not a whit"; cf. the phrases "not a straw," "not an atom," "not a button," "not a curse" (corrup. of "not a *kers* or cress").

Now: A.S. *nú*; cf. Lat. *nu-nc*. See § 164, under **When**.

Out: A.S. *út*, *út-e*, *út-an*, all adverbial, signifying outwards.

Oft, often: A.S. *oft*, Mid. Eng. *of-te-n*. A superlative form of comparative "ov-er." In Mid. Eng. we have the form *ofte*, to which an *n* was afterwards added. In Mid. Eng. *-e* was the common adverbial suffix.

Over: A.S. *ofer*, a comparative form of Old Aryan *up-a*, the stem of which we see in Eng. "*up*."

Well: A.S. *wel*; orig. "agreeably to a wish"; allied to *will*, to desire or be willing.

So: from A.S. *swá*; origin uncertain: apparently allied to Lat. *su-us*.

Yonder: adverb formed from *yon*, adj., "at a distance." "Yon" is from an old Relative stem, *ya*.

Ye-a, ye-s, answer respectively to A.S. *geá* and *gese*. "Yes" is a strengthened form of "yea," and was once supposed to be short for *geá sý* = yea, let it be. But the theory now held is—that the final *s* is due to A.S. *swá*. The stem is traced to the same Relative *ya*. The original sense was "in that way," "just so." Thus *yea*, *yes* are adverbs by etymology.

Ye-t, up to the present time, as in the phrase "not yet." Traced to the same root (*ya*) as the two preceding. Cf. Lat. *ja-m*, in which the root is the same.

Section 6.—The Forms of Prepositions.

169. Our prepositions were originally adverbs, which modified verbs, as, "He stood *by*," and served to point out more clearly the direction of the verbal action. By degrees they detached themselves from the verb and came to belong to nouns, furthering the disappearance of case-endings and assuming the peculiar office which they now hold.

Thus "motion to" was originally expressed by the Accusative alone, as it still is in the sentence, "He went home."

In Old English prepositions were followed by certain cases,—the Accusative, Dative, or Genitive. We still say that a preposition governs the Objective case; as *by the man*, *by me*, *by him*.

170. Simple Prepositions:—

At: A.S. *æt*; cognate with Lat. *ad*, as in "*ad*-jacent."

By: Goth. *bi*, which in A.S. was differentiated into the strong or accented form *bí* and the weak form *be*. The former became the preposition "by," and the latter the prefix "be."

Ere : before, A.S. *ǽr;* cf. *ear-ly*, from A.S. *ǽr-lic*.

For : A.S. *for*.

From : A.S. *fram, from;* Scand. *frá;* Mid. Eng. *fra, fro*. Hence the modern adverbial form "fro," as in the phrase "to and *fro*." The same root is seen in "for," "forth."

In : A.S. *in;* cognate with Lat. *in*, Gr. *en*.

Of, off : A.S. *of;* cognate with Lat. *ab*, Gr. *ap-o*. Shortened to *a* in "a-down" = of dune (from the hill), and to *o* in "o'clock."

On : A.S. *on;* cognate with Gr. *an-a*. Often shortened to *a*, as in "a-breast," "twice *a* day," etc.

> "Farewell, then, lady, *a* God's name," said the king.
>
> *Peveril of the Peak.*

The A.S. equivalent to "*a* God's name" was "*on* Godes naman." We now say "*in* God's name": but there is no authority for this in Old English.

Through : A.S. *ðurh;* cognate with Lat. "*tr*-ans" = across, as in "*trans*-gression."

Till : Northern dialect *til*, "to the time when."

To : A.S. *tó;* Der. adv. *too*.

Up : A.S. *up;* cognate with Lat. *s-ub*, Gr. *h-up-o*, from an old Aryan root "*up-a*," which appears also in ab-*ove*.

With : A.S. *wið*, which often meant "against," as in "*with*-stand."

Note.—There are also a few preps. of Romanic origin, which are met with in Mod. Eng. :—

Per, through : *per* cent, *per*force, *per* margin, *per*haps.

Versus, against : Australian cricketers *versus* Surrey.

Sans, Fr. (Lat. *sine*), without :—

> *Sans* eyes, *sans* teeth, *sans* taste, *sans* everything.—SHAKSPEARE.

Maugre, Fr. (*mal gré*, Old Fr.), in spite of : (rarely used).

171. Compound and Derivative Prepositions :—

(*a*) Comparative forms : comparative suffix *-ter*, cf. *ther* in *whe-ther;* or *-er*, as in *long-er* :—

Af-ter (adv., prep., conj.) : A.S. *æf-ter*, comp. of *af* = of = from. The word "after" denotes "farther off," "more distant" (comp.).

Note.—"*Aft*" is not an abridgment of *after*. In *af-t* the *t* is a suffix. Gothic *af-ta*. Cf. "*eft*-soons," "ab-*aft*" (= on by *aft*).

Near (adj., adv., and prep.) : Scand. *nær*, A.S. *neár*, comp. of A.S. *neáh* = nigh.

Ov-er : A.S. *of-er*, comp. of *-ove* in "ab-*ove*" (positive) : cognate with Lat. *s-up-er*, and Gr. *h-up-er*. (In A.S. we have "*uf*-an" (adv.), in Goth. *up*.)

Un-der : A.S. *un-der*.

(*b*) Prepositions compounded with adverbs or other prepositions :—

About : A.S. *á-b-útan*, short for *an-be-útan* = Eng. on-by-out.

Above : A.S. *á-b-ufan*, short for *an-be-ufan* = Eng. *on-by-ove* (up).

Athwart: Scand. *um þvert*, across; *um*=*on*=*a*, and adv. *þvert*, crossways.

Before: A.S. *be-foran*; *be*=by, and adv. *for-an*=in front.

Behind: A.S. *be-hindan*; adv. *hind-an*=at the back.

Beneath: A.S. *be-neoðan*; adv. *neoð-an*=downwards, from a base *ni*=down.

Beyond: A.S. *be-geondan*; adv. *geondan*=on the other side, across. See *yon*, *yonder*, adv., § 168.

But: A.S. *b-út-an*, short for *be* or *bi-út-an*=Eng. by-out.

Throughout, compound of *through* and the adv. *out*.

Underneath, compound of *under* and adv. *neoðan*=neath.

Unto, even to.—Not found in A.S. Put for *und-to*, where *to* is the usual prep. The origin of the *und* or *un* is Old Fries. *und*, which means "unto."

(*c*) Prepositions formed from Nouns:—

Against: A.S. *ongéan*, which meant *again* (adv.), or *against* (prep.). Origin of A.S. *géan* unknown. "Against" is formed with excrescent *t* from the Genitival adverb *a-yein-es* (Mid. Eng.).

Across, cross-wise.—The *a* is short for *on*. Mid. Eng. *cros*, Old Irish *cros*, borrowed from Lat. *cruc-em*, a cross. (This prep. is a hybrid, since the prefix is Teutonic and the noun Romanic.)

Among, amongst: A.S. *on mang* (lit. in a mixture or crowd); Mid. Eng. *a-monge*, or in the Genitival form *a-mong-es*, from which "amongst" has been formed with excrescent *t*.

Beside, besides.—The origin of these words is not quite the same, and this accounts for the difference of meaning that still attaches to them. "Beside" is from A.S. *be síd-an* ("by the side of"), where *-an* is a Dative suffix of the noun "side." "Besides" has the Genitival suffix *-es*, and was primarily an adverb, as it often is still, in the sense of "in addition." It has also come to be used as a prep. in the sense of "in addition *to*."

Down, short for *a-down*: A.S. *of-dúne*, from or off the dune (hill).

Till: Scand. *til*, originally a case (perhaps Accus. sing.) of a noun, *tili*, signifying aim or bent. Compound form "*un*-til."

(*d*) Prepositions formed from Adjectives:—

Along: A.S. *and-lang*, "over against in length." *A-long-es* (Gen. suffix) and *alongs-t* (with excrescent *t*) were once used.

Amid, amidst: A.S. *on-midd-an* (where *-an* is a Dative suffix), in the middle. In Mid. Eng. *amidde* and *amidde-s*, where *-s* is the Genitive suffix, which with excrescent *t* gave *amid-s-t*.

Anent, regarding, with reference to: A.S. *an-efen* or *on-efen* (in even). The *t* is excrescent.

Around (a hybrid, like "across"): Fr. *en rond*=Eng. *on round* =a-round.

Below.—"Low"=Scand. *lágr*, *lág*, "humble," "inferior," low."

Between: A.S. *be-twéon-um*, where *twéon-um* is the Dat. plur. of *twéon*, double, twain. Hence "between" is never used when more than *two* persons or things are referred to.

Betwixt: A.S. *be-tweoh-s*, where *tweoh*=double, from *twá*, two. The *s* is a Genitive suffix. Mid. Eng. *betwixe*, to which the excrescent *t* was added after the loss of the final *e*.

Since, for *sins*, which is short for Mid. Eng. *sithens*, in which the final *s* is the Gen. adverbial suffix. "Sithen" is a modification of A.S. *sīð ðám*, "after that." *Sīð* was originally an adj. signifying "late"; *ðám* is the Dative neuter of the Dem. pronoun (or Def. article).

Than: A.S. *ðænne* or *ðonne*, closely allied to *ðone*, Accus. Masc. of the Def. article. "Than" was frequently written as "then," and was originally the same word.

Towards.—The *s* is the Gen. adv. suffix. "Ward" is from A.S. *weord*, inclined, or turned to.

172. Participial or Verbal Prepositions.—These were originally Pres. or Past participles used absolutely, sometimes (*a*) with the noun expressed, and sometimes (*b*) with some noun understood.

(*a*) *The noun expressed*:—

Pending fresh orders = fresh orders *pending* or not yet given.

During the summer = the summer (en)*during* or still lasting.

Notwithstanding his anger = his anger not-*withstanding* or not preventing it.

All *except* one = all, one being *except*(*ed*).

The hour *past* sunset = the hour, sunset having *passed*.

All *save* one = all, one being *safe* (adj. Fr. *sauf*, Lat. *salv-us*) or reserved.

Note 1.—"Except" is not the Imperative mood used absolutely, but the Past participle (Lat. *except*-us), to which the Eng. suffix *-ed* has not been added. The participial origin is clear from the French use of the word *except-é*, and from the following passage in Milton:—

> God and his son *except* (being excepted),
> Created thing naught valued he nor shunned.

Note 2.—By the rule of Modern English grammar (see § 184), a noun used absolutely with a participle is in the Nom. case; as in "Fresh orders pending," where "orders" is in the Nom. absolute. But when "pending" becomes a preposition, and "orders" is placed after it as its object, the word "orders" is no longer Nom. but Objective. We still, however, find a Nom. pronoun after *save* or *saved* in Tudor English, and sometimes subsequently.

> All the conspirators save only *he*.—SHAKSPEARE.
> None save *thou* and thine, I've sworn,
> Shall be left upon the morn.—BYRON.

(*b*) *Some noun understood*: Impersonal absolute:—

Considering your age, you have done very well.

Owing to the long drought, the crops have failed.

Inform me *concerning*, *touching*, or *regarding* this matter.

173. Phrase Prepositions.—Two or more words habitually thrown together, and ending with a Simple preposition, may be called Phrase-prepositions or Prepositional phrases:—

By means of; because of; in front of; in opposition to; in spite of; on account of; with reference to; with regard to; for the sake of; on behalf of; instead of; in lieu of; in the place of; in prospect of; with a view to; in the event of, etc.

Note.—The phrases "*on this side*" and "*on board*" do not take a Simple prep. after them; as,

On this side the river. *On board* the ship.

Similarly the noun "*despite*" can be used as a preposition for the prepositional phrase "in spite of":—

Despite his riches, power, and pelf.—SCOTT.

SECTION 7.—THE FORMS OF CONJUNCTIONS.

174. Origin of Conjunctions.—Conjunctions are of comparatively late growth, and have sprung from other parts of speech, especially from pronouns, adjectives, adverbs, and prepositions, or from compounds of these.

Many of our conjunctions are identical in form with adverbs and prepositions, being, in fact, the same words in a different sense or a different connection; and the origin of these has been given already.

The few words remaining are described below:—

(*a*) Co-ordinative conjunctions:—

And: A.S. *and.* In A.S. it had two meanings—(1) moreover, something added; (2) if. Hence we have the phrase *an if*=if if (a mere reduplication).

But *an if* that evil servant shall say in his heart, etc.—*Matt.* xxiv. 48.

Both . . . and.—"Both" is of Scand. origin, *bá-ðir*, dual adjective; Scotch *baith.* Allied to A.S. *bá*, both; cf. Lat. "am-*bo*," Gr. "am-*pho.*" The suffix -*ðir* answers to "they," Nom. plur. of Def. art.

Also: compounded of *all* and *so.*

Either . . . or.—For "either," see above, § 122. For "or" see below.

Still (yet): A.S. *stille*, lit. quietly, even then.

Therefore: A.S. *for ðǽre*, because of that thing or reason, where some feminine noun is understood after *ðǽre*, the Dative Fem. of Def. art. Another, but less common form, is *therefor.* In A.S. the preposition "for" was spelt sometimes as *for* and sometimes as *fore*, and was followed by a Dative case. *Fore* was also adverbial.

Nevertheless, compounded of *never, the* (Instrumental case of Def. art.), and *less.* On the origin of "less," see § 126, II. This word was formerly *natheless*, from A.S. *ná*, not.

Or, a contraction of *outher, auther*, the Mid. Eng. forms. These words represent the A.S. *á-hwæþer.* (Observe that "or" is not a doublet of "either," as their derivations are different. "Either" is from *á-gi-*(or *ge-*)*hwæþer:* the mutation of the *á* caused by the *i* in *gi* gives *ǽghwæþer*, out of which came the Mid. and Mod. Eng. *either.* But "or" is from *á-hwæþer* without an intervening *gi* or *ge;* hence the *d* is not mutated, and we get the Mid. Eng. forms *outher*, *auther*, which in Mod. Eng. has been contracted to "or.")

Yet.—A.S. *get*, *git*; *get* was probably short for *ge tó*.

(*b*) Subordinative conjunctions :—

Because, a hybrid. Eng. *be*=by; Lat. *causa*, a cause.

As, a contraction of *also*. A.S. *eál-swá* (quite so).

Lest, for fear that, that not. Not connected with "least," but due to A.S. phrase *ðý lǽs ðe*, "for the reason less that" (cf. Lat. *quo minus*). The word *ðý* (for the reason) was dropped, and what remained of the phrase coalesced into "*lest*." *Lǽs*=less (adverb), and *ðe* is the indeclinable relative described in § 132 (spelt also as *þe*).

If: A.S. *gif*, which in other Teutonic languages appears as *ef*, *if*, and also in Mid. Eng. Cf. *op-* in Lat. "*op*-inionem."

Unless, if not, except. Formerly written *on lesse*; in the phrase *on lesse that*=in less than, or a less supposition than. Here the *un* of "unless" stands for the prep. "on."

Though: A.S. *ðeáh*, *ðéh*, from the Teutonic base *tha*, with suffix *-uh*.

CHAPTER VII.—SYNTAX.

Section 1.—Syntax of Cases.

Genitive or Possessive Case.

175. Qualitative Genitive.—Here the Genitive is equivalent to a descriptive or qualitative adjective :—

I'll break your *knave's* (=knavish) pate.—*Com. Err.* iii. 1, 74.
The *mother's* (=motherly) nature of Althea.—Lowell.

This idiom dates back to Old English :—

Wæs *micel-re sóthfæstnyss-e* wer (he was a man of much truthfulness=very truthful).—Beda, 3, 15.
Right as a *liu-es* (of life=living) creature she seemeth.—Gower, 2, 14.

176. "Of" followed by a Genitive.—This occurs in such phrases as "that book of James's," "that book of yours," etc. This construction is frequently met with in Chaucer, and has continued in constant use up to the present day :—

An old felawe (fellow, partner) *of youres.*—*Pardoneres Tale*, 210.
A trusty frende *of Sir Tristrams.*—Malory, *Morte d'Arthur*, 363, 8.

177. The Genitive for a Superlative.—This is seen in such a phrase as "in his heart of hearts" (in his deepest heart).

A servant of servants (the most abject of servants) shall he be.—*Genesis* ix. 25.

The idiom is a very old one :—

Eall-ra þrymm-a þrym (power of all powers, the greatest power).—*Elene*, 483.

That sprightly Scot of Scots, Douglas.—1 *Hen. IV.* ii. 4, 377.

178. Objective Genitive.—In such a phrase as "Cæsar's murderers," *Cæsar's* is called an Objective Genitive, because Cæsar was the object, not the agent, of the deed. This use of the Genitive is now becoming rather rare, but was not uncommon in Old English:—

Habbað God-es trúwan (have faith in God, lit. God's faith).—*Mark* xi. 22.

179. "Of" denoting apposition.—In expressions like "a fool of a man," "the land of Canaan," the "*of*" denotes apposition. This idiom is at least as old as the fifteenth century:—

And he was a ryght good knyght of a yonge man.—MALORY (15th century), *Morte d'Arthur*, 117, 34.

There was in þe castell a vii score prisoners of Frenchmen.—BERNERS (15th century), *Huon*, 90, 30.

180. Adverbial Genitive.—This has been described already in § 158. The Genitive as thus used might denote space, time, or manner. This use of the Genitive was common in Old English. Later on the Genitive was represented by "of," as it still is in many instances.

Wendon þa *óðr-es weg-es* hám-weard (they went home *of another way*).—*Chronicle*, 1006.

þis wæs þes *feórð-es geár-es* (this was *of the fourth year*).—*Chron.* 47.

Anyway-*s* afflicted or distressed.—*Prayer-book.*

There sleeps Titania sometime *of the night.*—*Midsummer Night's Dream*, ii. 1, 253.

The Dative Case.

181. Dative of Interest.—The noun or pronoun denoting the person to whose advantage or disadvantage something is done was put in the Dative case in Old English. The same construction, though now rather uncommon, is seen in Modern English, though what was once a Dative case is now called Objective:—

Bæd *him* hláfas wyrcan (prayed to make loaves *for him*).—*Crist and Satan*, 673.

Knock *me* at this gate and rap *me* well.—*Tam. Shrew*, i. 2, 11.

The Jew ate *me* a whole ham of bacon.—ADDISON.

"Archers," he cried, "send *me* an arrow through yon monk's frock."—SCOTT.

One Colonna cuts *me* the throat of Orsini's baker.—BULWER.

182. Reflexive Dative.—Here the verb is Intransitive, and the pronoun following is put in the Dative case. We call it Reflexive, because it relates to the same person as the subject to the verb.

> Beoth *eów* stille (be still *for yourselves*).—*Exodus* xiv. 14.
> Wæron *him* in Cent (they were *for themselves* in Kent).—*Chronicle*, 1009.
>
> But hear *thee*, Gratiano;
> Thou art too wild, too rude, and bold of voice.—*Mer. Ven.* ii. 2, 190.
> Vaulting ambition, that o'erleaps *itself*,
> And falls on the other side.—*Macbeth*, i. 7, 27.
> He overslept *himself* (slept too much for himself).

183. Adverbial Dative.—The Dative case-ending in *-um*, Singular or Plural—was used with an adverbial force, of which traces have survived in the two words "whilom" and "seldom." See § 159.

184. Dative Absolute.—In Old English the noun or pronoun in such constructions was in the Dative case; cf. the Ablative in Latin and the Genitive in Greek.

> Eów slǽpendum = you sleeping. (Here *slǽp-end-um* is the Dative plural of the present participle; and *eów* is the Dative plural of the Second Personal pronoun.)
>
> Hym spekynge þis þingis (him speaking these things).—WYCLIF'S *Bible, John* viii. 30.

The modern substitutes for the Dative Absolute are:—

(*a*) The Nominative, common even in Chaucer's time:—

> And *he* continuyng ever in stourdynesse.—*Clerkes Tale*, l. 700.

(*b*) The use of the preposition "with" in connection with a noun or participle following:—

> Besides, *with the enemy invading* our country, it was my duty to go in the campaign.—THACKERAY.

In Milton we meet with such phrases as "*me* overthrown," "*us* dispossessed," "*him* destroyed." It would be wrong to infer from this that the Dative Absolute was still lingering in use up to Milton's time. The poet was merely adopting, or attempting to reintroduce, the Latin idiom,—in which attempt he met with no followers.

We say "reintroduce" advisedly, because even in Old English the Dative Absolute was not a true Teutonic construction, but a mere imitation of the Latin Ablative Absolute.

185. Instrumental Dative.—In Old English the inflexion of the Dative case was used to express what is now denoted by the prepositions "by," "with":—

Stephanus wæs *stán-um* worpod (Stephen was killed with stones). —*Elene*, 492.

For þan ic hine *sweord-e* swebban nelle (therefore I will not kill him with sword).—*Beówulf*, 680.

One survival of the Instrumental case is the adverb *the* used with Comparative Adjectives, now spelt in the same way as the Indefinite article, but originally spelt as *ðý*. Another survival is *why*, A.S. *hwí*. Each of these, however, was a real Instrumental case, and not a Dative case used in an Instrumental sense.

186. Dative as Object.—In Old English the Dative was used (*a*) after certain adjectives, (*b*) as the object of Impersonal verbs, and (*c*) as the indirect object to some Transitive verbs. In Middle and Modern English this function has remained, except that the Dative is now called an Objective, and the preposition "to" or "for" is sometimes placed before the noun or pronoun.

(*a*) After certain adjectives :—

Léof *him* (dear to him). Gehýrsum *him* (obedient to him).

(In Mod. Eng. we can still omit the "to" after "near" and "like.")

(*b*) Object to impersonal verbs :—

Old Eng. Him gelamp (it happened to him).—*Genesis*, l. 1567.
Mid. Eng. Me thynketh, *me* semeth, *me* wondreth.
*Mod. Eng. Me*thinks, *me*seems, it shames *me*.

(*c*) Indirect object to Transitive verbs. Such verbs as *gif-an* (give), *lǽn-an* (lend), *unn-an* (grant), *secg-an* (say, tell), etc., were followed by an Indirect object in the Dative case in Old English. In Modern English the preposition "to" is sometimes put in. When no such preposition is expressed, the Dative is mistaken for an Accusative, so that if the voice of the verb is changed from Active to Passive, the Dative or Accusative becomes the subject to the verb,—a construction which among modern languages is peculiar to English :—

A book was given *him*.
He was given a book.

The Accusative Case.

187. Object of Transitive Verbs.—In Old English the object to a verb might be in the Genitive, Dative, or Accusative case. Most of the verbs then followed by a Genitive were in Middle English followed by an Accusative. In Modern English all the oblique cases that could be governed by verbs are lumped together under the name of Objective.

188. Cognate Accusative.—This construction occurs in the oldest English, and has been in constant use ever since:—

{ Þá leof-od-on heora líf.—*Chronicle*, 1086.
{ They lived their life.

{ He had bled so mychel blood.—*Alisaundre*, 5863.
{ He had bled so much blood.

189. Double Object.—In Old English, if verbs took a double object (as many verbs still do in Modern English), the cases of the nouns or pronouns might be grouped in three different ways—(*a*) two Accusatives, one of a person and the other of a thing; (*b*) an Accusative of the person and a Genitive of the thing; (*c*) an Accusative of the thing and a Dative of the person.

The last is the one that has survived to the present day, as we see from the fact that the preposition "to" may be used before the noun or pronoun denoting the person:—

He taught *my sons* Euclid.
He taught Euclid *to my sons.*

The first construction was rare in Old English. The following is an example:—

Hwæt héo *hine* bǽde (whatever she might ask him).—*Matt.* xiv. 7.

190. Objective Complement.—A noun used after a Factitive verb (such as verbs of naming, making, regarding, calling) in the Active voice is what we now call an Objective Complement. This complement, as in Modern English, was in the Accusative case:—

Hé *his englas* déð æðele gástas (he makes noble spirits (ghosts) his messengers or angels).—*Psalm* ciii. 5.

Note.—The Subjective Complement (that is, the noun used after Intransitive verbs like "becoming," etc.) was usually put in the Dative case with the preposition "to," after the verb *weorðan,* to become.

Cweð, þæt þás stánas *tó hláf-e* geweorðon (command that the stones shall become or turn to bread).—*Matt.* iv. 3.

191. Adverbial Accusative.—We now call this the Adverbial Objective. In Old English the Accusative could be used to denote time, space, and manner:—

Hé rícsade xvii *winter* (he reigned seventeen years).—*Chron.* 189.
He was sleeping the while (A.S. *þá hwíl-e*).

SECTION 2.—SYNTAX OF ADJECTIVES.

192. Nouns used as Adjectives.—In Modern English we meet with a few words, originally nouns, that are now used as adjectives, or as nouns and adjectives both. Examples of such words are, *cheap*, *chief*, *dainty*, *earnest*, *proof*.

A.S. *ceáp*, Mid. Eng. *chep*, meant originally "barter," "price." *Cheap* is now used only as an adjective.

Old French *chef*, *chief*, Mid. Eng. *chef*, *chief*, meant originally the "head"; cf. Latin *caput*, and *ker-chief*, Mid. Eng. *curchief*, that which covers the head. The word "chief" is now used either as an adjective or a noun.

Old French *daintie* (Lat. *dignitas*) meant originally "agreeableness." *Dainty* is now used either as an adjective or a noun.

A.S. *eornest* meant "seriousness"; now always an adjective except in the phrase "in earnest."

Profe (French, 1551) meant "a text," "evidence"; now sometimes used as an adjective, as in "a water-proof coat."

193. Adjectives used as Nouns.—In Old English this was as common as it is in Modern.

(*a*) *Ellipsis of noun after adjective*:—

Se *blinda*, gif he *blinde* lǽt, etc.—*Matt.* xv. 14.
(The blind (man), if he lead a blind (man).)
For he nought helpeth *needful* in his neede.—CHAUCER, *Man of Lawes Tale*, *Prologue*, 14.

(*b*) *Participles used as nouns.*—We have one example of this in Modern English:—*bygones.*

In A.S. there was a class of nouns ending in *nd*, which, though simply nouns in current use, can be traced back *etymologically* to Pres. Participles; cf. Latin *client-em*, orig. "hearing":—

Feónd (fiend): akin to Pres. Part. of *feón*, to hate.
Freónd (friend): akin to Pres. Part. of *freón*, to love.

Other examples in Old English are *hetend*, hater, enemy; *wígend*, warrior; *hǽlend*, the Healer, Saviour, etc. This group of words entirely disappeared in the later literature, leaving only "fiend" and "friend."

(*c*) *Abstract Neuters.*—This was common in Old English:—

Ne geald he yfel yfele (he paid not evil with evil).—*Elene*, 493.
A sudden *pale* usurps her cheek.—SHAKS. *Venus*, 589.
He may command them as well to *ill* as to *good*.—SPENSER, *State of Ireland*, p. 624, col. 2.

194. Origin and Character of the Articles.—The articles are adjectives, and not a separate part of speech. This is proved by their origin.

In Old English the Nom. singular masc. *se* and the fem. *seó* of the demonstrative adjective (which was chiefly used as a definite article) was derived from a base *sa*; but the Nom. neuter singular, and all the other cases, whether singular or plural, in all genders were formed from a base *tha*. Out of this base "*tha*" was formed the indeclinable A.S. relative *ðe*, and the declinable forms *ðe* and *ðéo* (Masc. and Fem.), which superseded *se* and *séo*. Hence came our Def. article *the*.

The Indefinite article comes from A.S. *án* (one), a Numeral adjective, that was declined throughout the Singular in all genders. In the Middle period of English *án* was differentiated into a regular Indefinite article by the loss of its accent and consequent shortening of the vowel. Thus *án* becomes *an*, as in Modern English; while the numeral *án* took the form of *ón*, which in Modern English is *one*. *A* is merely an abridgment of *an*.

Note.—It is therefore opposed to history as well as to reason to consider the Articles to be a distinct part of speech. It is opposed to reason, because whenever they are used they discharge, as their origin would imply, the function of Adjectives in limiting or defining the application of a noun. The universality of their use gives them an exceptional character, which distinguishes them from ordinary Adjectives; but this does not make them distinct parts of speech.

195. Definite Article.—In Old English the functions of the Definite article (expressed in the Nominative Masculine by *se*, "that," until *the* took its place) were much the same as in Modern. The following uses are worth noticing:—

(*a*) With proper names:—

Eart þú *se* Beówulf (art thou the Beowulf)?—*Beówulf*, 506.
The Douglas and *the* Hotspur both together
Are confident against the world in arms.—1 *Hen. IV*. v. 1, 117.
Stout Choiseul would discern in *the* Dubarry nothing but a wonderfully dizened scarlet woman.—CARLYLE, *Fr. Rev.* i. 1.

This, however, is rare in Modern English, except before proper names of rivers, as "*the* Thames"; mountain-ranges, as "*the* Alps"; groups of islands, as "*the* Hebrides."

(*b*) With names in the vocative case:—

Men *þá* leófestan (dearest men)!—*Blickling Homilies*, p. 61.
My lord *the* king, *the* king!—SHAKS. *Winter's Tale*, iii. 2, 143.

196. Indefinite Article.—The Indefinite article was placed before cardinal numerals, rarely in Old English, and frequently in Middle English. The numeral following is regarded as a Collective noun, similar to "a hundred," "a thousand," "a score," "a dozen," "a few," "a many" in Modern English:—

Man singe *án fiftig* sealmas for þone cyng (men shall sing a fifty psalms for the king).—*Laws of Æthelstan*, iv. 3.
So it fell that after the deth of his father about *a* vii yere, Kinge Charlemayn sent for him.—BERNERS, 210, 3.

Note 1.—In the phrase "a great many," the word "many" can be traced, not only to A.S. *manigu*, but to the Norman *meinee* (Old Fr. *meisnee*, Late Latin *mansionata*), a household troop. It occurs in the ballad of *Chevy Chase*:—

The Percy out of Northumberland came,
With him a great *meinee*.

Out of the word *meinee* we get the adj. "menial," which has no connection whatever, as has been supposed, with the word "manual," pertaining to the hand (Lat. *manus*).

Note 2.—In the phrase "many a," "many" is used in a Multiplicative sense, "many-times one."

Moni enne king (many a king).—LAYAMON, i. 281.

197. "One" in the sense of "a certain."—This idiom occurs in Middle English, though probably not in Old. In Modern English it is common.

Oon Grecus þat reigned there sometyme.—*Polychronicon*, 1, 175.

198. "Such and such."—In Modern English this phrase has an Indefinite force. In Old and Middle English the same phrase occurs, but in a Definite demonstrative sense, pointing to some preceding noun:—

Be *swilcum and be swilcum* þú miht ongitan, etc.—BOETH, 38, 1.
(By such and such things (those very things that have been mentioned) thou mayest understand, etc.)

SECTION 3.—SYNTAX OF PRONOUNS.

199. "Ye" supplanted by "you."—In Old English, and in the English Bible, *ye* (= A.S. *gé*) is a Nominative, and *you* (= A.S. *eów*) is an Accusative or Dative:—

Ye have not chosen me, but I have chosen *you*.—*John* xv. 16.

But prior to the date of the first Authorised Version some confusion had already been springing up in profane literature. Hence in the Elizabethan dramatists and later, when our language was still in some respects unsettled, we find *ye* and *you* apparently used indiscriminately, as if there were no difference between them:—

I do beseech *ye*, if *you* bear me hard.—*Julius Cæsar*, iii. 1, 157.
His wrath, which one day will destroy *ye* both.—*Par. Lost*, ii. 734.

Note.—*Ye* took the place of *you* in such examples as the above, because the unaccented *you* was pronounced as *y'*,—a sound very unlike that of the accented *you*. It was written as *ye*, because this spelling, though far from suitable, made a nearer approach to the sound of *y'* than the spelling of *you* did. We still say colloquially, "look *ee* here" for "look *ye* here."

200. "Thou" and "thee" supplanted by "you."—In the

thirteenth century onwards, and throughout the Tudor period, *you* was the more formal, distant, and respectful mode of address, and *thou* the more familiar, such as a father could use to a son, but not a son to a father.[1] Prior to the thirteenth century *þu*, *þou* (thou) was used as Singular on all occasions, and *gé*, *ye* (ye) as the Plural.

(1) *Grat.* I have a suit to *you*.
Bass. *You* have obtained it.
Grat. *You* must not deny me. I must go with *you* to Belmont.
Bass. Why, then *you* must. But hear *thee*, Gratiano;
Thou art too wild, too rude, and bold of voice.
Merchant of Venice, ii. 2, 187-190.

So long as the two friends are talking to each other in a formal way on a matter of business, they adopt the respectful and more distant *you*. But as soon as the one begins to address the other in a more confidential and intimate tone, he at once uses the more familiar *thee* and *thou*.

(2) All that Lord Cobham did was at *thy* instigation, *thou* viper! for I *thou* thee, *thou* traitor.

This language was used at Sir Walter Raleigh's trial (A.D. 1603), when Coke, finding that argument and evidence were wanting, insulted the illustrious prisoner by applying to him the familiar "*thou*."

(3) Kate, Kate, art *thou* not ashamed to deceive *your* father so?—GOLDSMITH, *She Stoops to Conquer*, Act iii.

He first addresses his daughter with *thou*; then, to remind her of the respect that she owes to him, he uses the more formal *your*.

Note 1.—"Thou" is retained in poetry and in addresses to the Deity, in both of which archaicisms are suitable.

Note 2.—Quakers used to address every one as *thou*, because (it is presumed) all men in their view were or ought to be friends and equals. They disowned the tone of distance and superiority implied by the more formal *you*.

201. **Self, my-self, him-self,** etc.

When "self" is added to a pronoun of the *First* or *Second* person, it is preceded by the *Possessive* case. But when it is added to a pronoun of the *Third* person, it is preceded by a pronoun in the *Objective* case. Thus we have:—

First and Second Persons.—My-self, our-selves. Thy-self, your-selves.

Third Person.—Him-self, her-self, it-self, them-selves.

---

[1] This question is worked out very fully by Prof. Skeat in *William of Palerne*, preface, p. xli. The results are embodied in Abbott's *Shakspearian Grammar*, pp. 153-158.

How is this to be explained? The word "self" was originally an adjective signifying "same," "actual," "identical." In the oldest English *silf* (self) was declined as an adjective with the preceding pronoun; as Nom. *ic selfa;* Gen. *mín selfes;* Dat. *mé silfum;* Accus. *mec silfne* (I the same; of me the same; to me the same; me the same). In the Tudor period and later *self* could still be used as an adjective:—

> On these *self* (=identical) hills.—RALEIGH.
> To shoot another arrow that *self* (=same) way
> Which you did shoot at first.—SHAKS. *Mer. Ven.* i. 1, 118.
> At that *self* moment enters Palamon.—DRYDEN, *Palamon*, 1838.
> His servant was healed in the *self-same* hour.—*Matt.* viii. 13.

But in later English "self" came to be also used as a noun, as we still see it used in such phrases as "a man's better *self*" (=the better side of his character); "she was beauty's self" (=a personification of beauty). Here the noun "self" is very correctly qualified by a noun in the Possessive case. Similarly in the First and Second persons we have "*my*-self," "*your*-self," etc., where the noun "self" is correctly qualified by the Possessives "my" and "your." The same construction occurs in what have now become provincial phrases, "his self," "their selves," in which "self" has been pluralised as a noun on the analogy of "shelf, shelves." "Self" is commonly used as a noun with the Third Personal pronoun in the Authorised Version of 1611; and Shakspeare has the phrase *our-self:*—

> Who *his* own *self* bare our sins.—1 *Peter* ii. 24.
> We will *our-self* in person to this war.—*Rich. II.* i. 4, 42.

But since the Tudor period "self" has retained its original function as an *adjective*, whenever it is compounded with the Third Personal pronoun:—

(1) He hurt *him*-self.
(2) He did it by *him*-self.
(3) He *him*-self did it.
(4) They *them*-selves did it.

In (1) and (2) there is no difficulty. In (3) and (4) we have the objectives *him* and *them* in what seems to be apposition with *he* and *they* respectively. But the apposition is apparent, not real. The construction is merely a survival of the Old English Dative, denoting agency. If these phrases were literally translated into Mod. Eng., they would be "*by* him-self," "*by* them-self," just as we still say sometimes, "He did it by himself," "They did it by themselves." But in Mod. Eng. the *by* is usually omitted, and the Reflexive or Emphatic pronoun is placed immediately after the subject to the verb, as if it were in apposition with it.

In the phrase "they them-*selves*," there is a confusion between "self" as a noun and "self" as an adjective; and since adjectives have now no plural forms, the phrase would be more correctly worded "they them-self." But it has been assimilated to the phrase "We our-*selves*." The latter is quite correct; for here "selves," Plural noun, is in apposition to "we," Plural pronoun, and is qualified by the Possessive pronoun "our."

202. Emphatic or Reflexive Possessive.—In Old English there were three ways in which a Possessive pronoun could be emphasised—(*a*) by *ágen* (own), (*b*) by *án* (one), and (*c*) by *self*, *silf*, or *sylf* (self). Modern English has retained only the first. The second was rare even in Old English.

(*a*) His *ágen* wíf (his own wife).—*Cura Pastoralis*, 397, 19.

(*b*) Ealle þás cynericu on his *ánes* æht geagnian (all these kingdoms in his own right to appropriate).—*Blickling Homilies*, 105, ix. 7.

Here *his ánes* mean literally "of him one," "of him alone."

(*c*) Crist cwæþ þurh his *sylfes* múþ (Christ spake through his own mouth).—*Blickling Homilies*, 59, 1.

203. Subject emphasised by Pronoun.—This is, in fact, a double subject. In order to emphasise the subject to a verb, a pronoun of the third person might be placed either (*a*) before, or (*b*) after, the noun. The same idiom has been retained in Modern English in poetry, but not in prose.

(*a*) And *he* Sanctus Georgius him tó Dryhtne gebad (and *he* St. George prayed to the Lord).—SWEET's *Old. Eng. Texts*, p. 178.

They tremble the sustaining crags.—TENNYSON, *In Memoriam*.

(*b*) Se oferspræca wer ne wierð *he* næfre gelǽred (the over-speaking or talkative man *he* will never be taught).—*Cura Pastoralis*, 278, 22.

My wife *she* was to go to her father's.—PEPYS's *Diary*, Jan. 2, 1659-60.

204. Relative referring to a Possessive Pronoun.—A.S. *mín* (from which we get "mine" and the shorter "my"), though declined like an adjective in AS.,[1] was originally a Genitive case signifying "of me." The same remark applies to "thine,"

---

[1] As an example in which these Genitives are inflected like adjectives, we may quote the following:—

Eall-*e* mín-*e* synd þýn-*e*, and þýn-*e* synd mín-*e* (all mine are thine, and thine are mine).—*John* xvii. 10.

"our," "your." Hence Possessive personal pronouns, including "his" and "her" as well as the four already named, are still sometimes used as antecedents to a Relative pronoun, and could be so used in Middle English also :—

> And for *his* love *that* deyd on rood.—*Richard Cœur de Lion*, 4469.
> (And for his love that died on the cross.)
> Poor is *our* sacrifice, whose eyes
> Are lighted from above.—NEWMAN.

The common phrase *in my despite* means "in spite of me"; cf. the obsolete phrase *maugre myn*, which in the Middle period of English meant the same thing. (*Maugre* is from Old French *maugré*, Mid. Fr. *malgré*, ill-will.)

205. Possessive Pronoun with Adjective-Noun.—When an adjective is used as a noun (see § 193), it could be coupled with a possessive pronoun in Old English, as it still is in Modern; cf. "his like," "his equal," "your elders," "your betters," etc.

> þá mé *yldra mín* ágeaf andsware (then *my elder* give me answer).—*Elene*, 462.
>
> *His per* in the world nas (his peer or like was not in the world). —ROBERT OF GLOUCESTER, l. 255.

206. "One" as Demonstrative Pronoun.—In Old, as in Modern, English the numeral "one" (A.S. *án*) could be used as a Demonstrative pronoun, to save the repetition of some noun that has gone before :—

> þæt *án* ongan fyrene fremman (that *one* (viz. the person previously named) began to work crimes).—*Beówulf*, 100, 101.

207. Which.—(*a*) as Interrogative; (*b*) as Relative :—

(*a*) According to present idiom, "which" as an Interrogative is used in a *selective* sense, and "who" or "what" in a *general* sense :—

> *What* book is that lying on the table there?
> *Which* of these books do you prefer?

In Old English *what* was not used as an adjective for qualifying nouns, and *hwilc* or *hwylc* (which) could be used in either sense.

> *Hwylc* (of what sort, who), is mín módor (my mother?)—*Matt.* xii. 48.

(*b*) "Which" as a Relative is now used only for Neuter (sex-less) antecedents, or for the names of young children and lower animals, when no question of sex arises about them. This restriction, however, is of recent date; for "who" *in the Nom. case* did not come into use at all as a *Relative* pronoun till the sixteenth century. Before this the Nom. had been used exclusively as an *Interrogative*, though the other cases were used as Relatives at a much earlier date:—

Our Father, *which* art in heaven.—*New Test.*
Then Warwick disannuls great John of Gaunt,
Which did subdue the greatest part of Spain.—3 *Hen. VI.* iii. 3.

208. "What" as an Interrogative.—In Old English, as in other Teutonic languages, *hwæt* (what, neuter of *hwā*) was used as a noun and followed by a noun in the Genitive case:—

Hwæt níw-*es*? (What new's or what of new? This is probably the origin of the phrase, *What news?* cf. Lat. *quid novi.*)

After the decay of the Genitive inflexion, the noun appeared to be in the Nominative case, and so *what* became an adjective, as it now is, qualifying the noun.

Even in Old English *hwæt* could be used predicatively for persons as well as for things:—

Hwæt synd þás? (who are these?)—*Gen.* xxxiii. 5.

209. "The whom," "the whose," "the which," etc.—In Middle English we find the Relative particularised by the Def. article. But modern idiom is against it, even in poetry:—

The whos power as now is falle.—GOWER, ii. 187.
Your mistress, from *the whom* I see
There's no disjunction.—*Winter's Tale*, iv. 4, 539.
'Twas a foolish guest,
The which to gain and keep he sacrificed all rest.—BYRON, *Childe Harold*, iii. 66.

210. "Who," "what," as Indefinite Demonstratives.—The Indefinite use of "who," "what," in the sense of *some one* or *something* dates back to Old English. Though modern idiom is against it, it has survived in the common word "somewhat" = something, and in the phrase "as who should say":—

And thus full ofte is lovë bought
For litel *what*, and mochel take, etc.—GOWER, ii. 275.
Come down and learn the little *what*
That Thomalin can sayne.—SPENSER, *Shep. Cal.* (*July*).
The cloudy messenger turns me his back
And hums, as *who* should say, You'll rue the time
That clogs me with this answer.—*Macbeth*, iii. 6, 41.

211. "That" for "who" or "which."—The form "that" is pre-eminently the *Restrictive* relative, and "who" or "which" the *Continuative*:—

This is the house *that* Jack built.
We went to York, *which* (=and this) is an old town.

This use of "that" as an indeclinable Relative pronoun is by no means modern. In Old Eng. the Demonstrative pronouns *sé*, *seó*, *þæt* were used as Relatives either by themselves or in conjunction with the indeclinable particle *þe*.

In Middle English *sé*, *seó*, and the particle *þe* disappeared at a very early period, leaving nothing but *þæt* (that) to do the work of a Relative.

The Neuter Singular *þæt* was becoming indifferent to gender and number even as early as the time of Alfred the Great:—

> Hé hæfde eahta and eahtatig coortona, þæt wé nú truman hátað (he had eight and eighty cohorts, that we now call "truma"). —*Orosius*, v. 12 (p. 240).

In the Tudor period and later, the Relative "that" yielded to the influence of "who" and "which" (both of which during the period named could be fortified, if necessary, by the Def. art. "the"), and almost disappeared. About Addison's time it again came into fashion, and has held its ground ever since as the Restrictive relative.

Addison, however, who was evidently not acquainted with the history of our language, protested against the change. In his "Humble Petition of 'Who' and 'Which'" he makes the petitioners say:—"We are descended of ancient families, and kept up our dignity and honour many years, till the Jack Sprat *that* supplanted us."

212. "That" for "what" or "that which."—This use of "that" has become archaic. It arose merely from the loss of Rel. *that* following the Demonstrative *that*. In A.S. the phrase was *that the* or *that that* (= that which):—

> We speak *that* (what) we do know, and testify *that* we have seen. —*New Test. John* iii. 11.
>
> I am possessed of *that* is mine.—SHAKSPEARE, *Titus* i. 1, 408.

213. "That" with the Genitive.—In such a phrase as "*that* of Paris," the word "that" is a Demonstrative pronoun pointing to some noun, the repetition of which is thereby saved.

This idiom can scarcely be traced back to Old English, but in Middle English instances occur:—

Old English:—

> Búton eówer rihtwísnys máre sý, þonne þǽra wrítera (except your righteousness is more than (that) of the scribes); in the A.S. no "that" is mentioned).—*Matt.* v. 20.

Middle English :—

I have seen many tymes *that* (*i.e.* the crown) of Paris and *that* of Constantynoble.—MAUNDEVILLE, p. 13.

214. "As" used as a Relative.—In the later Middle English, but not in Old English or in the early Middle, *as* (from A.S. *eál-swá*) was used as a Relative pronoun, not only after "such" or "same," but independently :—

The first Soudan was Zarocon, *as* was fadre to Sahaladyn.—MAUNDEVILLE, p. 36.

To those *as* have no children.—HOLLAND, *Plutarch's Morals*, 222.

This is out of date in Modern English, and has become a vulgarism, except after *such* and *same.*

SECTION 4.—SYNTAX OF VERBS.

215. Impersonal verbs.—Verbs used in the *third* person only, and without having a *personal* subject, are called Impersonal.

(*a*) Impersonal verbs denoting *physical* events were used with "it" in Old English, as now, and were not less common :—

Hit rínth = *it* rains. *Hit* fréoseth = *it* freezes.

(*b*) But verbs denoting *mental feelings* have undergone an important change. The Dative of the person (§ 186, *b*) has become the Subject, in the Nominative case. The change was gradual, and Impersonal verbs were more common in Shakspeare's time than now :[1]—

It yearns me not.—*Hen. V.* iv. 3, 26.
It dislikes me.—*Othel.* ii. 3, 49.
It likes us well.—*Hamlet*, ii. 2, 80.
So like you, sir.—*Cymb.* ii. 3, 59.

Note 1.—In the phrase "if you like," we now consider "you" to be the subject to the verb "like." Originally, however, the verb "like" was Impersonal, in the Subjunctive mood, and "you" was in the Dative case.

Note 2.—In Old English the "*it*" was omitted, whenever the Impersonal verb was connected with an object in the Dative case. This accounts for the curious forms that have survived in Modern English, such as *meseems, melists, methinks.*[2]

---

[1] "An abundance of Impersonal verbs is a mark of a very early stage in a language, denoting that a speaker has not yet arrived so far in his development as to trace his own actions and feelings to his own agency."—ABBOTT, *Shakspearian Grammar*, p. 208.

[2] "Thinks," the Impersonal verb, means "seems," and is derived from A.S. *thync-*; but the Personal verb "think" comes from A.S. *thenc-*; and *thenc* is allied to *thanc*, "thank," a kindly remembrance.

216. It is I.—In Old and Mid. Eng. the phrase was "it am I," out of which the Mod. Eng. "it is I" has been developed :—

Old English : "I it am."

Ic sylf hit eom }
I self *it am* }. = it is myself.—*Luke* xxiv. 39.

Mid. Eng. : "it am I."

I am thy mortel foo, and *it am I*
That loveth so hoote Emelye the brighte.—CHAUCER, *Knight's Tale*, A, 1736.

Mod. Eng. : "it is I."

It is not *he* that slew the man, *hit is I.*—*Gest. Rom.* 47 (p. 201).

Thus in Old and Mid. Eng. "it" is the *complement* to the verb "am"; while in Mod. Eng. it has become the *subject.* Hence any pronoun of any number or person can now be placed after "it is" as complement: "it is we," "it is you," "it is they," etc., instead of 'it are we," "it are you," etc.

217. "It is," "it was," for giving emphasis.—This device is found in Old English, but *þæt* (that) was used instead of "*it.*" In Mid. Eng. it was equally common; during this period it was developed by the current French phrase "*c'est,*" and "*that*" was changed to "*it.*"

þæt wæs on þone mónandæg, þæt Godwine becom (it *was* on Monday that Godwin came).—*Chronicle*, C. 1052.

In þe tyme bitwene Abraham and Moyses *it was* þat men come verst (first) to Engelond.—ROBERT OF GLOUCESTER, l. 204.

218. Interchange of Transitive and Intransitive.—One of the peculiarities of Modern English is that many Transitive verbs have acquired an Intransitive counterpart by dropping the Reflexive pronoun. Thus we say "He made merry," instead of "He made himself merry." The tendency to drop the Reflexive pronoun can be traced back to the earliest English :—

Old English :—

Seldon héo *baðian* wolde (seldom would she *bathe*).—BEDA, 4, 19.

Middle English :—

Þay maden as mery as any men moghten (they made as merry as any men might).—*Sir Gawayne*, 1953.

From the Intransitive sense thus acquired, the same Transitive verbs came also to be used in a Passive sense, but in the Active voice :—

Now quick desire hath caught the yielding prey,
And glutton-like she *feeds*, yet never *filleth.*
Venus and Adonis, 547.

Here "feeds" stands for "feeds herself" (Reflexive), and "filleth" stands for "is filled" (Passive).

219. Be, have.—In Old English the functions of "be" were for the most part the same as they are in Modern. But "be" has been encroached upon by "have" in three instances at least: (alluded to already in *Note* to § 144):—

(1) In the formation of the Perfect tense.

As has been explained in § 144, this tense was originally formed by "be" in Intransitive verbs, and by "have" in Transitive ones. Gradually, however, even in Old English, "have" lost the sense of possessing, and became a pure Auxiliary, *i.e.* a tense-forming verb. It could then be used with Intransitive verbs as freely as with Transitive ones, and in this capacity it has superseded "be."

"Be," however, is still used with some Intransitive verbs, though not quite in the same sense as "have."

"The flower *is* faded." *In what state* is the flower? Faded. No prominence is here given to the time of the fading. The verb "*is*" is not an Auxiliary, but an Intransitive verb of Incomplete Predication, to which the participle "faded" is the complement.

"The flower *has* faded." *By what time* was the fading of the flower completed? By the present time. The verb "*has*" is here Auxiliary, which with the word "faded" helps to form the Present Perfect tense of the verb "to fade."

Thus in the former *the state of the agent* is prominent, in the latter *the time of the action*.

(2) "Be," "have" with Infinitives:—

I am or was to go.
I have or had to go.

These two sentences mean much the same thing. The Infinitive in both expresses future time, combined sometimes with a sense of duty. The Infinitive is Gerundial. Both constructions have come down to us from Old English:[1]—

Hé is *tó cumenne* He is to come	=	Lat. Ille venturus est. Eng. He is about-to-come.
Thone calic the ic *tó drincenne* hæbbe The cup that I *to drink* have	=	The cup that I am about-to-drink.

From these examples it will be observed that in Old English the verb "*be*" was used when the verb following was *Intransitive*, and "*have*" when the verb following was *Transitive*. The

[1] Sweet's *Short Historical English Grammar*, ed. 1892, p. 130.

syntactical propriety of such distinction (which has been lost in Mod. English) is obvious.

Note.—It should be observed, however, that the Perfect Infinitive cannot be used after *have*, but only after the verb *be*. We can say, "I *was* to have gone" (that is, it was settled for me to go, only something prevented me); but we cannot say, "I *had* to have gone," nor can we say, "I *had* to have drunk."

(3) **Had as lief, had rather, had better, had as soon,** etc.—These phrases, preceded by a noun or pronoun in the Nom. and followed by a *to*-less or Simple Infinitive, are well-established idioms:—

I had as lief not be, as live to be
In awe of such a thing as I myself.—SHAKS. *Jul. Cæs.* i. 2, 95.
I had rather be a kitten, and cry mew.—1 *Hen. IV.* iii. 1, 129.

But the original construction was different. What is now the subject was in the Dative case (§ 186), and some form of the verb *be* was used where we now use *had*:—

Bot *lever* es *me* o myne thou have (but it is liever to me that you shall have (some) of mine).—*Cursor Mundi*, l. 2429.

But in the transition between the old and the present constructions we find the Dative case used with *had* instead of the Nominative, and the Nominative used with *be* instead of the Dative:—

Poor lady! *she were better* love a dream.—*Twelfth Night*, ii. 2, 27.
You were best hang yourself.—BEAUMONT AND FLETCHER.
Me rather had my heart might feel your love.—*Rich. II.* iii. 3, 192.

220. **Imperatives.**—In Old English, as in Modern, the only person in which the Imperative mood could be used was the second, Singular or Plural.

To express the first person the writer or speaker either used the first person Subjunctive (as we still do in poetry), or the word *uton* followed by an Infinitive. The verb *uton* answered the same purpose as the modern phrase "let us."

Upp-âhebben wé his naman (exalt we his name).—*Psalm* xxxiii. 2.
Uton faran (let us go).—*Luke* ii. 15.

221. **Do.**—This verb is used in various senses, the chief of which are exemplified in the sentences described below:—

(*a*) **How do you do?**—

The first *do* is the Auxiliary, which is used for asking a question in the present or past (Indefinite) tense.

The second *do* may be explained as an imitation, or rather

translation, of the French *faire*, in the old French sentence: *Comment faites-vous?* How do you make or do?

It has been also suggested that *do* is from A.S. *dúg-an*, to prosper. But the modern sound and spelling of *dúg* would be *dow*, like *cow* from A.S. *kú*. So this idea has been given up.

(*b*) **I do you to wit**:—

This quaint and almost obsolete expression means "I cause you to know." In Old English the verb *dó-n* (=do) meant (amongst other things) "cause," and this was very freely used in Middle English, when our language had lost the power of forming fresh Causal verbs, like *raise* from *rise*.

(*c*) **That will do**:—

The explanation usually given is that this *do* is not from A.S. *do-n*, but from A.S. *dúg-an*, to avail, to be sufficient (*Intrans.*), out of which we get the Adjective *dought-y*, valiant; and that hence the sentence "That will do" is equivalent to "That will suffice." But this explanation is untenable; for as shown in (*a*) the modern pronunciation and spelling of *dúg* would be *dow*, and not *do*. As an alternative explanation it might be said that "that will do" means "that will work," so that *do* is here a Transitive verb used Intransitively. Shakspeare has "I'll *do*, I'll *do*, and I'll *do*," where the verb *do* is evidently used Intransitively (see *Macbeth*, i. 3, 10).

222. Infinitive absolute.—In the English of the fourteenth century adverbial clauses of time, cause, or condition were rather frequently expressed by absolute constructions:—

> Boece withstod þat ordinaunce, *knowyng* al þis þe kyng hymself. (Boece withstood that ordinance, the king himself knowing all this.)—CHAUCER, *Boece*, bk. i. prose 4.
>
> The service *doon*, they soupen al by day.—*Squyeres Tale*, 289 (297).

In the first of these examples the participle used absolutely is *knowyng* (Present), and that in the second is *doon* (Past). As there was no future participle, how was future time to be expressed in the absolute construction?

To express future time, and yet retain the absolute construction, recourse was had to the Infinitive:—

> I dar the better aske of you a space
> Of audience, to schewen oure request;
> And ye, my lord, *to doon* right as yow leste.—*Clerkes Tale*, 49 (103).

In Modern English the Infinitive absolute is common:—

> The estate has been divided between us, *you to have* two-thirds, and *I* one.

223. Accusative with Infinitive.—This construction, with which we are so familiar in Latin, was common in Old English after such verbs as *biddan* (ask), *hátan* (bid), *seón* (see), *gehýran* (hear), *findan* (find) :—

(He) bæd him engla *weard geopenigean* uncúðe wyrd (he asked the *lord* of angels *to open* the unknown destiny).—*Elene*, 1101.

Later on, the same construction was extended to a great many other verbs, so that it has now become almost as common in English as in Latin :—

We saw *him come*. We suffered *him to come*.

224. Nominative with Infinitive.—This construction has been explained already in connection with the Infinitive absolute ; see § 122. But in the fifteenth century and even in Shakspeare we find the same construction used in other contexts :—

Thow to lye by our moder is to muche shame for us to suffre.—MALORY, *Morte d'Arthur*, p. 453, 4.

What he is indeed
More suits you to conceive than *I to speak of*.—*As You Like It*, ii. 2, 179.

In Modern English this construction is chiefly seen in exclamatory phrases or in absolute ones :—

I to be so foolish ! *He to deceive* me !
You to have one half, and *I* the other.

225. Past Participle in Active sense.—In Old English the Past participle could be used in an Active sense for qualifying nouns—an idiom which has survived to the present day :—

Yfele *geworht* man (a man full of evil works).—ÆLFRIC, *Hom.* ii. 476, 17.

The idiom continued all through the Middle period of our language, and is still common in the Modern :—

The *ravined* (=ravenous) salt-sea shark.—*Macbeth*, iv. 1, 24.
Fair-spoken ; better-spoken ; well-spoken. (All in Shakspeare.)

Compare "a *mistaken* man," *i.e.* a man who makes or has made many mistakes. (This participle or adjective can even be used as a complement : "You are *mistaken*," *i.e.* in error.) "A *learned* man," *i.e.* a man who has learned much. "A well-*read* man," *i.e.* one who has read much.

226. Gerundive or Noun-use of Participles.—In this construction a Participle is made to denote what would otherwise be expressed by a Gerund or Verbal noun. It was a common construction in Latin : "anno urbis *conditæ*," in the year of the city *built*, *i.e.* in the year of the *building* of the city. In our own language, however, it is not older than the sixteenth century. No instances occur in Old or even in Middle English.[1]

We have no right to be hurt at a *girl telling* me what my faults are.—THACKERAY.

There is always danger of *this disease appearing* (=the appearance of this disease) in the sound eye.—HUGH CONWAY.

Don't fear *me being* any hindrance to you.—DICKENS.

I ask where there could be pictures at Compton Green without *me knowing* it.—BESANT AND RICE.

Would you mind *me asking* you a few questions?—STEVENSON.

In the first of the following sentences "*being sent*" is a participle used Gerundively; in the second it is an actual Gerund or Verbal noun :—

(1) This prevented the letter *being sent*.
(2) This prevented the letter from *being sent*.

SECTION 5.—THE COMPLEX SENTENCE.

227. The Noun-Clause.—The first stage in the development of the noun-clause was to have no such particle as *that* for connecting the subordinate clause with the principal one. Even to this day the connective particle is often left out.

Simon . . . sægde hȳ drȳas wǣron.—*Juliana*, 301.
(Simon . . . said they sorcerers were.)

In the next stage some noun is made the object to the verb, before the subordinate clause is expressed :—

Ful wel þu *me* iseie, hwar ich was and hwat i dude.—*Old Eng. Homilies*, ed. Morris, First Series, p. 197.
(Full well thou sawest *me*, where I was and what I did.)

This construction is common in Tudor English and in the English Bible :—

---

[1] Mr. Kellner, however (in *Historical Syntax*, p. 262), quotes two examples of a much earlier date than the sixteenth century :—

(1) To-janes þo sunne risinde.—*Old. Eng. Misc.* p. 26.
(2) After the sunne goyng down.—WYCLIFF, *Gen.* xxviii. 11.

But here he appears to be mistaken. Ex. (1) is from Old Kentish Sermons that were copied by a Norman scribe, who betrays his imperfect knowledge of English by spelling the Verbal noun at first as *-inde*, then as *-inke*, and then at last correctly as *-inge*. The misspellings of such a scribe cannot be set up as an authority for Old English. The word *risinde* is not a pres. part. but a misspelling for *risinge*, a Verbal noun, and this noun is preceded by *sunne*, the *Genitive* case, which originally was spelt *sunnan*, then *sunnen*, then *sunne*. So example (1) means "at the time of the *sun's* rising," where "rising" (*risinde*) is a noun, and not a pres. part. Ex. (2) is equally clear. Here *sunne*, as before, is a Genitive case coupled with the verbal noun *goyng-down*.

I know *you* what you are.—*Lear*, i. 1, 272.
I know *thee* who thou art.—*New Test.*
Let me, my Lord, disclose unto your grace
This hainous tale, what mischief it contains.—*Gorboduc*, 627.

Compare Gen. xii. 14: "The Egyptians beheld the woman *that* she was very fair." Compare also: "And God saw *the light*, that it was good."—*Gen.* i. 4.

In the final stage no such intermediate noun is mentioned as object to the verb:—

I know what you are.
I know who thou art.
Let me, my Lord, disclose what mischief this heinous tale contains.

228. Adjective-Clause.—In the oldest form of the Adjective-clause the Relative, which is now used to connect the two sentences, was not mentioned:—

On þis geáre gefór Aelfred wæs æt Baðum geréfa.—*Chronicle*, 906.
(In this year died Alfred (who) was count at Bath.)
Sé fæder hire sealde áne þeówene Bala hátte.—*Genesis* xxix. 29.
(The father gave her a servant (who) was called Bala.)

In Tudor English the same construction is still rather common; but our more recent literature very rarely furnishes an example:—

I have a mind (which) presages.—SHAKS. *Mer. Ven.* i. 1, 175.
Were I Brutus,
And Brutus Anthony, there were an Anthony
(Who) would ruffle up your spirits, and put a tongue
In every wound of Cæsar.—SHAKS. *Jul. Cæs.* iii. 2, 230.
'Tis distance (that) lends enchantment to the view.—CAMPBELL.

229. Adverb-Clause.—Adverb-clauses introduced by *though*, *if*, etc., were formed in the same way in Old English as in Modern. But instead of using correlative particles like *where* . . . *there*, *when* . . . *then*, the custom in Old English was to use the same particle for both clauses, whenever this was possible:—

þær þín goldhord ys, *þær* ys þín heorte.
(Where thy treasure is, there is thy heart.)—*Matt.* vi. 21.
þonne hit dagian wolde, *þonne* tóglád hit.
(When it was about to dawn, then it vanished.)—*Chronicle*, C. 979.

There is one survival of this parallelism, which our language is never likely to part with, viz. *the* . . . *the* before comparatives; as "*the* more, *the* merrier." This has come down to us from the earliest English. See § 164, and § 185.

CHAPTER VIII.—COMPOUND WORDS.

230. When two Simple words are joined together, the word so formed is called a *Compound;* as *ink-pot, drinking-water.*

Compound words are subdivided into—

I. **Unrelated,** or those in which the Simple words are not connected together by any grammatical relation. (These have been also called Juxta-positional.)

II. **Related,** or those in which there is some grammatical relation between the component words. (These have been also called Syntactical.)

SECTION 1.—UNRELATED OR JUXTA-POSITIONAL COMPOUNDS.

231. In all compounds of this class the word that stands *first* defines the one that stands second :—

Thus "*horse-race*" means that kind of race which is run by *horses,* and not by boats or by men or by anything else. But "*race-horse*" means that kind of horse which is used for *racing,* and not for ordinary riding, or for drawing a carriage.

232. Compound Nouns can be formed as follows :—

(1) A noun preceded by another noun :—

Oil-lamp, lamp-oil ; ear-ring, ring-finger ; rail-way, way-side.

(2) A noun preceded by a Gerund :—

Cooking-stove, looking-glass, drinking-water, bathing-place.

Note.—The *-ing* is not always used ; as in *wash-house,* not *washing-house ; grind-stone,* not *grinding-stone,* etc.

(3) A noun preceded by an adverb :—

By-word, by-path, under-tone, under-wood, up-land, in-land.

233. Compound Adjectives can be formed as follows :—

(1) An adjective preceded by a noun, denoting—

(*a*) *Some point of resemblance :—*

Snow-white (=white like snow), blood-red, coal-black, sky-blue.

(*b*) *Some point of reference :—*

Air-tight (=tight against air), fire-proof, head-strong, heart-broken, book-learned, top-heavy, colour-blind, blood-thirsty.

(*c*) *The cause or source of the quality :—*

Home-sick (=sick for home), purse-proud, heaven-born.

(*d*) *The extent or measure of the quality :—*

Skin-deep (=deep as the skin), world-wide, breast-high, life-long.

(2) A noun (with suffix *-ed*) preceded by a noun :—

Chicken-hearted, hook-nosed, ox-tailed, web-footed, cow-houghed.

(3) An adjective or participle preceded by an adjective :—

Red-hot, dark-brown, bright-blue, dead-alive, luke-warm.

234. Compound Verbs can be formed as follows :—

(1) A verb preceded by a noun :—

Hen-peck, brow-beat, top-dress, back-bite, hood-wink, way-lay.

(2) A verb preceded by an adjective :—

Safe-guard, rough-hew, white-wash, rough-shoe, dumb-founder.

Section 2.—Related or Syntactical Compounds.

235. Compound Nouns can be formed as follows :—

(1) A verb Transitive followed by its Object :—

A tell-tale (one who tells tales), a cut-throat, a pick-pocket.

(2) A verb Transitive (with suffix *-er* or *-ing*) preceded by its Object :—

Shoe-maker, tax-payer ; engine-driving, house-building, etc.

Note.—The "*er*" and the "*ing*" are not always used, as in *tooth-pick*, not *tooth-picker ; blood-shed*, not *blood-shedding.*

(3) A verb qualified by an adverb :—

(*a*) *When the adverb precedes the verb :—*

An out-turn, an out-look, an out-fit, an up-start, an in-let.

(*b*) *When the adverb is placed after the verb :—*

A run-away, a cast-away, a break-down, a break-up, a fare-well.

Note.—Some compounds of this class have two forms ; *set-off* or *off-set ; turn-out* or *out-turn ; look-out* or *out-look.*

(4) A noun qualified by an adjective :—

A noble-man, a half-penny, a mad-man, a sweet-heart, mid-day.

(5) A noun qualified by a participle :—

(*a*) *Present Participle :—*

Humming-bird, loving-kindness, spinning-top, finishing-stroke.

Note.—The "*ing*" is not always used ; as in *screech-owl*, not *screeching-owl ; glow-worm*, not *glowing-worm.*

(*b*) *A verb with the force of a Past or Passive participle :—*

Hump-back = humped-back ; lock-jaw = locked-jaw.

(6) A noun qualified by a Possessive noun :—

Sales-man (for sale's-man), bats-man, oars-man, Tues-day, kins-man, herds-man, crafts-man, bees-wax, states-man, sports-man.

Note 1.—In some compounds the apostrophe is retained before the *s :—stone's-throw, king's-bench, cat's-paw, heart's-ease, land's-end.* The noun *spokes-man* has been formed by a false analogy.

Note 2.—The following compounds, since the first noun is not Possessive, are of the Unrelated or Juxta-positional class :—*boat-man, sea-man, oil-man, wood-man, cart-man, plough-man*, etc.

(7) A noun in apposition with a noun or pronoun :—

Washer-woman ; he-goat, she-goat ; man-servant, maid-servant.

236. Compound Adjectives can be formed as follows :—

(1) A noun preceded and qualified by an adjective :—

Evil-hearted, hot-headed, long-tailed, one-sided, red-coloured.

(2) A noun as object to the Pres. part. of a Trans. verb :—

A *heart-rending* sight ; a *time-serving* man ; a *soul-stirring* story.

(3) A noun as object to some preposition :—

An *over-land* (over the land) journey ; an *underhand* trick.

237. Verbs can be compounded with adverbs :—

(*a*) When the adverb precedes the verb. (Uncommon.)

Back-slide, cross-question, over-awe, under-state, with-hold.

(*b*) When the verb precedes the adverb. This is very common. The two words are written separately ; as *turn out, come on*, etc. (But in *don* (=do on), *doff* (=do off) they are compounded.)

238. Phrase Compounds.—Such compounds are sometimes used as nouns, and sometimes as adjectives :—

Forget-me-not (noun) ; hand-and-glove (friends that fit each other as closely as hand and glove) ; man-of-war ; would-be (adj. used for one who intended to be or do something, but was stopped) ; barrister-at-law ; note-of-hand ; ticket-of-leave ; Jack-o'-lantern ; hole-and-corner (adj. clandestine) ; son-in-law ; four-in-hand ; spick-and-span new (lit. spike and spoon new ; new as a nail or spike just made, or a spoon (chip) just cut).

Section 3.—Disguised Compounds.

239. Agnail : A.S. *ang-nægl*, a nail or hard knob that gives pain (*ang-*) ; the modern corrupted form is "hang-nail." See p. 177.

As : short for *al-so ;* A.S. *eál-swá* (quite so).

Atone : *at-one*, to reconcile or make *at one*.

Auger : corruption of *nauger ;* A.S. *nafu-gár*, from *nafu*, a nave, and *gár*, a piercer. "A nauger" was changed to "an auger."

Aught : A.S. *á-wiht*, one whit, anything whatever.

Back-gammon : a back-game ; A.S. *bæc* (back), *gamen* (game).

Bandog : Mid. Eng. *band-dogge*, a dog tied by a band, a watch-dog or ferocious dog.

Barley : A.S. *bær-lic*, that which is like *bear* or *bere* (barley). The last syllable has no connection with A.S. *léac*, a plant.

Bay-window : a window having a "bay" or recess ; not the same word as "bow-window."

Barn : A.S. *bere-ern*, a place (A.S. *ærn* or *ern*) for keeping barley.

Beldam : a hag. Ironical : Fr. *belle*, beautiful, and *dame*, lady.

Bilberry: Scand. *böllr* (a ball), and *bær* (a berry).

Biscuit: *bis* (twice, Lat.), and Fr. *cuit*, Lat. *coctus*, cooked.

Brannew: for *brand-new*, new from the brand or fire.

Bridal: put for *bride-ale*, that is, a bride-feast. A.S. *brýd, ealu.*

Bride-groom: for *bride-goom;* A.S. *guma*, a man. In Mid. Eng. the Fr. *grome* was substituted for A.S. *guma.*

Brimstone: Mid. Eng. *bren-stoon*, burning stone.

Buck-wheat: from *beech-wheat*, because the grain resembles the mast of a beech-tree.

Bulwark: properly bole-work, from Scand. *bolr*, the stem or trunk of a tree; cf. Fr. *boulevard.*

Bylaw: a town-law or municipal law; from Scand. *by*, town. Not compounded with the adverb *by.*

Cenobite: one of a brotherhood of monks; Gr. *koinos*, together; *bios*, life.

Chaffer: for *cheap-fare;* A.S. *ceáp*, bargain; *far-u*, journey.

Cobweb: A.S. *coppa*, a head (only known in the compound *átor-coppa*, a thing with poison in its head, a spider).

Colporteur: hawker; Lat. *coll-um* (neck), *port-ator* (carrier).

Constable: Old Fr. *conestable*, Lat. *comes stabuli*, count of the stable.

Coverlet: Old Fr. *covre*, to cover; and *lit*, Lat. *lectum*, a bed.

Curfew: Old Fr. *covre-feu*, a fire-cover.

Daisy = day's-eye, A.S. *dæges edge.*

> That well by reason it men callen may
> The *dayesie*, or else the eye of day.—CHAUCER.

Dismal, gloomy: Old Fr. *dis mal*, Lat. *dies mali*, evil days.

Distaff: A.S. *distæf* for *dise-* (a bunch of flax) *stæf* (a staff).

Earwig: ear-creeper; *wig* from A.S. *wic-ga*, one that runs.

Eaves-dropper, one who stands under droppings from the eaves of a house, to listen to what is said inside the room.

Elbow: A.S. *el-boga* or *eln-boga*, lit. arm (*eln*), bending (*boga*).

Fellow: Scand. *fé-lag-i*, a partner in a *fé-lag*, from *fé*, property (Eng. *fee*), and *lag*, an association or laying together.

Filibuster, Span.: a corruption of Eng. *free-booter*; from Dutch *vrij* (free), and *buit*, booty, plunder.

Filigree: formerly spelt as *filigrane;* Span. *filigrana;* Lat. *filum*, a thread, and *granum*, a thread.

Friday: A.S. *Frige-dæg*, day of *Frigu* (Love, Venus).

Fur-long = furrow-long, the length of a furrow.

Futtocks, for *foot-hooks.*

Gaffer, gammer: Eng. *grand-father* (hybrid); Fr. *grand-mère.*

Garlic: A.S. *gár-léac*, spear-leek; from *gár*, spear.

Gantlet, gauntlet (in the phrase "to run the gauntlet"). Confused with *gauntlet*, a glove. The older form was *gantlope*, from Swedish *gat-lopp*, lit. "a gate-leap," where *gate* means street or way. To run the gauntlet is to run down a lane formed by two files of soldiers, who strike the offender as he passes.

Gospel: A.S. *gód-spell*, "good story": trans. of *ev-angelium.*

Gossamer: lit. *goose-summer.* The provincial English name is *summer-goose;* so called from the downy appearance of the film.

Gossip, lit. a sponsor in baptism; *god*, and *sib*, "related."

Grunsel, groundsill, threshold; from *ground* and *sill*.

Haberdasher: a seller of small wares; said to be from Old Fr. *hapertas*, with Eng. suffix *-er* (a hybrid word). But Dr. Murray says "origin unknown."

Handicap: hand i' (th') cap; a mode of drawing lots.

Handiwork: here the *i* answers to A.S. *ge*; as in A.S. *hand-ge-weorc*. In *handicraft* the *i* has been inserted by analogy.

Handsel, hansel: the first instalment of a bargain (Scand.). Lit. *hand-sale*, the conclusion of a bargain by shaking hands.

Harbinger: Old Fr. *herberge-our;* lit. one who goes before to secure a *herberge* (lodging for an army). (See next word.)

Harbour (Scand.): *her-bergi*, army-shelter. Old Fr. *herberge*.

Hawthorn: A.S. *haga*, a hedge, and *thorn*.

Heifer: A.S. *héah-fore*, from *héah* (high, full-grown), and *fore*, cognate with Greek *poris*, a heifer; A.S. *fearr*, a bull. See § 104.

Henchman: Mid. Eng. *hensman, henchman*, a page; probably from A.S. *hengst*, a horse, and *man;* hence lit. "a groom."

Heyday: high-day; Mid. Eng. *hey*, high.

Hobby-horse: a horse-shaped toy; Sc. *hoppe*, a mare.

Hobnob: A.S. *hæbban*, to have, and *næbban*, not to have.

Humbug: from *hum*, to cajole, and *bug*, a terror.

Husband: lit. house-dweller; Scand. *hús-bóndi*.

Hussy, short for house-wife; A.S. *hús-wíf* (the house-woman).

Hustings, properly *husting;* from A.S. *husting*, borrowed from Icelandic *hús-þing*, "house-thing"; a meeting of the house.

Icicle: A.S. *ís-gicel*, from *ís*, ice, and *gicel*, a small piece of ice.

Kerchief: Old Fr. *covre-chef*, cover-to-the-head (*chef*).

Lady: A.S. *hláf-dige*, loaf-kneader.

Lammas: A.S. *hláf-mæsse*, loaf-mass: observed on 1st August.

Lamprey: a kind of shell-fish; lit. a licker of rocks; Lat. *lamb-ere* (to lick), and *petra* (a rock).

Leman: A.S. *léof-mann*, dear one, from *léof*, lief, dear.

Lichgate: corpse-gate, from A.S. *líc*, a corpse.

Limpet: another form of *lamprey*. See **Lamprey.**

Livelihood: Mid. Eng. *livelode*, A.S. *líf* (life), and *lád*, a way.

Lord: A.S. *hláf-ord*, probably for *hláf-weard*, a loaf-keeper.

Lukewarm: lit. warm-warm; Mid. Eng. *leuk, luke*, tepid.

Malady, sickness; Lat. *malus*, bad; *habitus*, condition.

Malaria: Lat. *mala*, bad; *aria*, air.

Mermaid: lake-maid, water-nymph; from A.S. *mere*, a lake.

Midriff: A.S. *mid-rif;* from *mid* (middle), and *hrif* (belly).

Midwife: from A.S. *mid*, with, and *wíf*, woman; female helper.

Mildew: A.S. *mele-deáw*, honey-dew; A.S. *mele, mil*, honey.

Misletoe: lit. bird-lime twig; A.S. *mistel* (that which has *mist* or bird-lime), and *tán*, a twig.

Mulled-ale: corrupt of *mould-ale*, a funeral feast; cf. *bridal*, or marriage-feast.

Monday: A.S. *Mónan-dæg*, day of the moon.

Narwhal: the sea-unicorn; lit. corpse-whale, from Icel. *nár* (a corpse), and *hvalr*, a whale; so called from its pallid colour.

Naught, not: for *ne aught*. See **Aught.**

Neighbour: A.S. *neáh* (nigh), and *búr*, a husbandman.

Nickname: lit. an additional name. The *n* has been wrongl attached from *an*; hence "an eke-name" > a nickname.

Nightingale: A.S. *nihte-gale*, a singer by night.

Nostril: A.S. *nos-þyrl*, nose-thirl, or nose-hole.

Parboil: orig. to boil thoroughly; Lat. *per*, and *bullire*. Bu now "to boil partially," through confusion with *part*.

Prose: Lat. *pro* (forward), and *versa* (turned); shortened to *prors* and then to *prosa*, a forward or unembellished speech.

Puttock: *put*, a contraction of *poult* or *pullet*, and *hawk*; hen lit. a hawk that seizes pullets.

Quagmire: formerly *quake-mire*, a quaking mire.

Ransack: Icel. *rann*, a house, and *sæk-ja*, to search.

Rearmouse, a bat; A.S. *hrére-mús*, a fluttering or flying mouse.

Saturday: A.S. *Sætern-dæg* or *Sæter-dæg*, day of Saturn.

Scotfree, free from paying *scot* or *shot*, contribution.

Sennight, seven nights, a week.

Shelter: A.S. *scild-truma*, a shield-troop, a squadron or guard.

Sheriff: A.S. *scír-réfa*, a shire-reeve, officer of the shire.

Sirloin: from Old Fr. *sur* (over, upon), and *longe* (loin).

Sledge-hammer: lit. a hammer-hammer; A.S. *slecge*, hammer.

Somersault: Old Fr. *soubre-soult*; *soubre* = Lat. *super*, over; *sau* = Lat. *saltus*, a leap.

Soothsayer, one who says sooth or truth.

Squirrel: Lat. *skiur-ellus*, dim. of Gr. *ski-urus* (shadow-tailed).

Stalwart: A.S. *stǽl-wyrðe*; *stǽl*, foundation, and *wyrðe*, worthy

Starboard: A.S. *stéorbord*, steerboard; the steersman's deck.

Stark-naked: Mid. Eng. *start-naked*, lit. "tail-naked."

Step-child: A.S. *stéop-cild*, an orphaned child.

Steward: A.S. *stí-weard*, keeper of sties and cattlepens.

Stickleback, the little fish with stickles (prickles) on its back.

Stirrup: A.S. *stíg-ráp*, a rope to climb up by.

Sunday: A.S. *Sunnan-dæg*, day of the sun.

Tadpole, a *toad* nearly all head or *poll*.

Tantamount: Lat. *tantus*; Fr. *à mont*, towards the mountain.

Thursday: A.S. *Thunres-dæg*, day of Thor or Thunder.

Topsy-turvy: orig. *topsy-tervy*. *Top-so-turvy* afterwards alter to *top-side-turvy*, as *up-so-down* was changed to *up-side-down*. *Tur* means overturned, from A.S. *torfian* (to throw), Mid. Eng. *terven*.

Trade-wind, wind of a certain trade, tread, or trend (path).

Tramway, a railroad on *trams* (sleepers).

Tuesday: A.S. *Tíwes-dæg*, day of Tíw or Mars.

Twilight: lit. double (*i.e.* doubtful) light: from A.S. *twí-*, doub

Valhalla: Icel. *val-r*, the slain; *hall*, a hall.

Vinegar: Fr. *vin* (Lat. *vin-um*), and *egre* (Lat. *acre*, sour).

Walrus: Dutch *walrus*; Danish *hval-ros*, a whale-horse.

Wanton, undisciplined; A.S. *wan*, lacking; *togen*, disciplined.

Wassail: from A.S. *wes hál*, be thou whole or hale.

Wednesday: A.S. *Wódnes-dæg*, the day of Woden.

Wellaway, an exclamation of sorrow; sometimes corrupted *welladay*; A.S. *wá lá wá*, woe! lo! woe!

Whitlow: a corruption of *quick-flaw*; a flaw in the *quick*.

Wilderness, for *wildern*-ness: A.S. *wild* (wild), *déor* (deer, anim

Window: lit. "wind-eye"; Icel. *vindr* (wind), and *auga* (an eye).
Woman: A.S. *wif-man; wif*, a female, and *mann*, person.
Woof: A.S. *ó-wef*, for *on-wef*, lit. web on or across the weft.
World: lit. age of man; A.S. *wer*, man; *ældu*, old age.
Yesterday, from A.S. *geostra* (yester) and *dæg* (day).
Zoo-phyte, animal-plant: Gr. *zoön* (animal), *phuton*, plant.

Section 4.—Mistaken or Apparent Compounds.

240. Acorn.—Not compounded of A.S. *ác* (oak) and *corn*. A.S. *æcern*, fruit of the field; from *æcer*, a field; cognate with Lat. *ager*.

Blind-fold.—"Fold" is not connected with "fold," but is a corruption of *feld-en* or *fell-en*, to strike.

Belfry.—Not compounded with *bell*. Old Fr. *ber-freit*, of Teutonic origin; *ber* or *berg*, to protect, and *freit*, a place of safety.

Battle-ment.—Not from *battle*, but from Fr. *bastile*, a fortress.

Bondage.—Not from "bond," but from A.S. *bonda*, a serf.

Caterpillar.—Not compounded with *pillar*. Fr. *chate*, a she-cat, and *peleuse* (Lat. *pilosa*), hairy. Old Fr. *chatepeleuse*, a weevil.

Chincough.—Not from *chin*, but *chink*=kink, a catch in the breath.

Counterpane.—Old Fr. *contre-poinct*, Lat. *culcita puncta*, a quilt punctured or stitched. In older English counterpoint was used:—

Embroidered coverlets or *counterpoints* of purple silk.—North.

Country-dance.—This word has been wrongly included among compounds of mistaken origin. It is an English word signifying "rustic dance"; but it was borrowed by the French and misexplained as *contre-danse*, a dance in which the partners stand opposite (*contra*) each other.

Crayfish.—Old Fr. *crevisse*; Old High Germ. *crebis*, a crab.

Curtail.—Old Fr. *curt-ault*, Lat. *curt-us*, with suffix *-ault*.

Frontispiece.—Old Fr. *frontispice*, Late Lat. *fronti-spicium*, a front view.

Grey-hound, Sc. *grey* (dog), and *hundr* (hound).

Gridiron.—Mid. Eng. *gridire*, Lat. *craticula*. In Mid. Eng. the word for "iron" was *iren* or *ire*. *Gridire* was changed to *gridiron*, because the *ire* was supposed to signify "iron."

Hand-cuff.—Apparently for *hand-cops*: *cops* means manacle.

Hang-nail.—Not compounded with *hang*. See **Agnail**, § 239.

Hiccough.—A misspelling for *hiccock*, dim. of *hic* or *hick*, a catch in the voice imitative of the sound. Cf. "hacking cough."

Hogshead.—More correctly *ox-head*. Dutch *oxhoofd*, ox-head.

Humble-pie.—Not compounded with *humble*, but *umble*, the entrails of a deer, given as a perquisite to the men who helped in the chase.

Iron-mould.—Not compounded with *mould*, but with *mole*, spot.

Isinglass.—Dutch *huyzen-blas*, sturgeon-bladder, from which isinglass is made. The *g* after the *n* is intrusive; the *b* before the *l* has been lost.

Island.—No connection with Fr. *isle*, Lat. *insula*. A.S. *íg-land*, in which *íg* alone means "island."

Lanthorn.—Lat. *lanterna;* misspelt, because *horn* was once used for making the sides of lanterns.

Lapwing.—A.S. *hleap-wince*, "one who turns about in running."

Lime-house, a proper name of a place; for *lime-oast*, lime-kiln.

Loadstone, a stone that *leads;* A.S. *lád*, a way or course.

Lute-string.—Not compounded either with *lute* or *string;* for *lustring*, Fr. *lustrine*, a sort of lustrous silk. Lat. *lustr-are*, to shine.

Mungoose, an ichneumon: Indian word *mangús*.

Mushroom.—Old Fr. *mouscheron*, an extension of *mousse*, moss.

Night-mare, an incubus; A.S. *niht* (night), and *mara* (a crusher).

Peacock.—The word *pea* is borrowed from Lat. *pa-vo*, Gr. *ta-os*.

Pea-jacket.—Dutch *pij*, a coat of coarse woollen stuff.

Penthouse.—Corrupt. of Fr. *a-pentis*, Lat. *appendicium*, appendage.

Periwig.—Not compounded with *wig; wig* is itself the short of *periwig*. Fr. *perruque*, from Lat. *pil-um*, hair.

Pick-axe.—Mid. Eng. *pikois, pikeis*, a mattock; cf. Lat. *spic-a*.

Policies (insurance paper).—No connection with *policy*. Gr. *poly* (many), *ptukon* (a fold), a writing in many folds. Late Lat. *polecticum*.

Porpoise.—Old Fr. *por-peis*, Lat. *porcus*, pig, and *piscis*, fish.

Posthumous.—Not compounded with Lat. *humus*, the ground. A misspelling for *postumus*, "the last," superlative of *post*.

Primrose.—Not compounded with *rose*. Mid. Eng. *primerole*, dim. of Late Lat. *prim-ula*, which is itself a dim. of Lat. *prim-a*.

Rakehell.—For Mid. Eng. *rakel*, Scand. *reikall*, a vagabond.

Rein-deer.—Not compounded with *rein*. Sc. *hreinn*, a deer.

Rosemary.—Lat. *ros* (dew), *marinus* (maritime).

Runagate.—A corruption of *renegade;* Lat. *re*, again, and *negatus*, denied; one who has denied his faith.

Sandblind.—Lit. "half-blind"; A.S. *sám*, half, Lat. *semi*.

Sangreal.—Wrongly traced to *sang* (blood), *real* (royal, not real); the word is *san* (holy), *greal* or *grail* (dish). "The Holy Grail."

Service-tree, a kind of wild pear. Corruption of Mid. Eng. *serv-es*, plural, A.S. *syrf*, borrowed from Lat. *sorb-us*. Cf. *sorb*-apple.

Shamefaced.—For *shame-fast;* cf. "sted-fast": A.S. *sceam-fæst*.

Slow-worm.—A.S. *slá-wyrm*, a worm or snake that slays.

Sovereign.—Late Lat. *super-aneus;* cf. *foreign*, Lat. *for-aneus*.

Surcease.—Fr. *sursis*, pp. of the verb *surseoir;* Lat. *super-sedere*.

Surround.—For *sur-ound;* Lat. *super*, over, and *und-are*, to flow.

Titmouse.—Scand. *tittr*, little; A.S. *máse*, small bird.

Touchy.—Corruption of *tetchy*, from Mid. Eng. *tetch*, a whim.

Turmoil.—From Fr. *tremouille*, the hopper of a mill, so called because it is constantly in motion; Lat. *trem-ere*, tremble.

Uproar.—Not compounded of *up* and *roar*. Dutch *op-roer*, where *op* means "up," and *roer* means "commotion"; allied to A.S. *hrer-an*, to flutter; cf. **Rearmouse.** "Roar" is from A.S. *rár-ian*.

Wall-eyed, "with a beam in the eye." Scand. *vagl*, a beam.

Walnut.—Not compounded with *wall*, but with A.S. *wealh*, foreign.

Wiseacre.—Dutch *wijs-segger*, a wise-sayer.

Witchelm.—A.S. *wice*, bending; cf. *wicker*, made of twigs.

Yeoman.—Old Fris. *ga-man*, a villager, from *ga*, a village.

SECTION 5.—HYBRID COMPOUNDS.

(*Compounds made up of words taken from different languages.*)

241. Arch-fiend: Gr. *arch* (chief); A.S. *féond* (enemy, hence fiend).

Bandy-legged: Fr. *bandé* (bound); Scand. *leggr* (leg).

Bank-rupt: Du. *banck* (bench, table); Lat. *rupt-us* (broken).

Beef-eater: Fr. *boef*, *bœuf* (beef); Eng. *eater*, one who eats his master's beef; a servant. (The theory which made it a corruption of Fr. *buffetier*, a waiter at a side-board, has been disproved in Skeat's *Student's Pastime*, pp. 157, 158.)

Black-guard: Eng. *black* (A.S. *blæc*); Fr. *guard*.

Cause-way: Old Fr. *caucie* (Lat. *calciata*), paved; *way* (A.S. *wæg*).

Foumart: a pole-cat; A.S. *fúl* (foul); Fr. *marte* (a marten).

Grandfather, grandmother: Fr. *grand* (great); Eng. *father*, *mother*.

Haut-boy: Fr. *haut*, high; Dutch *bosch*, wood.

Heir-loom: Fr. *heir* (Lat. *her-es*); Eng. *loom* (A.S. *ge-lóma*, a tool).

Holly-hock: A.S. *hálig* (holy); Celt. *hoc-ys* (mallow). The flower was indigenous to the Holy Land.

Inter-loper: Lat. *inter* (between), and Du. *looper* (runner).

Kerb-stone: Lat. *curv-us* (curved), and A.S. *stán* (stone).

Knight-errant: Eng. *knight;* Lat. *errant-em* (wandering).

Life-guard: A.S. *líf* (life); Fr. *guard*.

Macadamised: Gael. *mac* (son); Heb. *Adam;* Greek *-ise* or *-ize*, and Eng. suffix *-d*.

Mari-gold: Heb. *Mary;* Eng. *gold:* so called from its colour.

Nuncheon: Mid. Eng. *none-schenche*, "noon-drink": Lat. *nona*, ninth hour, noon; and A.S. *scenc-an*, to pour out drink.

Nut-meg: A.S. *hnut-a* (a nut); Mid. Eng. *muge*, Lat. *musc-us*.

Orchard: A.S. *ort-geard;* from Lat. *(h)ort*-us, garden; A.S. *geard*, yard. (The theory which identifies the first syllable with A.S. *wort* is now exploded.)

Os-trich: Lat. *avis* (bird); Gr. *struth-ion* (a kind of bird).

Par-take, for *part-take*: Lat. *part-em*, Eng. *take* (from Sc. *tac-a*).

Pas-time: Fr. *pass*-er, to move onward; A.S. *tim-a* (time).

Pent-roof: sloping roof. Fr. *pente*, a slope; A.S. *hróf*, a cabin.

Piece-meal: Fr. *piece* (part); A.S. *mǽl* (a portion or time).

Pur-blind: orig. *pure-blind*; Lat. *purus*, A.S. *blind*.

Rigmarole: Sc. *ragmenni* (coward); Lat. *rotula* (a little wheel, hence *roll*). A coward's roll; a long stupid story.

Salt-cellar: A.S. *sealt* (salt); Fr. *salière*, L. *salarium*, saltholder.

Sorb-apple: Lat. *sorb-us* (a wild tree); A.S. *æppel* (apple).

Spike-nard: Lat. *spic-atus* (spiked); Sanskrit *nalad-a* (nard).

CHAPTER IX.—TEUTONIC PREFIXES AND SUFFIXES.

242. Derivatives, Compounds.—A word derived from *one* Simple word is called a *Derivative;* whereas a word formed by the junction of *two* or more Simple words is called a *Compound.*

Thus *man-like* is a Compound, of which the component words are *man* and *like.* But *man-ly* is a Derivative, because *ly* is not a separate word, but merely a suffix added to the word *man.*

Derivatives are subdivided into two main classes :—

I. **Primary**, when one word is formed out of another by some change in the body of the word.

II. **Secondary**, when a new word is formed by adding some affix (either prefix or suffix) to some given stem.

Thus *men* is a Primary derivative, because it is formed from *man* by vowel-mutation (see § 77); but *man-ly* is a Secondary derivative, because it is formed by adding the suffix *-ly* to the word *man*. Observe, however, that words, whose difference from one another consists of *vowel-gradation*, do not belong to the class of Primary derivatives under any circumstances. Such words are co-radical; that is, one is not derived from another (see § 3, *Note* 3, and § 78). Again, *graze* is a Primary derivative, because this verb is formed from the noun *grass* by changing *ss* to *z;* but *grass-y* is a Secondary derivative, because it is formed by adding the adjective-suffix *-y* to *grass*.

243. Root, stem.—The *root* of a word is that essential part of it, which it has in common with a group of cognate words.

Thus from the Teutonic root *būg* (Mod. Eng. *bow*) we got *buxom*, lit. *bow-some*, *i.e.* pliant; *bow*, a weapon (A.S. *boga*); *bight*, a coil of rope (A.S. *byht*). All these are from an Aryan root *bheugh*, which appears in Lat. *fug*-ere, to flee, Gr. *pheug*-ein, to flee, Sanskrit *bhuj*, to bend. See also the Aryan root *pa*, exemplified in *Note* 3 to § 3.

A *stem* is the form assumed by the root, before a suffix is added to it.

Thus in *loved* the root is *lov* (A.S. *luf*), the stem is *lov-e* (A.S. *luf-o*), and the suffix is *-d* (A.S. *-de*). Here *d* is the *derivative* suffix added to the stem *love*, and *-e* is the *formative* suffix, with the help of which the stem *love* is formed. Similarly in the A.S. Infinitive *luf-i-an*, *luf* (as before) is the root, *luf-i* is the stem (consisting of the root combined with the formative suffix *-i*), and *-an* is the flexional or Derivative suffix, which makes the Infinitive. To take one more example :—*stones*. Here *ston* (A.S. *stán*) is the root; the stem is *stán-a ; -s* is the (Derivative) Nom. Plural suffix (A.S. *stán-a-s*, Mod. Eng. *stones*).

A stem may therefore be more strictly defined as "a root combined with some formative suffix, to which a derivative suffix can be added."

Note 1.—So far as we know, roots never existed as independent words. Thus *luf* (the A.S. root) has never been seen alone. A word is reduced to its root, after all formative and derivative suffixes have been cut off. The root which remains is merely a theoretical form, useful for etymological purposes.

Note 2.—Such a word as *luf* is an *English root*,—that is, it is the simplest form to which the word can be reduced in English. It has other forms in other Aryan languages; thus in Sanskrit it has the form *lubh*. The phrase *English root* means "the form that an Aryan root assumes in the English language."

244. Prefixes, Suffixes, Affixes.—A prefix is a particle placed at the beginning of a stem; a suffix is one placed at the end of it. The name "affix" may be given to either.

Prefixes alter the meanings of words, while suffixes alter their functions.

Thus there is a radical difference of meaning between *teach* and *un-teach*, *bid* and *for-bid*, *con-vert* and *sub-vert*, *pro-ceed*, *pre-cede*, and *suc-ceed*.

On the other hand, suffixes form nouns, adjectives, verbs, and adverbs, and hence they change the function of a word, that is, they make it of one part of speech or another. Thus the stem *dark* becomes a noun in *dark-ness*, a verb in *dark-en*, and an adverb in *dark-ling* and *dark-ly*.

SECTION 1.—TEUTONIC PREFIXES.

245. These are either (*a*) Separable, or (*b*) Inseparable.

(*a*) **Separable**, or such as have a separate existence as independent words. Words so formed might be called Compounds; and in fact are so called for convenience in § 235 (3), *a*, *b*. But the name "Compound" is usually restricted to those words of which the component parts are nouns, adjectives, or verbs; whereas the name "Separable prefix" is for the most part restricted to adverbs and prepositions. Words formed with separable prefixes or separable suffixes are a connecting link between Compounds and Derivatives.

After (A.S. *æft*, *æfter*, prep. and adverb):—*after*-wards, *after*-thought, *after*-math (a second mowing), *after*-life, *after*-sails, etc.

Al-, **l**- (A.S. *eal*, Eng. *all*, adverbial):—*al*-one, *l*-one, *al*-most, *al*-ready, *al*-together, *al*-so, *al*-mighty, *al*-though, *al*-way (A.S. *ealne weg*), *al*-ways (Mid. Eng. *alles weis*).

At- (*at*):—*at*-one, *at*-one-ment, etc.

By (A.S. *bí*):—*by*-path, *by*-word, *by*-way, *by*-election.

Note.—*By*-law is excluded; lit. "town-law"; once spelt *bir*-law, *bur*-law; from *bær* or *býr* (Scand.), a town; cf. Grims-*by*, etc. § 33.

Fore (A.S. *fore*, before):—*fore*-cast, *fore*-tell, *fore*-see, *fore*-head, *fore*-lock, *fore*-thought, *fore*-runner, *fore*-stall, *fore*-man, *fore*-ground, *fore*-leg, *fore*-bode, *fore*-father, *fore*-noon, *fore*-doom.

Forth:—*forth*-coming, *for*(th)-ward, *forth*-with.

Fro (Scand. *frá*, from): *fro*-ward (opp. to *to*-ward, as in un-*to*-ward).

In- (A.S. *in*):—*in*-to, *in*-sight, *in*-bred, *in*-land, *in*-let, *in*-mate, *in*-step, *in*-born, *in*-come, etc.

Mis- (A.S. *mis*, Eng. *miss*, in the sense of wrongly):—

With A.S. words and stems:—*mis*-become, *mis*-behave, *mis*-believe, *mis*-deed, *mis*-deem, *mis*-sent, *mis*-give, *mis*-lay, *mis*-lead, *mis*-like, *mis*-name, *mis*-shape, *mis*-time, *mis*-understand.

With stems of Scand. origin:—*mis*-call, *mis*-hap, *mis*-take.

With stems of Lat. or *Fr. origin* (all hybrids):—*mis*-apply, *mis*-

calculate, *mis*-carry, *mis*-conceive, *mis*-conduct, *mis*-construe, *mis*-date, *mis*-demeanour, *mis*-employ, *mis*-fortune, *mis*-govern, *mis*-guide, *mis*-inform, *mis*-interpret, *mis*-judge, *mis*-place, *mis*-print, *mis*-pronounce, *mis*-quote, *mis*-represent, *mis*-rule, *mis*-spend, *mis*-term, *mis*-use, etc. (Different from the *mis* in *mis-chief.*)

Note.—The Lat. prefix *dis-* is sometimes interchanged with Eng. *mis-*. Thus we have *mis*-believe and *dis*-believe, *mis*-trust and *dis*-trust, *mis*-like and *dis*-like.

Off- (*of, off*) :—*off-ing* (what is seen of the sea at some distance from the shore), *off*-spring, *off*-shoot, *of*-fal (*off* + fall, that which falls off), *off*-set, *off*-scouring, *off*-hand.

Note.—This prefix sometimes takes the form of *a-*, as in *a*-down ; see below under **A**- (*b*) **Inseparable.**

On- (A.S. *on*, Mid. Eng. *on* ; allied to *in*) :—*on*-set, *on*-slaught, *on*-ward, *on*-wards, *on*-to (double preposition).

Note.—This prefix appears as *an* in *an*-on (=on one), and as *a* in a large number of words like *a*-foot ; see below under **A**- (*b*) **Insep.**

Out-, ut- (A.S. *út*) :—*out*-let, *out*-cast, *out*-side, *out*-landish, *out*-spoken, *out*-look, *out*-come, *out*-break, *out*-post, *out*-house, *out*-cry, *out*-set ; *ut*-ter, *ut*-most, *ut*-ter-most.

Note.—This prefix makes Intransitive verbs Transitive in the sense of surpassing :—

Out-live (live beyond or longer than), *out*-shine (surpass in shining), *out*-run (run ahead of), *out*-vote (defeat by votes), *out*-weigh, *out*-general (surpass in generalship), "*out*-Herods Herod" (*Shaks.* surpasses Herod in wickedness).

Over- (A.S *ofer*, compar. of *-ove*, above) :—*over*-look (to look over a thing without perceiving it), *over*-flow, *over*-due, *over*-coat (a coat that is worn over another coat), *over*-cast, *over*-whelm, *over*-throw.

Note.—This prefix is often used to denote *excess*, as an equivalent to the adverb *too*, "beyond the proper mark" :—

Over-eat (eat too much), *over*-sleep (sleep beyond the time), *over*-eager (too eager), *over*-step (step beyond, trangress), *over*-shoot (as, a mark), *over*-worked (worked too much), *over*-fond (too fond), *over*-value (value too highly), *over*-tax, etc.

In the word "*or*-lop," the prefix *or*- is a disguised form of *over*—the lowest deck of a vessel, the deck laid *over* the beams in the hold (of Dutch origin).

Thorough, through :—*thorough*-fare, *through*-out, *thorough*-bred, *thorough*-paced, *through*-carriage, *through*-ticket.

Note.—In Shakspeare we find *thorough* used as a prep. =*through* ; as, *thorough* fire, *thorough* bush, *thorough* flood, etc.

To- (A.S. *tó*, prep.) : *to*-day (A.S. tó dæg-e), *to*-gether, *to*-morrow, *to*-night, *to*-ward.

Under (A.S. *under*) :—*under*-let, *under*-growth, *under*-go, *under*-stand, *under*-ling, *under*-neath, *under*-mine, *under*-sell, *under*-told.

Note.—This prefix also denotes *deficiency*, or too little :—

Under-paid, *under*-fed, *under*-valued, etc.

Up- (A.S. *up*) :—*up*-start, *up*-shot, *up*-braid, *up*-hold, *upp*-er.

Wel-, well- (A.S. *wel*, agreeable to a will or wish) :—*wel*-fare, *wel*-come, *well*-bred, etc.

With (A.S. *with*, against or back) :—*with*-stand, *with*-hold, *with*-draw.

Note.—In the compound noun "*with*-drawing-room," the prefix *with* has been dropped and the word has become "drawing-room."

Note.—To denote bigness, strength, or coarseness we use as prefixes the nouns *bull*, *horse*, and *tom*.

Bull :—*bull*-dog, *bull*-faced, *bull*-finch, *bull*-fly, *bull*-frog, *bull*-head (kind of fish), *bull*-terrier, *bull*-weed, *bul*-rush (?), *bull*-mastiff.

Horse :—*horse*-chestnut, *horse*-fish, *horse*-laugh, *horse*-leech, *horse*-play, *horse*-radish, *horse*-weed, *horse*-wood (West Indian tree).

Tom :—*tom*-boy (a romping girl), *tom*-fool, *tom*-noddy, *tom*-rig (a hoiden), *tom*-tit, *tom*-cat (a big male cat).

(*b*) **Inseparable**, such as cannot be used as separate words :—

A- (*of*) :—*a*-down (A.S. *of-dune*, off a hill or dune), *a*-kin (of kin), *a*-new, *a*-fresh, *a*-light (to descend from, A.S. *of-líht-an*).

A- (*on*, the commonest value of the prefix *a*) :—*a*-foot, *a*-miss, *a*-float, *a*-fore (A.S. *on-foran*), *a*-light (adv.), *a*-light (verb, to light on, A.S. *on-líht-an*), *an*-on (in one), *a*-bed, *a*-board, *a*-thwart (in the cross), *a*-hunting (in or for hunting), *a*-thinking (in the act of thinking), *a*-jar (on the jar), *a*-mong (A.S. *on*-mang, in a mixture), *a*-like (A.S. *on*-líc), now-*a*-days.

A- or **an**- (A.S. *and*-, against) :—*a*-long (A.S. *and*-lang, over against in length) ; *an*-swer (A.S. *and*-swer-ian, to swear or speak back).

A- (A.S. *án*, one) :—*a*-ught (á-wiht), n-*a*-ught.

A- (A.S. *á*, intensive) :—*a*-rise, *a*-waken, *a*-maze, *a*-rouse, *a*-weary, *a*-shamed, *a*(c)-cursed, *a*(f)-fright, *a*(c)-knowledge.

Note.—In the three words last named, the A.S. *á* has been confounded with the Lat. suffix *-ad*, which by assimilation to *c* or *f* can become *ac* or *af*.

A- (*at*, in North. Eng. used for *to*, to express the Gerundial Infin.) :—*a*-do (in the phrase *much a-do*=much to do), *t*-wit (short for *at*-wit-en, to reproach).

A- (A.S. *ge*, Mid. Eng. *i*, *y*) :—*a*-ware (A.S. *ge*-wær, Mid. Eng. *i*-war or *y*-war) ; *a*(f)ford (A.S. *ge*-forth-ian, to further).

Note.—**An hungred.**—The sentence "He was an hungred" occurs frequently in the Authorised Version of 1611 ; but in the Revised Version of 1885 it has been changed to "he hungered." The *an* appears to have been substituted for the prefix *a* (A.S. *of*), which was confounded with the Indefinite article. *An hungered*=Mid. Eng. *a-hungred*=Mid. Eng. *of-hungred*. Thus *of* > *o* > *a* > *a*(*n*).

Be- (by). (1) It forms Transitive verbs out of nouns and adjectives :—*be*-calm, *be*-dew, *be*-friend, *be*-fit, *be*-numb, *be*-guile, *be*-fool, *be*-night, *be*-troth, *be*-stow (A.S. *stow*=place, noun), *be*-chance, (*Shaks.*).

(2) It makes Intrans. verbs Trans. :—*be*-moan, *be*-lie, *be*-speak, *be*-think.

(3) It intensifies verbs :—*be*-daub, *be*-smear, *be*-seech (=*be*-seek), *be*-get, *be*-stir, *be*-sprinkle, *be*-take, *be*-deck, *be*-gin, *be*-wray (A.S. *wrég-an*, to accuse).

(4) It helps to form nouns :—*be*-hoof, *be*-quest, *be*-half, *be*-hest.

(5) It helps to form adverbs or preps. :—*be*-sides, *be*-low, *be*-neath, *be*-fore, *be*-tween, *b*-ut (be + out).

(6) It has a privative force in :—*be*-head.

Note 1.—In the verb *be*-lieve the *be* has been substituted for *ge* (A.S. *ge*-lȳf-an, to *be*-lieve).

Note 2.—*Be*-have is a derivative of *have*, with a pronunciation due to *behāviour*, which simulated a French noun with a Fr. suffix.

E- (A.S. *ge*, Mid. Eng. *i*-, *e*-) :—*e*-nough (A.S. *ge*-nóg, Mid. Eng. *i*-noh, *e*-nogh).

E- (Dutch *ont*, A.S. *and*, see above **A**-, **an**-) :—*e*-lope (akin to *leap*, Dutch, *ont*-hlop-en). (This word came to us through the Anglo-Fr. form *a*-lop-er.)

For (through, thoroughly ; related to *from* ; distinct from *fore*) :—

Intensive :—*for*-bear, *for*-give, *for*-lorn, *fr*-et (A.S. *for*-et-an, to eat up).

Privative and depreciatory :—*for*-bid, *for*-sake, *for*-get, *for*-swear (swear falsely), *fore*-go (go without, a bad spelling of *for*-go).

Note.—In *for*-feit and *for*-close or *fore*-close, the prefix is Romanic ; see § 253 (16).

Fore (before) :—*fore*-bode, *fore*-tell, *fore*-cast, *fore*-father, *fore*-noon (hybrid).

Gain (A.S. *gegn*, against) :—*gain*-say (say or speak against).

I- (A.S. *ge*) :—*i*-wis (A.S. *ge*-wis, Mid. Eng. *y*-wis, or *i*-wis, "certainly"; wrongly written in Mod. Eng. as *I wis*, as if *wis* were a verb), hand-*i*-work (A.S. hand-*ge*-weorc).

N- (Indefinite article, *an*, from which the *n* has been wrongly attached to the open vowel of the following noun) :—*n*-ewt (for *an ewt*), *n*-ickname (for *an eke-name*), *n*-ugget (for *an ingot*).

Note.—In Shakspeare we find *n-uncle*, *n-aunt*, which have probably been formed from *mine uncle*, *mine aunt*. The phrase *for the n-once* has come from *for then once*.

N- (A.S. *ne*, negative prefix ; cf. Lat. *non*) :—*n*-o (A.S. *ná*), *n*-ay (from *ne* + aye), *n*-aught or *n*-ought (A.S. *ná*-wiht, not a whit), *n*-either, *n*-ever, *n*-or (short for A.S. *n*-óther, also spelt as *n-ówther*, *n-áwther*, a contracted form of *n-áhwæðer*), *n*-illy-will-y (nill I or he + will I or he), hob-*n*-ob (A.S. *hæbb-an ne hæbb-an*, have or not have).

Or- (A.S. *or*-, signifying "out") :—*or*-deal (A.S. *or*-dél, a dealing out, a judgment), *or*-ts (leavings, from A.S. *or*, and *et*-an, to eat ; that is, "uneaten").

Note.—In the phrase "odds and ends" the *odds* is a Norse spelling of *ords*, beginnings (A.S. *ord*, a point or beginning), not of *orts*.

To- (A.S. *tó*, intensive prefix) :—*to*-break (split open : "all to-brake his head" = utterly smashed his head : Judges ix. 53). This was a common prefix in A.S., but is now seen in only one word "to-brake," which is obsolescent.

Twi- (A.S. twí, double):—*twi*-n, *twi*-ce, *twi*-light, *twi*-bill (a two-edged bill), *twi*-ne, *twi*-st, *twi*-g, *twi*-ll.

Un- (A.S. *un*, negative prefix):—*un*-truth, *un*-told, *un*-ripe, *un*-real, *un*-wise, *un*-called-for.

Un- (A.S. *un*, a verbal prefix, signifying the *reversal* of an action; akin to A.S. *and*-, "against"; see above under **An-**):—*Un*-tie, *un*-teach, *un*-say (withdraw what has been said), *un*-learn, *un*-lock, *un*-fold, *un*-bolt, *un*-twine, *un*-do, *un*-deluged (cleared of the deluge, *Campbell*).

Note 1.—In *un*-loose the *un* is merely intensive.

Note 2.—The suffix *un*-, when added to nouns, sometimes forms verbs that have the sense of reversal; as,

Un-sex, *un*-earth (=*ex*-hume), *un*-horse.

Un- (not in A.S.; put for *und*, Old Frisian):—*un*(*d*)-to, *un*(*d*)-til.

Wan (privative, like -*un*):—*wan*-ton (A.S. *wan*-towen, untrained). So also *wan*-hope (obsolete), "hopelessness."

Y- (A.S. *ge*, Mid. Eng. *i*, *y*):—*y*-wis (corrupted to "I wis"), *y*-clept. (This prefix has already appeared as *a*- in *a*-ware, A.S. *ge*-wær, Mid. Eng. *i*-war; as *e*- in *e*-nough, A.S. *ge*-nóh; and as *i* in hand-*i*-work, A.S. hand-*ge*-weorc.)

Section 2.—Suffixes.

A. *Noun-forming.*

246. Separable, or once separable.—Words so formed might, as in the case of words formed with separable prefixes, be called Compounds. They differ from ordinary compounds only in two points—(*a*) the suffixed word is attached to other words so frequently as to constitute *a class*, whereas an ordinary compound stands alone; (*b*) most of the suffixed words have not completely retained their separate and independent meaning.

Note.—In this and the following chapters hybrids are marked with an asterisk. The word "hybrid" is used with various degrees of strictness. In this book, if the stem belongs to one Teutonic language and the suffix to another, the word so formed is not counted as a hybrid. Thus *fellowship* is not counted a hybrid, because *fellow* is Scandian and *ship* A.S.; nor is *landscape* counted a hybrid, because *land* is A.S., and *schap* Dutch. Nearly all the suffixes, however, included under the name Teutonic are Anglo-Saxon. Hybrids are words composed of *heterogeneous* elements, such as Teutonic with Romanic (as in *hindr-ance*), Teutonic with Greek (as in *heathen-ism*), Romanic with Greek (*gloss-ary*).

(1) **-craft** (skill; A.S. *cræft*, force, skill): forms Abstract nouns:—

Leech-*craft* (medical science or skill), speech-*craft* (skill in the use of words), wood-*craft*, handi-*craft* (the *i* has been inserted in imitation of "hand-i-work," A.S. *hand-ge-weorc*).

Depreciatory sense:—*priest-*craft*, *state-*craft*, witch-*craft*.

(2) **-dom** (A.S. *dóm*, judgment, jurisdiction: Eng. *doom*).—Attached chiefly to nouns, but also to adjectives; cf. *wis-dom*, *free-dom*.

Abstract sense:—*duke-*dom*, earl-*dom*, free-*dom*, *martyr-*dom*, *pope-*dom*, thral-*dom*, *serf-*dom*, wis-*dom*, *prince-*dom*.

Concrete sense:—king-*dom*, *Christen-*dom*, heathen-*dom*.

Recent formations (mostly humorous);—beadle-*dom* (Dickens), Bumble-*dom* (Dickens), Czar-*dom*, flunkey-*dom*, rascal-*dom* (Carlyle), scoundrel-*dom* (Carlyle), tinker-*dom*, bore-*dom*.

Excluded words:—

Seldom: *seld*=rare, *-om* for *-um*, Dative Plural suffix (see § 159).

Random: Old Fr. *randon*, violent haste.

(3) **-fare** (A.S. *far-u*, a journey; from *far*-an, to go):—

Thorough-*fare* (a through passage, a much-frequented road), wel-*fare*, chaf-*fer* (now a verb; formerly a noun=cheap-fare), war-*fare* (lit. a war-going, a military expedition).

(4) **-herd** (A.S. *heorde*, *hirde*, one who keeps a *heord* or *herd*):—

Shep-*herd*, swine-*herd*, cow-*herd*, neat-*herd*.

Note.—This is no longer used for forming fresh words; and some examples, such as *hog-herd*, *goose-herd*, have become obsolete.

Excluded word:—

Pot-sherd, from *pot*, and *sherd* or *shard*, a fragment (A.S. *sceard*, a thing cut).

(5) **-hood, -head** (A.S. *hád*, state, degree, form): chiefly Abstract. Attached chiefly to nouns, but also to adjectives, as in *likelihood*, *falsehood*:—

-head.—God-*head*, maiden-*head*.

-hood.—Boy-*hood*, child-*hood*, girl-*hood*, hardi-*hood*, knight-*hood*, likeli-*hood*, maiden-*hood*, man*hood*, *priest-*hood*, woman-*hood*, wife-*hood*, widow-*hood*.

Concrete sense:—neighbour-*hood*, *false-*hood*, sister-*hood* (collective), brother-*hood* (collective, sometimes abstract).

Excluded word:—

Livelihood: A.S. *líf-lád*, Mid. Eng. *live-lode*, life-leading.

(6) **-lock, -ledge** (*-lock* is from A.S. *lác*, Mid. Eng. *lok*, sport or play (noun); but *-ledge* is from A.S. *lǽc*-an (*verb*, formed by vowel-mutation from *lác*-ian, through the influence of *i*), Mid. Eng. *lech*-en, Mod. Eng. *-ledge*; cf. verb "ac-know-*ledge*"); now almost obsolete as a suffix, but once common:—

Wed-*lock*; know-*ledge*.

(7) **-lock, -lic** (A.S. *leác*, a plant; hence Eng. *leek*):—

Hem-*lock*, char-*lock*, house-*leek*, gar-*lic* (spear-plant, *gár*=spear).

Excluded word :—

Barley : A.S. *bere*, barley. The *ley* is derived from *lic*, like, and not from *léac*, a plant (Dr. Murray).

(8) **-man** (A.S. *mann*, which meant person of either sex). In many words this has taken the place of the old suffix *-ere* or *-er*, denoting agent. In "fish-*er-man*" both suffixes are seen. In "cart-*er*," "cart-*man*," either suffix is seen.

Boat-*man*, *post-*man*, dust-*man*, midship-*man*, oars-*man* (observe the *s*, man *of the oar*), sports-*man* (man of sport), spokes-*man* (Mid. Eng. speke-*man* ; in "spokesman" the *s* is intrusive, based on the analogy of *sportsman*, etc.), wo-*man* (a corruption of *wif-man*, that is, a female person), alder-*man* (formed with A.S. *ealdor*, elder, chief).

(9) **-monger** (A.S. *mang-ere*, a dealer in mixed goods ; cf. the verb *ming-le*) : often used in a depreciatory sense :—

Iron-*monger*, coster-*monger*, fish-*monger*, sausage-*monger*, *cheese-*monger*.

Depreciatory sense :—news-*monger*, gossip-*monger*, crotchet-*monger*, *grievance-*monger*, *ballad-*monger*, *scandal-*monger*, *verse-*monger* (*Ben Jonson*, = poet-aster, rhyme-ster).

I had rather be a kitten and cry mew
Than one of these same metre ballad-*mongers*.
Henry IV. iii. 1, 133, 134.

With eagle-pinion soaring to the skies,
Behold the ballad-*monger* Southey rise.—BYRON.

(10) **-red** (A.S. *rǽden*, rule, counsel, condition).— Once a common suffix, as in Mid. Eng. *frend-rede*, "friendship" ; *sib-rede*, "relationship" :—

Hat-*red*, kin-d-*red* (here the *d* is intrusive ; Mid. Eng. *kin-rede*).

Proper names.—Mild-*red* (mild in counsel), Ethel-*red* (noble in counsel), Un-*rede* (without counsel ; misspelt as Un-*ready*, as if it meant "ill-prepared").

Note.—The second half of *quand-ary*, Mid. Eng. *wand-reth*, is not now traced to this suffix.

(11) **-red** (A.S. *rǽd*, rate, reckoning) :—

Hund-*red* (from A.S. *hund* = Lat. *cent*-um, a hundred).

(12) **-ric** (A.S. *rice*, dominion, jurisdiction ; allied to Lat. *reg*-num, rule).—Once common, as in A.S. heofon-*rice* = kingdom of heaven ; A.S. abbod-*rice* = jurisdiction or office of abbot ; A.S. cyne-*rice*, Mid. Eng. king-*rice* = kingdom :—

*Bishop-*ric* (the only example left).

Note.—The *rake* of *drake* is not connected with *ric* ; see p. 92.

(13) **-ship** (A.S. *scipe*, form, shape, mode) : Abstract suffix. Attached chiefly to nouns, but also to adjectives, as in *hardship* :—

Friend-*ship*, hard-*ship*, lord-*ship*, town-*ship*, wor-*ship* (for "worth-ship"), clan-*ship*, fellow-*ship*, kin-*ship*.

In later use.—Owner-*ship*, *relation-*ship*, teacher-*ship*, lady-*ship*, *professor-*ship*, *author-*ship*, horseman-*ship*, workman-*ship*, *scholar-*ship*, *citizen-*ship*, *tutor-*ship*, *master-*ship*, steward-*ship*, son-*ship*, king-*ship*, *court-*ship*, *clerk-*ship*, *member-*ship*, etc.

Note.—"Land-*scape*" was borrowed from Dutch "land-*schap*" in the seventeenth century. Milton uses the word "land-*skip*" (A.S. *scipe*), but not "land-*scape*." *Ship*, however, is the only true form of the suffix in Mod. English.

(14) **-son** : a patronymic in the Northern dialect :—

Ander-*son*, Collin-*son*, David-*son*, etc.

(15) **-stead** (A.S. *stede*, a place) :—

Home-*stead*, bed-*stead*, in-*stead* of, Hamp-*stead*, Berkham-*stead*.

(16) **-tree** (A.S. *tréow* or *tréo*, sawn timber ; Scand. *tré*) :—

Axle-*tree*, roof-*tree*, rood-*tree* (=cross ; obsolete, though we still have the hymn beginning with, "Bound upon the accursëd *tree*").

(17) **-ward** (A.S. *weard*, guardian, keeper).—Once commonly used for a suffix, as in the obsolete words, ape-*ward*, hay-*ward*, bear-*ward*.

Ste-*ward* (from A.S. *stigo*, a sty or stall for keeping domesticated animals ; A.S. *stíweard* ; see § 239).

French form : *guard*. Hence van-*guard*, rear-*guard*, *black-*guard*.

(18) **wife** (A.S. *wíf*, woman, married or unmarried ; cf. the phrase "an old wife's tale" = an old woman's tale).

Fish-*wife* (a woman who sells fish), mid-*wife* (an attendant woman ; no connection with *meed*, pay, or reward ; from A.S. *mid* = with), house-*wife* (the woman of the house), huss-*y* or huzz-*y* (contracted forms of "house-*wife*").

(19) **-wright** (A.S. *wyrht-a*, a workman, from *wyrc*-an, to work, which by vowel-mutation is formed from A.S. *weorc*, work) :—

Ship-*wright*, wheel-*wright*, cart-*wright*.

247. Inseparable.—These suffixes may have once been separate and independent words, or have been derived from such. But the separate words, if they ever existed, cannot now be traced.

(20) **-d, -de** (sometimes of the same origin as the Past part. suffix of Weak verbs).—Nouns formed with this suffix usually denote the result of some action, and can generally be traced to some verbal stem :—

Bloo-*d* (cf. A.S. *blów*-an, to blow or bloom, the blood being the life), bran-*d* (either a fire-brand or a bright sword ; cf. A.S. *beorn*-an, to burn), brea-*d* (fermented flour; cf. A.S. *breów*-an, to brew), dee-*d* (the thing done), floo-*d* (cf. A.S. *flów*-an, to flow), gle-*de* (a burning coal; cf. A.S. *glów*-an, to glow), mea-*d* (the thing mown), see-*d* (the thing sown; cf. A.S. *sáw*-an), spee-*d* (cf. A.S. *spów*-an, to succeed), threa-*d* (cf. A.S. *þráw*-an, to twist or whirl), su-*ds* (things *sodden*; A.S. *seóð*-an, to seethe), shar-*d* or sher-*d* (the thing cut; A.S. *scear-d*).

Note.— -*d* or -*ed* or -*t* is also the suffix for forming the Past tense in verbs of the Weak conjugation; as *loved*, *dragged*, *slept*; but this is quite distinct from the suffix of the Past Participle; see § 3. The same suffix is sometimes attached to a foreign phrase such as Lat. *non plus*, so as to form a new verb, as in *nonpluss-ed*.

(21) **-el, -le, -l** (A.S. = *el*), sometimes used in the compound form **-er-el**. This suffix is used in two main senses—(*a*) in the sense of diminutive, though the diminutive sense has not always remained; (*b*) to denote the agent, instrument, or result of some action.

(*a*) *Diminutive* — **-el, -l, -le, -er-el**:—

Ax-*le*, bram-b-*le* (A.S. *bróm*, the plant broom; the *b* is intrusive), bund-*le* (A.S. *bund*, a bundle), freck-*le* (cf. *fleck*, a spot), gir-*l* (cf. *gör*, a child), heck-*le* or hack-*le* or hatch-*el* (dim. of *haak*, a hook or curved instrument), hov-*el* (dim. of A.S. *hof*, a house), hurd-*le* (from a base *hurd*; cf. *crat*-es, a hurdle), icic-*le* (A.S. *is-gic-el*; "gicel" means a small piece), kern-*el* (A.S. *corn*, grain), knuck-*le* (dim. of a base *knok*, a bone), snai-*l* (little creeper, dim. of A.S. *snag*-a (theoretical form; cf. *sneak*), nav-*el* (dim. of A.S. *naf*-a, the boss or nave of a wheel), nipp-*le* (dim. of *neb* or *nib*, a beak or nose), nodd-*le* (dim. of *knod*, a variant of *knot*, A.S. *cnott*-a), nozz-*le* (dim. of *nose*, A.S. *nos*-u), padd-*le*, perhaps dim. of *spade*), prick-*le* (dim. of *prick*), snaff-*le* (dim. of Dutch *snabbe*, bill, beak; cf. *snap*), spang-*le* (dim. of A.S. *spange*, a metal clasp), speck-*le* (dim. of *speck*), stick-*le* (dim. of *stick*), thrott-*le* (dim. of *throat*), wrink-*le* (a little twist; cf. *wring* (verb), to twist).

From Latin through Teutonic.—Sick-*le* (A.S. sic-*ol*, Lat. sec-*ula*; from verb *sec*-are, to cut, hence *seg*-ment), ti-*le* (A.S. tig-*el*, Lat. teg-*ula*; from verb *teg*-ere, to cover), mang-*le* (Dutch mang-*el*-en, to mangle; Lat. *mang-an-um*).

-erel (*often used in a depreciatory sense*).—Cock-*erel* (a young cock), pik-*erel* (a little pike), mong-*rel* (a puppy of mixed breed), *mack-*erel* (a fish with little spots), dott-*erel* (a kind of bird), dogg-*erel* (contemptible poetry; origin of base unknown), wast-*rel* (a spendthrift), gang-*rel* (a vagabond; used by Scott).

(*b*) *Agent, instrument, or result of action*:— **-el, -le, -l**:—

Aw-*l* (that which pierces; A.S. aw-*el*), bead-*le* (one who proclaims; A.S. *béod*-an, to bid[1]), beet-*le* (a heavy mallet, a thing that *beats*), beet-*le* (an insect, a thing that *bites*; A.S. *bít*-an, to bite), cripp-*le* (one who *creeps* or crawls; A.S. *créop*-an, to creep), gird-*le* (a thing that *girds*; A.S. *gyrd*-an), lad-*le* (that by which we *lade* or

[1] *Beadle* really came to us through Old Fr. *bedel*, a proclaimer or messenger; this came from a Frankish verb co-radical with *béod*-an.

dip out liquid), brid-*le*, sadd-*le* or sett-*le* (a thing to *sit* on), shov-*el* (a thing to *shove* with; A.S. *scof*-ian), shutt-*le* (a thing to *shoot* with; A.S. *scot*-ian), skitt-*le* (a variant of *shuttle*), spin-d-*le* (a thing to *spin* with; the *d* is intrusive), spitt-*le* (the result of *spitting*; A.S. *spitt*-an), sti-*le* (a thing to climb by; A.S. *stig*-an, to climb), swiv-*el* (that which turns on a pin; A.S. *swif*-an, to revolve), tack-*le* (that which *takes* or grasps), teas-*el* (a *teas*-er, a thing for *teas*-ing or carding wool), thim-b-*le* (a thing to use the *thumb* with; A.S. *þuma*; the *b* is intrusive), thist-*le* (tearer; from A.S. þist-*el*; base *thins*, to pull or tear), watt-*le* (the result of twining; base *wat*), tread-*le* or tredd-*le* (a thing to tread with), ridd-*le* (a large sieve), scoundr-*el*.

Monosyllabic forms ending in -l:—fow-*l* (that which flies; A.S. *fug*-ol), hai-*l* (A.S. *hag*-ol or *hag*-al), sai-*l* (that which endures the wind; A.S. *seg*-el), sou-*l* (A.S. *saw*-el), tai-*l* (A.S. *tæg*-el), stoo-*l* (that which *stands* firm; A.S. *stól*, a seat), pai-*l* (A.S. *pæg-el*).

Peculiar word:—

Riddle: A.S. *rǽdelse* (in which the *else* is a double suffix made up of -*el* and -*se*); from *rǽd*-an, to interpret.

(22) **-en, -n, -on**, in five different senses:—

(*a*) *Diminutive sense*: **-en** (A.S. *en*):—

Maid-*en* (A.S. mægd-*en*), chick-*en* (A.S. cic-*en*, parallel formation to a diminutive of *cocc*, a cock; of imitative origin).

Excluded words:—

Kitten: not a dim. of *cat*, but Eng. rendering of Fr. *kitoun*.

Mitten: from Old Fr. *mitaine*, a winter glove; origin doubtful.

Mizzen: from Old Fr. *misaine*, a sail in a ship; derived from Late Lat. *median*-us.[1]

Kitchen: Lat. *coquina*, a cooking-room; whence A.S. *cicen* for *cycen*.

(*b*) *Feminine suffix* **-en** (A.S. *-en*):—

Vix-*en* (A.S. fyx-*en*, Fem. of *fox*; on the mutation of *o*, see § 77, 6).

Obsolete words:—gyd-*en* (goddess), wylf-*en* (she-wolf), mynch-*en* (Fem. of *munec*, monk; cf. *Minchin* (now Mincing) Lane, "Nun's Lane").

(*c*) *Agent*: **-en, -n, -on**:—

Hav-*en* (that which holds, from the base of the verb *to have*), mai-*n* (A.S. *mæg*-en, that which *may* or is able), rai-*n* (that which moistens; cf. Lat. *rig*-are), su-*n* (that which begets; cf. Lat. so-*l*), thor-*n* (that which pierces), tok-*en* (that which points out), wag-*on* or wai-*n* (that which carries; cf. *weigh*).

---

[1] There is a difference between *Low* Latin and *Late* Latin. Low Latin is a French or Teutonic word turned into Latin,—not true Latin at all: thus *beghardus* (from which we get our word *beggar*) was coined from French, and the French word was formed from Teutonic elements. Late Latin is genuine Latin, though late, that is, post-classical; as *medi-anus*, a late form of *medius*.

(*d*) *Passive sense*, allied to Past part. suffix *-en* :—

Bair-*n* (that which is born), burd-*en* (that which is borne ; A.S. *byrð-en*, a load), loa-*n* (that which is lent).

(*e*) *Plural suffix :* **-en, -n** :—

Ox-*en*, childre-*n*, brethre-*n*, ki-*ne* (cý-*en*). Obs.: hose-*n*, shoo-*n*, etc.

(23) **-er, -r** (A.S. *-or, -er*) : instrument or result of action :—

Lai-*r* (a thing to *lie* on ; A.S. *leg-er*), stai-*r* (a thing to climb by ; A.S. *stig*-an, to climb) ; tim-b-*er* (material to build with ; Teutonic base, *tem*, to build ; cf. Lat. *dom*-us, a house), tind-*er* (anything to kindle a fire by ; A.S. *tend*-an, to light a spark), thun-d-*er* (A.S. *þun*-or, thunder ; *þun*-ian, to make a noise), wat-*er* (from a root *wad ;* cf. Eng. *wet*), wond-*er* (A.S. wund-*or*, that from which one turns aside ; allied to A.S. *wand*-ian, to turn aside), hung-*er* (A.S. hung-*or*, base *hung*-, to shrink), ang-*er* (base *ang*-, to be in pain ; cf. Lat. *ang*-or, Eng. *ang*-uish).

(24) **-er, -ier, -yer, -ar, -or.**—All these are different spellings of A.S. *-ere* or *-iere*, originally a male agent or doer. The spellings *-ier, -yer* have been extended by the influence of Anglo-French, which formed the suffix *-ier* from the Lat. suffix *-arius.*

-er :—rid-*er*, sing-*er*, mill-*er*, *min-*er*, robb-*er*, spid-*er* (for spinn-*er*), full-*er*, sow-*er*, angl-*er*, fish-*er*-man, garden-*er*, drumm-*er*, common-*er*, wagon-*er*, *villag-*er*, fing-*er* (=catch-*er* ; A.S. *fón*, pp. *fang*-en, to seize or catch ; cf. *fang*).

With Proper names :—London-*er*, British-*er* (United States).

Recent formations :—*photograph-*er*, *biograph-*er*.

-ar :—li-*ar*. (The *-ar* is due to such Romanic words as *schol-ar.*)

-or :—sail-*or*. (The *-or* is due to such Romanic words as *author*, or such parallel words as *visit-or, visit-er.*)

-ier, -yer :—cloth-*ier*, *court-*ier*, coll-*ier*, glaz-*ier*, graz-*ier*, hos-*ier*, law-*yer*, saw-*yer*.

Excluded word :—

Begg-ar[1] : Low Latin *beg-hard*-us, from which *begg-ar* has been formed by the loss of final *d*. Out of *beggar* we have coined the verb *beg*.

(25) **-ing** (A.S. *-ing*) *:* used for three different purposes :—

(*a*) *Diminutive*, but in this sense usually preceded by *l*, so as to make *ling*, which see below. It sometimes signifies a part of a whole.

Wild-*ing* (a wild or uncultivated plant), farth-*ing* (the *fourth* part of a whole), trith-*ing* (a *third* part of a whole ; cf. *Riding* of Yorkshire), *penn-*y* (A.S. pen-*ing*, a little pawn), stock-*ing* (dim. of *stock*), shill-*ing* (small money ; from base *shil*, to divide), lord-*ing* (a little lord), sweet-*ing* (a term of endearment).

Trip no further, pretty *sweeting*,
Journeys end in lovers' meeting.

[1] See footnote on previous page.

(*b*) *Patronymic*, son of; hence, belonging to:—

Edgar Athel-*ing* (Edgar the prince, from A.S. *æthele*, noble), k-*ing* (short for kin-*ing;* A.S. cyn-*ing*, man of noble kin), vik-*ing* (man of a *vik*, creek or bay), Brown-*ing*, Hard-*ing*, Mann-*ing*, Bark-*ing* (in Essex, the abode of the *Barkings*), Buck-*ing*-ham (the home or residence of the *Buckings*), Nott-*ing*-ham, Whitt-*ing*-ton, Kens-*ing*-ton.

(*c*) *Names of fish*:—

Whit-*ing* (named from its whiteness), herr-*ing* (the fish that comes in shoals; A.S. *hær*-ing, *hær* = army or host).

(26) **-ing** (A.S. *-ung* or *-ing*): usually attached to verb-stems, so as to form a noun. Sometimes, by analogy, attached to nouns and adverbs. Such nouns are usually abstract, since they denote the doing of something; but sometimes, especially in the Plural number, they are used in a concrete sense. (This must not be confounded with the Pres. Participial suffix *-ing*.)

Learn-*ing* (A.S. leorn-*ing* or leorn-*ung*), follow-*ing* (A.S. fylg-*ing*; it sometimes means a company of followers), *ceil-*ing* (the top lining of a room), *lin-*ing* (that which lines; cf. Lat. *lin*-um, flax; A.S. *lín*; Eng. *lin*-en), morn-*ing* (short for morwen-*ing*), even-*ing* (A.S. ǽfen-*ung*), leav-*ings* (scraps left uneaten), mend-*ings* (scraps to mend with), air-*ing* (taking the air), out-*ing*, off-*ing* (that part of the sea just *off* the shore), inn-*ings* (at cricket), borrow-*ings* (things borrowed), end-*ings* (final letters or syllables, suffixes), trapp-*ings* (things that trap or adorn).

(27) **-kin** (rare in A.S.; chiefly due to the borrowing of Middle Dutch words ending in *-ken*):—

(*a*) *Diminutive*, sometimes with a sense of contempt or endearment:—

Bump-*kin* or bum-*kin* (a thick-headed fellow; Dutch, *boom*, a bar or block), cana-*kin* (a small can or pot, *Shaks.*), cat-*kin* (lit. a little cat; a loose spike of flowers resembling a cat's tail), fir-*kin* (the fourth part of a barrel; Dutch, *vier*, four; cf. Eng. *farth*-ing), jer-*kin* (a jacket; dim. of Dutch *jurk*, a frock), kilder-*kin* (the eighth part of a vat; lit. a little child, from Dutch *kind*, a child), mani-*kin* or mana-*kin* (a little man), lamb-*kin* or lambi-*kin*, pip-*kin* (dim. of pipe), *nap-*kin* (dim. of Old Fr. *nape*, a cloth), lad-*kin* (dim. of *lad*), grimal-*kin* (cat; gray-Mald (= Maud, Matilda) -*kin*).

(*b*) *Patronymic*, son of:—

Peter-*kin* (hence Per-*kin*, Per-*kins*), Daw-*kin* (David-*kin*), Sim-*kin* (Simon-*kin*), Wil-*kins* (William-*kin*), Jen-*kins* (John-*kin*), Haw-*kins* (Hal- or Harry-*kin*).

Excluded word:—

Welkin, from A.S. *wolcn-u* (clouds), plural of *wolcen*, a cloud.

(28) **-ling** (double dim., *-el*, *-ing;* see (25) above).—Some-

times it implies endearment or contempt. Must not be confounded with adverbial suffix *-ling*.

With nouns.—Cod-*ling*, duck-*ling*, gos-*ling*, star-*ling* (base A.S. *stær*, the bird that we now call starling), lord-*ling*, fop-*ling*.

Indirectly related to the noun.—Strip-*ling* (a lad as thin as a *strip*, not grown out), seed-*ling* (a plant sprung from a seed), nest-*ling*, world-*ling*, sap-*ling*, wit-*ling* (one of very little wits), year-*ling*, ster-*ling* (short for Easter-*ling*, formerly a name for the Hanse merchants in London), dump-*ling*, ground-*ling* (a spectator in the pit of a theatre), *chamber-*lain* (for chamber-*ling*, a man of the chamber).

With adjectives.—Dar-*ling* (for *dear*-ling), first-*ling*, fat-*ling*, weak-*ling*, young-*ling*, fond-*ling*.

With verbs.—Ean-*ling* or yean-*ling* (a lamb just born, from *ean* or *yean*, to bring forth young), wean-*ling* (a child or other animal just weaned), shear-*ling* (a young sheep that has undergone one year's shearing), change-*ling*, found-*ling* (Mid. Eng. *fund*-ling, from *fund*-en, pp. of *find*), hire-*ling*, nurse-*ling*, shave-*ling* (a man shaved; hence a monk, so named in derision), starve-*ling*, suck-*ling*.

With adverbs.—Under-*ling*, hild-*ing* or hinder-*ling* (A.S. *hinder-ling*, one who goes behind or is inferior to his ancestors).

Note.—The *ling* looks so like a Pres. part. that it may have helped to form or suggest Frequentative verbs ending in *-le*; as *suckling*, *suckle*; *fondling*, *fondle*.

(29) **-m, -me -om** (A.S. *-m*, *-ma*; cf. Lat. *-mus*, cul-*mus*; Gr. *-mos*, cala-*mos*), generally attached to verb-stems :—

Bar-*m* (yeast, A.S. beor-*ma*; *bréow*-an, to brew), bar-*m* (lap, A.S. bear-*m*; *ber*-an, to bear), bes-*om* (A.S. bes-*ma*, a broom), bloo-*m* (*blów*-an, to bloom or flourish), blo-ss-*om* (*blów*-an, with double suffix *-st* and *-ma*; A.S. blo-*st-ma*), bos-*om* (A.S. bós-*ma*), doo-*m* (A.S. dó-*m*, a thing set or done; verb *dó-n*), fath-*om* (A.S. fæð-*m*; the base is allied to *pat* in "pat-ent," open; a fathom is the space reached by the extended arms), gloo-*m* or gloa-*m*-ing (dusk, twilight; A.S. gló-*m*; *glów*-an, to glow), hel-*m* or hel-*m*-et (armour for the head; A.S. hel-*m*; *hel*-an, to cover), na-*me* (A.S. na-*ma*; cf. Lat. no-*men*), qual-*m* (A.S. cweal-*m*, a pestilence; *cwel*-an, to cower or *quail*), sea-*m* (A.S. seá-*m*; verb *siw*-ian, to sew), stor-*m* (A.S. stor-*m*, lit. that which lays low; of the same root as Eng. *stir*, Lat. *ster*-n-ere), strea-*m* (A.S. streá-*m*, that which flows; base *stru*), swar-*m* (A.S. swear-*m*, that which hums; base *swar*, to hum), tea-*m* (A.S. teá-*m*, animals harnessed in a row; A.S. *téon*, to draw).

Excluded words:—

Beam, broom, harm, dream, foam; the *m* is radical.

Transom, lintel or cross-beam; corrupt. of Lat. *transtrum*.

Ransom, from an Old Fr. form of *redemption*.

Flotsam, jetsam, abridgments of Anglo-French *flotteson*, *jettison*. "Flotteson" is from the verb *floter*, to float, Late Lat. *fluctation*-em. *Jettison* is from Late Latin *jactation*-em, goods thrown out of a ship.

(30) **-nd, -and, -end** (the old suffix of the Pres. participle of

verbs: Northern dialect, *-and;* Midland, *-ende;* Southern, *-inde;* cf. Lat. *ant*-em, *ent*-em).

Err-*and* (a message, business; A.S. ær-*ende*, from a root *ar;* not from Lat. *err-ant-em*, though probably cognate), fie-*nd* (orig. Pres. part. of A.S. *féo-n*, to hate), frie-*nd* (orig. Pres. part. of A.S. *fréo-n*, to love), tid-*ings* (Southern Eng. tid-*ind*-e), wi-*nd* (A.S. wi-*nd*, from a root *wá*, to blow; cf. Lat. ve-*nt*-us), husba-*nd* (Scand. hús-bo-*nd*-i, house-dweller).

(31) **-ness** (A.S. *-nis*, *-nes*, *-ness;* this is a compound suffix, subdivisible into *n-es-s*, in which the *n* belonged originally to some noun stem, and the *es-s* is supposed to stand for *es-t* or *es-tu;* see below, No. 34): Abstract suffix, combined as freely with Romanic as with Teutonic stems.

With adjectives.—Dark-*ness*, liveli-*ness*, holi-*ness* (A.S. *hálig-nes*), *rigid-*ness*, *artful-*ness*, etc.

With nouns (rare).—Nothing-*ness*, wilder-*ness* (wild-deer-ness; A.S. *wilder-n*, belonging to wild animals).

With verb.—Wit-*ness* (concrete sense; testimony or testifier).

Excluded word.—

Harness: Old Fr. *harnois*, equipment; of the same root as *iron*.

(32) **-ock** (A.S. *-uc;* but probably the real suffix is *-c*, the *u* being either a separate suffix or part of the stem. In *stir-k*, dim. of *steer*, we have the original suffix *-c* or *-k*): diminutive suffix.

Bull-*ock*, hill-*ock*, humm-*ock* (dim. of *hump*), butt-*ock* (stem word *bot;* cf. "*butt*-end"), padd-*ock* (a toad; stem word *padd-a*), par-*k* (A.S. pearr-*oc;* cf. A.S. *sparr*-an, to enclose), padd-*ock* (merely a modern respelling of Mid. Eng. *parr-ok*, A.S. *pearr-oc*), pinn-*ock* (a hedge-sparrow; origin of base uncertain), matt-*ock* (A.S. matt-*uc*, Welsh mat-*og*, in which the *-og* is a cognate suffix), shamr-*ock* (Irish *seamr-og*).

Scotch dialect.—Wif-*ock*, ladd-*ock*, lass-*ock*, wif-*uk*-ie (double diminutive).

Proper names.—Poll-*ock* (from *Paul*), Bald-*ock* (from Bald-win), Matt-*ock* and Madd-*ox* (from *Matthew*), Wil-c-*ock* or Wil-c-*ox* (from *William*).

Excluded words:—

Puttock, futtocks (see § 239).

Fetlock: the *lock* or tuft of hair behind a horse's pastern-joint. *Fet* is allied to *foot*.

Hassock: Welsh *hesgog*, sedgy; material for covering a footstool.

Bannock, a cake: from Gaelic *bonnach*, a cake.

Cassock, from Fr. *casaque*, Ital. *casacca*, an outer coat.

Hammock: West Ind. *hamaca*.

Pibroch: Gael. *piobair* (piper), and *eachd* (merely a suffix expressing the same as *-age* in "bagg-*age*").

Havoc: old Fr. *havot*, by the substitution of *c* for *t;* see § 59.

(33) **-ow, -w** (A.S. *-we, -wa*) :—

The suffix appears as **-ow** *in*—

Mead-*ow* (A.S. mǽd-*we*, Dat. case of *mǽd-u*), barr-*ow* (wheel-barrow, that which bears; Mid. Eng. bar-*owe;* A.S. *ber*-an, to bear or carry), mall-*ow* (A.S. mal-*we;* cf. Lat. mal-*ua;* from a base *mal*, soft), shad-*ow* (A.S. *scead-we*, Dat. case of *scead-u*), sparr-*ow* (A.S. spear-*wa*, a flutterer; from root *spar*, to flutter), wid-*ow* (A.S. wid-*we*, wid-*uwe;* the base is *widh*), yarr-*ow* (the plant milfoil; that which dresses or puts in order; A.S. *gear-we*, yarrow; cf. A.S. *gear-u*, ready; cf. *gear*).

The suffix appears as **-w** *in*—

Stra-*w*, de-*w*, sno-*w*, cla-*w*, sto-*w* (a place).

Excluded words :—

Pillow, Lat. *pulvinus* (A.S. *pyle*, Mid. Eng. *pil-we*).

Window, elbow (see § 239).

(34) **-st, -t, -est** (A.S. *-st, -t, -est*) :—

Harv-*est* (A.S. hærf-*est*, autumn; orig. crop; from a base *carp;* cf. Lat. *carp*-ere, to gather in), earn-*est* (seriousness; cf. phrase "in earnest"; now used as adj.; base *arn*), twi-*st* (base *twi*, double), tru-*st* (base *true*), try-*st* (variant of *trust*), wris-*t* (base *wrīð*-an, to turn; "wrist" is that which turns the hand about), rus-*t* (lit. redness; A.S. *rūs-t;* of the same root as *red*, *rudd*-y), gri-*st* (corn to be ground; base *gri;* cf. "grind"), mi-*st* (A.S. mi-*st;* base A.S. *míg*-an, to sprinkle; cf. Lat. *ming*-ere), bla-*st* (base A.S. *bláw*-an, to blow).

Excluded word :—

Nest: A.S. *nest;* allied to Lat. *nis-dus*, which has become *nidus*. Traced to *ni-sd-as*, a place to sit down in.

(35) **-ster** (A.S. *-es-tre*, a compound suffix; cf. Lat. *-as*, and *-ter*, as in "poet-*aster*"). Used in A.S. solely as a Fem. suffix; but in Mid. Eng. this restricted use was soon set aside in many words. Now denotes trade, occupation, etc., and often in a depreciative sense.

Fem. suffix.—Spin-*ster* (the only word left): bæc-*estre*, tæp-*estre*, sæm-*estre*, etc., all of which were Fem. forms denoting female *baker*, *tapster*, *seamster*, are now obsolete.

Trade.—Huck-*ster* (orig. fem. of *huck*-er, now spelt as *hawk*-er), team-*ster*, tap-*ster*, malt-*ster*, song-*ster*, drug-*ster* (now superseded by drugg-*ist*), palmi-*ster*, up-hol(d)-*ster*-er (the final "er" is superfluous), Brew-*ster* (the trade term is now *brew-er*), Web-*ster* (weav-er).

Depreciatory sense.—Rhyme-*ster* (cf. Romanic equivalent poet-*aster*), young-*ster*, pun-*ster*, trick-*ster*, road-*ster*, tongue-*ster* (Tennyson), game-*ster*, fib-*ster*, slack-*ster*.

Other senses.—Hol-*ster* (leathern case for a pistol; A.S. *hel*-an, to cover), bol-*ster* (from its round shape; base, *bole*, cf. *boil*).

Excluded words :—

Monster: Lat. *monstrum*, a prodigy or monster.

Lobster: A.S. *loppestre*, a corrupt form of *lopust*, Lat. *locusta*,

Eng. *locust;* in which the voiceless *c* or *k* has been substituted for the voiceless *p* (see § 59).

Foster: A.S. *fóstor*, nourishment; allied to *fóda*, food.

(36) **-t, -th**; chiefly an Abstract suffix, but also used to denote the result of an action; attached to verbal stems, common nouns, and adjectives:—

-th:—bir-*th* (A.S. *ber*-an, to bear), ber-*th* (a variant of "birth"), bro-*th* (A.S. *breów*-an, to brew), grow-*th*, steal-*th*, til-*th*, tru-*th* or tro-*th* (A.S. *treówe*, true), dep-*th*, ru-*th* (rue), mon-*th* (A.S. *móna*, moon; *móna-ð*, a lunation), dea-*th* (A.S. *deá-ð*), dear-*th*, wid-*th*, heal-*th* (A.S. *hál*, whole), leng-*th*, slo-*th*, weal-*th*, streng-*th*, ki-*th* (kindred, acquaintance; A.S. cý*ð-ðe;* base *cúð*, known), warm-*th*, fil-*th* (A.S. *fúl*, foul), mir-*th* (A.S. *merg*, merry), you-*th* (young-*th*).

Note 1.—The earliest form of the suffix was *-ith*, which produced by means of the *i* the vowel-mutation in *length*, *breadth*, *strength* (from *long*, *broad*, *strong*); see § 77 (6).

Note 2.—Another form of this suffix was *-et* (not Diminutive like the Romanic *-et* in "eagl-*et*"): this appears in A.S. *þicc-et*, now written *thick-et*.

-t (this form of the suffix appears after *f*, *gh*, *n*, *r*, and *s*, because after these letters the original *t* is retained):—drough-*t* (A.S. *drýge;* hence *dry*), heigh-*t*, thef-*t*, drif-*t* (A.S. *dríf*-an, to drive), shrif-*t* (A.S. *shríf*-an, to impose a penance), rif-*t* (Scand. *rif*-a, to rive or tear), thrif-*t* (Scand. *thríf*-a, to thrive), ligh-*t* (A.S. leóh-*t;* cf. Lat. *luc*-em, light), haf-*t* (lit. that which is held, hence "handle"; A.S. *haf-*, base of *habb*-an, to hold), shaf-*t* (of a spear, lit. that which is *shaven* smooth: A.S. *scaf*-an, to shave), though-*t*, draugh-*t* or draf-*t* (A.S. *drag*-an, to draw), weigh-*t*, hef-*t* (a *heav*-ing), brun-*t* (Scand. *brun*-a, to advance with the speed of fire; cf. *burn*), fros-*t* (A.S. *freós*-an, to freeze), sleigh-*t* (of the same root as *sly*), fligh-*t*, migh-*t* (base A.S. *mæg*, may), gif-*t* (A.S. *gif*-an, to give).

Excluded word:—

Faith.—Anglo-Fr. *feid*, Lat. *fid*-es; the *d* was pronounced *th* from the first; but *d* was written, because Fr. had no such symbol as *th*.

(37) **-ter, -ther, -der** (A.S. *-dor*, *-ðer*, *-der*), agent or instrument:—

Mo-*ther*, bro-*ther*, daugh-*ter*, fa-*ther*, spi(n)-*der* (the insect that spins; the *n* is lost, as in *tooth*, Lat. *de*(*n*)*t*-em), rud-*der* (A.S. ró-*ðer*, rowing implement; A.S. *rów*-an, to row), fod-*der* (A.S. fód-*dor*, that which feeds), blad-*der* (base *bláw*-an, to blow), la-*ther* (A.S. leá-*ðor*, "that which washes"; A.S. *leáh*, lye, a mixture of ashes and water).

Abstract sense.—Laugh-*ter* (A.S. hleah-*tor*), slaugh-*ter* (base *slay;* A.S. *slah*-an, to kill), mur-*der* (A.S. mor-*ðor*).

(38) **-y, -ey, -ie** (A.S. *-ig*): generally diminutive:—

Bod-*y* (A.S. bod-*ig;* the root is unknown), hon-*ey* (A.S. hon-*ig*), iv-*y* (A.S. íf-*ig*), bird-*ie*, lass-*ie*, ladd-*ie*, dadd-*ie* or dadd-*y*, dogg-*ie*, wif-*ie*, don-k-*ey* (double diminutive; on *k* or *c*, see above under

-ock; perhaps from A.S. *dunn*, dun-coloured), Will-*ie*, Johnn-*y*, Bill-*y*, Bets-*ie*, Lizz-*ie*.

Excluded words:—

Puppy: Fr. *poupée*, Lat. *pupa*, a girl, doll.
Lady, loaf-kneader: A.S. *hláf*, a loaf; *dige*, kneader; see p. 175.
Monkey: Old Ital. *monicchio*, dim. of *mona*, an ape.
Money: Mid. Eng. *moneie*, Old Fr. *moneie*, Lat. *moneta*, a mint.
Valley: Old Fr. *valee*, Ital. *vallata*, formed like a valley.

(39) **-y** (A.S. *-e*, the place of action):—

Smith-*y* (A.S. smiðð-*e*, a smith's workshop), steth-*y* (a place for a steth or anvil).

Excluded word:—

Lobby: Low Lat. *lobia*, a gallery or covered way.

B. *Adjective-forming.*

248. Separable, or formerly separable:—

(1) **-fast** (A.S. *fæst*, firm, sure):—

Stead-*fast* (Mid. Eng. stede-*fast*, firm or fast in its stead or place), shame-*faced* (a misspelling for shame-*fast*, Mid. Eng. scham-*fast*, A.S. sceam-*fæst*).

(2) **-fold** (A.S. *feald*): added to cardinal numbers:—

Two-*fold*, three-*fold*, mani-*fold*, etc.

(3) **-ful** (A.S. *ful*, that is, full):—

With Abstract nouns.—Hope-*ful*, play-*ful*, fear-*ful*, dread-*ful*, regret-*ful*, truth-*ful*, etc. (Freely added to nouns of Romanic origin; as, power-*ful*, deceit-*ful*, grace-*ful*, grate-*ful*, etc.)

With Common noun.—Master-*ful* (not the same sense as master-*ly*).

With Concrete nouns, but without changing them into Adjectives.—Pocket-*ful* (a full or filled pocket, as much as would go into a pocket), hand-*ful*, mouth-*ful*, basket-*ful*, spoon-*ful*, etc.

Excluded words:—

Forget-ful: a mistaken rendering of A.S. *forgit-el*.
Wake-ful: a mistaken rendering of A.S. *wac-ol*.

(4) **-less** (A.S. *léas*, loose or free from; merely another form of the Scand. *lauss*; has no connection whatever with the comparative adjective or adverb *less*); it answers the purpose of a negative, and can be added to almost any noun in the language, of whatever origin:—

With nouns (very common).—Fear-*less*, hap-*less*, luck-*less*, care-*less*, *sense-*less*, hope-*less*, worth-*less*, *grace-*less*, etc.

With verbs (rare).—*Resist-*less*, *fade-*less*, *cease-*less*, reck-*less*.

To quarrel with your great oppose-*less* wills.—*King Lear*, iv. 6.

(5) **-like** (A.S. *líc*, like or similar).—In older words, the

suffix is usually *-ly*,—in more modern ones it is *-like*. For **-ly**, see below, § 249 (21).

-like: God-*like*, life-*like*, war-*like*, business-*like*, lady-*like*, workman-*like*, *scholar-*like*, home-*like*, war-*like*, *court-*like* (or court-*ly*), *saint-*like* (or saint-*ly*).

'Tis as man-*like* to bear extremities, as God-*like* to forgive.—FORD.

(6) **-right** (A.S. *riht*), direction :—

Up-*right*, down-*right*.

(7) **-some, -som** (A.S. *sum*, of the same root as Eng. *same*) :—

(*a*) *With nouns* :—burden-*some*, win-*some* (A.S. *wyn*, joy), *trouble-*some*, grue-*some*, hand-*some*, love-*some* (Tennyson), game-*some*, *toil-*some*, frolic-*some*, *mettle-*some*, *quarrel-*some*, etc.

(*b*) *With adjectives* :—glad-*some*, ful-*some*, whole-*some*, weari-*some*, lis-*som* (lithe-*some*), dark-*some* (in poetry), whole-*some*.

(*c*) *With Verbs* :—irk-*some*, tire-*some*, meddle-*some*, *noi-(an-noy) -*some*, loath-*some*, cumber-*some*, bux-*om* (A.S. *búg*-an, to bend; original meaning, pliant, yielding) :—

The joyous playmate of the *buxom* breeze.—COLERIDGE.

(8) **-teen** (A.S. *tén*, Eng. *ten*), ten by addition; **-ty** (A.S. *tig*), ten by multiplication :—

Four-*teen*, fif-*teen*, etc. ; twen-*ty* (A.S. twen-*tig*), thir-*ty*, for-*ty*, etc.

Note.—In thir-*teen* (=three+ten) the *r* has changed its place by metathesis. In fif-*teen* (=five+ten) the *v* has been changed to voiceless *f* by contact with voiceless *t*; see § 57, Rule I.

(9) **-ward** (A.S. *weard*, inclined or turned to; A.S. *weorth-an*, to become) :—

Fro-*ward* (A.S. from-*weard*, about to depart), way-*ward* (away-*ward*), for-*ward* (fore-*ward*), west-*ward*, home-*ward*, awk-*ward* (Mid. Eng. *auk* or *awk*, transverse, strange, crooked), back-*ward*, to-*ward* (the adjective is now used only in the negative form un-to-*ward*), in-*ward*, out-*ward*, up-*ward*, down-*ward*.

(10) **-wart** (A.S. *weorth*, Eng. *worth* or *worthy*) :—

Stal-*wart* (worthy of its *stǽl* or foundation ; cf. such compounds as sea-*worthy*, trust-*worthy*).

(11) **-wise** (A.S. *wís*, knowing, wise).

Right-*wise*, misspelt as right-*eous* (wise in what is right); weather-*wise*; penny-*wise*.

249. Inseparable :—

(12) **-d, -ed** (Past participial ending of Weak verbs; A.S. *-d*): applied also to noun-stems :—

Love-*d*, lai-*d*, *place-*d*, *pai-*d*, etc., nake-*d* (pp. of *nake*, to strip, which occurs in Chaucer), etc.

Bal-*d* (Celt. *bal*, a white streak), col-*d* (cf. Lat. *gel*-u, noun; *gel-id*-us, adjective), lou-*d* (A.S. hlú-*t*; cf. Gr. *klu-t*-os), wil-*d* (actuated by *will*, unrestrained), dea-*d* (A.S. *deád*), wretch-*ed* (made a wretch), letter-*ed*, boot-*ed* (with boots on), land-*ed*, gift-*ed*, ragg-*ed*, green-eye-*d*, etc.

(13) **-el, -le, -l** (A.S. *-ol, -el*).—There was once a large number of adjectives with this suffix; cf. *thanc-ol* (*thanc*, thought), *het-ol* (*het-e*, anger):—

Britt-*le* (A.S. *breót*-an, to break), fick-*le* (A.S. ge-*fic*, a fraud), id-*le* (A.S. íd-*el*), ev-*il* (A.S. yf-*el*), fou-*l* (A.S. fú-*l*: cf. Lat. *pu*-tridus), litt-*le* (A.S. lyt-*el*; base *lut*, to deceive; cf. *lout*), mick-*le* (A.S. myc-*el*; cf. Gr. *meg-al*-o, great), rake-*hell* (a misspelling of A.S. rak-*el*, rash, dissolute; cf. Eng. *rake*), scrann-*el* (Scand. *skran*, thin, lean, dry; cf. prov. Eng. *scrann-y*:—

Grate on their *scrannel* pipes of wretched straw.—MILTON'S *Lycidas*.

(14) **-en, -n** (Past participial suffix of Strong verbs):—

Drunk-*en*, hew-*n*, mow-*n*, bitt-*en*, forlor-*n* (A.S. *for-lor-en*, pp. of *for-leós*-an, to lose utterly, the *s* having become *r* as in "was," "were"), froz-*en* (A.S. *fror-en*, pp. of *freós*-an, to freeze; hence Eng. *frore*), op-*en* (lit. that which is *up*).

(15) **-en, -n** (A.S. *-en*, made of, pertaining to; cf. Lat. *-in*-us, as in "can-*in*-us," canine, pertaining to a dog):—

Beech-*en*, wood-*en*, earth-*en*, wheat-*en*, wooll-*en*, silk-*en*, lin-*en* (A.S. *lín*, flax; hence "lin-*en*" was orig. an adj.), leather-*n*, silvern-*n* (nearly obsolete), asp-*en* (now used as noun like "lin-*en*"), heath-*en* (man of the *heath*; now used chiefly as noun; cf. Lat. "pag-*an*-us," man of the village), oat-*en* (made of oat-straw), swi-*ne* (orig. an adjective, cf. Lat. su-*in*-us):—

Tempered to the *oaten* flute.—*Lycidas*.

Metaphorical sense:—gold-en (gold-like), braz-*en*, flax-*en*.

(16) **-er, -est** (signs of Comp. and Superl.):—

Hott-*er*, hott-*est*, etc.; be-*st* (short for bet-*est*).

(17) **-er, -r** (A.S. *-or, -er*).—Once rather common. Not connected with Comparative suffix:—

Bitt-*er* (A.S. bit-*or* or bit-*er*, biting; A.S. *bít*-an, to bite; cf. phrase "bitter words," that is, cutting words), slipp-*er*-y (A.S. slip-*or*, with added *y*; A.S. *slip*-an, to slip), fai-*r* (A.S. fæg-*er*).

(18) **-ern** (perhaps allied to "run"; A.S. *irn*-an): direction:—

North-*ern*, south-*ern*, east-*ern*, west-*ern*, north-*er*-ly (with *n* omitted), south-*er*-ly, etc.

(19) **-ing** (Pres. part. suffix; earliest form *-inde* (Southern dialect), which was superseded by *-inge, -ing*; see § 142):—

Charm-*ing*, astonish-*ing*, middl-*ing* (added to adj. *middle*).

Note.—The Pres. participles of Trans. verbs become like real adjectives, when they are not followed by an object:—

It astonishes me = it is astonishing (= wonderful, marvellous) *to* me.

(20) **-ish, -sh, -ch** (A.S. *-isc*; cf. Gr. *iskos*, Lat. *iscus*, Fr. *esque*): these are diminutive suffixes, and hence, like most other diminutive suffixes, *-ish* is largely used in a depreciatory sense.

(*a*) *Depreciatory.*—Rom-*ish*, book-*ish*, mawk-*ish*, out-land-*ish*, heathen-*ish*, woman-*ish* (fit for a woman, but not fit for a man), child-*ish*, baby-*ish*, *monk-*ish*, boy-*ish*, upp-*ish* (saucy, pert), boor-*ish*, churl-*ish*, *brut-*ish*, fiend-*ish*, wolf-*ish*, *devil-*ish*, swine-*ish*, snobb-*ish*, fopp-*ish*, *pop-*ish* (not the same sense as "papal"; cf. *popish* practices, *papal* supremacy), peev-*ish*, *hipp-*ish* (subject to morbid fancies, = hyp-*ish*: cf. *hypochondria*), etc.

(*b*) *Denoting a slight degree or tendency*:—

With adjectives.—*Pal-*ish*, redd-*ish*, dark-*ish*, *long-*ish*, old-*ish*, etc.

With verbs.—Snapp-*ish* (inclined to *snap*), mop-*ish*, fre-*sh* (A.S. *fersc*, perhaps by mutation of the *a* from *far-isc*, inclined to go or move; A.S. *far*-an, to go; as *fresh* water, opposed to stagnant water; cf. the phrase "*fresh* breeze," "*fresh*-et," a running stream).

With nouns.—Wasp-*ish*, fool-*ish*, swin-*ish*, slav-*ish*, prud-*ish*, rogu-*ish*.

(*c*) *Denoting language or nationality*:—

Ir-*ish*, Wel-*sh*, Fren-*ch* (Frank-*ish*), Span-*ish*, Turk-*ish*, Scot-*ch*.

(21) **-ly** (an unemphatic and "inseparable" form of A.S. *-lic*); see above, § 248 (5):—

With nouns.—God-*ly* (pious), woman-*ly*, man-*ly*, maiden-*ly*, ghost-*ly*, ghast-*ly*, *miser-*ly*, *scholar-*ly*, home-*ly*, sister-*ly*, brother-*ly*, father-*ly*, mother-*ly*, slattern-*ly*, friend-*ly*, *beggar-*ly*, un-manner-*ly*, love-*ly*, king-*ly*.

Note.—In all these words, if the stem has a good sense, *-ly* has a good sense also, and therefore is altogether opposed in meaning to *-ish*. Thus woman-*ly*" means "worthy of a woman," "befitting a woman"; but woman-*ish*" means "worthy of a woman, but *unworthy of a man*."

With adjectives.—Like-*ly* (probable), live-*ly*, lone-*ly*, etc.

Note.—The force of *-ly* in composition with adjectives usually implies "rather," in this point resembling *-ish* in the (*b*) sense:—

Sick-*ly* (rather sick, inclined to be sick), poor-*ly*, clean-*ly*, weak-*ly*, good-*ly*, kind-*ly*, elder-*ly* (not old, but rather old).

(22) **-most** (A.S. *mest*, compounded of one Superl. *-ma*, and another *-est*; see § 123, 4):—

Fore-*most*, in-*most*, ut-*most*, hind-*most*, etc.

(23) **-ow, -w** (A.S. *-we*, *-u*):—

Call-*ow* (A.S. cal-*u*), fall-*ow* (A.S. feal-*u*), mell-*ow* (Mercian mer-*we*), narr-*ow* (A. S. near-*u*), sall-*ow* (A.S. sal-*u*), yell-*ow*, fe-*w* (A.S. fea-*we*), ra-*w* (A.S. hreá-*we*), slo-*w*, tr-*ue* (A.S. treó-*we*), holl-*ow*.

(24) **-t, -th** (A.S. *-t*, *-ð*: other forms of the suffix *-d* described above under (12):—

(*a*) *-t*, chiefly preceded by verb-stems ending in *f*, *gh*, *l*, *n*, *p*, *s*:—
Clef-*t*, ref-*t*, lef-*t*, brough-*t*, bough-*t*, sough-*t*, taugh-*t*, wrough-*t*,

fel-*t*, spil-*t*, burn-*t*, mean-*t*, pen-*t*, kep-*t*, slep-*t*, swep-*t*, wep-*t*, bles-*t*, los-*t*, etc.

Swif-*t* (from a base *swip*, to revolve; cf. *swiv*-el), brigh-*t* (from a base *bhreg*; cf. Lat. *flag*-rare), ligh-*t*, righ-*t* (A.S. rih-*t*; base *reg*; cf. Lat. *rec*-tus), sligh-*t* (allied to *slay*, beaten flat), straigh-*t* (orig. pp. of *strecc*-an, to stretch), sal-*t* (orig. an adjective; A.S. *seal-t*, as in *sealt wæter*, salted water; root *sal*; cf. *sal*-ient, per *salt*-um = by a bound), tar-*t* (A.S. tear-*t*, tearing, bitter; A.S. *ter*-an, to tear), won-*t* (orig. pp. of A.S. *wun*-ian, to dwell).

(*b*) *-th*. (Chiefly used for forming Ordinals.)

Un-cou-*th* (A.S. cú-*ð*, pp. of *cunn*-an, to know; hence "uncouth" = unknown, strange, unsightly), sou-*th* (A.S. sú-*ð*, "the *sunned* quarter"). Four-*th* (A.S. feór-*þa*, made four), fif-*th*, etc. (cf. Lat. *t* in quar-*tus*, quin-*tus*).

Excluded word:—

Both: of Scand. origin. A.S. *bá*, two, both; cf. Lat. am-*bo*; *th* means "the," "they." Hence *both* means "the two."

(25) **-ther** (A.S. *-ðer*, Comparative suffix; see § 123, 3):—

O-*ther*, whe-*ther*, ei-*ther*, ne-*ther*, fur-*ther*, etc.

Excluded word:—

Rather: comparative of obsolescent *rathe* (early).

(26) **-y** (A.S. *-ig*; after the loss of *g* the *i* was changed to *y*):—

With nouns.—Might-*y*, craft-*y*, char-*y* (A.S. cear-*ig*, full of *care*; A.S. *cear-u*), sill-*y* (A.S. sæl-*ig*, lit. "time-*ly*,"—then "luck-*y*,"—lastly "simple"), storm-*y*, dusk-*y*, drear-*y* (A.S. dréor-*ig*; from *dréor*, gore), dought-*y* (A.S. *dýht-ig*; from the root *dúg*-an, to be sufficient), empt-*y* (A.S. æmt-*ig*, lit. full of leisure; A.S. *æmt*-a, leisure).

With verbal or other stems.—An-*y* (A.S. ǽn-*ig*, *án* = one; the vowel-mutation is caused by the *i* of *-ig*), man-*y* (A.S. man-*ig*), bus-*y* (A.S. *bys-ig*), dizz-*y* (A.S. dys-*ig*; cf. *doze*), heav-*y*, wear-*y* (A.S. wér-*ig*; A.S. *wór*, a moor, a swampy place), naught-*y* (cf. *naught*, from A.S. *ná wiht* = not a whit, nothing).

Excluded word:—

Every: a compound formed of A.S. *ǽfre*, ever, and *ælc*, each; § 122.

C. *Adverb-forming*; see §§ 157-164.

250. Separable, or formerly separable:—

(1) **-meal** (A.S. *mǽl*, a time, also time for food; hence the Eng. noun *meal*, a repast. The suffix *meal* is an abridged form of A.S. *mǽlum*, Dative Plural):—

*Piece-*meal* (the only example now in use, and this is a hybrid; in Mid. Eng. we had flok-*mele*, by flocks or companies; pound-*mele*, a pound at a time, etc.).

(2) **-ward, -wards** (A.S. *weard*, inclined or turned to; see *-ward* explained above as an adj. suffix). The adj. is usually *ward*, and the adv. *wards*. The *s* in *wards* is the Genitive adverbial suffix :—

Back-*ward* or back-*wards*, down-*ward* or down-*wards*, etc.

(3) **-way, -ways**: the *s*, as in the preceding, is an old Genitive or Possessive :—

Al-*way*, (more commonly) al-*ways*; straight-*way* (immediately), any-*way*, no-*way*. (In Mid. Eng. we had *alles weis* (Gen. adj. and Gen. noun) for *always*; and in A.S. *ealne weg* (Accus. case) for *alway.*)

(4) **-wise** (A.S. *wís*-e, Accus. *wís*-an, manner; the suffix in Mod. Eng. is from the Accusative. The Accus. wís-*an* became in Mid. Eng. wís-*e*, and finally *wise*) :—

No-*wise*, like-*wise*, cross-*wise*, class-*wise* name-*wise* (name by name), other-*wise*, etc.

251. Inseparable.—Some of these are due to case-endings, all of which, except the Genitive or Possessive case-endings, have become obsolete :—

(5) **-ly** (A.S. *líc-e*; *líc-e* was the A.S. form of Gothic *leïk-o*. In Mod. Eng. the *lic-e* is reduced to *-ly*. First the suffix *e* and then the final *c* fell off, leaving only *li* or *ly*) :—

Hard-*ly*, on-*ly*, bad-*ly*, utter-*ly*, happi-*ly*, etc.

(6) **-s, -ce, -se** (in A.S. *-es* is the Genitive suffix of Neuter and strong Masculine nouns; and this suffix was often used adverbially in A.S.; as dæg-*es*, by day) :—

El-*se* (A.S. ell-*es*), need-*s*, whil-*es*, on-*ce* (A.S. án-*es*), twi-*ce*, thri-*ce*, be-side-*s*, un-aware-*s*, alway-*s*, sometime-*s*, eft-soon-*s*, side-way-*s*, hen-*ce* (Mid. Eng. henn-*es*), then-*ce*, when-*ce* (Mid. Eng. whenn-*es*), wondrou-*s* (for wonder-*s*), again-*s*-t (the *t* has been added to Mid. Eng. ayein-*es*), among-*s*-t (formerly *amonges*).

(7) **-om** (A.S. *-um*, a suffix of the Dative case) :—

Whil-*om* (A.S. hwíl-*um*, at times), seld-*om* (A.S. seld-*um*).

(8) **-ling, -long** (A.S. *-lung-a*, later *-ling-a*, in which the *a* was a Genitive plural case-ending) :—

Dark-*ling*, grovel-*ling*, head-*long* (by the confounding of *ling* with *long*), side-*long* (now used as adj., as in the phrase "a side-long glance").

(9) **-er, -re** (A.S. *-re* and *-r*) :—

Ev-*er* (A.S. æf-*re*), nev-*er* (A.S. næf-*re*), he-*re* (A.S. *hér*), whe-*re* S. hwǽr).

(10) **-n** (A.S. *-nne*, probably allied to Accus. Masc. as in A.S. *hwo-ne*, Accus. Masc. of *hwá*, who :—

Whe-*n* (A.S. hwæ-*nne*), he-*n*-ce, tha-*n*, the-*n*, the-*n*-ce.

(11) **-ther** (A.S. *der*) :—

Hi-*ther*, thi-*ther*, whi-*ther*.

D. *Verb-forming.*

252. (1) **-en, -n** (a causal suffix, but formed from the *-en* of the pp. of Strong verbs). In A.S. there was a class of causal verbs formed by adding the causal Infin. suffix *-ian* to a Strong past part., as *ág(e)n-ian*, to make one's own, formed with pp. *ágen* (from which we get our adjective "own"). When the Infin. suffix was lost, no suffix was left but that of *-en* or *-n*. As this had been associated with causal verbs, it became an independent causal suffix, and can now be added to adjectives and even to nouns :—

With adjectives.—Bright-*en*, black-*en*, broad-*en*, cheap-*en*, dark-*en*, deaf-*en*, deep-*en*, fast-*en*, fresh-*en*, gladd-*en*, hard-*en*, less-*en*, lik-*en*, madd-*en*, moist-*en*, quick-*en*, redd-*en*, rip-*en*, rough-*en*, sadd-*en*, sharp-*en*, short-*en*, etc.

With nouns.—Fright-*en*, dis-heart-*en*, height-*en*, length-*en*, strength-*en*, hast-*en* (Intrans.), list-*en* (Intrans., from A.S., *hlyst*, a hearing), glist-*en* (Intrans., from a base *glis-*; cf. *glitt*-er).

Ow-*n*, drow-*n* (A.S. *drunc(e)n*-ian, the base *drunc-en* being pp. of *drinc*-an, to drink), faw-*n* (Scand. *fagna*, allied to A.S. *fægn*-ian, where *fægn* = fain, rejoiced), learn-*n* (A.S. *leorn*-ian, from the weak grade of the base of verb *lǽr*-an, to teach), op-*en* (A.S. *open*-ian).

(2) **-k** (frequentative or intensive) :—

Hear-*k*, hear-*k*-en, lur-*k* (Scand. *lure*, to lie in wait), scul-*k* (allied to *scowl*), smir-*k* (akin to *smile*, *smir*-en), stal-*k* (A.S. *stæl*, a stalk or stem; has been wrongly connected with the verb *steal*), wal-*k*, smir-*ch* (weakened form of "smer-*k*"; Mid. Eng. *smer*-en, to smear).

Doubtful word :—

Talk, generally considered to be a frequentative of *tell*, but without authority. In other Aryan languages the root *talc* or *talk* means to interpret; and the Russian verb *tolkováte* also means simply "to talk." In English it seems to be a frequentative of *tell* both in form and signification.

(3) **-se** (A.S. *s*-ian) :—

Clean-*se* (A.S. *clæne*, clean), rin-*se* (base *rein*, *ren*, pure), clap-*s* (now written *clasp*), grap-*s* (now written *grasp*, akin to grope), gap-*s* (now written *gasp*, base *gap*-a; cf. *gape*), glim-p-*se* (akin to *gleam*), bles-*s* (Mid. Eng. *blessen*, A.S. *blœ́d*-*s*-ian, formed from *blód* (blood), with the suffix *s*, the *o* being changed to *e* by mutation).

(4) **-sk** (of Scand. origin : *-sk* stands for *sik*, which means self. Hence verbs of this class are reflexive ; two only remain) :—

Ba-*sk* (bathe or warm oneself), bu-*sk* (prepare oneself).

(5) **-le, -el, -l** (chiefly frequentative ; sometimes denotes mere continuance, and sometimes has a causal or transitive force, as *start-le*, cause to start) :—

Verbs of imitative origin.—Babb-*le*, cack-*le*, crack-*le*, chuck-*le*, gabb-*le*, gigg-*le*, gobb-*le*, jang-*le*, jing-*le*, mumb-*le*, ratt-*le*, rumb-*le*, rust-*le*, tatt-*le*, tink-*le*, warb-*le*, whist-*le*.

The stem, to which the suffix is attached in the following examples, is usually a verb, which thereby becomes either frequentative or transitive. Sometimes, however, the stem is a noun or adj. :—

(*a*) *Frequentative, or denoting continuance* :—

Crimp-*le*	crimp (verb).	Rust-*le*	Sc. rust-a (to stir).
Crumb-*le*	crumb (noun).	Scramb-*le*	scrape (verb).
Crump-*le*	cramp (verb).	Scuff-*le* / Shuff-*le*	shove (verb).
Dabb-*le*	dab (verb).	Scutt-*le*	scud (verb).
Dazz-*le*	daze (verb).	Snar-*l*	sneer (verb).
Dibb-*le*	dip (verb).	Sniv-*el*	sniff (verb).
Draw-*l*	draw (verb).	Snuff-*le*	snuff (verb).
Dribb-*le*	drip (verb).	Spark-*le*	spark (noun).
Drizz-*le*	A.S. dréos-an.	Stradd-*le*	stride.
Dwind-*le*	A.S. dwín-an.	Strugg-*le*	Sc. strjúk-a, to strike.
Gamb-*le*	game (noun).	Stumb-*le*	Sc. stumr-a, to trip.
Gobb-*le*	Old Fr. gob-er.	Swadd-*le*	swathe (verb).
Grumb-*le*	Dutch grumm-en.	Tink-*le* / Ting-*le*	Mid. Eng. tink-en (to ring).
Hagg-*le*	hack (verb).	Tramp-*le*	tramp (verb).
Hobb-*le*	hop (verb).	Trund-*le*	trend (verb).
Humb-*le*	hum (verb).	Tumb-*le*	A.S. tumb-ian.
Hurt-*le* / Hur-*l*	hurt (verb).	Tuss-*le*	touse (verb).
Hust-*le*	Dutch hots or	Twink-*le*	Mid. Eng. twink-en.
Jing-*le*	jink, chink (verb).	Wabb-*le*	whap (verb).
Jogg-*le*	jog (verb).	Wadd-*le*	wade (verb).
Knee-*l*	knee (noun).	Wagg-*le*	wag (verb).
Mew-*l*	mew (verb).	Wai-*l*	woe (noun) ; A.S. *wá*.
Ming-*le*	A.S. meng-an.	Warb-*le* / Whir-*l*	Mid. Eng. wherf-en.
Mizz-*le*	mist (noun).	Wau-*l*	Mid. Eng. waw-en.
Nest-*le*	nest (noun).	Wrang-*le*	wring (verb).
Nibb-*le*	nip (verb).	Wrest-*le*	wrest (verb).
Padd-*le*	pat (verb).	Wrigg-*le*	A.S. wrig-ian.
Ramb-*le*	Mid.Eng.ram-en(roam).		
Rif-*le*	Sc. hríf-a (to seize).		

(*b*) *Causal* :—

Curd-*le*	curd (noun).	Start-*le*	start (verb).
*Jost-*le*	joust (verb).	Stif-*le*	stiff (adj.).

Excluded words :—

Tremble : Fr. *trembler*, Low Lat. *trem-ul-are*. The *b* in *tremble* is intrusive ; cf. *hum-b-le*, from Lat. *hum-il-is*.

Gargle : Old Fr. *gargouill-er*, to gargle.

Gurgle : Ital. *gorgoli-are*, to purl, bubble.

Grovel, darkle, sidle : verbs formed from the adverbs *grovling*, *darkling*, *side-long*, mistaken for Pres. participles.

Broil : this is a French frequentative ; *bruiller*, from Old Fr. *bruir*, to roast.

Travel: a doublet of *travail:* Ital. trav-*aglio*, Late Lat. trav-*aculum*.

(6) **-er, -r.** This is merely another form of *-el*, *-l*, the *l* being changed to *r*.

Verbs of imitative origin.—Chatt-*er*, clatt-*er*, jabb-*er*, gibb-*er*, patt-*er*, simm-*er*, titt-*er*, twitt-*er*, mutt-*er*, whisp-*er*.

Other verbs, formed with verbal or noun stems :—

Blund-*er*	Sc. blund-a (to doze).	Shimm-*er*	A.S. scím-an.
Blust-*er*	blast (noun).	Simp-*er*	Scand. simp (noun).
Clamb-*er*	clamb (verb).	Slabb-*er*	Dutch slav-en.
Falt-*er*	falt (base).	Slobb-*er*	Dutch slav-en.
Flick-*er*	flick (verb).	Be-spatt-*er*	spit (verb).
Flutt-*er*	A.S. flot-ian (float).	Splutt-*er*	spurt (verb).
Glimm-*er*	gleam (verb).	Sputt-*er*	spout (verb).
Glitt-*er*	glint (verb).	Stagg-*er*	Scand. staka (verb).
Hank-*er*	hang (verb).	Swagg-*er*	sway, swag.
Ling-*er*	Mid. Eng. leng-en.	Wand-*er*	wend, wind (verb).
Mutt-*er*	mut- (base).	Welt-*er*	A.S. wealt-an.
Patt-*er*	pat (verb).	Whimp-*er*	whine (verb).

(7) **-y** (the *i* of the Infin. suffix -*i*-an) :—

Ferr-*y* (A.S. fer-*i*-an), tarr-*y* (Mid. Eng. tar-*i*-en).

Note.—Verbs of Fr. origin sometimes formed the Infin. in *-ien* in Mid. Eng., as if they had come from Teut. *-ian*. The form *-ien* with the loss of *-en* became *-y ;* as Mid. Eng. sal-*i*-en, Mod. Eng. sall-*y* (Fr. saill-*i*-r, Lat. sal-*ire*) ; Mid. Eng. mar-*i*-en, Mod. Eng. marr-*y* (Fr. mar-*i*-er, Lat. marit-*are*).

CHAPTER X.—ROMANIC PREFIXES AND SUFFIXES.

Section 1.—Prefixes.

(*Hybrids are marked with an asterisk.*)

253. Romanic prefixes.—Under this heading we include Latin and neo-Latin (French).

(1) **A-, ab-, abs-** (*from, away*) :—

A-vert, *a*-vocation.

Ab-hor, *ab*-use, *ab*-ject, *ab*-normal, *ab*-surd, *ab*-olish.

Abs-tract, *abs*-ent, *abs*-tain, *abs*-cond.

(2) **Ad-** (to): by assimilation to the following consonant, it becomes *ab-*, *ac-*, *af-*, *ag-*, *al-*, *an-*, *ap-*, *ar-*, *as-*, *at-*, *a-*:—

Ad-vice, *ad*-join, *ad*-monish, *ad*-ore, *ad*-here, *ad*-opt, *ad*-apt.

Note.—*Advance*, *advantage* do not belong to this list. They are from Lat. *ab ante*; the *d* is intrusive. *Adventure* is from Fr. *aventure*, in which the *a* is a Fr. prefix from Lat. *ab*, which in English was wrongly changed to *ad*.

Ab-breviate (*ab*-brevi-are, Lat.), *a*-bridge (*a*-breg-ier, Fr.).
Ac-custom, *ac*-cept, *ac*-cede, *ac*-cent, *ac*-cuse.

Note.—"*A*(*c*)-know-ledge" is not a Romanic word. The *a* is a disguised form of the prefix *on*; see above, p. 186.

Af-flict, *af*-fix, *af*-fection, *af*-filiate, *af*-fable, *af*-firm.

Note.—*A*(*f*)-*ford* is from A.S. *ge-forth*-ian; *a*(*f*)-*fair* is from a Fr. phrase *à faire*, to do.

Ag-grieve, *ag*-gravate, *ag*-gregate, *ag*-gressor, *ag*-grandise.
Al-lege, *al*-lot, *al*-lure, *al*-low, *al*-lay, *al*-leviate, *al*-lude.
An-nounce, *an*-nex, *an*-nul, *an*-nihilate.
Ap-proach, *ap*-pear, *ap*-peal, *ap*-point, *ap*-pease, *ap*-pal, *ap*-pend.
Ar-rive, *ar*-rears, *ar*-rest, *ar*-rogant, *ar*-ray, *ar*-range.
As-sent, *as*-sert, *as*-sume, *as*-certain, *as*-sail, *as*-sign.
At-tend, *at*-tain, *at*-tract, **at*-tach, *at*-tempt, **at*-tack.
A- (final *d* being lost): *a*-spect, *a*-scribe, *a*-vow, **a*-bet, *a*-bate.

Note.—*Ad*- is not changed to *am*- before words beginning with *m*; cf. *ad*-monish. The first syllable of the words *ammunition* and *ammiral* (Milton) are not from Latin *ad*. "Ammunition" is from Old Fr. *amunition*, a soldiers' corruption due to putting *l'amunition* for *la munition*. "Ammiral" is from Arabic *amir*, prince; see p. 44.

(3) **Ambi-, amb-, am-** (*around, on both sides*):—

Ambi-dexterous, *amb*-iguous, *amb*-ient, *amb*-ition, *am*-putate.

(4) **Ante-, anti-, ant-** (*before*):—

Ante-cedent, *ante*-chamber, *ante*-diluvian, *ante*-date, **ante*-room.
Anti-cipate, *anci*-ent (Late Lat. *anti*-anus).
Ant-erior, *ant*-ique, *ant*-ic.

Note.—The form *anti* is the older form, from which *ante* resulted, the *e* being substituted for *i* through absence of emphasis; cf. *mare*, the sea; *mari*-time, pertaining to the sea. It is a cognate form to the Gr. prefix *anti*-, though the latter is differently used and means "against," in such words as *anti*-podes, etc.

(5) **Bene-** (*well*):—

Bene-fit, *bene*-volent, *bene*-diction, *ben*-ison, *bene*-ficence.

(6) **Bis-, bi-, bin-** (*twice, two*):—

Bis-cuit (Lat. *bis coctus*, twice cooked), *bis*-sextile (leap-year).
Bi-ped, *bi*-gamy, *bi*-lateral, *bi*-ennial, *bi*-sect, *bi*-lingual, **bi*-cycle (two-wheeled, Gr. *cyclos*, wheel), *bi*-as (origin of *as* unknown), *bi*-cuspid, *bi*-lateral.
Bin-ocular, *bin*-ary.

(7) **Circum-, circu-** (*around*) :—

Circum-spect, *circum*-ference, *circum*-stance, *circum*-vent.
Circu-it, *circu*-itous.

(8) **Con-** (*with*).—By assimilation to the following consonant it becomes *col-*, *com-*, *cor-*, or *co-*. Sometimes changed in French to *coun-* :—

Con-tend, *con*-trive, *con*-flict, *con*-verge, *con*-fluence, *con*-cur.
Col-lapse, *col*-lege, *col*-lect, *col*-league, *col*-lision, *col*-lusion.
Com-mand, *com*-mend, *com*-pete, *com*-bat, *com*-merce, *com*-pound.
Cor-rupt, *cor*-rect, *cor*-rode, *cor*-respond, *cor*-roborate.
Co-alesce, *co*-heir, *co*-habit, *co*-equal, *co*-gnate.
Coun-tenance, *coun*-cil, *coun*-sel.

(9) **Contra-, contro-, counter-**, through Fr. *contre* (against) :—

Contra-dict, *contr*(*a*)-ary, *contr*(*a*)-alto, *contra*-vene, *contra*-st.
Contro-vert, *contro*-versy.
Counter-act, *counter*-sign, *countr*-y, *counter*-feit, *counter*-part, *contr*-ol (short for *counter*-roll).

Note.—In the word "en-counter," "counter" appears a stem, to which *en-* is prefixed.

(10) **De** (*down, away from, astray, reversal, intensive*) :—

De (*down*) : *de*-scend, *de*-grade, *de*-crease, *de*-spair, *de*-jected.
De (*away from*) : *de*-part, *de*-duce, *de*-duct, *de*-camp, **de*-tach.
De (*astray*) : *de*-viate, *de*-lirious, *de*-bauch, *de*-lude, *de*-face.
De (*reversal*) : *de*-odorise, *de*-plete, *de*-cipher, *de*-merit.
De (*intensive*) : *de*-liver, *de*-clare, **de*-file, *de*-fend, *de*-fraud.

Note.—"De" (*down*) is sometimes used as the opposite to "ad" (*up*) : *de*-preciate, *ap*-preciate ; *de*-scend, *a*(*d*)-scend ; *de*-clivity, *ac*-clivity. Sometimes it is used as the opposite to *in-* or *en-* : *de*-crease, *in*-crease ; *de*-throne, *en*-throne ; *de*-camp, *en*-camp ; *de*-cline, *in*-cline ; *de*-sist, *in*-sist.

(11) **Demi-** (*half*) :—

Demi-god, *demi*-official, *demi*-quaver.

(12) **Dis-, di-** ; **dif-** before words beginning with *f* :—

Dis- (*asunder, aside*) : *dis*-tract, *dis*-member, *dis*-miss, *dis*-perse ; *di*-vert, *di*-gress, *di*-vorce ; *dif*-fer, *dif*-fuse, etc.

Dis- (*intensive*) : *dis*-annul, *dis*-sever, *di*-minish, *di*-rect.

Dis- (*oppositive* or *negative*) : con-fident, *dif*-fident ; facility or faculty, *dif*-ficulty ; ease, *dis*-ease ; please, *dis*-please ; honour, *dis*-honour ; like, *dis*-like ; agree, *dis*-agree ; repute, *dis*-repute ; grace, *dis*-grace ; console, *dis*-consolate ; figure, *dis*-figure-ment ; per-suade, *dis*-suade ; as-sent, *dis*-sent ; similar, *dis*-similar ; en-courage, *dis*-courage ; credit, *dis*-credit ; loyal, *dis*-loyal ; deign, *dis*-dain.

Dis- (*reversal, undoing something done*) : enchant, *dis*-enchant ; infect, *dis*-infect ; illusion, *dis*-illusion ; as-sociate, *dis*-sociate ; array, *dis*-array ; cover, *dis*-cover ; close, *dis*-close ; mount, *dis*-mount ; arm, *dis*-arm; appear, *dis*-appear; continue, *dis*-continue; charge, *dis*-charge; prove, *dis*-prove; burden, *dis*-burden; join, *dis*-join; colour, *dis*-colour; praise, *dis*-praise; en-franchise, *dis*-franchise.

(13) **Duo-, du-**, Fr. **deu-, do-, dou-** (*two*):—

Duo-decimal, *du*-et, *du*-el, *du*-al, *dou*-ble, *deu*-ce, *dou*-bt, *du*-bious, *do*-zen, *du*-plex, *du*-plicity.

(14) **Ex-, e-** (*off, out*): appears as *ef-*, when followed by *f*:—

Ex-ample, *ex*-alt, *ex*-tract, *ex*-pel, *ex*-amine, *ex*-plain.
E-ducate, *e*-lapse, *e*-normous, *e*-manate, *e*-rect, *e*-ject.
Ef-frontery, *ef*-fort, *ef*-fect, *ef*-fulgence, *ef*-fervesce.

Note.—Prefixed to a Common noun, the *ex* may denote loss of office; as, **ex*-king (dethroned king), *ex*-judge (retired or dismissed judge), *ex*-empress (formerly empress).

(15) **Extra-, exter-** (beyond). "Extra" is from *exter-â*, Abl. Fem. of *exter-us*:—

Extra-ordinary, *extra*-vagant, *extr*(*a*)-aneous, *exter*-nal, *exter*-ior, *extr*-eme.

(16) **For-** (Lat. *foris*, out of doors; Old Fr. *for-*):—

For-feit (Lat. *foris* factum), *for*-close (misspelt as *fore*-close).

(17) **In-** (*into*, or *in*, sometimes merely intensive): Fr. **en-, em-**; it becomes *il-*, *im-*, *ir-* before certain consonants, as shown below:—

In-ject, *in*-vade, *in*-vert, *in*-close, *in*-furiate, *in*-fest, *in*-vest.
Il-lusion, *il*-lustrate, *il*-lumine, *il*-lative, **il*-logical.
Im-merse, *im*-pute, *im*-pose, *im*-press, *im*-pede.
Ir-ruption, *ir*-rigate, *ir*-ritate, *ir*-radiate.
En- (Fr.): *en*-tice, *en*-treat, *en*-ter, *en*-title, *en*-quire, *en*-dued.
Em- (Fr.): *em*-ploy, *em*-bark, *em*-brace, *em*-barrass.

Note 1.—In some words the prefix may be spelt either as *in* or *en*: *in*-close or *en*-close, *in*-dorse or *en*-dorse, *in*-twine or *en*-twine, *in*-circle or *en*-circle, *im*-bitter or *em*-bitter, *in*-sure or *en*-sure.

Note 2.—This prefix, placed before a noun or adjective, makes a Transitive verb:—

**En*-dear, *en*-rich, *en*-large, **en*-slave, *en*-title, **em*-body, *im*-peril, *en*-danger, **en*-trust, **em*-bitter, **en*-thral.

Note 3.—The Fr. form *en-* must not be confounded with the Greek *en-*, as in the word "*en*-cyclical," though Gr. *en* and Lat. *in* are ultimately the same.

(18) **In** (not): it becomes *il-*, *im-*, *ir-*, *i-* before certain consonants:—

In-firm, *in*-tact (un-touched), *in*-fant (not speaking), *in*-decent.
Il-legal, *il*-literate, *il*-legible, *il*-liberal.
Im-passive, *im*-pious, *im*-pervious, *im*-penetrable, *im*-mense.
Ir-rational, *ir*-regular, *ir*-reverence, *ir*-religious.
I-gnoble, *i*-gnominy, *i*-gnorance.

Note.—The Lat. *in-* and the Eng. *un-* are equivalent; hence some words are spelt both ways: *in*-frequent or *un*-frequent, *in*-cautious or *un*-cautious, *in*-stable or *un*-stable, *in*-apt or *un*-apt, *in*-extinguishable or *un*-extinguishable.

(19) **Ind-, indi-** (Old Lat. *indo*, extension of *in;* cf. Gr. *endon*, within):—

Ind-igent, *ind*-i-genous.

(20) **Infra-, infer-** (*beneath*): *infra* is from *infer-â*, Fem. Abl. of *infer-us*:—

Infer-ior, *infer*-nal.

(21) **Inter-**, Fr. **entre-, enter-** (*between, among*). It appears sometimes as *intel-*:—

Inter-preter, *inter*-est, *inter*-course, *inter*-nal, *inter*-pose, *inter*-fere.
Intel-lect, *intel*-ligible.
Enter-tain, *enter*-prise.

(22) **Intro-, intra-** (*within*):—

Intro-duce, *intro*-spection, *intro*-it; *intra*-mural, *intra*-cellular, *intra*-dos (interior curve of an arch), *intra*-tropical; *intr*-insic.

(23) **Juxta-** (*close by*):—

Juxta-position, *joust* (verb), **jost*-le.

(24) **Male,- mali-**, Fr. **mal-** (*badly*):—

Male-factor, *male*-volence; *mali*-gnant; *mal*-ice, *mal*-content, *mal*-ady, *mal*-apert, *mal*-aria, *mal*-inger, *mal*-treat, *mal*-versation, *mal*-ison (=*male*-diction).

(25) **Mis** (from Lat. *minus*, badly; distinct from Eng. *mis-*):—

Mis-adventure, *mis*-chief, *mis*-alliance or *mes*-alliance, *mis*-chance, *mis*-count, *mis*-creant, *mis*-nomer.

(26) **Ne-, neg-** (not):—

Ne-farious, *ne*-uter; *neg*-otiate, *neg*-lect.

(27) **Non-** (not):—

Non-sense, *non*-entity, *non*-age, *non*-descript.

Note.—"Non" is much less emphatic than "in-" or "un-"; the former is merely *negative*, denoting the negation or absence of something; the latter is *positive*, and denotes the presence of some opposite quality. Compare *non*-religious with *ir*-religious (profane), *non*-Christian with *un*-Christian (unworthy of a Christian), *non*-famous with *in*-famous (disreputable), *non*-professional with *un*-professional (unworthy of the profession).

But in some words the *non* has become emphatic; as *non*-sense (rubbish), *non*-entity (one not worth noticing).

(28) **Ob-** (*in front of, against*): takes the form of *oc,- of-, op-, os-*, or *o-*, according to the consonant following:—

Ob-tuse, *ob*-it, *ob*-ituary, *ob*-ese, *ob*-durate, *ob*-ject, *ob*-long, *ob*-verse, *ob*-scure.

Oc-casion, *oc*-cur, *oc*-cupy, *oc*-cult, *oc*-ciput (back of the head).

Of-fer, *of*-ficer, *of*-fend.

Op-pose, *op*-portune, *op*-press, *op*-probrious.

Os- (from an older form *obs*-; cf. *ab*-, *abs*-) : *os*-tensible.

O-mit, *o*-mission.

(29) **Pene**- (almost) :—

Pen-ultimate, *pen*-insula.

(30) **Per**-, Fr. **par**- (through):—

Per-form, *per*-spire, **per*-haps, *per*-secute, *per*-fect, *pel*-lucid.

Par-don, *par*-amount, *par*-amour, *par*-son, *par*-lous (Shakspeare).

Note.—*Per*, like the Teutonic *for*, sometimes passes from the notion of *thoroughness* to that of going *too far* or going *in a wrong direction* :—

Per-vert, *per*-sist, *per*-jure, *per*-fidy, *per*-ish, *per*-dition.

(31) **Post**- (*after*) :—

Post-script, *post*-date, *post*-pone, *post*-humus (a misspelling for *post*-umous, Lat. *post*-umus, the superl. of *post*).

(32) **Por**- (from Old Lat. *port* ; cf. Eng. *forth*) :—

Por-tend, *pol*-lute.

(33) **Pos**-, **possi**-, **pot**- (Lat. *potis*, powerful) :—

Pos-sess, *pot*-ent, *possi*-ble (Lat. *possi*-bilis for *poti*-bilis).

(34) **Pre**- (Lat. *præ*, before) :—

Pre-caution, *pre*-pare, *pre*-dict, *pre*-ference, *pre*-tend.

(35) **Preter**- (beyond) :—

Preter-natural, *preter*-ite.

(36) **Pro**-, Fr. **pour**, whence *por*-, *pur*- (*before*, *instead of*) :—

Pro-fession, *pro*-ject, *pro*-pose, *pro*-noun, *pro*-mise, *pro*-ffer, *pro*-vident, *pro*(d)-igal.

Pour-tray, *por*-trait, *pur*-vey, *pur*-pose, *pur*-sue, *pur*-port, *pur*-loin.

(37) **Quad**-, **quadr**-, **quart**- (Lat. *quatuor*, *quart*-us, four, fourth) :—

Quadr-angle, *quadr*-ant, *quadr*-ennial, *quadr*-i-lateral, *quadr*-ille, *quadr*-oon (for *quart*-oon, one who is, in a fourth part, black), *quadr*-u-ped, *quadr*-u-ple, *quar*-antine (Lat. *quadraginta*, forty).

(38) **Quasi** (*as if, in pretence*) :—

Quasi-judge (a sham or pretended judge).

(39) **Quondam** (*formerly*) :—

Quondam-judge (a former judge).

(40) **Quinque** (*five*), **quintus** (*fifth*) :—

Quinqu-ennial (five-yearly), *quintu*-ple, *quint*-essence.

(41) **Re-** (*back, again*), **red-** (before vowels) :—

Re-course, *re*-act, **re*-new, *re*-join, **re*-fresh, **re*-call, **re*-cast, **re*-set, **re*-lay.

Red-eem, *red*-undant, *red*-olent, *red*-integration.

Note.—The insertion of a hyphen after *re* alters the sense by giving the prefix the emphatic sense of *again* or *afresh.*

Recover (get back), re-cover (cover again) ; redress (set right), re-dress (dress again) ; rejoin (answer), re-join (join again, return to) ; reform (make better), re-form (form again) ; recollect (remember), re-collect (collect again) ; recount (enumerate), re-count (count again) ; return (go or give back), re-turn (turn a second time) ; resort (go), re-sort (sort out afresh).

(42) **Retro-** (*back* or *backwards*) :—

Retro-cession, *retro*-grade, *retro*-spection, *retro*-version.

(43) **Se-** (*apart from*), **sed-** (before vowels) :—

Se-clude, *se*-parate, *se*-cret, *se*-cure, *se*-duce, *se*-cede, *sed*-ition.

(44) **Semi-** (*half; cf. demi-*) :—

Semi-circle, **semi*-colon, *semi*-breve.

(45) **Sine-** (*without*) :—

Sine-cure (pay without care or work).

(46) **Sub-** (*under*) : is changed to *suc-*, *suf-*, *sug-*, *sum-*, *sup-*, *sur-*, *sus-*, *su-*, according to the consonant following :—

Sub-ject, *sub*-join, *sub*-tend, *sub*-stance, *sub*-orn, *sub*-vert.
Suc-ceed, *suc*-cumb, *suc*-cour, *suc*-cinct.
Suf-fer, *suf*-focate, *suf*-fice, *suf*-frage, *suf*-fix, *suf*-fuse.
Sug-gest (Lat. *sub* + ger-ere, *gest*-us, to carry on).
Sum-mon (Lat. *sub* + *mon*-ere), *sum*-mons (noun, Fr. *semonce*).
Sup-port, *sup*-pose, *sup*-plant, *sup*-press, *sup*-plement.
Sur-reptitious, *sur*-rogate.
Sus-tain, *sus*-pend, *sus*-ceptible.
Su-spect (Lat. root, *spec*-ere, *spect*-us, to see).

Note 1.—When *sub* is prefixed to an adjective, it often means *rather* (cf. Eng. suffix *-ish*) ; *sub*-acid (slightly acid), *sub*-tropical (nearly tropical), *sub*-tepid (= warm-*ish*).

Note 2.—When *sub* is prefixed to a noun, it denotes subordination or inferiority of rank.

Sub-judge (the judge of a lower court), *sub*-committee (a smaller committee working under a larger one), *sub*-deputy, *sub*-heading, *sub*-division.

Note 3.—Sometimes *sub-* has a prepositional force ; as *sub*-montane (situated under mountains), *sub*-marine, *sub*-terranean, *sub*-lunary.

(47) **Subter-** (under) :—

Subter-fuge.

(48) **Super-**, Fr. **sur-** (*above, over, beyond*) :—

Super-lative, *super*-sede, *super*-ficial, *supr*-eme.

Sur-pass, *sur*-cease, *sur*-charge (an *over*-charge), *sur*-face, *sur*-vive, *sur*-mount, *sur*-prise, *sur*-name, *sur*-plus, *sur*-plice.

Note.—"Super" is sometimes used in the sense of "very," as *super*-fine = very fine; and sometimes in the sense of excess, as *super*-fluous.

(49) **Trans-, tra-** (across):—

Trans-mit, *trans*-it, *trans*-late, *trans*-form, *trans*-gress, *tran*(s)-scend.

Tra-duce, *tra*-verse, *tra*-ffic, *tra*-dition, *tra*-itor.

Prepositional force.—*Trans*-Atlantic (across the Atlantic), *trans*-Alpine, *trans*-continental, *trans*-oceanic.

(50) **Tri-**, Fr. **tre-** (*three, thrice*):—

Tri-angle, *tri*-ad, *tri*-colour, *tri*-pod, *tri*-dent, *tri*-ennial, etc.

Tre-ble, *tre*-foil.

(51) **Ultra-** (*beyond, excessively*):—

Prepositional: ultra-montane (beyond the mountains), *ultra*-marine (beyond the seas).

Qualifying: ultra-radical (an extreme radical), *ultra*-liberal, *ultra*-Tory.

(52) **Vice-**, Fr. **vis-** (*instead of*):—

Vice-roy, *vice*-regent, *vis*-count.

254. Disguised prefixes.—Mainly through French, the Latin prefixes named below have been disguised in the words placed after them:—

Ab-: *av*-aunt (Lat. *ab ante*), *v*-an-guard (Fr. *av*-ant-garde), *adv*-ance, *adv*-antage (the last two derived from Fr. av-ant, with an intrusive *d* between the *a* and the *v*).

Ad-: *ex*-cise (Dutch *aksiis*, corruption of Old Fr. *assise*, a tax; Lat. *ac* or *ad sess*-us, from *sedere*, to sit).

Ante-: *an*-cestor (Old Fr. *an*-cessour, Lat. *ante*-cessor, one who goes before).

Bi-: *ba*-lance (Fr. *ba*-lance, Lat. *bi*-lancem, having two scales).

Con-, co-: *cu*-stom (Lat. *con*-suetumen), **cur*-ry (verb, Old Fr. *con*-roi), *co*-ver (Old Fr. *co*-vrir; Lat. *co*-operire), *co*-venant (Old Fr. *con*-venant), *co*-unt (verb, Fr. *con*-ter, Lat. *com*-putare), *co*-unt (noun, Lat. *com*-item), *co*-uch (Old Fr. *cou*-cher; Lat. *col*-locare), *co*-st (Lat. *con*-stare), *co*-il and *cu*-ll (Old Fr. *coi*-ller, Lat. *col*-ligere), *co*-stive (Lat. *con*-stipatus), *cou*-sin (Lat. *con*-sobrinus), *cu*-rfew (O. Fr. *co*-vre-feu, covering of fires), *ke*-rchief (O. Fr. *co*-vre-chef, covering to the head).

De-: *di*-stil (Lat. *de*-stillare).

Dis-, di-: *des*-cant, *des*-habille (state of undress), *des*-sert (the last course at dinner), *de*-feat, *de*-fy, *de*-luge (Lat. *di*-luvium), *s*-pend (Lat. *dis*-pendere), *s*-tain (for *dis*-tain), *de*-bark (Fr. *des*-barquer, to land from a ship).

Ex-, e-: *a*-mend (but *e*-mendation), *a*-skance (*ex*-cansare, to go aslope), *a*-bash (Old Fr. *es-bahiss*, imitative), *af*-fray (Low Lat. *ex*-frediare), *a*-fraid (pp. of *affray*), *a*-ward (Old Fr. *es*- = Lat. *ex*- warder), *as*-tonish (Old Fr. *es*-tonner, Late Lat. *ex*-tonare), *es*-cape (Old Fr. *es*-caper, Lat. *ex* cappâ, out of one's cape), *es*-planade (Lat. *ex*-planata), *es*-cort (Lat. *ex*-correctus, corrigere), *es*-cheat (Old Fr. *es*-chet, pp. of *es*-cheoir, Lat. *ex*-cadere), *es*-say (Old Fr. *es*-sai, a trial; Low Lat. *ex*-agium, a trial of weight), *é*-carté (game at cards, lit. discarded), *is*-sue (Old. Fr. *is*-sué, Lat. *ex*-ire), *s*-ample (Mid. Eng. *s*-ample, Old Fr. *es*-semple, Lat. *ex*-emplum), *s*-carce (Late Lat. *scarpsus*, short for *ex*-cerptus), *s*-corch (Old Fr. *es*-corcher, Lat. *ex*-cortic-are, take off bark or rind), *s*-courge (Old Fr. *es*-corgie, Lat. *ex*-coriata, flayed off), *s*-ombre (*ex* umbrâ, from the shade), *s*-camp (Old Fr. *es*-camper), *s*-camper (run away), *s*-luice (Lat. *ex*-clusa), *s*-cour (*ex*-curare), *s*-ewer (*ex*-aquaria), *s*-prain (Old Fr. *es*-praindre, Lat. *ex*-primere), *s*-quare (Lat. *ex*-quadrare; so also *s*-quadron).

Extra-: *stra*-nge (Lat. *extr*(*a*)-aneous, external).

Intra-: *entr*-ails (Old Fr. *entr*-ailles, Late Lat. *intr*(*a*)-alia).

In- (*in*): *an*-oint (Lat. *in*-unctus), *am*-bush (Low Lat. *im*-boscare, to set in a bush).

In- (*not*): *en*-emy (Lat. *in*-imicus, hence *in*-imical).

Juxta-: *joust* (Late Lat. *juxt*-are), *jost*-le (freq. of Mid. Eng. *joust*-en).

Male-: *mau*-gre (in spite of, Fr. *mau* = Lat. male, *gré* = gratum, pleasing; hence the word means "ill-pleasing," "unpleasant").

Non-: *um*-pire (older form *num*-pire, Old Fr. *non*-per, peerless; *a numpire* was changed to *an umpire*).

Per-: *pil*-grim (Ital. *pellegrino*, Lat. *per*-egrinus), *par*-don (Lat. *per*-don-are), *par*-son (Lat. *per*-sona, lit. a mask, because an actor's voice *sounded through* it).

Post-: *pu*-ny or *puis*-ne (Old Fr. *puis*-né, Lat. *post*-natus, younger, born after; hence inferior in rank).

Pre-: *pre*-ach (Old Fr. *pre*-cher, Lat. *præ*-dicare), *pro*-vost (Old Fr. *pro*-vost or *pre*-vost, Lat. *præ*-positus, one placed in authority), *pr*-ize, *pr*-ison (Lat. *pre*-hensum, *pre*-hendere).

Pro-: *pr*-udent (short for Lat. *pro*-videntem, one who looks before him).

Re-: *re*(*n*)-der (Fr. *ren*-dre, Lat. *red*-dere), *r*-ally (Fr. *r*-allier, Lat. *re* + alligare, to bind together), *r*-ansom (Old. Fr. *ra*-enson, Lat. *red*-emptionem), *ru*-nagate (corrupt form of *re*-negade, Lat. *re*-negatus, pp. of *re*-negare, to deny one's faith).

Retro-: *rear*-guard (older spelling *rere*-ward), *rere*-dos.

Se-: *s*-ober (Lat. *se*, apart; *ebrius*, intoxicated), *s*-ure (a short form of *se*-cure (Lat. *se*-curus).

Semi-: *sin*-ciput (lit. half the head, the fore part of the head).

Sub-: *su*-dden (Lat. *sub*-itaneus, Old Fr. *so*-dain), *so*-journ (Lat. *sub* + diurn-are, to stay, Old Fr. *so*-journ-er), *s*-ombre (traced by some to *sub*-umbrâ, under the shade; but see above, under **Ex**).

Super-: *sopr*-ano, *sover*-eign (older and more correct spelling *sovr*-an; no connection with *reign*, nor with the last syllable of Lat. *supremus*; derived from Late Lat. super-*aneus*), *su*-zer-ain (Late Lat. *sur*-ser-anus, Lat. *su*-rsum for *sub*-versum, upwards).

Trans-: *tres*-pass, *tre*-ason, *tres*-tle (a support for a table, a cross-beam; Late Lat. *trans*-tellum, dim. of *trans*-trum), *tranc*-e (Fr. *trans*-e, Lat. *trans*-itum, a passing away).

Tri-: *tra*-mmel (Fr. *tra*-mail, Lat. *tri*+macula, a net).

Ultra-: *outr(a)*-age (Old Fr. *oltr*-age, cf. Ital. *oltr*-aggio, excessive violence).

SECTION 2.—SUFFIXES.

(*Hybrids are marked with an asterisk.*)

A. *Noun-forming.*

255. (1) **-ace** (Lat. *-atio*, *-atium* or *-acem*; Fr. *-ace*, *-asse*):—

Popul-*ace*, terr-*ace* (Fr. terr-*asse*), pinn-*ace*, grim-*ace*, men-*ace*, furn-*ace*, sol-*ace*, pref-*ace*, pal-*ace*, sp-*ace*.

Excluded word:—

Place: Fr. *place*, Lat. *platea*, Gr. *plateia*, Fem. adj. "broad."

(2) **-ade** (Lat. *-ata*, Fem. of *-atus*; Span. *-ada*; Ital. *-ata*; Fr. *-ade*): forms Collective and Common nouns:—

Collective.—Balustr-*ade* (a series of balusters or banisters), colonn-*ade* (a line of columns), cavalc-*ade* (procession of horsemen), brig-*ade*, cannon-*ade* (a general discharge of cannon), fusil-*ade*, ambusc-*ade* (troops in ambush), barric-*ade* (a line of barriers), stock-*ade* (a line of stocks), palis-*ade* (a fence of pales), arc-*ade* (a line of arches).

Common.—Casc-*ade*, crus-*ade*, tir-*ade*, masquer-*ade*, esplan-*ade*, rodomont-*ade*, par-*ade*, escal-*ade*, char-*ade*, pom-*ade*, promen-*ade*, broc-*ade*, seren-*ade*, com-*rade* (originally a company, now a person), gascon-*ade* (Abstr. boasting), pasquin-*ade*, lemon-*ade* (Fr. limon-*ade*, Sp. limon-*ada*), *block-*ade*, marmal-*ade*, faç-*ade* (the face of a building), enfil-*ade*, gren-*ade* (a war missile).

Recent formations.—Orange-*ade*, ginger-*ade* (formed on the analogy of lemon-*ade*).

Disguised suffix.—Ball-*ad* (Fr. ball-*ade*, from Late Lat. ball-*ata*, ball-*are*, to dance), cust-*ard* for crust-*ade* by misplacement of the *r*.

Naturalised words.—Arm-*ada* (Spanish, from Lat. arm-*ata*, classis), son-*ata* (Ital.).

Excluded word:—

Cockade, a knot of ribbon on a hat; Fr. coqu-*arde* (Fem. form of suffix *-ard*), Anglicised in imitation of words ending in *-ade*.

(3) **-ado** (Lat. *-atus*, Masc.; Span. *-ado*, Masc.; *-ada*, Fem.; in English *-ado* was sometimes wrongly put for Fem. *-ada*):—

Desper-*ado*, reneg-*ado* (now superseded by reneg-*ade*), carbon-*ado* (broiled meat, substituted for Fem. carbon-*ada*), bastin-*ado* (substituted for Fem. bastin-*ada*), arm-*ado* (twice used by Shakspeare for Fem. arm-*ada*, a fleet), torn-*ado* (a hurricane, substituted for Fem. torn-*ada*), brav-*ado* (for Span. brav-*ada*).

(4) **-age** (Lat. *-aticum*, Late Lat. *-agium*, Fr. *-age*):—

Collective sense.—Foli-*age*, plum-*age*, *bagg-*age*, herb-*age*, assembl-

age, mile-*age*, cord-*age*, lugg-*age*, tent-*age*, *equip-*age*, sewer-*age*, pastur-*age*.

Abstract sense.—Cour-*age*, *bond-*age*, *till-*age*, *pilot-*age*, vassal-*age*, pill-*age*, marri-*age*, hom-*age*, *shrink-*age*, tutel-*age*, person-*age* (sometimes = person), pilgrim-*age*, peer-*age*, *dot-*age*, pupil-*age*, brigand-*age*, *stopp-*age*, espion-*age*, *cribb-*age*, *cleav-*age*, *scrimm-*age*, wast-*age*, umbr-*age*, villen-*age*, tall-*age*, verbi-*age*.

Place of action, etc.—Hermit-*age*, *cott-*age*, parson-*age*, vill-*age*, anchor-*age*, pass-*age*, messu-*age*.

Result or instrument of action.—*Break-*age*, *leak-*age*, coin-*age*, *band-*age*, voy-*age*, outr-*age*, *age* (Lat. æt-*aticum*), mess-*age*, mortg-*age*, dam-*age*, rav-*age*, badin-*age*, persifl-*age*, ensil-*age*, *rumm-*age*, vint-*age*, append-*age*, appan-*age*, mir-*age*, advant-*age*, *herit-*age*, *pott-*age*, aver-*age*, vis-*age*.

Cost of action.—*Broker-*age*, post-*age*, cart-*age*, carri-*age*, *halt-*age*, *wharf-*age*, porter-*age*, pilot-*age*, salv-*age*, demurr-*age*, tonn-*age*, *pound-*age*, *freight-*age*.

Agent.—Sav-*age* (Lat. silv-*aticus*, Fr. *sauvage*, a man of the woods, spelt as *salvage* by Spenser), host-*age* (Late Lat. obsid-*aticus*, one who remains behind with the enemy).

Imitations:—

Langu-*age*, cabb-*age*, bever-*age*, surplus-*age*, saus-*age*.

Excluded words:—

Hemorrhage: the final *age* is here part of the root of a Greek verb.

Selvage, lit. "self-edge," from Old Dut. *self-egge*; hence the syllable -*age* in "selvage" is a corruption of *egge* or *edge*.

Presage: the final -*age* is part of the Lat. root *sag-ire*, to perceive; whence our own words "*sage*," "*sag*-acious."

Spinage, or **spinach**: Lat. spin-*aceus*, a vegetable with prickly leaf.

Rage, a variant of *rave*, Lat. *rab*-ies. "Outrage," however, is not compounded of *out* + *rage*, but is composed of the suffix *age* + Lat. *ultra*, beyond, Fr. *outr*-: outr-*age*.

(5) **-al, -als**, Lat. -*alis*, -*ale*, Sing., -*alia*, Neut. Plur.; hence the suffix -*als* has a plural form in English. But the Lat. -*alia* gradually became -*aille* in French, which is a Fem. Singular suffix; and this became -*al* or -*le* in English. Thus we have Lat. batt-*alia*, Old Fr. bat-*aille*, Mid. Eng. bat-*ail*, Mod. Eng. batt-*le*:—

-*als*: victu-*als*, nupti-*als*, spous-*als*, entr-*ails*, initi-*als*, credenti-*als*, vit-*als*.

-*al*, -*el*, -*le*: forms Abstract and other nouns.

With verbs.—Refus-*al*, *bestow-*al*, propos-*al*, tri-*al*, *upheav-*al*, committ-*al*, avow-*al*, *betroth-*al*, *withdraw-*al*, remov-*al*, arriv-*al*, surviv-*al*, repris-*al*, puzz-*le* (formerly spelt *apposayle*, *apposaile*, and *apposelle*; lit. that which *poses* or *puzzles*).[1]

---

[1] Skeat's *Student's Pastime*, ed. 1896, p. 131. Dr. Murray has further shown that *apposayle* was a substitute for *opposayle*, so that the original verb was *oppose*.

With nouns or adjectives.—Cardin-*al*, can-*al* (hence chann-*el*), minstr-*el* (Old Fr. *menestral*, Lat. *ministralis*, a retainer), capit-*al* (hence catt-*le*, chatt-*els*), memori-*al*, hospit-*al* (hence hot-*el*, host-*el*, and the now almost obsolete spitt-*le*, spit-*al*), fu-*el*, jew-*el* (Lat. joc-*ale*), rasc-*al*, festiv-*al*, miner-*al*, anim-*al*, funer-*al*, individu-*al*, gener-*al*, etc.

Excluded words:—

Vassal, from Low Lat. vass-*allus*, an extended form of *vassus*, a servant.

Wassail, from A.S. *wes hál*=be hale, words used in drinking to one's health.

Burial, A.S. *byrgels*, a tomb, Mid. Eng. *buriel.*

(6) **-an, -ain, -on, -en** (Lat. *-anus;* Fr. *-ain*, *-en*) denotes person or agent, though originally an adjective suffix :—

-an: public-*an*, civili-*an*, artis-*an*, partis-*an* (Late Lat. partiti-*anus*), de-*an* (Lat. dec-*anus*), sacrist-*an*, veter-*an*, republic-*an*, pag-*an*, histori-*an*, pedestri-*an*, equestri-*an*.

Religious titles: Wesley-*an*, Luther-*an*, Rom-*an*, Anglic-*an*, etc.

-ain: capt-*ain*, chief-*tain*, vill-*ain*, sover-*eign* (a misspelling for sover-*an*, Lat. super-*aneus*).

-on: sext-*on* (a variant of sacrist-*an*).

-en: citiz-*en*, deniz-*en*, scriv-*en*-er (Late Lat. scrib-*an*-us), *ward-*en* (variant of *guard-*ian*).

-ian.—The *i* is inserted before the *-an* for the sake of euphony :—

*Politic-*ian*, *rhetoric-*ian*, precis-*ian*, barbar-*ian*, statistic-*ian*, *guard-*ian*, *dialectic-*ian*, *logic-*ian*, *music-*ian*, etc.

Ital-*ian*, Russ-*ian*, Egypt-*ian*, Christ-*ian*, Norweg-*ian*, Eton-*ian*, Harrov-*ian*, etc.

-ana (Lat. Neut. Plur.), a new formation :—Shakspeari-*ana* (sayings of Shakspeare), Virgili-*ana*, Johnsoni-*ana*.

Note.—Camp-*aign* (military movements), champ-*aign* (open plain), champ-*agne* (kind of wine) are all derived from Latin "camp-*ania.*" Peas-*ant* (O.F. pais-*an*), anci-*ent* (Late Lat. anti-*anus*), pheas-*ant* (Lat. Phasi-*ana* avis, the bird of the river Phasis),—in all these words the final *t* is excrescent.

(7) **-ance, -ence** (Lat. *-antiam*, *-entiam;* French *-ance*); it forms Abstract nouns :—

-ance: arrog-*ance*, petul-*ance*, endur-*ance*, abund-*ance*, radi-*ance*, dist-*ance*, eleg-*ance*, ordin-*ance*, ordn-*ance*, circumst-*ance*, nuis-*ance* (Fr. nuis-*ance*, from *nuis-ant*, *nuire*, to hurt; Lat. *nocere*).

Modern formations:—griev-*ance*, brilli-*ance*, allegi-*ance*, repent-*ance*, assist-*ance*, resist-*ance*, complais-*ance*, compli-*ance*, defi-*ance*, alli-*ance*, *hindr-*ance* (for hinder-*ance*), *guid-*ance*, abey-*ance*, pleas-*ance*, acquaint-*ance*.

-ence: obedi-*ence* (cf. the Fr. form obeis-*ance*), influ-*ence*, innoc-*ence*, ess-*ence*, sil-*ence* (Lat. sil-*entium*), abs-*ence*, cad-*ence* (hence the Fr. form ch-*ance*), consequ-*ence*, provid-*ence* (hence prud-*ence*, Lat. prud-*entia*), penit-*ence* (hence the Fr. form pen-*ance*).

(8) **-ancy, -ency.**—A more modern form of *-ance* and *-ence* :—

-ancy : brilli-*ancy*, const-*ancy*, inf-*ancy*, piqu-*ancy*, ten-*ancy*, pli-*ancy*, occup-*ancy*.

-ency : excell-*ency*, reg-*ency*, urg-*ency*, frequ-*ency*, clem-*ency*, innoc-*ency*, insolv-*ency*, dec-*ency*, etc.

Concrete sense. Vac-*ancy* (a vacant place), emerg-*ency* (an emergent event), depend-*ency* (a country dependent on another), constitu-*ency* (a body of constituents).

(9) **-and, -end** (Lat. *-andus, -a, -um, -endus, -a, -um*, Gerun. Pass. ; Fr. *-ande* or *-ende*) :—

Divid-*end* (the thing to be divided), multiplic-*and*, vi-*and* or vi-*ands* (Lat. viv-*enda*), deod-*and*, leg-*end*, preb-*end*, reprim-*and* (a reproof, lit. a thing to be repressed), rever-*end* (usually an adject., Lat. rever-*endus*, Masc.), preb-*end*-ary, prov-*ende*-r (with intrusive *r*), lav-*ende*-r (Lat. *lavanda*, Fem.).

Naturalised Lat. words :—Memor-*andum*, add-*endum*, corrig-*endum*, ag-*endum*, not-*andum*, refer-*endum*.

Excluded words :—

Stipend, from Lat. stipend-*ium*, where the *end* is part of the stem and not a suffix.

Errand, husband : both Teutonic, see § 247 (30).

(10) **-ant, -and, -ent** (Lat. *-antem, -entem ;* Fr. *-ant*), originally an adject. suffix ; chiefly denotes an agent. Several nouns, which had no such suffix in Latin, have come to us through the French ; all these end in *ant* :—

-ant, -and : merch-*ant*, *ped-*ant* (from Greek root, *pais, paida*, a pupil), *tru-*ant* (from Celtic root), ten-*ant*, combat-*ant*, confid-*ant*, depend-*ant*, pend-*ant* (anything hanging), command-*ant*, claim-*ant*, brig-*and*, inhabit-*ant*, serv-*ant* (other forms, serje-*ant* or serge-*ant*), command-*ant*, attend-*ant*, assist-*ant*, miscre-*ant*, *warr-*ant*, coven-*ant*, inst-*ant*, remn-*ant* (a residue, the things remaining).

Naturalised Fr. word : savant (a man of research ; Fr. sav-oir, Lat. sap-ere).

Note.—On the Greek suffix **-ant**, see below.

-ent : stud-*ent*, tang-*ent*, rod-*ent*, torr-*ent*, cli-*ent*, pati-*ent* (sometimes adj.), reg-*ent*, presid-*ent*, depend-*ent*, adher-*ent*, etc.

Excluded words :—

Vagr-ant, confused with Lat. root *vag*, to wander, which would give vag-*antem ;* but probably from Anglo-French *wakerant*, from Old H. Germ. verb *walgern*, to walk about, the suffix *-ant* being added.

Peas-ant, from Old Fr. pais-*ant* or pais-*an*, another form of pag-*an*, the suffix being *-anus* and not *-antem*.

Pheas-ant ; here, too, the suffix is not *-antem*, but *ana ;* Lat. Phasi-*ana* avis, the bird of the river Phasis ; see above (6), *Note*.

(11) **-ar** (Lat. *-aris, -are*) ; originally an adj. suffix, and still chiefly so :—

Schol-*ar*, pill-*ar*.

(12) **-ard, -art** (Low Lat. *-ardus;* Old Fr. *-ard* or *-art*).—The real origin of the suffix is Teutonic *hart*, which found its way into Latin and French, and thence into English. It forms chiefly personal nouns, and often in a depreciatory sense, implying some kind of excess :—

Persons.—Drunk-*ard*, dull-*ard*, slugg-*ard* (Sc. *slouch*, *slug*), dot-*ard*, nigg-*ard*, cow-*ard* (Old Fr. cou-*ard*, a hare; from Lat. *cauda*, a tail; named from the bob-tailed hare), bast-*ard*, lagg-*ard*, Loll-*ard*, wiz-*ard* (= witt-ish-*ard*), bragg-*ard*, dast-*ard* (from *dazed*), stink-*ard*, blink-*ard*.

Other animals.—Buzz-*ard* (inferior falcon), mall-*ard* (a wild drake), reyn-*ard* (orig. a man's name), hagg-*ard* (a wild hawk), pilch-*ard*.

Inanimate things.—Blizz-*ard*, plac-*ard*, tank-*ard*, can-*ard*, pet-*ard*, poni-*ard*, billi-*ards*, stand-*ard*, must-*ard*.

Nation.—Spani-*ard*, Savoy-*ard*, Lomb-*ard*.

Recent formations.—Dynamit-*ard*, commun-*ard*.

Disguised suffixes.—Cock-*ade* (misspelling of Fr. coqu-*arde*). Cost-*er*-monger (for cost-*ard*, an apple). Duff-*er* (North. dowf-*art;* from *dowf*, stupid, dull; lit. *deaf*). Begg-*ar* (Low Lat. *beghardus;* see above, p. 191). Lumb-*er*-room (lit. a pawn-room; from Lomb-*ard*, because the first pawnbrokers were Lombards).

Excluded words :—

Lizard : Lat. *lacerta*, Fr. *lezard*, Mid. Eng. *lesarde*.

Orchard = *ort* + *yard*, "garden-garden" (see p. 179, **Orchard**).

Boulevard : a corruption of *bulwark*.

Custard, for *crustade*, by the shifting of *r;* Old Fr. *croustade* (a pie made of crust); Lat. *crustata*, from *crusta*, a crust.

Leopard = *leo* + *pardus*, a lion-pard.

Steward : A.S. *sti-weard*, keeper of sty or pen.

Bustard, formerly *bistarde*, Lat. *avis tarda*, a slow bird.

Scabbard : Old Fr. *escau-berc;* Mid. Eng. *scau-berc* or *scau-bert*, a protecting case, lit. a cover-cover.

Hazard : Span. *azar*, the die; the *d* is excrescent.

Gizzard : Mid. Eng. *gis-er*, with excrescent *d*.

Stalwart : Mid. Eng. *stal-worth*, foundation-worthy.

Sweetheart, wrongly supposed to be a corruption of *sweet-ard*. It is the modern form of Mid. Eng. *swete herte*, sweet heart.

Rampart, Old Fr. *rempar*, "put again in a state of defence." Lat. *re* (again) + *im* + *par*-are. The *t* is excrescent.

Haggard, lean, orig. *hagged;* confused with "haggard," a wild falcon.

Spikenard, for *spiked-nard*, nard furnished with spikes.

(13) **-ary, -aire, -ar, -er, -eer, -ier, -or** (Latin *-arius*, Fr. *-aire*, *-ier*, *-er*) : denotes agent or person :—

-ary : lapid-*ary*, statu-*ary*, dignit-*ary*, justici-*ary*, voluptu-*ary*, *ary*, mission-*ary*, vision-*ary*, secret-*ary*, sect-*ary*, *apothec-*ary*, *ry*, incendi-*ary*, advers-*ary*, antiqu-*ary*, prebend-*ary*, not-iss-*ary*, vot-*ary*, *dromed-*ary*, actu-*ary*, lumin-*ary*.

months : Janu-*ary*, Febru-*ary*.

-aire, -air: million-*aire*, doctrin-*aire*, cors-*air*.

-ar: vic-*ar*, Templ-*ar*, burs-*ar* (Late Lat. burs-*arius*, purse-bearer).

-er (often confused with Teutonic suffix *-er*): arch-*er* (arcu-*arius*), *butch-*er* (A.S. *bucca*, a male deer, buck), *butl-*er* (for bottl-*er*), messeng-*er*, scaveng-*er*, carpent-*er*, passeng-*er*, marin-*er*, practition-*er*, carpent-*er*, ush-*er* (osti-*arius*), port-*er*, falcon-*er*, treasur-*er*, forest-*er*, pension-*er*, offic-*er* (offici-*arius*), farm-*er* (Late Lat. firm-*arius*), sumpt-*er* (Late Lat. sagmat-*arius*), cutl-*er* (Lat. cultell-*arius*; *cultell*-um, dim. of *culter*, a coulter or knife), millin-*er* (probably from Milan-*arius*, a dealer in goods brought from Milan), partn-*er* (Late Lat. portion-*arius*).

-eer: volunt-*eer*, auction-*eer*, *crotchet-*eer*, mountain-*eer*, mutin-*eer*, pion-*eer*, pamphlet-*eer*, mulet-*eer*, car-*eer* (not denoting agent), target-*eer*, chariot-*eer*, buccan-*eer*, musket-*eer*.

-ier: financ-*ier*, cash-*ier*, sold-*ier* (Late Lat. solid-*arius*, a mercenary), brigad-*ier*, caval-*ier*, fusil-*ier*, prem-*ier* (prim-*arius*), farr-*ier* (ferr-*arius*), gondol-*ier*, cuirass-*ier*, cour-*ier*, terr-*ier* (terr-*arius*, a dog that pursues rabbits, etc., at their holes).

-or: chancell-*or* (cancell-*arius*), bachel-*or* (baccal-*arius*, lit. the holder of a small farm, called in Late Lat. *baccalaria*).

Notes on peculiar words:—messeng-*er*, scaveng-*er*, passeng-*er*,—in all these the *n* is intrusive: the original spellings were messag-*er*, etc.

Prison-*er*,—this has a Passive sense.

Practition-*er*, parishion-*er*, scriven-*er*,—in all these the final *-er* was unnecessary. "Practic-*ian*" and "parish-*ian*" were once used like "optic-*ian*." "Scriv-*en*-er" is from Late Lat. scrib-*anus*, a writer.

"Sorcer-*er*" contains a double suffix: a second *er* is added to Fr. sorc-*ier*, Lat. sort-i-*arius*.

"Squi-*re*," from Lat. scut-*arius* (one who has armorial bearings), contains this suffix in a very disguised form.

Excluded words:—

Burgl-ar, for burgl-*or*, Low Lat. burgul-*ator*.

Liar: the suffix *-ar* is a disguised form of Teutonic *-er*.

Begg-ar: the suffix is a disguised form of *-ard*; see (12).

(14) **-ary, -ier, -ar, -er** (Lat. *-arius, -a, -um*, Fr. *-iere*):—

Place or collection: libr-*ary*, gran-*ary* (hence garn-*er*), estu-*ary*, semin-*ary*, infirm-*ary*, penitenti-*ary*, reliqu-*ary* (a casket for relics), sanctu-*ary*, dispens-*ary*, avi-*ary*, ros-*ary*, vocabul-*ary*, arm-*ory* (for arm-*ary*, Late Lat. arm-*arium*).

Other senses: sal-*ary*, coroll-*ary*, centen-*ary*, annivers-*ary*, burgl-*ary*, diction-*ary*, dow-*ry* (Late Lat. dot-*arium*), vag-*ary*, summ-*ary*.

Latin suffix unchanged: aqu-*arium*, sanit-*arium*, honor-*arium*.

-ier: pann-*ier* (a bread basket, Lat. pan-*arium*), chandel-*ier* (a collection of lights).

-ar, -er: cell-*ar* (Lat. cell-*arium*), mort-*ar*, calend-*ar*, lard-*er*, sauc-*er*, dow-*er*, garn-*er* (variant of gran-*ary*), *gart-*er*, gutt-*er*, barri-*er*, pray-*er*, panni-*er*, antl-*er* (from Late Lat. ant-ocul-*arium*, that which is in front of the eye), osi-*er* (Late Lat. os-*aria*), ew-*er* (aqu-*aria*, a water-vessel), salt-cell-*ar* (salt-sal-*arium*, a salt-salt-holder; the first *salt* being superfluous).

Excluded words :—

Boundary, corruption of bound-*er-y*.

Attainder, **remainder**, **rejoinder**,—in these words the final *-er* represents the final **-re** of the French Infinitive ; as, attaind-*re*.

(15) **-arian** (double suffix, Lat. *-ari*, *-anus*): denotes agent or person :—

Libr-*arian*, *gramm-*arian*, latitudin-*arian*, veget-*arian*, valetudin-*arian*, octogen-*arian*, antiqu-*arium*, unit-*arian*.

(16) **-aster** (double suffix, *as-ter*, allied to Teut. *es-tre*): forms diminutive nouns in a depreciatory sense.

Poet-*aster*, ole-*aster* (the wild and inferior olive), critic-*aster* (lately coined by Swinburne), pil-*aster* (a small square pillar).

Excluded words :—

Disaster = evil star, from *dis* and *astrum*, a star.

Alabaster ; said to be derived from the name of a town in Egypt.

(17) **-ate** (from the Latin suffixes shown below) :—

(*a*) From *-atus*, *-ata* (Masc. or Fem. of Pass. part.).—Originally an adject. suffix, but also used for forming nouns :—

Advoc-*ate*, cur-*ate*, candid-*ate*, inebri-*ate*, leg-*ate*, associ-*ate*, reneg-*ade* (hence runag-*ate*, corrupted form, supposed to represent "run a gate").

(*b*) From *-atum* (Neuter of Pass. Part.) :—

Postul-*ate* (a thing demanded as needing no proof), f-*ate*.
Imitated in chemical terms : nitr-*ate*, hydr-*ate*, sulph-*ate*, etc.
Words with Lat. suffix : desider-*atum*, ultim-*atum*.

(*c*) From *-atem* (Accus. of nouns ending in *-as*): denoting agent :—

Prim-*ate*, magn-*ate*, potent-*ate*.

(*d*) From *-atus* (Fourth declension of Latin nouns): denoting office, and sometimes collection with office :—

Office : consul-*ate*, diacon-*ate*, noviti-*ate*, patriarch-*ate*, magistr-*ate* (originally the office, now the holder), st-*ate*, triumvir-*ate* (office or government of triumvirs).

Collection : episcop-*ate* (the body of bishops ; cf. episcop-*acy* for office of bishop), elector-*ate* (the whole body of electors in a constituency), *syndic-*ate*, sen-*ate*.

Excluded word :—

Apostate : from Greek apo-*stat*-es, one who stands off from or abandons his creed.

(18) **-cre**, **-chre** (Lat. *-crum*) :—

Lu-*cre*, sepul-*chre* (Mid. Eng. sepul-*cre*).

Excluded word :—

Massacre : origin uncertain ; the last syllable seems to have been formed in imitation of the above.

(19) **-cule, -cle** (Lat. *-culus*, *-cula*, *-culum*, Fr. *-cle*): a double Diminutive suffix, consisting of *cu* + *lus* (on *-ulus* see below, under (54) **-ule**):—

-cule: reti-*cule*, animal-*cule*, mole-*cule*.

Naturalised Latin words: curri-*culum*, reti-*culum*.

-cle: corpus-*cle*, clavi-*cle* (collar-bone, Lat. clavi-*cula*, dim. of clav-*is*), vesi-*cle*, parti-*cle*, arti-*cle*, versi-*cle*, pinna-*cle*, taberna-*cle*, cuti-*cle*, mus-*cle*, un-*cle* (from Lat. avun-*culus*), carbun-*cle*, pani-*cle*, ventri-*cle*, pelli-*cle*, gridd-*le* (Lat. crati-*culum*), bug-*le* (Lat. bu-*c-ulus*, double dim. of *bos*).

In a sense not Diminutive: mira-*cle* (hence marv-*el*), vehi-*cle*, specta-*cle*, obsta-*cle*, ora-*cle*, tenta-*cle* (feeler of an insect), recepta-*cle*, man-a-*cle*, ser-*aglio* (Ital. from Late Lat. ser-*aculum*).

Excluded words:—

Chronicle, from Greek root: Old Fr. *chronique*, Mid. Eng. *cronike*, *cronicle*. The *l* is intrusive.

Icicle = Anglo-Saxon *is* + *gicel*, a bit of ice; see § 247, (21) (*a*).

(20) **-cy, -sy, -acy** (Lat. *-tia*, as frequen-*tia*, frequen-*cy*):—

-acy.—Concrete nouns and adjectives ending in *-ate* were formed into Abstract nouns ending in *-acy*:—

Magistr-*ate*, magistr-*acy*. Prel-*ate*, prel-*acy*. Cur-*ate*, cur-*acy*. Advoc-*ate*, advoc-*acy*. Intim-*ate*, intim-*acy*. Intric-*ate*, intric-*acy*. Priv-*ate*, priv-*acy*. Accur-*ate*, accur-*acy*. Obstin-*ate*, obstin-*acy*. Delic-*ate*, delic-*acy*. Effemin-*ate*, effemin-*acy*. Degener-*ate*, degener-*acy*. Prim-*ate*, prim-*acy*. Leg-*ate*, leg-*acy* (Concrete).

By degrees *-acy*, *-cy*, and *-sy* became independent suffixes:—

-acy: pap-*acy*, lun-*acy*, suprem-*acy*, episcop-*acy*.

-cy: *idiot-*cy*, *bankrupt-*cy*, secre-*cy*, captain-*cy*, chaplain-*cy*, baronet-*cy*, ensign-*cy*, *diploma-*cy*.

-sy: minstrel-*sy*. (This must not be confounded with the Greek suffix *-sy*; as pal-*sy*.)

(21) **-ee, -ey, -y** (Lat. Masc. *-ātus*, Fr. *-é*, or Lat. Fem. *-āta*, Fr. *-ée* (see above (17) **-ate**):—

(*a*) *-ee*; denotes the person for whom or to whom something is done, the corresponding active agent being denoted by *-or* or *-er*:—

Legat-*ee*, trust-*ee*, grant-*ee*, pay-*ee*, nomin-*ee*, examin-*ee*, mortgag-*ee*, patent-*ee*, less-*ee*, transfer-*ee*, bail-*ee*, refer-*ee*, consign-*ee*, assign-*ee*.

Imitations: debauch-*ee*, devot-*ee*, absent-*ee*, refug-*ee*, grand-*ee*.

French words in current use: employ-*é*, protég-*é*, habitu-*é* (one habituated), rou-*é*.

(*b*) *-y -ey* (this is the weaker form of *-ee*):—

(1) From *-atus*, Masc. Pass. Part., Fr. *-é*:—deput-*y* (deput-*atus*, one deputed), attorn-*ey*, all-*y* (allig-*atus*, one bound).

(2) From *-atus*, Fr. *-é*, Fourth declension of Latin nouns:—clerg-*y* (cleric-*atus*), treat-*y* (tract-*atus*), duch-*y* (duc-*atus*), count-*y* (comit-

atus, Old Fr. comit-*é*, a province, the jurisdiction of a count), committ-*ee* (comit-*atus*, Fr. comit-*é*, as before, but in a Collective sense).

Note.—The spelling of *committee* has been influenced by the verb *commit.* Some derive the word from *commit;* according to this "committ-*ee*" would be a body of men to whom something is committed.

(3) From *-ata*, Fr. *-ée*, Fem. Pass. Part. :—jur-*y* (jur-*ata*), lev-*y*, arm-*y*, countr-*y* (contr-*ata*), entr-*y*, journ-*ey* (diurn-*ata*, hence journ-*al*), chimn-*ey* (camin-*ata*), destin-*y* (destin-*ata*), cov-*ey*, part-*y* (part-*ita*), vall-*ey* (from Ital. vall-*ata*, Fr. vall-*ée*, Lat. vall-*is*), jell-*y* (Lat. gel-*ata*, con-gealed, stiffened by cold), voll-*ey* (vol-*ata*), jett-*y* (O. F. jett-*ée*).

French word in current use :—soir-*ée* (evening party, Lat. ser-*ata*).

Excluded words :—

Guarantee has no connection with the suffix *-ee;* a misspelling of Old Fr. garant-*ie* (Eng. garrant-*y*), originally the Fem. of Pres. part. of French verb *garantir.*

Bull-y (Old Low Germ.); formerly spelt bull-*aert*, a noisy fellow.

Repartee : Fr. repart-*ie*, Fem. part. of repart-*ir*, to answer with a threat.

Enemy : Old Fr. *enemi*, Lat. *inimicus* (for the loss of *c*, see § 42).

(22) **-el, -le, -l, -elle** (Lat. *-ellus*, *-a*, *-um ;* Fr. *-el*, *-elle*) : Diminutive suffix. (Cognate with A.S. suffix **-el**, which see in p. 189.)

-el, *-le*, *-l* : lib-*el*, pomm-*el* (dim. of Lat. *pom*-um, an apple), timbr-*el* (dim. of *timbre*), pann-*el*, bush-*el* (Low Lat. busc-*ellus*), bow-*el* (Lat. bot-*ellum*), mod-*el*, citad-*el*, mors-*el*, chanc-*el* (Lat. canc-*elli*, Plural), chap-*el*, gru-*el* (Low Lat. grut-*ellum*, Old Fr. gru-*el*), scutt-*le* (scut-*ella*, dim. of *scutra*, a tray ; cf. "coal-scuttle"), lev-*el* (dim. of Lat. *libra*, a balance), lint-*el* (dim. of *limit*), eas-*el* (Lat. as-*ellus*), gao-*l* (dim. of *gabia*, a cage), tunn-*el* (dim. of Late Lat. *tunna*), petr-*el* (dim. of *Peter*, because that apostle walked on the waves), parc-*el* (Low Lat. partic-*ella*, French parc-*elle*), dams-*el* (Lat. dominic-*ella*, French damois-*elle*), cast-*le* (Lat. cast-*ellum*), vea-*l* (Lat. vit-*ellus*), mant-*le*, fard-*el* (bundle), mant-*el*, *shamb-*les* (A.S. scam-*el*, Lat. scab-*ellum*).

-ello, Ital. form of suffix : violon-c-*ello*, dim. of violone.

-elli, Ital. and Latin plural : vermi-c-*elli* (little worms).

-elle, *-ella* : bagat-*elle*, umbr-*ella*, cinder-*ella*, fem-*ale* (disguised form of Old Fr. fem-*elle*, Lat. fem-*ella*, dim. of *femina*).

Note.—In the words par-*c-el*, dam-*s-el*, vermi-*c-elli*, and violon-*c-ello*, we have two diminutive suffixes, *-c* and *-el*, *-elli* or *-ello.* Par-*c-el* = parti-*c-ella* ; dam-*s-el* = domini-*c-ella.*

Naturalised Latin word :—cereb-*ellum* (lobe of the hind or inferior brain).

(23) **-el, -le, -ele** (Lat. *-ela :* no connection with the preceding suffix) :—

Quarr-*el* (Lat. quer-*ela*), sequ-*el*, tut-*el*-age, client-*ele*, cand-*le*.

(24) **-en** (Lat. *-enus, -ena, -enum*) :—

Ali-*en* (ali-*enus*), ven-*om* (disguised from Lat- ven-*enum*), chai-*n* (from cat-*ena*).

(25) **-eny, -iny** (Lat. *-inium, -inia*) :—

Larc-*eny* (latroc-*inium*), ignom-*iny* (ignom-*inia*).

(26) **-ern** (Lat. *-erna*) :—

Tav-*ern*, cav-*ern*, lant-*ern*, cist-*ern*.

Excluded words :—

Lectern : from Late Lat. *lectrinum*, a reading-desk.
Postern : Old Fr. post-*erle*, Lat. post-*erula*, a little back door.
Slattern, an untidy woman ; Scand. origin.
Pastern, Old Fr. past-*uron ;* this joint was so called because a horse at *pasture* was tethered by the *pastern*.

(27) **-esse** (Gr. *-issa*, Late Lat. *-issa*, Fr. *-esse*) : feminine suffix :—

Poet-*ess*, count-*ess*, *godd-*ess*, *shepherd-*ess*, etc.

(28) **-ess** (Lat. *-ensis*, as in Carthageni-*ensis*) : originally an adjective suffix; see **-ese** in § 256 (15) :—

*Burg-*ess* (Low Lat. burg-*ensis*), *marqu-*ess* or *marqu-*is* (Low Lat. march-*ensis*, governor of a march or frontier).

(29) **-et, -ot, -ette, -let** (French *-et*, Fem. *-ette*, origin unknown. The form *-let* is compounded of two suffixes, *-l* and *-et*) : Diminutive suffix :—

-et : pell-*et*, *helm-*et* (A.S. *helm*, a covering), clar-*et*, bull-*et*, bill-*et*, tick-*et*, lanc-*et*, carp-*et*, coron-*et*, turr-*et*, *fresh-*et*, *pock-*et* (from pouch or poke), hatch-*et* (from hack), latch-*et*, pick-*et* (from peak), *brack-*et*, fill-*et*, clos-*et*, baron-*et*, trump-*et* (Fr. *trompe*), sonn-*et* (Ital. son-*etto*, dim. of *sound*, not of *song*), *cabin-*et*, sign-*et*, cask-*et*, *lock-*et*, isl-*et*, tabl-*et*, fever-*et*, cellar-*et*, flower-*et*, circl-*et*, bracel-*et* (from Old Fr. bracel), cors-*et*, cru-*et*, marmos-*et* (a small American ape), gull-*et* (from Old Fr. goule, the throat), cad-*et*, crotch-*et*, wick-*et* (small gate), varl-*et* (for vasl-*et*, dim. of vassal, servant ; also spelt val-*et*), banqu-*et* (but dim. force is now lost ; Fr. *banc*), jack-*et* (Old Fr. jaqu-*ette*, dim. of *jaque*, a coat of mail), agl-*et* (a tag of lace, dim. of Lat. *ac*-us, a needle), dock-*et*, *buck-*et* (A.S. *búc*, a pitcher), gobb-*et* (a mouthful, Old Fr. *gob*, a gulp), pack-*et*, *budg-*et*, bouqu-*et* (pronounced bookā), canzon-*et* (Ital. *canzone*, a hymn or song), gobl-*et* (dim. of Old Fr. *gobel*, a cup), mall-*et* (a small *mall* or wooden hammer), summ-*it* (Fr. somm-*et*), *ankl-et.

The young of animals :—pull-*et*, lever-*et* (from Lat. *lepor-em*), eagl-*et*, *owl-*et*, cygn-*et*.

Imitations without diminutive force :—castan-*et*, martin-*et*, doubl-*et*, riv-*et*.

Naturalised Ital. words :—stil-*etto*, fals-*etto*.

-ot : chari-*ot*, ball-*ot*, fag-*ot* (origin doubtful), piv-*ot* (dim. of *pipe*,

a peg), spig-*ot* (little spike), parr-*ot* (from Fr. Pierr-*ot*, little Peter), galli-*ot* (a small galley).

-ette: statu-*ette*, toil-*ette*, corv-*ette*, *coqu-*ette*, roul-*ette*, pirou-*ette*, silhou-*ette*, novel-*ette*, cigar-*ette*, *etiqu-*ette*, *waggon-*ette*, bassin-*ette* or -*et*, oper-*etta* (Ital. form of -*ette*), *Henri-*etta*, *brun-*ette*, gaz-*ette*, ros-*ette*, mignon-*ette*, vign-*ette*, paroqu-*ette*, pal-*ette*, bayon-*et* (orig. Fr. bayon-*ette*, from Bayonne, where the weapon was first made), quart-*ette*, quint-*ette*.

-let: *brook-*let*, *leaf-*let*, rivu-*let*, *root-*let*, *gaunt-*let* (Scand. *gant*, a glove), *ham-*let*, *stream-*let*, front-*let*, chap-*let*, *roof-*let*, cut-*let* (Fr. cote-*lette*, formerly coste-*lette*, a little rib), cabrio-*let*, flageo-*let*, tart-*let*, ring-*let* (once a little ring, now a curl of hair), trout-*let*, gob-*let* (Lat. *cupa*, *cup-ellus*, Fr. *gobel*, a vat).

Without diminutive force:—*arm-*let*, *neck-*let*, cors-*let*.

Peculiar words:—In "martlet" and "anklet" the suffix is -*et*, not -*let*: Ankl-*et*, martl-*et*. The last is a doublet to "martin-*et*," in which the *n* of the base has been changed to *l*; cf. *postern* from Old Fr. *posterne* or *posterle*, Lat. *posterula*.

Excluded words:—

Com-et: from Lat. com-*eta*, long-haired.
Cover-let is from Old French covre-*lit*, a *bed*-cover.
Out-let means a letting out (of the verb *let*).
Magnet: Lat. *magnetem* (lapidem), loadstone.
Gauntlet, misspelt for *gatlopp*; see § 239 under **Gauntlet**.
Racket or **raquet**, a battledore: Arab. *rāhat*.
Trivet: tri-*vet*, Latin tri-*pod*-em, A.S. tre-*fet*.

(30) **-ic** (Lat. *-icus*, *-ica*, *-icum*; Greek *-ikos*): originally an adjective suffix, and chiefly so still:—

Persons:—fanat-*ic*, lunat-*ic*, mim-*ic*, scept-*ic*, rust-*ic*.
Things:—mus-*ic*, fabr-*ic*, mosa-*ic* (Lat. musa), ton-*ic*, por-*ch* (Lat. port-*icus*, for-*ge* (Lat. fabr-*ica*), sil-*k* and ser-*ge* (Lat. ser-*icum*), per-*ch* (Lat. per-*ca*).
Disguised suffix:—enemy (Lat. inim-*icus*).

(31) **-ice, -ish** (Lat. *-ix*, *-icem*):—

Pom-*ice*, rad-*ish*, ra-*ce* (from rad-*icem*), cocka-tr-*ice*, cica-tr-*ice*.
Naturalised Lat. words in -ix or -ex:—append-*ix*, ind-*ex*, vert-*ex*, ap-*ex*, vort-*ex*, ma-tr-*ix*. *Feminine suffixes:*—testa-tr-*ix*, execu-tr-*ix*.

(32) **-ice, -ise, -ess, -esse** (from Lat. suffixes named below):—

(*a*) From *-itius*, *-itium*, Masc. or Neuter; Fr. *-ice*:—

Nov-*ice*, apprent-*ice*, surpl-*ice* (Lat super + pell-*icius*), solst-*ice*.

(*b*) From *-itia* or *-ities*, Fr. *-esse*: Abstract suffix:—

-ice: serv-*ice*, just-*ice*, mal-*ice*, avar-*ice*, not-*ice*, coward-*ice*, pent-*house* (corruption of Fr. pent-*ice*; see § 240 under **Penthouse**).
-ise: exerc-*ise*, franch-*ise*, merchand-*ise*, treat-*ise*.
-ess: prow-*ess*, larg-*ess*, dur-*ess*, lach-*es* (Fr. lach-*esse*), car-*ess*, fin-*esse*, dis-tr-*ess*, rich-*es* (Fr. rich-*esse*, mistaken for an Eng. Plural), fortr-*ess* (Old Fr. fort-el-*esce*, Late Lat. fort-al-*itia*).

Excluded words:—

Pract-ice: of Greek origin, through Fr. pract-*ique*.

Advice: through Old Fr. *à vis*, according to my opinion.

Amice: from Lat. am-*ictus*, Fr. am-*ict*, Old Fr. am-*is*.

Crevice: Old Fr. crev-*asse*, Lat. crep-*acea*.

Pumice: Lat. pum-*icem*.

Bodice (stays): corruption of bod-*ies*, which was the old spelling, plural of *body*.

Caprice: from Ital capr-*iccio*, a whim; Fr. *caprice*.

Burgess, marquis: the suffixes in these words are traced to the Lat. suffix -*ensis* (stems, *burg*, a fort, and *march*, a frontier). See (28).

(33) **-il, -ile, -le** (Lat. -*illus*, -*illa*, -*illum*; Span. -*illo*, -*illa*): Diminutive suffix:—

Pup-*il* (dim. of Lat. pup-*us*, a boy), codic-*il*, sea-*l* (sig-*illum*), trif-*le*, pest-*le* (Lat. pist-*illum*) ais-*le* (Lat. ax-*illa*), imbec-*ile* (Lat. imbec-*illus*), past-*ille* (Lat. past-*illum*), quadr-*ille*, tass-*le* (tax-*illum*), kett-*le* (cat-*illus*).

Naturalised Lat. words:—max-*illa*, bac-*illus*.

Spanish form of suffix:—peccad-*illo*, armad-*illo*, punct-*ilio* (corruption of Spanish punt-*illo*), guer-*illa* (little war, irregular fighting).

Note.—The suffix -*il* or -*el* is sometimes formed from the double diminutive suffix -*ic-ulus*, -*a*, -*um*, in which the *c* has been lost in passing through French.

Lent-*il* (Lat. lenti-*c-ula*), per-*il* (Lat. per-*ic-ulum*, danger), appar-*el* (for appar-*il*, Lat. appar-*ic-ulus*), fenn-*el* (Lat. fœn-*ic-ulum*).

Excluded words:—

Postil: probably an abridgment of *post illa verba*.

Devil: Greek *diabolos*, A.S. *deóful* or *deófol*.

Missile: Lat. *miss-il-e*, an arrow or lance; Lat. suffix -*ilis*, -*ile*.

Foss-il: Lat. *foss-il-e*, that which may be dug out.

(34) **-ine, -in** (Lat. -*inus*, -*ina*, -*inum*; Fr. -*ine*): originally an adjective suffix, and still chiefly so:—

Persons or other animals:—libert-*ine*, concub-*ine*, gobl-*in*, Carol-*ine*, pilgr-*im* (Ital. pellegr-*ino*), dolph-*in*, verm-*in* (from Lat. verm-*inus*, of the root *vermis*, a worm); cous-*in* (Fr. cous-*in*, Late Lat. cos-*inus*, short form of consobr-*inus*, the child of a mother's sister; wrongly traced to Lat. *consanguineus*).

Things:—columb-*ine*, cuis-*ine*, doctr-*ine*, eglant-*ine*, rout-*ine*, *tambour-*ine*, fam-*ine*, medic-*ine*, rav-*ine*, quarant-*ine*, viol-*in*, res-*in* or ros-*in*, carb-*ine* (once denoted person), bullet-*in*.

Chemical words, etc.:—quin-*ine*, vacc-*ine*, turpent-*ine*, case-*in*, iod-*ine*, peps-*ine*, floril-*ine*, gelat-*ine*, glycer-*ine*, coca-*ine*.

Newly-formed trade words:—brilliant-*ine*, butter-*ine*, margar-*ine*.

Excluded words:—

Paraffine, from Lat. *parum* (=little)+*affinis*: so named from its having very little affinity with alkali.

Sardine, a small kind of fish. From *Sardin-ia*, the island.

(35) **-in**, Lat. *-inem*, Accus. of *-o*) :—

Marg-in (Lat. marg-*inem*), orig-*in*, virg-*in*.

Excluded word :—

Chagrin, a French word, once said to be of Turkish origin.

(36) **-ion, -on** (Lat. *-ionem*, Accus. of *-io*) : Abstract suffix, but often has a Concrete sense. Whenever this suffix is preceded by *t*, or *s*, these letters belong to the stem of the word, and are not part of the suffix :—

Un-*ion*, opin-*ion*, rebell-*ion*, relig-*ion*, domin-*ion* (hence *dungeon*), fash-*ion* (from *fact*), suspic-*ion*, falch-*ion*, bast-*ion*, stanch-*ion*, vermil-*ion*, on-*ion*, leg-*ion*, battal-*ion*, bull-*ion*, gangl-*ion*, etc.

Perdit-*ion*, fract-*ion*, posit-*ion*, lot-*ion*, adopt-*ion*, etc.

Occas-*ion*, cohes-*ion*, collis-*ion*, explos-*ion*, collus-*ion*, mans-*ion*.

Double forms : those which come nearer to Latin than French are called "learned" :—

Learned.	*Popular.*	*Learned.*	*Popular.*
Poti-*on*	pois-*on*.	Orat-*ion*	oris-*on*.
Redempt-*ion*	rans-*om*.	Venat-*io* (L.)	venis-*on*.
Rat-*io*	reas-*on*.	Prehens-*io* (L.)	pris-*on*.
Lect-*ion*	less-*on*.	Comparat-*io* (L.)	comparis-*on*.
Sat-*io* (L.)	seas-*on*.	Fus-*ion*	fois-*on*.
Benedict-*ion*	benis-*on*.	Ars-*io* (L.)	ars-*on*.
Maledict-*ion*	malis-*on*.		

(37) **-ito** (Span. diminutive) :—

Musqu-*ito* (a little fly, Lat. *musca*, a fly), negr-*ito* (small negro of the East Indies).

(38) **-ive, -iff** (Lat. *-ivus*, Fr. *-if*) : originally an adjective suffix ; generally had an Active meaning :—

-ive : representat-*ive*, fugit-*ive*, conservat-*ive*, nat-*ive*, mot-*ive*, alternat-*ive*, incent-*ive*, initiat-*ive*, explet-*ive*, prevent-*ive*.

-iff : cait-*iff* (another form of capt-*ive*), plaint-*iff*, bail-*iff*.

Passive sense :—capt-*ive* (a prisoner), miss-*ive* (a letter).

Excluded word :—

Olive, from Lat. *oliva*.

(39) **-lence** (Lat. *-lentia*) : double suffix compounded of *-l* and *entia* (-ence) :—

Pesti-*lence*, vio-*lence*, viru-*lence*, turbu-*lence*, corpu-*lence*, opu-*lence*.

(40) **-me, -m** (Lat. *-men*, Fr. *-me*) :—

Cri-*me* (Lat. cri-*men*), volu-*me*, régi-*me*, char-*m* (Lat. car-*men*), legu-*me*, real-*m* (Late Lat. regali-*men*).

Naturalised Latin words :—o-*men*, grava-*men*, regi-*men*, bitu-*men*, acu-*men*, speci-*men*, sta-*men*.

Disguised suffix:—leav-*en* (Lat. lev-*amen*, Fr. lev-*ain*), nou-*n* (Lat. no-*men*), cost-*ume* and cust-*om* (Lat. consuet-*umen*, Old Fr. cost-*ume* and cust-*ume*).

(41) **-ment** (Lat. *-mentum*, French, *-ment*: a double suffix, made up of *men* and *tum*; cf. Gr. *-ma-to-*):—

(*a*) *Abstract sense*:— conceal-*ment*, *fulfil-*ment*, judg-*ment*, commence-*ment*, enchant-*ment*, punish-*ment*, *bewilder-*ment*, *bereave-*ment*, enjoy-*ment*, agree-*ment*, *refresh-*ment*, *atone-*ment*, attach-*ment*, employ-*ment*, treat-*ment*, etc.

(*b*) *Concrete sense*:—pay-*ment*, frag-*ment*, argu-*ment*, emolu-*ment*, announce-*ment*, detri-*ment*, *rai-*ment*, depart-*ment*, instru-*ment*, ele-*ment*, rudi-*ment*, sedi-*ment*, incre-*ment*, firma-*ment*, *gar-*ment*, orna-*ment*, imple-*ment*, compli-*ment*, comple-*ment*, supple-*ment*, induce-*ment*, chastise-*ment*, nourish-*ment*, vest-*ment*, mo-*ment*, docu-*ment*, *acknowledge-*ment*, excre-*ment*, parlia-*ment*, *bewitch-*ment*, pig-*ment*, regi-*ment*, *allot-*ment*, manage-*ment*, escarp-*ment*, seg-*ment*.

Excluded word:—

Parchment. Here the *t* is excrescent. The word is derived from Pergamus, where parchment was first made.

(42) **-mony** (Lat. *-monium*, *-monia*, Fr. *-moine*):—

Acri-*mony*, testi-*mony*, sancti-*mony*, matri-*mony*, patri-*mony*, parsi-*mony*, cere-*mony*, ali-*mony*.

(43) **-o** (Lat. *-um* or *-us*, Ital. and Spanish *-o*): this suffix has been imported into English unchanged, and most of the words ending with it are naturalised foreign words:—

Embarg-*o*, manifest-*o*, studi-*o*, grott-*o*, nunci-*o*, oratori-*o*, junt-*o*, volcan-*o*, indig-*o* (from Indic-*us*), came-*o* (Ital. camme-*o*), virtuos-*o*, incognit-*o* (unknown, Pass. part. *in-cognit*-us), seragli-*o* (Eastern harem), domin-*o*, tors-*o*, lass-*o*, portic-*o*, brav-*o* (in Ital. a daring fellow), mott-*o*, carg-*o*, flaming-*o* (Span. flamenc-*o*), punctili-*o* (Span. puntill-*o*), gust-*o* (Ital. or Span. form of Eng. *gust*, Lat. *gust*-us), mulatt-*o*, fresc-*o*, mosquit-*o*, casin-*o*, negr-*o*, embrogli-*o*, scenari-*o*, pian-*o*, fiasc-*o*.

Imitations:—curi-*o* (short for *curiosity*), mang-*o* (an Eastern fruit).

Proper names:—Barnat-*o*, Bernard-*o*, Chatt-*o*, Antoni-*o*, etc.

Excluded words:—

Farrago, a medley or hotch-pot; a Latin noun in the Nominative case.

Lumbago, pain in the loins: similar to the above.

Limbo; the original phrase is *in limbo* (in the borders of hell), where *limbo* is the Ablative case of Lat. *limbus*.

Olio: mistaken form of Span. *olla*, Lat. *olla* (Fem.).

Akimbo = in a bent position, perhaps of Scand. origin, in any case *not* Romanic.

Embryo, formerly *embryon*, of Greek origin.

Echo, halo, hero: Greek words; the *o* is the Nom. Gr. ending.

Memento: naturalised as a noun, but really the Imperative mood of Lat. verb *memini*, and hence naturalised as an English noun.

Innuendo (misspelt as *inuendo*); naturalised as a noun, but really a Lat. gerund in the Ablative case = by giving a nod or hint.

Folio, quarto, duodecimo, proviso,—all of these are Latin Ablatives.

(44) **-on** (Lat. *-onem*, Accus. of *-o*; also Lat. *-onus*, *-ona*):—

Men and other animals:—fel-*on*, pige-*on*, glutt-*on*, cap-*on*, li-*on*, simplet-*on* (double suffix *-et* + *on*), champi-*on*, compani-*on*, scorpi-*on*, drag-*on*, falc-*on*, mas-*on*, sculli-*on*, mini-*on*, sturge-*on*, salm-*on*, postili-*on*, stalli-*on*, marchi-*on*-ess, bis-*on*, patr-*on*, matr-*on*.

Other meanings:—apr-*on*, carb-*on*, gamm-*on*, *bac-*on*, bat-*on*, penn-*on*, pris-*on*, gall-*on*, serm-*on*, mutt-*on*, *butt-*on*, carri-*on*, tal-*on*, clari-*on*, tend-*on*, cauldr-*on*, chaper-*on* (orig. a kind of hood), garris-*on*.

Disguised suffixes:—kitt-*en*, Mid. Eng. kit-*oun*, Fr. chatt-*on*. (The common explanation that kitt-*en* is dim. of "cat" is erroneous.) Burd-*en*, "refrain of a song," Fr. bourd-*on*, Low Lat. burd-*onem*.

Excluded words:—

Gammon, nonsense: **A.S.** *gamen*; hence Eng. *game*.

Surgeon, of Gr. origin: *chir-urge-on* = hand-worker.

Horizon: Gr. Pres. part., "the bounding or limiting circle."

Gnomon (index of a dial): naturalised Greek word.

Colon (a clause; hence a stop-mark): naturalised Greek word.

Mastodon (an extinct elephant): of Greek origin: *mast*-os, the female breast, and *odont*, a tooth.

Skeleton: naturalised Greek word, "a dried body."

Pentagon, hexagon, etc.; of Greek origin: pentag-*on*-os, etc.

Cannon: of Gr. origin through French *canon*, orig. a gun-barrel.

Canon (lit. rule): a naturalised Greek word.

Nuncheon: Mid. Eng. *none-chenche*, "noon-drink"; see p. 179. Quite distinct from *luncheon*.

Luncheon, of Scand. origin; from *lunch* = lump, a hunk of bread; see (45). But *luncheon* might be a misspelling of *lunch-in(g)*.

Ribbon: of Celtic origin: Mid. Eng. *riban*. In *riband* the final *d* is excrescent.

(45) **-oon, -one, -on** (Fr. *-on*, Ital. *-one*): augmentative:—

-oon: ball-*oon* (a large ball), sal-*oon* (Fr. *salle*, an ordinary room), pont-*oon* (a large punt), cart-*oon* (a large chart or picture), bass-*oon* (a large bass instrument), gall-*oon* (aug. of *gala*, festival), mushr-*oom* (Fr. mouscher-*on*, an augmented form of *mousce*, moss).

-one: tromb-*one*, viol-*one*.

-on: flag-*on* (a large flask), galle-*on* (a large galley; cf. *galli-ot*, a small galley), milli-*on*, medalli-*on* (a large medal), squadr-*on* (a large squad (Lat. *quadra*, a troop), lunche-*on* (aug. of *lunch?*), caparis-*on* (aug. of *cape*), buni-*on* (a round lump formed in the flesh, aug. of *bun*, allied to *bunch*), gabi-*on* (a *large* basket filled with earth, aug. of *gabia*, a cage).

Not augmentative:—quadr-*oon*, musket-*oon*, macar-*oon*, mar-*oon*, harp-*oon*, drag-*oon*, buff-*oon*, poltr-*oon*, bat-*oon*, coc-*oon*, fest-*oon*, lag-*oon*.

Excluded words:—

Baboon: Low Lat. *babewynus* (A.D. 1295), Fr. *babouin*.
Moonsoon (a trade wind); of Arab. origin: *mausim*, a season.
Racoon, from the American Indian name of the animal.
Shalloon (light woollen stuff): from *Chalons*, a town in France.
Lampoon: from the exclamation *lampons*, let us drink.
Cyclone: Gr. *kukton*, pres. part. "circling"; a wind that circles.
Typhoon: Chinese *ta*, great, and *fung*, wind. It has been respelt as *typhoon* on account of the Gr. *tuphon* or *tuphos*, a whirlwind.

(46) **-or, -our, -eur, -er, -eer** (from Latin suffixes named below). These denote agent or person:—

(*a*) From Lat. *-or*, Old Fr. *-our*, Mid. Fr. *-eur*, denoting agent. This suffix is added to the stem of the Pass. part. of Latin verbs.

-or: act-*or*, monit-*or*, spons-*or*, audit-*or*, progenit-*or*, assess-*or*, tut-*or*, oppress-*or*, vict-*or*, confess-*or*, edit-*or*, exhibit-*or*, orat-*or*, conduct-*or*, profess-*or*, trait-*or* (Lat. tradit-*or*), doct-*or*, cens-*or*, auth-*or* (Lat. auct-*or*), debt-*or*, credit-*or*, imitat-*or*, success-*or*, aggress-*or*, testat-*or*, execut-*or*, ancest-*or* (Lat. antecess-*or*), vend-*or* (Lat. vendit-*or*).

Imitations:—conquer-*or*, cultivat-*or*, *warri-*or*, tail-*or* (Fr. *tailler*, to cut). *New words*:—refrigerat-*or*, incubat-*or*, demonstrat-*or*.

-our: troubad-*our* (naturalised Provençal word), *herberge-our* (now spelt *harbinger*).

-eur: amat-*eur*, collaborat-*eur*, connoiss-*eur*, colport-*eur*, literat-*eur*, persifl-*eur*.

(*b*) From Lat. *-ator*: denotes agent like the preceding, but is formed from Latin verbs of the First conjugation by adding *-ator* to the stem of the Present tense. In Old French the *t* was weakened, and then finally dropped, as in *emper-eor*, *sauv-eor* (hence English savi-*our*).

-or: emper-*or* (Lat. imper-*ator*), govern-*or* (gubern-*ator*), jur-*or* (Lat. jur-*ator*), counsell-*or* (Lat. consili-*ator*), councill-*or* (concili-*ator*), raz-*or* (Late Lat. ras-*ator*), proct-*or* (procur-*ator*), savi-*our* (salv-*ator*), solicit-*or* (sollicit-*ator*).

-er, -eer: preach-*er* (predic-*ator*), compil-*er* (compil-*ator*), found-*er* (fund-*ator*), juggl-*er* (jocul-*ator*), enchant-*er* (incant-*ator*), command-*er* (Fr. command-*eur*, Lat. commend-*ator*), engin-*eer* (ingeni-*ator*), lev-*er* (lev-*ator*, lifter), divin-*er* (divin-*ator*), interpret-*er* (interpret-*ator*), coron-*er* (coron-*ator*), groc-*er* (wholesale dealer, Old Fr. *gros*, great).

Disguised suffix:—burgl-*ar*, a misspelling for "burgl-*or*," from Low Lat. burgul-*ator*.

Excluded words:—

Attaind-er, rejoind-er, remaind-er.—Here the final *-er* represents the French Infinitive ending *-re*, as "attaind-*re*."

(47) **-or, -our, -eur** (Lat. *-or*, Old Fr. *-our*, Mod. Fr. *-eur*): this suffix denotes Abstract *qualities* or *states*, and must not be confounded with the preceding:—

-or: err-*or*, langu-*or*, trem-*or*, splend-*or*, pall-*or*, stup-*or*,—these are all naturalised Latin or French words.

-our: fav-*our*, hon-*our*, col-*our*, ard-*our*, lab-*our*, sav-*our*, flav-*our*, dol-*our*, clam-*our*, ranc-*our*.

Imitations:—*behavi-*our*, demean-*our*.

Naturalised French word:—am-*our* (hence the phrase "am-*our* propre" = self-esteem; hence the word "param-*our*," which now denotes lover; orig. *par amour*, with love).

-eur: grand-*eur*, haut-*eur*, liqu-*eur* (not abstract, another form of liqu-*or*).

-ore: commod-*ore* (short for Mid. Dutch command-*eur*, borrowed by the Dutch from French, Lat. commend-*ator*).

Excluded words:—

Neighbour = nigh + bour, a near husbandman. See above, p. 175.

Scissors, wrongly derived from Lat. *scind-ere*, to cut, *sciss-or*, a cutler. It really comes from Old Fr. cis-*oires*, shears; plural of *cisel*, chisel. The root word is Lat. *cæd*-ere, *cæs*-um, to cut.

Armour, from Lat. *armatura*; see below under (55) **-ure**.

(48) **-ory, -or, -our, -er** (Lat. *-oria* or *-orium*, Fr. *-oire*): chiefly denotes place:—

-ory: dormit-*ory*, rect-*ory*, deposit-*ory*, hist-*ory* or st-*ory*, mem-*ory* (hence mem-*oir* or mem-*oirs*), observat-*ory*, territ-*ory*, orat-*ory*, repert-*ory*, refect-*ory*, fact-*ory*, invent-*ory*, lavat-*ory*, laborat-*ory*, purgat-*ory*, direct-*ory*, consist-*ory*, conservat-*ory*, promont-*ory*, offer-t-*ory*.

Denoting agent (Lat. *-orius*): signat-*ory*, deposit-*ory* (person or thing).

-orium: sens-*orium*, sanat-*orium*.

-oir: boud-*oir* (lit. a room for a lady to sulk in, from Fr. *boud-er*, to sulk, akin to *pout*), mem-*oir*.

-or: mirr-*or* (Late Lat. mirat-*orium*), man-*or*.

-our: parl-*our* (Low Lat. parlat-*orium*, Fr. parl-*oir*).

-er: mang-*er* (Lat. manducat-*orium*, Fr. mange-*oire*), dorm-*er* (dormit-*orium*), cens-*er* (incens-*orium*), count-*er* (computat-*orium*), lav-*er* (lavat-*orium*, Old Fr. lav-*oir*).

Excluded words:—

Arb-our: Lat. herb-*arium*, Mid. Eng. *herb-ere* or *erb-ere*.

Arm-ory, for arm-*ary*, Lat. arm-*arium*, place for keeping arms; see above under (14) **-ary**.

(49) **-ry, -ery** (French *-rie* or *-erie*, formed by the addition of the Abstract suffix *-ie* (see below under (56) **-y**) to the French ending -(*i*)*er*. In English also the final *y* was associated with the personal suffix *-er*, as in fish-*er*-*y*. In such words, therefore, *-ery* is a hybrid suffix.

Collective:—machine-*ry*, artill-*ery*, statione(r)-*ry* (articles dealt in by a station-*er*, one who occupies a stand or station), jewel-*ry* or jewell-*ery*, tenant-*ry*, peasant-*ry*, upholste(r)-*ry*, *crock-*ery*, *rook-*ery*, *rock-*ery*, *fern-*ery*, *heron-*ry*, caval-*ry*, infant-*ry*, Jew-*ry*,

Irish-*ry*, fine-*ry*, spice-*ry*, batt-*ery*, gent-*ry*, poult-*ry*, drape-*ry*, *yeoman-*ry*, trinket-*ry*, cannon-*ry*, scene-*ry*, *pigg-*ery*, etc.

Abstract:—*slave-*ry*, *witch-*ery*, cook-*ery*, *trick-*ery*, *husband-*ry* *housewife-*ry*, mason-*ry*, *drudge-*ry*, *herald-*ry*, rival-*ry*, pageant-*ry*, carpent-*ry*, *surge-*ry* (contracted from surgeon-*ry*), pleasant-*ry*, brave-*ry*, gallant-*ry*, *chemist-*ry*, *bribe-*ry*, *rogue-*ry*, *treach-*ery*, musket-*ry*, *mock-*ery*, revel-*ry*, bigot-*ry*, *devil-*ry*, *pedant-*ry*, sorc-*ery*, *outlaw-*ry*, *pope-*ry*, *coquet-*ry*, *monk-*ery*, buffoon-*ery*, *canon-*ry*, *thiev-*ery*, *sophist-*ry*, trump-*ery*, forest-*ry*, forge-*ry*, join-*ery*, embroid-*ery*, fool-*ery*, casuist-*ry*, dentist-*ry*, poet-*ry*, fai-*ry* (properly an enchantment, now a *fay* or elf, Lat. *fata*).

Place with sense of multitude:—cemet-*ery*, collie-*ry* (=collier+*ry*), laund-*ry*, nunn-*ery*, cutl-*ery* (Lat. cultell-*arium*, from *culter*, a knife, confused with *cut*), nurse-*ry*, *bake-*ry*, *shrubb-*ery*, *rock-*ery*, treasur-*y* (short for treasure-*ry*), hostel-*ry*, butte(r)-*ry* (from butle(r)-*ry*, bottle(r)-*ry*), pant-*ry*, scull-*ery* (from Lat. *scutella*, a dish), dean-*ery*, *brew-*ery*, *chumm-*ery*, *baptist-*ry*, found-*ry*, *dai-*ry* (from *deye*, a milk-woman), batt-*ery*, cream-*ery*, chanc-*ery* (Lat. cancell-*aria*, the record room of a chancellor), etc.

Result of action:—poet-*ry*, tapest-*ry*, forge-*ry*, gallant-*ries* (plur.), pleasant-*ries*.

(50) **-t** (Lat. *-tus*, *-ta*, *-tum*, Pass. part.):—

Fac-*t* (hence fea-*t*), counterfei-*t*, frui-*t* (cf. usufruc-*t*), join-*t* (cf. junc-*t*-ure), poin-*t* (cf. punc-*t*-uation), deb-*t*, sain-*t*, sui-*t*, concei-*t*, receip-*t*, ren-*t* (Late Lat. ren-*dit*-a, for red-*dit*-a, Fr. ren-*te*), retor-*t*, pac-*t* or compac-*t*, can-*t*, tac-*t*, strai-*t*, trai-*t*, etc.

Peculiar word:—

Ink (Old Fr. *enque*, Lat. *encaust*-um, lit. "burnt in"; of Gr. origin).

(51) **-ter, -tre** (Lat. *-trum*, Gr. *-tron*):—

Clois-*ter*, thea-*tre*, lus-*tre*, spec-*tre*, scep-*tre*, fil-*tre*, mons-*ter*, canis-*ter* (Lat. canis-*trum*, a reed basket).

Naturalised Lat. word:—spec-*trum*.

Excluded words:—

Goitre, a swelling on the throat; Lat. *guttur*, a throat.

Disaster: *dis*+*astr*-um; the *str* is radical: cf. *star*.

Note.—The words *theatre*, *sceptre*, and *filtre* are formed from Greek words, which became naturalised in Latin.

(52) **-tude** (Lat. *-tudo*, *-tudinem*): Abstract suffix:—

Longi-*tude*, forti-*tude*, apti-*tude* (hence atti-*tude*), alti-*tude*, desue-*tude*, vicissi-*tude*, soli-*tude*, decrepi-*tude*, lassi-*tude*, etc.

Concrete sense:—multi-*tude*.

(53) **-ty** (Lat. *-tas*, *-tatem*, Fr. *-té*): chiefly Abstract:—

Abstract sense:—cruel-*ty*, frail-*ty*, boun-*ty*, beau-*ty*, feal-*ty*, pover-*ty*, liber-*ty*, certain-*ty*, du-*ty*, royal-*ty*, loyal-*ty*, plen-*ty*, hones(t)-*ty*, varie-*ty*, pie-*ty*, pi-*ty*, mod-es-*ty*.

Authori-*ty*, falsi-*ty*, reali-*ty*, personali-*ty*, longevi-*ty*, simplici-*ty*, abili-*ty*, antiqui-*ty*, vani-*ty*, etc.

Concrete sense :—real-*ty*, personal-*ty*, commonal-*ty*, admiral-*ty*, proper-*ty*, ci-*ty*, universi-*ty*, royal-*ty* (share of profit), dain-*ty* (O. F. dain-*tie*, Lat. digni-*tatem*), penal-*ty*, *oddi-*ty* (with Sc. stem *odd*, to which an *i* has been added for the sake of euphony).

Naturalised French word :—naive-*té*.

The suffix *-ty* is especially added to adjectives ending in *-al*, *-an* or *-ane*, *-ar*, *-ble*, *-ile*, *-ive*, *-ous* or *-ose* :—

-al : vitali-*ty*, formali-*ty*, finali-*ty*, mortali-*ty*, etc.
-an or *-ane* : humani-*ty*, urbani-*ty*, insani-*ty*, Christiani-*ty*, etc.
-ar : regulari-*ty*, familiari-*ty*, vulgari-*ty*, populari-*ty*, etc.
-ble : possibili-*ty*, abili-*ty*, nobili-*ty*, culpabili-*ty*, etc.
-ile : servili-*ty*, senili-*ty*, facili-*ty*, agili-*ty*, frail-*ty*, etc.
-ive : captivi-*ty*, nativi-*ty*, passivi-*ty*, relativi-*ty*, etc.
-ous or *-ose* : curiosi-*ty*, verbosi-*ty*, generosi-*ty*, pomposi-*ty*, etc.

(54) **-ule, -le** (Lat. *-ulus*, *-ula*, *-ulum*, Fr. *-le*) :—

Diminutive sense :—pill-*ule*, glob-*ule*, nod-*ule*, pust-*ule*, caps-*ule*, sched-*ule*, chasub-*le* (Late Lat. casab-*ula*), circ-*le*, cup-*ola* (Ital. form of Lat. cup-*ula*, a little cup).

Not diminutive :—ridic-*ule*, vestib-*ule*, fab-*le*, pimp-*le* (from Lat. pap-*ula*), tab-*le*, tit-*le*, stab-*le*, peop-*le*, buck-*le*, ang-*le* (Lat. ang-*ulus*), fidd-*le* (apparently from Lat. vid-*ula*, a viol).

Disguised suffixes :—rol-*l* (Lat. rot-*ula*, hence the naturalised French word, rôle), chapt-*er* (Fr. chapit-*re*, Lat. capit-*ulum*), funn-*el* (Lat. infundib-*ulum*), poster-*n* (poster-*ula* porta, a little back gate ; Old Fr. poster-*le* or poster-*ne*, by changing the *l* into *n*).

Excluded words :—

Kennel, from Mid. Eng. ken-*el*, Old Fr. chen-*il*, Lat. can-*ile*, a dog's house.

Principle, manciple, these are from Lat. *principium*, *mancipium* ; by the insertion of *l* they have been modernised to *principle*, *manciple*.

(55) **-ure** (Lat. *-ura*, Fr. *-eur*) :—

Abstract sense :—cult-*ure*, *seiz-*ure*, capt-*ure*, nat-*ure*, rapt-*ure*, rupt-*ure*, cens-*ure*, depart-*ure*, stat-*ure*, junct-*ure*, clos-*ure*, verd-*ure*, moist-*ure*, forfeit-*ure*, nurt-*ure*, sepult-*ure*, compos-*ure*, press-*ure*, calent-*ure*.

Concrete sense :—apert-*ure*, fig-*ure*, furnit-*ure*, creat-*ure*, pict-*ure*, curvat-*ure*, indent-*ure*, feat-*ure*, meas-*ure*, fixt-*ure*, vest-*ure*, script-*ure*, joint-*ure*, caricat-*ure*, advent-*ure*, past-*ure*, ligat-*ure*.

Disguised suffixes :—us-*ury* (Lat. us-*ura*), arm-*our* (Lat. armat-*ura*, Old Fr. arm-*eure*), tent-*er* (properly tent-*ure*, from Lat. tent-*ura*, a frame for stretching cloth).

Excluded words :—

Leis-ure, pleas-ure have been Anglicised in imitation of the above. Leis-*ure* is from French Infinitive lois-*ir*, and pleas-*ure* from Fr. Infin. plais-*ir*.

Treas-ure is from Fr. trés-*or*, Lat. thes-*aurus*, Gr. thes-*auros*.

Sinecure, Lat. *sine curâ*, without care.

Cynosure, Gr. *kunos oura*, the tail of the Lesser Bear.
Epicure, Gr. *Epikouros*, the name of a philosopher.
Debenture, from the phrase *debentur mihi*, they are due to me.

(56) **-y** (from the Lat. suffixes named below); on the *-y* suffix derived from *-ate* and equivalent to *-ee*, see (21).

(*a*) From *-ia* or *-ea*, French *-ie* :—

Famil-*y*, galler-*y* (Lat. galer-*ia*), comed-*y*, traged-*y*, fur-*y*, cop-*y*, victor-*y*, infam-*y*, histor-*y* or stor-*y*, miser-*y*, *treacher-*y*, perfid-*y*, ignomin-*y*, Arab-*y*, Arcad-*y*, Ital-*y*, eyr-*y* (Low Lat. ar-*ea*, eagle's nest).

Disguised suffix :—abb-*ey* (Low Lat. abbat-*ia*).

Imitations :—*jealous-*y*, *bastard-*y*, *simon-*y*, courtes-*y*, nav-*y*, beggar-*y*.

Entire suffix :—As-*ia*, Austr-*ia*, Ind-*ia*, Austral-*ia*.

(*b*) From *-ium* :—

Stud-*y*, augur-*y*, remed-*y*, monaster-*y*, master-*y*, myster-*y*, ministr-*y*, subsid-*y*, jo-*y* (Lat. gaud-*ium*), prodig-*y* (Lat. prodig-*ium*).

Naturalised words :— od-*ium*, aquar-*ium*, cran-*ium*, med-*ium*, *trapez-*ium*, *bacter-*ium*, *pandemon-*ium*, exord-*ium*, proscen-*ium*, equilibr-*ium*, residu-*um*.

(*c*) From *-ies* :—

Progen-*y*, luxur-*y*, effig-*y*, compan-*y* (Late Lat. compan-*ies*, taking food together).

Naturalised words :—rab-*ies*, spec-*ies*, superfic-*ies*, conger-*ies*.

Excluded words :—

Daisy, from Anglo-Saxon *dæges edge*, the eye of day.
Jeopardy = Old Fr. *jeu parti*, a divided game; hence a risk.

B. *Adjective-forming.*

256. (1) **-able** (Lat. *-abilis*): see below under **-ble** (13).

(2) **-aceous** (Lat. *-aceus*), made of :—

Farin-*aceous* (made of farina, a fine flour), argill-*aceous* (made of argilla, clay), test-*aceous* (having a hard shell), sapon-*aceous* (soapy), herb-*aceous* (having the nature of herbs).

Disguised suffixes :—cuir-*ass* (noun; Lat. cori-*aceus*, made of *corium*, leather). Crev-*ice*, Old Fr. crev-*asse*, Lat. crep-*acea*.

(3) **-acious** (Lat. *-ax*, *-ac-is*), a double suffix made up of *-ac* and *-is*: the *-is* has been changed to *-ious*, on the model of words like "illustr-*is*" (Lat.), "illustr-*ious*" (Eng.) :—

Ten-*acious*, loqu-*acious*, mend-*acious*, ver-*acious*, cap-*acious*, contum-*acious*.

Note.—Similarly from *-ox*, *-ocis*, we get the following :—

Prec-*ocious*, atr-*ocious*.

(4) **-al** (Lat. *-alis*, Fr. *-al* or *-el*), pertaining to :—

Vit-*al*, mort-*al*, reg-*al* or roy-*al*, leg-*al* or loy-*al*, accident-*al*, speci-*al*, gener-*al*, mutu-*al*, equ-*al*, natur-*al*, annu-*al*, habitu-*al*, cordi-*al*, alluvi-*al*, circumstanti-*al*, margin-*al*, proportion-*al*, patern-*al*, terrestri-*al*, celesti-*al*, *baptism-*al*, *phantasm-*al*, *phenomen-*al*, *ephemer-*al*, ceremoni-*al*, parti-*al*:—

-*al* is frequently added to the suffix -*ic*, so as to produce the compound suffix -*ical*:—

*Polit-*ical*, *whims-*ical*, *diabol-*ical*, *iron-*ical*, *anatom-*ical*, *com-*ical*, *dramat-*ical*, *botan-*ical*, *trag-*ical*, *angel-*ical*, *polem-*ical*, fanat-*ical*, nonsens-*ical*, *heret-*ical*, *mag-*ical*, *lackadais-*ical*, *grammat-*ical*, *pragmat-*ical*, *Druid-*ical*, *surg-*ical*, *myth-*ical*, *mathemat-*ical*, poet-*ical*, *dogmat-*ical*, *scept-*ical*, inim-*ical*.

-*al* is frequently joined to the Abstract suffixes -*ment*, -*ure*, and -*ion*, so as to form adjectives:—

Experiment-*al*, department-*al*, instrument-*al*, detriment-*al*, etc.

Architectur-*al*, structur-*al*, natur-*al*, scriptur-*al*, pastor-*al* (for pastur-*al*).

Sensation-*al*, option-*al*, exception-*al*, devotion-*al*, fraction-*al*, intention-*al*, nation-*al*, etc.

-*ial*: after the syllables -*ant* or -*ent*, when these are Pres. Participles of Latin verbs, but not when the suffix is -*ment*, Lat. *mentum*. In the former case the suffix is -*anti* (stem of Pres. Part.) + *ālis*. In the latter the suffix is -*ment* + *ālis*.

Circumstant-*ial*, confident-*ial*, essent-*ial*, prudent-*ial*, provident-*ial*, penitent-*ial* (but fundament-*al*, detriment-*al*, ornament-*al*, instrument-*al*, department-*al*, etc.).

Note.—According to the above rule "transcendent-*al*" and "accident-*al*" should have had the suffix -*ial*, since in both words -*ent* is a Pres. Part. These words are therefore exceptional.

(5) **-an, -en, -ain, -ane** (Lat. -*anus*, Fr. -*ain*, -*en*):—

-*an*, -*en*: pag-*an*, hum-*an*, sylv-*an*, mea-*n* and mizz-*en* (Late Lat. medi-*anus*), sull-*en* (Late Lat. sol-*anus*, solit-*aneus*), suburb-*an*, barbari-*an*, pedestri-*an*, republic-*an*, diluvi-*an*, crustace-*an*, patrici-*an*, plebei-*an*.

Proper adjectives:—Rom-*an*, Christi-*an*, Mahommed-*an*, Luther-*an*, Anglic-*an*, Elizabeth-*an*, Armeni-*an*, Phœnici-*an*, etc.

-*ain*: cert-*ain*, germ-*ain*.

-*ane*; mund-*ane*, hum-*ane*, submont-*ane*.

-*ean*: the -*anus* in Latin was sometimes preceded by *æ* or *e*, as, -*æanus* or -*eanus*, Eng. -*ean*:—

Hercul-*ean*, subterran-*ean*, Europ-*ean*, Chald-*ean*, Pythagor-*ean*.

(6) **-arian**, compounded of -*ari* + -*an*; see below under (10) **-ary**:—

Unit-*arian*, agr-*arian*, humanit-*arian*, antiqu-*arian*, sect-*arian*, necess-*arian*. (In *barbarian* the -*ar* belongs to the stem of the word.)

(7) **-aneous** (Lat. *-aneus*) :—

Cut-*aneous* (*cutis*, skin), extr-*aneous* (*extra*, outside), instant-*aneous*, contempor-*aneous* (*con* + *tempor-*, time), simult-*aneous* (*extra*, outside) same time), miscell-*aneous*.

Disguised suffix :—

For-eign, a misspelling for for-*an*, Lat. for-*aneus*, "out of doors"; cf. sover-*eign* for sovr-*an*, Lat. super-*aneus*.

(8) **-ant, -ent** (Lat. *-antem*, *-entem*, Pres. part.; Fr. *-ant*) :—

-ant : arrog-*ant*, import-*ant*, ignor-*ant*, *blat-*ant*, petul-*ant*, abund-*ant*, predomin-*ant*, eleg-*ant*, dist-*ant*, radi-*ant*, etc.

Borrowed from French :—brilli-*ant*, pleas-*ant*, complais-*ant*, re-pent-*ant*, defi-*ant*, compli-*ant*, *ramp-*ant*, trench-*ant*, poign-*ant* (Lat. form pung-*ent*), recre-*ant* (one who recants or gives in).

-ent : emin-*ent*, innoc-*ent*, obedi-*ent*, abs-*ent*, pres-*ent*, preval-*ent*, promin-*ent*, penit-*ent*, insolv-*ent*, etc.

Confid-*ent* (noun form, confid-*ant*), depend-*ent* (noun form, depend-*ant*).

(9) **-ar** (Lat. *-aris*, Fr. *-ier* or *-aire*) :—

Sol-*ar*, lun-*ar*, famili-*ar*, regul-*ar*, singul-*ar*, vulg-*ar*, schol-*ar* (noun, but orig. adject., hence we now say schol-ar-*ly* for adject.).

(10) **-ary, -arious** (Lat. *-arius*, Fr. *-aire*) :—

-ary : contr-*ary*, necess-*ary*, ordin-*ary*, legend-*ary*, tempor-*ary*, stipendi-*ary*, solit-*ary*, second-*ary*, station-*ary*, capill-*ary*, residu-*ary*, sedent-*ary*, obitu-*ary*, etc.

-arious : nef-*arious*, greg-*arious*, multif-*arious*, prec-*arious*.

Note.—The suffix *-ary* is often added to nouns ending in *-ment* :—document-*ary*, parliament-*ary*, moment-*ary*, fragment-*ary*, ele-ment-*ary*, rudiment-*ary*, compliment-*ary*, supplement-*ary*, etc.

(11) **-ate, -atic** (Lat. *-atus*, *-aticus*); see below under (30) **-t** and under (18) **-ic**. A compound suffix.

(12) **-ble** (Lat. *-plex*, Fr. *-ple*), fold :—

Dou-*ble* (du-*plex*), tre-*ble* (= Fr. and Eng. tri-*ple* = Lat. tri-*plex*).

(13) **-ble, -able, -ible, -uble** (Lat. *-bilis*), generally in a Passive sense. Preceded by *a*, *i*, or *u*, according to the Latin verb with which it is connected. But *-able* has become an independent suffix, and can be attached to nouns as much as to verbs, and to Teutonic as well as Romanic stems. Sometimes, but far less commonly, *-ible* is similarly used.

(*a*) Added to verb-stems :—

Passive sense :—laud-*able*, ar-*able* (fit to be ploughed), *eat-*able*, ed-*ible* (= eat-*able*), *read-*able*, intellig-*ible*, *drink-*able*, percept-*ible*, vis-*ible*, suit-*able*, *blam-*able*, fee-*ble* (Old Fr. foi-*ble* for floi-*ble*, Lat. fle-*bilis*, lamentable), *teach-*able*, *unsearch-*able*, sol-*u-ble* or solv-

able, mo-*bile* or move-*able*, tang-*ible*, aud-*ible*, *answer-*able*, *regrett-*able*, enjoy-*able*, horr-*ible*, *break-*able*, conquer-*able*, assail-*able*.

Active sense:—favour-*able*, terr-*ible*, agree-*able*, change-*able*, con-form-*able*, comfort-*able*, cap-*able*, ami-*able*.

Either sense:—sens-*ible*, soci-*able* (usually active).

(*b*) Added to noun-stems :—

Manage-*able*, marriage-*able*, peace-*able*, *sale-*able*, market-*able*, *laugh-*able*, account-*able* (=responsible), avail-*able*, objection-*able*, fashion-*able*, season-*able*, service-*able*, reason-*able*, treason-*able*, palate-*able*, companion-*able*, action-*able*, question-*able*, duti-*able*, forc-*ible*, *gull-*ible*.

(*c*) Added to prepositional verbs, but scarcely yet admitted :—

Come-at-*able*, get-at-*able*, reli-*able* (the last is much used, but is open to objection, as it omits the preposition *on*).

Excluded word ;—

Humble, from Lat. hum-*ilis*; the *b* is inserted for the sake of euphony.

(14) **-esc-ent** (Lat. Pres. part. of verbs in *-esc-o*): inceptive :—

Qui-*escent*, conval-*escent*, evan-*escent*, incand-*escent*, efferv-*escent*, obsol-*escent* (beginning to go out of use), irid-*escent*, excr-*escent*, erub-*escent* (turning red), liqu-*escent* (beginning to melt).

(15) **-ese** (Lat. *-ensis*, Anglo-Fr. *-eis*) :—

Denoting country or language:—Chin-*ese*, Malt-*ese*, Portugu-*ese*, Siam-*ese*, Japan-*ese*, etc.

Denoting literary style:—Johnson-*ese* (a pompous and formal style), Carlyl-*ese* (a fervid and poetical style), journal-*ese* (a newspaper style).

Disguised suffix:—court-*eous*, Anglo-French curt-*eis*.

Naturalised word:—a-manu-*ensis* (copyist).

Note.—In the word "for-*ens-ic*" an *ic* has been added to Lat. *for-ens-is*, so as to make *forens*(*i*)-*ic*; cf. *extrinsic*.

(16) **-esque** (Lat. *-iscus*, Fr. *-esque*): orig. Diminutive :—

Grot-*esque*, pictur-*esque*, burl-*esque*, arab-*esque*, statu-*esque*.

(17) **-et** (Old Fr. *-et*, Ital. *-etto*) :—

Dulc-*et*, russ-*et*.

(18) **-ic, -ique** (Lat. *-icus*, *-iquus*, Fr. *-ique*) :—

-ic: publ-*ic*, domest-*ic*, gener-*ic*, rust-*ic*, civ-*ic*, barbar-*ic*, class-*ic*, magnet-*ic*, aquat-*ic*, mim-*ic*, lymphat-*ic*, errat-*ic*.

Proper adjectives:—Kelt-*ic*, German-*ic*, Hanseat-*ic*, Asiat-*ic*, etc.

-ique: ant-*ique*, obl-*ique*, un-*ique*.

Compound suffix **-at-ic** :—aqu-*atic*, lun-*atic* (noun), fan-*atic* (noun).

(19) **-id** (Lat. *-idus*, Fr. *-ide*) :—

Ac-*id*, pall-*id*, morb-*id*, viv-*id*, rig-*id*, plac-*id*, liv-*id*, ferv-*id*, tim-*id*, tum-*id*, hum-*id*, turb-*id*, hybr-*id*, val-*id*, rap-*id*, vap-*id*, stup-*id*, flu-*id*, sol-*id*, etc.

Note.—In French the suffix sometimes disappears, as Lat. *nit-idus*, Fr. *net*, Eng. *neat*. Sometimes the suffix is changed into *-e*, as Lat. *pall-idus*, Old Fr. *pall-e*, Eng. *pal-e*.

(20) **-ile, -il, -eel, -le, -el** (Lat. *-ĭlis* from verb-stems, *-īlis* from noun-stems; Fr. *-ile*):—

-ile: frag-*ile*, juven-*ile*, ster-*ile*, infant-*ile*, doc-*ile*, fac-*ile*, duct-*ile*, serv-*ile*, puer-*ile*, text-*ile*, sen-*ile*, vir-*ile*, ag-*ile*, etc.
-il: fra-*il* (from frag-*ile*), civ-*il*.
-eel: gent-*eel* (other forms, gent-*ile*, gent-*le*).
-le, -el: subt-*le*, gent-*le*, ab-*le*, hum(b)-*le*, cru-*el* (Lat. crud-*elis*).

Note.—In the suffix *-ile* there is often a depreciatory sense, as in the Teutonic suffix *-ish*. Thus infant-*ile* = child-*ish*; serv-*ile* = slav-*ish*. Puer-*ile* is invariably used in a depreciatory sense. Contrast the meanings of "infant-*ile*" and "infant-*ine*"; "sen-*ile*" and "veter-*an*." There is nothing depreciatory, however, in *vir-ile* = manly, *doc-ile* (teachable).

(21) **-ine, -in** (Lat. *-inus*, Fr. *-ine*):—

Div-*ine*, sup-*ine*, clandest-*ine*, mascul-*ine*, lacustr-*ine*, femin-*ine*, infant-*ine* (not depreciatory, like "infant-*ile*"), libert-*ine* (now used as a noun), genu-*ine*, mar-*ine*, sangu-*ine*, *adamant-*ine* (Greek stem), sal-*ine*, sup-*ine* (from Lat. *sub*), prist-*ine*, pilgr-*im* (Lat. peregr-*inus*, Ital. pellegr-*ino*.

Adjectives formed from Latin names of animals:—leon-*ine*, fel-*ine*, can-*ine*, asin-*ine*, elephant-*ine*, aquil-*ine* (generally in a metaphorical sense), bov-*ine*, equ-*ine*, vulp-*ine*, ov-*ine*, lup-*ine*.
Proper adjectives:—Alp-*ine*, Philist-*ine*, Lat-*in*.

(22) **-ior** (Latin Comparative suffix, unchanged in English):—

Pri-*or*, super-*ior*, infer-*ior*, jun-*ior*, sen-*ior*, etc.

(23) **-ive** (Lat. *-ivus*, Fr. *-if*; hence bail-*iff*, plaint-*iff*, cait-*iff*, in English nouns): generally in an Active sense:—

Recept-*ive*, amat-*ive*, curat-*ive*, abus-*ive*, act-*ive*, pass-*ive*, pens-*ive*, sensit-*ive*, extens-*ive*, nat-*ive* (hence na-*ive*), fugit-*ive*, sport-*ive*, *talkat-*ive*, relat-*ive*, furt-*ive*, rest-*ive* (Lat. *re* + *sto*, resist), coerc-*ive*, tentat-*ive*, inquisit-*ive*, argumentat-*ive*, retribut-*ive*, combat-*ive*.

Note.—The student will observe the difference in meaning between "reflect-*ive*" and "reflex-*ive*"; the former has the stem of the Present tense, the latter that of the Pass. part. The last is the kind of stem to which the suffix *-ive* is usually added.

(24) **-lent** (Lat. *-lentus* or *-lens*, *-lentem*):—

Pesti-*lent*, corpu-*lent*, opu-*lent*, escu-*lent*, vio-*lent*.
Excluded words:—

Malevolent, benevolent, insolent must be divided for etymological purposes as malevol-*ent*, benevol-*ent*, insol-*ent*, as their suffix is *-ent*, not *-lent*; the *l* is part of the stem.

(25) **-me** (Lat. Superlative suffix *-mus*).—

Pri-*me*, extre-*me*, supre-*me*.

(26) **-monious** (Lat. *-monius*) :—

Queri-*monious*, sancti-*monious*, cere-*monious*, *har-*monious*.

(27) **-ory, -orious** (Lat. *-orius*, Fr. *-oire*) : usually in an Active sense :—

Dilat-*ory*, compuls-*ory*, perempt-*ory*, conciliat-*ory*, illus-*ory*, amat-*ory*, migrat-*ory*, obligat-*ory*, consolat-*ory*, valedict-*ory*, laudat-*ory*, statut-*ory*, defamat-*ory*, permiss-*ory*, transit-*ory*, curs-*ory*, damnat-*ory*, etc.

Cens-*orious* (cf. *-erious*, in delet-*erious*).

Note.—In labori-*ous*, the suffix is *-ous*, the *ori* being part of the stem-word.

(28) **-ous, -ose** (corresponding to suffixes (*a*) and (*b*) named below) : *ous* is largely used as an independent suffix. It indicates the possession of some quality in a high degree ; cf. Teutonic suffix *-ful* :—

(*a*) Lat. *-osus*, Fr. *-eux* :—

-ous :—glori-*ous*, furi-*ous*, call-*ous*, fam-*ous*, querul-*ous*, numer-*ous*, peril-*ous* (parl-*ous* in Shakspeare), curi-*ous*, ponder-*ous*, studi-*ous*, preci-*ous*, gener-*ous*, odi-*ous*.

-ose :—verb-*ose*, grandi-*ose*, joc-*ose*, bell-ic-*ose* (double suffix), oti-*ose*, mor-*ose*, *comat-*ose*, adip-*ose* (Lat. *adip*-em, fat).

(*b*) Lat. *-us* :—

Tremend-*ous* (Lat. tremend-*us*), ardu-*ous*, posthum-*ous*, anxi-*ous*, superflu-*ous*, querul-*ous*, sedul-*ous*, assidu-*ous*, egregi-*ous*, ovipar-*ous*, cutane-*ous*, surreptiti-*ous*, etc.

As an independent suffix *-ous* is added (*a*) to Adject.-stems, (*b*) to Noun-stems, which had no connection with Lat. *-osus* or *-us* :—

(*a*) *Adject.-stems* :—felicit-*ous*, atroci-*ous*, expediti-*ous*, efficaci-*ous*, precipit-*ous*, loquaci-*ous*, dexter-*ous*, mendaci-*ous*, feroci-*ous*, illustri-*ous*, etc.

(*b*) *Noun-stems* :—joy-*ous*, *lusci-*ous* (corruption of lust-i-*ous*), *up-roar-i-*ous*, pite-*ous*, *hazard-*ous*, marvell-*ous*, chivalr-*ous*, riot-*ous*, beaute-*ous*, *treacher-*ous*, plente-*ous*, *murder-*ous*, *slander-*ous*, danger-*ous*, mischiev-*ous*, burglari-*ous*, adventur-*ous*, larcen-*ous*, ceremoni-*ous*, sanctimoni-*ous*, *boister-*ous* (lengthened from Mid. Eng. boist-*ous*, noisy, from *boist*, noise), raven-*ous*, *hein-*ous*.

Excluded words :—

Righte-ous, a corruption of Mid. Eng. *right-wis* = wise in what is right. The *e* has been inserted to help out the sound on the analogy of *beauteous*, *aqueous*, *piteous*, etc.

Gorgeous : Old Fr. *gorgias*, brilliant.

Courte-ous = Anglo-Fr. *curt-eis*, where the *-eis* represents the Lat. suffix *-ensis*. The word has been refashioned to resemble "aque-ous," "pite-ous," etc.

Wondr-ous, a corruption of the Mid. Eng. Genitival adverb *wond-*

ers. "Wondrous" is now much used as an adjective, but is still an adverb in poetry, as "wondrous wise," "wondrous wild," etc. "Wondrous-ly" is seldom or never seen as an adverb.

(29) **-ple** (Lat. *-plex*, Fr. *-ple*; see above under (13) **-ble**):—

Sim-*ple*, tri-*ple* (=tre-*ble*), quadru-*ple*, sup-*ple*.
Naturalised Lat. words:—du-*plex*, com-*plex*.
Note.—In sing-*le* the *-le* is a short form of *-ule* from Lat. *-uli*.

(30) **-t, -ate, -ete** or **-eet, -ite, -ute**.—These are the English equivalents of Lat. *-tus*, *-atus*, *-etus*, *-itus*, *-utus*, all of which are Pass. participial suffixes. The suffix *-ate* (cf. the parallel case of **-able**) has become an independent suffix, which can be added to nouns or adjectives:—

-t (here *-e* for *-us* is not required for the pronunciation):—
Exact, exempt, elect, abrupt, blest, abject, devout, content.
Adjectives:—modest, honest.
-ate: orn-*ate*, separ-*ate*, anim-*ate*, fortun-*ate*, priv-*ate*, accur-*ate*, effemin-*ate*, degener-*ate*, etc.
Independent suffix:—affection-*ate*, rose-*ate*, insens-*ate*, passion-*ate*.
-ete, *-eet*: compl-*ete*, obsol-*ete*, discr-*eet*.
-ite: defin-*ite*, recond-*ite*, erud-*ite*, exquis-*ite*, pol-*ite*, contr-*ite*.
-ute: destit-*ute*, hirs-*ute*, ac-*ute*, absol-*ute*, resol-*ute*, min-*ute*.

Note.—The suffix *-ate*, when it is used for forming nouns, can take the forms of *-ee* or *-y* (see above under Noun-suffixes, § 255 (21) **-ee**). Hence we sometimes have two forms, as priv-*ate*, priv-*y*.

(31) **-und, -ond** (Lat. *-undus*, Fr. *-ond*):—

Morib-*und*, rubic-*und*, joc-*und*, rot-*und* or ro-*und*. Sec-*ond*, vagab-*ond* (noun).

(32) **-urn** (Lat. *-urnus*):—

Tacit-*urn*, aub-*urn* (Late Lat. *alb-urnus*), noct-*urn*-al, di-*urn*-al.

(33) **-y** (Lat. *-ivus*, Anglo-French *-if*).—The *f* was retained in Early and Middle English, but dropped off by degrees, leaving *-i*, which is now written as *-y*.

*Hast-*y*, *joll-*y*, mass-*y*, test-*y*, touch-*y* (for tetch-*y*, freakish).

Adverb suffixes.—There are no adverbial suffixes of Latin origin, but adjectives ending in *-ble* form adverbs in *-bly*, as *horrible*, *horribly*, on the analogy of the Teutonic adverbial suffix *-ly*.

C. *Verb-forming.*

For the ways in which English verbs have been formed from Latin ones, the reader can refer to § 40.

257. (1) **-ate** (Lat. *-atus*, Pass. participle).—The suffix has become naturalised, and has been used for forming new verbs, to which there is no Latin equivalent :—

Agit-*ate*, moder-*ate*, stimul-*ate*, cre-*ate*, etc.

Modern formations :—captiv-*ate*, gradu-*ate*, accentu-*ate*, vaccin-*ate*, differenti-*ate*, isol-*ate*, incapacit-*ate*, *assassin-*ate*, *filtr-*ate*, alien-*ate*, superannu-*ate*, compassion-*ate*, etc.

(2) **-er** (from Fr. Infin. *-re* or *-ir*, Lat. *-ere*) :—

Rend-*er* (Fr. rend-*re* or *-er*, Lat. rend-*ere*).

(3) **-esce** (Lat. *-esco*), inceptive :—

Efferv-*esce*, coal-*esce*, acqui-*esce*, efflor-*esce*.

(4) **-fy** (Lat. *-ficare*, Fr. *-fier*).—Added to nouns and adjectives for forming Causal verbs :—

Magni-*fy* (to make great), signi-*fy*, simpli-*fy*, modi-*fy*, terri-*fy*, edi-*fy*, stupe-*fy*, ampli-*fy*, rami-*fy*, fructi-*fy*, Frenchi-*fy*.

(5) **-ish** (Fr. *-iss*, Pres. part. suffix of several verbs in *-ir*, as in "flor-*iss*-ant," where the *-iss* is really derived from the Lat. inceptive *-esc*, "flor-*esc*-entem") :—

Establ-*ish*, pun-*ish*, fin-*ish*, nour-*ish*, garn-*ish*, publ-*ish*, van-*ish*, flour-*ish*, cher-*ish*, abol-*ish*, ban-*ish*, relinqu-*ish*, fam-*ish*, per-*ish*, extingu-*ish*, dimin-*ish*, demol-*ish*, etc.

Disguised suffix :—pun-*ch*, short for pun-*ish*.

(6) **-y** (Fr. *-i* in the Infin. suffix *-i-er* ; cf. A.S. *-i* in the Infin. suffix *-i-an*) ; see above, p. 205.

Marr-*y* (Fr. mar-*i*-er), sall-*y* (Fr. saill-*i*-r), carr-*y* (O. F. carr-*i*-er).

CHAPTER XI.—GREEK PREFIXES AND SUFFIXES.

Section 1.—Prefixes.

258. A-, an-, am- (*not ;* like English *un-*) : *an*-archy, *an*-æsthetic, *an*-ecdote, *an*-odyne, *an*-onymous, *a*-symptote, *a*-theism, *a*-pathy, *am*-brosial, *a*-trophy, *an*-omalous, *a*-byss (lit. bottomless), *a*-tom, *a*-pterix (the wingless), *a*-maranth, *a*-mnesty, *a*-sbestos, *a*-sphyxia.

Amphi- (*about, on both sides*) : *amphi*-theatre, *amphi*-bious.

Ana-, an- (*up to, again*) : *ana*-chronism, *ana*-tomy, *ana*-logy, *ana*-lysis, *an*-eurism, *ana*-gram, *ana*-thema, *ana*-pæst, *an*-choret.

Anti-, ant- (*against*) : *anti*-podes, *anti*-type, *anti*-thesis, *anti*-dote, *anti*-Christ, **anti*-fat, **anti*-bilious, **anti*-socialist, *anti*-pathy ; *ant*-agonist, *anth*-em (Gr. *anti*-phona), *ant*-arctic.

Apo-, aph- (*from*) : *apo*-logy, *apo*-state, *apo*-strophe, *aph*-orism, *aph*-æresis, *aph*-elion, *apo*-stle, *apo*-plexy, *apo*-thecary, *apo*-gee, *apo*-theosis.

Arch-, archi-, arche- (*chief, head*) : *arch*-heretic, *arch*-bishop, *arch*-angel, *arch*-enemy, *archi*-tect, *arche*-type, an-*arch*-y, *archi*-pelago, *arch*-aic, *arch*-ives.

Auto-, auth- (*self*): *auto*-graph, **auto*-car, *auto*-maton, *auto*-nomy, *auto*-biography, *auth*-entic, *aut*-opsy.

Cata-, cath-, cat- (*down*): *cata*-ract, *cath*-edral, *cata*-strophe, *cat*-echism, *cath*-olic, *cata*-comb, *cata*-clysm, *cata*-logue, *cat*-egory, *cata*-pult, *cata*-rrh.

Dia- (*through*): *dia*-meter, *dia*-logue, *dia*-dem, *dia*-gonal, *dia*-lysis, *dia*-phragm, *dia*-pason, *dia*-rrhœa, *dia*-lect, *dia*-phanous, *dia*-tribe, *dia*-gram, *dia*-gnosis, *dia*-betes, *di*-æresis, *dia*-bolical. The prefix is disguised in *dea*-con (Gr. *dia*-konos), *de*-vil (Gr. *dia*-bolos).

Dis-, di- (*in two*): *dis*-syllable, *di*-ptera, *di*-stich, *di*-glott, *di*-ploma, *di*-phthong, *di*-lemma.

Dys- (*ill*): *dys*-peptic, *dys*-entery.

Ec-, ex- (*out, from*): *ex*-odus, *ex*-orcise; *ec*-stasy, *ec*-clesiastic, *ec*-centric, *ec*-lipse, *ec*-logue.

En- (*in*): *en*-thusiasm, *en*-demic, *en*-caustic, *en*-cyclical, *en*-ergy, *em*-piric, *em*-porium, *em*-pyrean, *em*-phasis, *el*-lipsis, *en*-comium.

Endo- (*within*): *endo*-gamous, *endo*-genous.

Epi-, eph-, ep- (*upon*): *epi*-gram, *ep*-och, *epi*-taph, *eph*-emeral, *epi*-stle, *epi*-phany, *ep*-ode (something sung after), *epi*-cene (of common gender).

Eso- (*within*): *eso*-teric.

Eu-, ev- (*well*): *eu*-phony, *eu*-phemism, *eu*-logy, *ev*-angelist.

Exo- (*without*): *exo*-teric, *exo*-tic, *exo*-gamous.

Hemi- (*half*): *hemi*-sphere, *hemi*-stich. (Disguised in *me*-grim, Gr. *hemi*-cranion, half the skull.)

Hepta-, hept- (*seven*): *hepta*-gon, *hept*-archy.

Hetero- (*different*): *hetero*-dox, *hetero*-geneous.

Hexa- (*six*): *hexa*-meter, *hexa*-gon.

Homeo- (*similar*): *homeo*-pathy.

Homo-, hom- (*same*): *homo* geneous, *hom*-onym.

Hyper- (*above*): *hyper*-bole, *hyper*-critical, *hyper*-borean. (The *hyper*- in the two words first given denotes *excess, too much;* cf. *super*- in *super*-fluous.)

Hypo-, hyph- (*under*): *hypo*-crite, *hypo*-thesis, *hyph*-en, *hypo*-chondria.

Meta-, meth-, met- (*after, substitution*): *meta*-phor, *meth*-od, *met*-onymy, *meta*-morphosis, *meta*-physics, *meta*-thesis, *met*-eor.

Mono-, mon- (*single, alone*): *mono*-graph, *mon*-archy, *mon*-astery, *mon*-ody, *mon*-k. (Disguised in *min*-ster, Gr. *mon*-asterion.)

Palin- (*again*): *palin*-ode, *palim*-psest.

Pan-, panto- (*all*): *pan*-theist, *pan*-oply, *pan*-orama, *pan*-acea, *panto*-mime, *pan*-demonium.

Para-, par- (*beside*): *para*-phrase, *para*-ble, *par*-allel, *para*-site, *para*-digm, *para*-dox, *para*-bola, *para*-graph, *par*-ody, *para*-phernalia, *para*-gon, *par*-allax, *par*-oxysm, *par*-helion, *par*-ish, *para*-lysis (hence *pa*-lsy).

Note.—The Greek *para* is quite distinct from *para* in *para*-chute, *para*-pet, *para*-sol. These are from Fr. *parer*, to guard against.

Penta- (five): *penta*-meter, *penta*-teuch, *penta*-polis, *penta*-gon.

Peri- (*around*): *peri*-meter, *peri*-phrasis, *peri*-od, *peri*-gee, *peri*-phery, *peri*-staltic.

Poly- (*many*): *poly*-syllable, *poly*-theist, *poly*-glot.

Pro- (*before*): *pro*-gramme, *pro*-logue, *pro*-phet, *pro*-boscis, *pro*-blem, *pro*-gnathous, *pro*-gnostic.

Pros- (*towards*): *pros*-ody, *pros*-elyte.

Pseudo-, **pseud**- (*false*): *pseudo*-critic, *pseud*-onym.

Syn- (*with*): *syn*-thesis, *syn*-agogue, *syn*-tax, *sym*-pathy, *syl*-lable, *syl*-logism, *sym*-bol, *sym*-metry, *syn*-dicate, *sy*-stem.

Tele- (*afar*): *tele*-graph, *tele*-phone, *tele*-gram.

Tetra- (*four*): *tetra*-gon, *tetra*-hedron, *tetr*-arch, *tetra*-syllable, *tra*-pezium (*tetra-peza*, a four-footed bench).

Tri- (*thrice* or *three*): *tri*-pod, *tri*-syllable, *tri*-gonometry.

U- (*not*, properly *ou*): *u*-topia (the land of no-where).

SECTION 2.—SUFFIXES.

(*Hybrids are marked with an asterisk.*)

A. *Noun-forming.*

259. (1) **-ac** (Gr. *-akos*, an adjective suffix in Greek):—

Mani-*ac*, demoni-*ac*.

(2) **-ad, -id**, chiefly used with proper names for country, nymph, poem, etc.

-ad: Tro-*ad* (the country about Troy), Ili-*ad* (poem about Ilium or Troy), Dunci-*ad* (epic of Dunces), Dry-*ad* (wood nymph), Lusi-*ad* (the Portuguese epic), mon-*ad* (a unit), tri-*ad* (a union of three), myri-*ad*, dec-*ade*.

-id: Æne-*id* (the story of Æneas), Nere-*id* (water nymph), Theba-*id* (the story of Thebes).

Excluded word:—

Druid, from Celtic *druidh*, a soothsayer.

(3) **-ant** (Gr. *-antem*, *-antes*):—

Gi-*ant*, eleph-*ant*, adam-*ant*, sycoph-*ant*.

(4) **-asm** (Gr. *-asmos*, *-asma*): chiefly Abstract:—

Enthusi-*asm*, pleon-*asm*, sarc-*asm*, iconocl-*asm*, ch-*asm*, phant-*asm* (other form, phant-*om*), sp-*asm*, mi-*asma*, phant-*asma*.

> Between the acting of a dreadful thing
> And the first motion, all the interim is
> Like a phant-*asma* or a hideous dream.—SHAKSPEARE.

(5) **-ast** (Gr. *-astes*), agent:—

Enthusi-*ast*, gymn-*ast*, iconocl-*ast*, encomi-*ast*.

Excluded word:—

Bombast: Pers. *bandash*, carded cotton, hence in English "padding or inflated language."

(6) **-e** (Greek suffix unchanged), syllabic *ē* :—

Epitom-*e*, catastroph-*e*, acm-*e*, apostroph-*e*.

(7) **-ic, -ics** (Gr. *-ikos*, *-ica*, Neut. Plur.) : *-ic* denotes agent, or some art or science ; *-ics* denotes only some art or science. The English plural is in imitation of the Greek Plural :—

-ic. Agent : heret-*ic*, mim-*ic*, scept-*ic*, crit-*ic*, polem-*ic*, agnost-*ic*, ecclesiast-*ic*, cyn-*ic*, cler-*ic* or cler-*k*. (Cf. Lat. suffix *-ic* in lunat-*ic*, fanat-*ic*, etc.)

Some art, science, or quality :—log-*ic*, mus-*ic*, mag-*ic*, phys-*ic*, arithmet-*ic*, characterist-*ic*.

-ics : phys-*ics*, eth-*ics*, opt-*ics*, econom-*ics*, mathemat-*ics*, polit-*ics*, gymnast-*ics*, tact-*ics*, obstetr-*ics*, hermeneut-*ics*, cosmet-*ics*, statist-*ics*, stat-*ics*, dynam-*ics*, metaphys-*ics*, phonet-*ics*.

Note 1.—When the Latin *-an* is added to *-ics* to denote agent, the final *s* is dropped, and the vowel *i* is added :—

Optic(s)-*ian*, physic(s)-*ian*, statistic(s)-*ian*, politic(s)-*ian*.

Note 2.—The adjective suffix *-al* is frequently added to *-ic* :—

Optic-*al*, physic-*al*, statistic-*al*, politic-*al*, heretic-*al*, sceptic-*al*, critic-*al*, etc.

Excluded word :—

Antics, an imitation of the Greek nouns ; but the stem *antic* is from Lat. *antiqu*-us, ancient.

(8) **-ine** (Gr. *-in-e*, Fr. *-ine*) :—

Hero-*ine* (Gr. *he-ro-i-ne*, four syll.), Czar-*ina*.

Note.—The suffixes in Landgrav-*ine*, Margrav-*ine* came through Dutch.

(9) **-isk, -esque** (Gr. *-iskos*, Fr. *-esque*) : Diminutive :—

Aster-*isk*, basil-*isk*, obel-*isk*.

(10) **-ism** (Gr. *-ismos*) : Abstract. Very widely used ; can be freely added to Romanic and Teutonic stems, as well as to Greek ones :—

Greek stems :—patriot-*ism*, bapt-*ism*, despot-*ism*, critic-*ism*, barbar-*ism*, sch-*ism*, archa-*ism*, soph-*ism*, rheumat-*ism*, the-*ism*, euphem-*ism*, euphu-*ism*, solec-*ism*, dogmat-*ism*, magnet-*ism*, aneur-*ism*, anachron-*ism*, mechan-*ism*, organ-*ism*.

Romanic stems (hybrid words) :—fatal-*ism*, formal-*ism*, rational-*ism*, secular-*ism*, plagiar-*ism*, pagan-*ism* (corrupted to Payn-*im* or Pain-*im*), optim-*ism*, pessim-*ism*, de-*ism*, social-*ism*, commun-*ism*, vulgar-*ism*, manner-*ism*, somnambul-*ism*, etc.

Teutonic stems (hybrid words) :—heathen-*ism*, tru-*ism*, wittic-*ism* (from adj. *witty*, to which a *c* has been added for the sake of euphony).

The suffix is much used for denoting (*a*) religious belief, (*b*) language or style :—

(*a*) *Religious belief*:—Hindu-*ism*, Buddh-*ism*, Mahommedan-*ism*, Roman-*ism*, Protestant-*ism*, Method-*ism*, sceptic-*ism*, *ritual-*ism*, Unitarian-*ism*, Puritan-*ism*, athe-*ism*, Calvin-*ism*.

(*b*) *Language or style*:—Anglic-*ism*, Gallic-*ism*, Latin-*ism*, Scottic-*ism*, Cockney-*ism*, Yankee-*ism*, American-*ism*, provincial-*ism*, vulgar-*ism*.

Recent formations:—hypnot-*ism*, mesmer-*ism*, jingo-*ism*, Chauvin-*ism*, *union-*ism*, *separat-*ism*, agnostic-*ism*, *toady-*ism*, *ventrilo-qu-*ism*.

(11) **-ist** (Gr. -*istes*): the concrete counterpart to -*ism*, and covering much the same ground: denotes agent:—

Some art, science, or profession:—*art-*ist*, dramat-*ist*, *ocul-*ist*, *dent-*ist*, *natural-*ist*, botan-*ist*, *chem-*ist*, psalm-*ist*, monopol-*ist*, *annal-*ist*, *novel-*ist*, *lingu-*ist*, *vocal-*ist*, *instrumental-*ist*, *copy-*ist*, *Oriental-*ist*, *flor-*ist*, *tobacco(n)-*ist*, taxiderm-*ist*.

Some kind of theory or creed:—pap-*ist*, *dual-*ist*, mon-*ist*, *commun-*ist*, *ego-*ist*, *altru-*ist*, *fatal-*ist*, *secular-*ist*, *scient-*ist*, *rational-*ist*, the-*ist*, *de-*ist*, anarch-*ist*, *royal-*ist*, theosoph-*ist*, evangel-*ist*, method-*ist*, *real-*ist*, *ideal-*ist*, etc.

Some peculiarity of habit or character:—*optim-*ist*, *pessim-*ist*, *extrem-*ist*, *alarm-*ist*, *ego(t)-*ist*, *formal-*ist*, dogmat-*ist*, *manner-*ist*, *opportun-*ist*, *casu-*ist*, soph-*ist*, theor-*ist*, *terror-*ist*, *piet-*ist*, *quiet-*ist*, bigam-*ist*.

Recent formations:—*Nihil-*ist*, *union-*ist*, *separat-*ist*, *spiritual-*ist*, *jingo-*ist*.

(12) **-ite, -it** (Gr. -*ites*): denotes agent of some kind:—

National titles:—Ishmael-*ite*, Canaan-*ite*, Israel-*ite*.

Habit or character:—cosmopol-*ite*, erem-*ite* or herm-*it*, anchor-*ite* or -*et*.

Sect or faction:—Parnell-*ite*, Pusey-*ite*, Ibsen-*ite*, Irving-*ite*, Jesu-*it*, Jacob-*ite*, Carmel-*ite*.

Scientific terms:—dynam-*ite*, anthrac-*ite*, etc.

Excluded word:—

Favour-ite, the fem. of the French participle *favori*.

(13) **-m, -me** (Gr. -*ma*, Fr. -*mme*):—

The-*me*, sche-*me*, progra-*mme*, cli-*me* (Gr. *clima*, *climat-os*; hence clim-*ate*), proble-*m*, theore-*m*, axio-*m*, poe-*m*, apophtheg-*m*, syste-*m*, diade-*m*, emble-*m*, anagra-*m*, stratage-*m*, telegra-*m*, phleg-*m*, para-dig-*m*.

Naturalised Greek words:—dra-*ma*, stig-*ma*, ecze-*ma*, panora-*ma*, diora-*ma*, ene-*ma*, diplo-*ma*, enig-*ma*, aro-*ma*, asth-*ma*, dog-*ma*.

Excluded words:—

Anthem: Gr. *anti-phona*, Anglo-Saxon *antefn*, later *antem*: no connection with the suffix -*m*.

Phantom: corruption of Gr. phant-*asm*, Old Fr. fant-*osme*.

Balsam, balm: in these the *m* is part of the stem.

(14) **-oid** (Gr. *eid*-os, form or kind, preceded by *o*, which gives the compound -*oid*):—

Anthrop-*oid*, negr-*oid*, metall-*oid*, musc-*oid* (moss-like), tabl-*oid*, trapez-*oid*, rhomb-*oid*, aster-*oid*, aner-*oid*, etc.

(15) **-on** (Greek suffix, unchanged) :—

Naturalised words : phenomen-*on*, criteri-*on*, automat-*on*.

(16) **-ot** (Gr. *-otes*) : denotes agent or title :—

Zeal-*ot*, *patri-*ot*, idi-*ot*, Iscari-*ot*, Cypri-*ot*.

(17) **-sy, -se** (Gr. *-sis*, Fr. *sie*) : chiefly Abstract :—

-sy : drop-*sy*, pal-*sy*, phren-*zy* or fren-*sy*, epilep-*sy*, catalep-*sy*, here-*sy*, pleuri-*sy*, apoplexy, aposta-*sy*.

-se : eclip-*se*, ellip-*se*, ba-*se*, apocalyp-*se*, phra-*se*, paraphra-*se*.

Naturalised Greek words :—ba-*sis*, analy-*sis*, the-*sis*, parenthe-*sis*, antithe-*sis*, synthe-*sis*, paraly-*sis* (hence pal-*sy*), neuro-*sis*, diagno-*sis*, exege-*sis*, cri-*sis*, empha-*sis*, synop-*sis*, periphra-*sis*, probos-*cis*, elephantia-*sis*, metamorpho-*sis*, syneri-*sis* (cf. metropol-*is*, acropol-*is*).

Excluded word :—

Minstrelsy, a misspelling for minstel-*cy*, with Lat. suffix *-cy*.

(18) **-t, -te** (Gr. *-tes*, *-te*, Lat. *-ta*) :—

Prophe-*t*, plane-*t*, poe-*t* (Gr. or Lat.), die-*t*, aposta-*te*, come-*t*.

(19) **-tre, -ter** (Gr. *-tron*, Lat. *-trum*) :—

Cen-*tre*, me-*tre*, me-*ter*, phil-*tre*, diame-*ter*, thea-*tre*, scep-*tre*, fil-*ter*.

(20) **-y** (Gr. *-ia*, Lat. *-ia*) : chiefly Abstract :—

Monarch-*y*, academ-*y*, energ-*y*, agon-*y*, philosoph-*y*, physiolog-*y*, anarch-*y*, democrac-*y*, astronom-*y*, sympath-*y*, iron-*y*, antholog-*y*, categor-*y*, pharmac-*y*, poes-*y*, monod-*y*, parod-*y*, monoton-*y*, monopol-*y*, polit-*y*, peripher-*y*, orthograph-*y*, euphon-*y*, symphon-*y*, harmon-*y*, autonom-*y*, Deuteronom-*y*, autops-*y*.

Naturalised Greek words :—man-*ia*, dyspeps-*ia*, hydrophob-*ia*, utop-*ia*, pneumon-*ia*, pharmacopœ-*ia*, morph-*ia*, panac-*ea*.

Imitation :—orthodox-*y* (from Gr. ortho + dox-*a*).

(21) **-ysm** (Gr. *-usmos*) :—

Catacl-*ysm*, parox-*ysm*.

B. *Adjective-forming.*

260. (1) **-ac** (Gr. *-akos*) :—

Demoni-*ac*, Syri-*ac*, *ili-*ac*.

(2) **-ic** (Gr. *-ikos*, similar to the Lat. *-icus*) :—

Authent-*ic*, lacon-*ic*, empir-*ic*, climat-*ic*, spasmod-*ic*, opthalm-*ic*, scen-*ic*, aromat-*ic*, frant-*ic*, schismat-*ic*, monast-*ic*, hero-*ic*, rheumat-*ic*, dogmat-*ic*, erot-*ic*, econom-*ic*, academ-*ic*, drast-*ic*, dramat-*ic*, com-*ic*, trag-*ic*, period-*ic*, graph-*ic*, iamb-*ic*, letharg-*ic*, caust-*ic*, æsthet-*ic*, archa-*ic*, chromat-*ic*, emphat-*ic*, organ-*ic*, despot-*ic*, cathol-*ic*, eccentr-*ic*, diplomat-*ic*, autocrat-*ic*.

The Greek suffix *-ic* is often compounded with the Latin

suffix *-al*, the addition of which usually modifies the force of the adjective :—

Period-*ic*, period-*ical*; polit-*ic*, polit-*ical*; dramat-*ic*, dramat-*ical*; trag-*ic*, trag-*ical*; com-*ic*, com-*ical*.

(3) **-astic** (Gr. *-astikos*, the adjective of *-ast*) :—

Pleon-*astic*, sarc-*astic*, bomb-*astic*, enthusi-*astic*, fant-*astic*, ecclesi-*astic* (chiefly used as a noun : adj. form is ecclesi-*astical*).

(4) **-istic** (Gr. *-istikos*, the adj. of *-ist*) :—

Patr-*istic*, eulog-*istic*, evangel-*istic*, *lingu-*istic*, *egot-*istic*-al, the-*istic*, *real-*istic*, method-*istic*-al, *art-*istic*, soph-*istic*-al.

C. *Verb-forming.*

261. -ize, -ise (Gr. *-izein*, Fr. *-iser*).—Generally spelt with *s*, and rightly so, since the suffix came to us through the Fr. *-iser*. This suffix is very widely used. It converts (*a*) an adjective into a Transitive verb; (*b*) a noun into a Transitive or Intransitive one :—

(*a*) *Human-*ise*, *brutal-*ise*, *general-*ise*, *special-*ise*, *real-*ise*, *moral-*ise*, *vital-*ise*, *popular-*ise*, *solemn-*ise*, *aggrand-*ise*, *minim-*ise*, *modern-*ise*, *secular-*ise*, *national-*ise*, *rational-*ise*, *equal-*ise*, *civil-*ise*, *util-*ise*, *mobil-*ise*, *fertil-*ise*, *neutral-*ise*, *local-*ise*, bapt-*ize*, *fratern-*ise*.

With proper names :—Anglic-*ise*, Indian-*ise*, Christian-*ise*.

Transitive verbs :—

(*b*) Harmon-*ise*, magnet-*ise*, *summar-*ise*, *scrutin-*ise*, emphas-*ise*, systemat-*ise*, method-*ise*, monopol-*ise*, mesmer-*ise*, scandal-*ise*, symbol-*ise*, *subsid-*ise*, evangel-*ise*, *terror-*ise*, dramat-*ise*, *patron-*ise*, *colon-*ise*, *author-*ise*, *jeopard-*ise*, *capital-*ise*, *memorial-*ise*, apolog-*ise*, ostrac-*ise*.

Intransitive verbs :—

*Tempor-*ise*, theor-*ise*, botan-*ise*, *sermon-*ise*, tyrann-*ise*, sym-path-*ise*, philosoph-*ise*.

Recent formations :—Gorgon-*ise* (Tennyson; to have the effect of a Gorgon upon a thing; to petrify it). Bowdler-*ise* (an expurgated edition of Shakspeare was published by a Mr. Bowdler. Hence to Bowdlerise a book is to eliminate whatever is not fit to be read).

CHAPTER XII.—SUMMARY OF RESULTS IN PREFIXES AND SUFFIXES.

262. Hybrids.—As a general rule Teutonic affixes are added to Teutonic stems, Romanic to Romanic, and Greek to Greek.

But all these prefixes and suffixes have now become naturalised in English, and hence many Derivative words are of mixed origin. Such words are called Hybrids or half-breeds, § 246, *Note*.

(*a*) Teutonic stems with Romanic prefixes :—

En-dear, *en*-snare, *per*-haps, *demi*-god, *re*-call, *counter*-work.

(*b*) Teutonic stems with Romanic suffixes :—

Starv-*ation*, stream-*let*, godd-*ess*, lusci-*ous*, scrimm-*age*, drink-*able*, fern-*ery*, block-*ade*, atone-*ment*, talkat-*ive*, forbear-*ance*, bond-*age*.

(*c*) Romanic stems with Teutonic prefixes :—

Under-estimate, *un*-deceive, *be*-siege, *a*-cross, *after*-piece, *over*-turn.

(*d*) Romanic stems with Teutonic suffixes :—

False-*hood*, priest-*craft*, quarrel-*some*, bishop-*ric*, rapid-*ly*, merci-*ful*, duke-*dom*.

Note 1.—On hybrid *compounds*, see list in chap. viii. § 241.
Note 2.—For a hybrid *suffix*, see **-ery**, as "fish-*er-y*," § 255 (49).

263. Comparative Results.—The comparative results of what is shown in chaps. ix.-xi. are exemplified below :—

(*a*) Affixes denoting a *moderate* degree of some quality :—

-ish, Teut.: black-*ish* (rather black), sweet-*ish* (rather sweet).
-ly, Teut.: clean-*ly*, sick-*ly*, elder-*ly*, weak-*ly*.
Sub-, Rom.: *sub*-acid (rather acid), *sub*-tropical (almost tropical).

(*b*) Suffixes denoting a *high* degree of some quality :—

-ful, Teut.: *plenti-*ful*, wonder-*ful*, *taste-*ful*, truth-*ful*.
-ous, **-ose**, Rom.: verb-*ose*, numer-*ous*, fam-*ous*, odi-*ous*.

Note.—The equivalence of these two suffixes is shown by the pairs of words in which they appear. Thus we have: *plenti-*ful*, plente-*ous*; *beauti-*ful*, beaute-*ous*; *bounti-*ful*, bounte-*ous*; *piti-*ful*, pite*ous*; *joy-*ful*, joy-*ous*; *grace-*ful*, graci-*ous*.

(*c*) Prefixes signifying the undoing of something done :—

Un-, Teut.: *un*-bolt, *un*-tie, *un*-lock, *un*-fold.
Dis- or **di-**, Rom.: *dis*-mount, *dis*-appear, *dis*-arm.
De-, Rom.: *de*-throne, *de*-camp, *de*-tach, *de*-odorise.

(*d*) Prefixes and Suffixes denoting a negative :—

Un-, Teut.: *un*-happy, *un*-safe, *un*-ready.
-less, Teut.: hap-*less*, law-*less*, hope-*less*.
N-, Teut.: *n*-one, *n*-ever, *n*-either, *n*-or.
Dis-, **di-**, Rom.: *dis*-quiet, *dif*-ficult, *dif*-fident, *dis*-honour.
In-, Rom.: *in*-human, *ir*-regular, *im*-moral, *il*-legible.
Ne-, **neg-**, **non-**, Rom.: *ne*-farious, *neg*-lect, *non*-sense.
A- or **an-**, Greek: *a*-pathy, *an*-archy, *am*-brosial.

(*e*) Suffixes indicating the Feminine gender :—

-ster, Teut.: spin-*ster*.
-en, Teut.: vix-*en*.
-ess: Rom.: lion-*ess*, temptr-*ess*, tigr-*ess*.

(*f*) Prefixes indicating something bad :—

Mis-, Teut. (from *miss*) : *mis*-take, *mis*-deed, *mis*-hap.
Male-, **mal-**, Rom.: *male*-factor, *mal*-treat.
Mis-, Rom. (from *minus*) : *mis*-use, *mis*-fortune.
Dys-, Greek : *dys*-entery, *dys*-pepsia.

(*g*) Prefixes indicating something good :—

Well-, Teut.: *wel*-fare, *wel*-come, *well*-being.
Bene-, Rom.: *bene*-volent, *bene*-fit, *bene*-diction.
Eu-, Greek : *eu*-phemism, *ev*-angelist, *eu*-phony.

(*h*) Suffixes denoting diminutives, endearment, or contempt :—

Teutonic :—

-el, **-le**, **-erel** : kern-*el*, padd-*le*, dott-*erel*.
-en : maid-*en*, chick-*en*.
-ing : wild-*ing*, sweet-*ing*.
-ling : dar-*ling*, strip-*ling*, weak-*ling*, under-*ling*.
-kin : bump-*kin*, manni-*kin*, lamb-*kin*, fir-*kin*.
-ock : hill-*ock*, bull-*ock*, humm-*ock*, padd-*ock*.
-y, **-ie** : bird-*ie*, dogg-*y*, lass-*ie*, Charl-*ey*, Johnn-*y*.

Romanic :—

-aster : poet-*aster*, pil-*aster*.
-ule, **-le** : pill-*ule*, sched-*ule* ; circ-*le*, chasub-*le*.
-cule, **-cle** : animal-*cule*, mole-*cule* ; parti-*cle*, pinna-*cle*.
-el, **-le**, **-l**, **-elle** : parc-*el*, kett-*le*, vea-*l*, bagat-*elle*.
-et, **-ot**, **-ette**, **-let** : bill-*et*, ball-*ot*, statu-*ette*, *brook-*let*.
-ito : mosqu-*ito*, negr-*ito*.

Greek :—

-isk : aster-*isk*, obel-*isk*.

(*i*) List of Suffixes forming Abstract Nouns :—

Teutonic :—

-craft : witch-*craft*, *priest-*craft*, handi-*craft*.
-dom : free-*dom*, *martyr-*dom*, *pope-*dom*, *duke-*dom*.
-hood, **-head** : maiden-*head*, likeli-*hood*.
-lock, **-ledge** : wed-*lock*, know-*ledge*.
-red : hat-*red*, kind-*red*.
-ric : *bishop-*ric*.
-ing : learn-*ing*, hunt-*ing*, etc.
-ness : dark-*ness*, nothing-*ness*.
-ship : friend-*ship*, wor-*ship*, owner-*ship*, *citizen-*ship*.
-t, **-th** : heigh-*t*, sigh-*t* ; tru-*th*, dear-*th*, etc.
-ter, **-der** : laugh-*ter*, slaugh-*ter*, mur-*der*.

Romanic :—

-age : cour-*age*, hom-*age*, umbr-*age*, *bond-*age*.
-al : refus-*al*, tri-*al*, arriv-*al*, surviv-*al*.
-ance, **-ence**, **-ancy**, **-ency** : dist-*ance*, prud-*ence*, const-*ancy*, urg-*ency*.
-ate : consul-*ate*, noviti-*ate*, patriarch-*ate*.
-cy, **-sy**, **-acy** : secre-*cy*, minstrel-*sy*, prel-*acy*.
-ice, **-ise**, **-ess**, **-es** : serv-*ice*, franch-*ise*, prow-*ess*, rich-*es*.

-ion : relig-*ion*, suspic-*ion*, fash-*ion*, fact-*ion*.
-lence : opu-*lence*, viru-*lence*, corpu-*lence*.
-ment : judg-*ment*, enjoy-*ment*, attach-*ment*.
-mony : acri-*mony*, parsi-*mony*, matri-*mony*.
-or, -our, -eur : err-*or*, fav-*our*, grand-*eur*.
-ry, -ery : *husband-*ry*, *trick-*ery*.
-tude : lassi-*tude*, forti-*tude*.
-ty : cruel-*ty*, authori-*ty*.
-ure : cult-*ure*, *seiz-*ure*, nat-*ure*, verd-*ure*.
-y : perfid-*y*, luxur-*y*, master-*y*, infam-*y*.

Greek :—

-asm, -ism : sarc-*asm*, *optim-*ism*.
-ic, -ics : log-*ic*, eth-*ics*.
-sy, -se : drop-*sy*, apocalyp-*se*.
-y : monarch-*y*, energ-*y*, sympath-*y*.

(*j*) List of Suffixes denoting agent or person :—

Teutonic :—

-man : boat-*man*, wo-*man*, midship-*man*, fisher-*man*.
-el, -le : bead-*le*, cripp-*le*, scoundr-*el*.
-er, -ier, -yer, -ar, -or : rid-*er*, cloth-*ier*, law-*yer*, li-*ar*, sail-*or*.
-ster : huck-*ster*, malt-*ster*, trick-*ster*, rhyme-*ster*.
-ter, -ther, -der : mo-*ther*, fa-*ther*, sis-*ter*, daugh-*ter*, spi-*der*.
-nd : fie-*nd*, frie-*nd*, wi-*nd*, husba-*nd*.

Romanic :—

-an, -ain, -on, -en, -ian : public-*an*, capt-*ain*, citiz-*en*, sext-*on*, guard-*ian*.
-ant, -ent : merch-*ant*, tru-*ant* ; stud-*ent*, presid-*ent*.
-ard, -art : *wiz-*ard*, Spani-*ard*, *bragg-*art*.
-ary, -aire, -ar, -er, -eer, -ier, -or : statu-*ary*, million-*aire*, vic-*ar*, arch-*er*, volunt-*eer*, cash-*ier*, chancell-*or*.
-ate, -ee, -ey, -y : candid-*ate*, *trust-*ee*, attorn-*ey*, deput-*y*.
-ine, -in : libert-*ine*, gobl-*in*.
-on : fel-*on*, glutt-*on*, mas-*on*, sculli-*on*.
-or, -our, -eur, -er : aggress-*or*, troubad-*our*, amat-*eur*, preach-*er*.

Greek :—

-ac : mani-*ac*, demoni-*ac*.
-ast : enthusi-*ast*, inconocl-*ast*.
-ic : heret-*ic*, scept-*ic*, crit-*ic* (cf. Lat. lunat-*ic*).
-ist : psalm-*ist*, anarch-*ist*, the-*ist*.
-ite, -it : cosmopol-*ite*, erem-*ite*, Jesu-*it*.
-ot : zeal-*ot*, patri-*ot*, Cypri-*ot*.

(*k*) List of Adjective Suffixes that convey a Passive sense :—

-d, -ed, -t, Past part. Teut. : love-*d*, kill-*ed*, brough-*t*.
-able, -ible, -uble, Rom. : laud-*able*, ed-*ible*, sol-*uble*

(*l*) List of Adjective Suffixes conveying an active sense :—

-ing, Pres. part. Teut. : astonish-*ing*, amus-*ing*.
-ive, Rom. : recept-*ive*, amat-*ive*, curat-*ive*.
-ory, -orious, Rom. : illus-*ory*, cens-*orious*.
-erious, Rom. : delet-*erious*.

(*m*) List of Suffixes having a depreciatory force :—

Teutonic for forming Nouns :—
-craft : *priest-*craft*, *state-*craft*, witch-*craft*.
-ling : hire-*ling*, ground-*ling*, under-*ling*, world-*ling*, weak-*ling*.
-monger : *ballad-*monger*, *crotchet-*monger*, *grievance-*monger*.
-erel, -rel : mong-*rel*, dogg-*erel*, dott-*erel*, *wast-*rel*.
-ster : trick-*ster*, young-*ster*, rhyme-*ster*.
Romanic for forming Nouns :—
-ard : cow-*ard*, *drunk-*ard*, *slugg-*ard*, dot-*ard*.
-aster : poet-*aster*, critic-*aster*.
Teutonic for forming Adjectives :—
-ish : Rom-*ish*, woman-*ish*, child-*ish*, baby-*ish*, upp-*ish*, *slav-*ish*.
Romanic for forming Adjectives :—
-ile : puer-*ile* (=child-*ish*), infant-*ile* (=baby-*ish*), serv-*ile* (=slav-*ish*).

(*n*) List of Suffixes having an augmentative force :—

Teutonic :—
-le (frequentative verb) : dabb-*le*, grumb-*le*, wagg-*le*, etc.
-er (freq. verb) : sputt-*er*, be-spatt-*er*, wand-*er*, etc.
Romanic :—
-ard (excess to a fault) : *blizz-*ard*, *lagg-*ard*, *drunk-*ard*.
-oon, -one (augment. noun) : ball-*oon*, bass-*oon*, tromb-*one*.

(*o*) List of Suffixes denoting patronymics :—

Teutonic :—
-ing : Vik-*ing*, k-*ing* (A.S. cyn-*ing*), Brown-*ing*, Mann-*ing*.
-son : Ander-*son*, Collin-*son*, David-*son*.
-kin : Peter-*kin* (hence Per-*kin*), Sim-*kin* (Simon-*kin*), Wil-*kin*-s.

(*p*) List of Prefixes and Suffixes by which Transitive Verbs can be formed from an Adjective or Noun :—

Be-, Teut : *be*-friend, *be*-calm, *be*-numb, *be*-little.
-en, Teut. : dark-*en*, length-*en*, hast-*en*, lik-*en*.
-se, Teut. : clean-*se*, rin-*se*, glimp-*se*.
-le, Teut. : start-*le* (start), jost-*le* (joust), stif-*le* (stiff).
In-, **en-**, Rom. : *im*-peril, **en*-dear, **em*- or *im*-bitter.
-fy, Rom. : magni-*fy*, modi-*fy*, stupe-*fy*.
-ise or **-ize**, Greek : *human-*ise*, *brutal-*ise*, *galvan-*ise*.

(*q*) Suffixes denoting Collection or Place. All Romanic.

-ade : arc-*ade* (collection of arches), colonn-*ade*, *balustr-*ade*.
-age : foli-*age*, plum-*age*, *bagg-*age*, *lugg-*age*, equip-*age*.
-ary : *gloss-*ary*, ros-*ary*, libr-*ary*, gran-*ary*.
-ory : invent-*ory*, consist-*ory*, fact-*ory*, dormit-*ory*.
-ry, -ery : tenant-*ry*, gent-*ry*, caval-*ry*, machin-*ery*.

264.—*Latin and Greek equivalent Prefixes :—*

Ambi- (L.)	amphi- (G.)	on both sides.	Semi- (L.)	hemi- (G.)	half.
Ab- (L.)	apo- (G.)	from.	Super- (L.)	hyper- (G.)	above.
Ex- (L.)	ec- (G.)	out of.	Sub- (L.)	hypo- (G.)	under.
In- (L.)	en- (G.)	in, into.	Pro- (L.)	pro- (G.)	before.
Indo- (L.)	endo- (G.)	within.	Tri- (L.)	tri- (G.)	thrice.

265. The same Affix from different Sources.—Sometimes we find a suffix or prefix that has one form and spelling, but comes from more than one source. The following are the principal examples:—

(1) **mis-** (Teut. *miss*, wrongly): *mis*-deed, *mis*-hap, *mis*-take.
,, (Rom. *minus*, less, badly): *mis*-count, *mis*-chief, *mis*-nomer, etc.
(2) **a-** (Teut.): *a*-down (for *of*), *a*-foot (for *on*), *a*-long (for *and*), *a-ught* (for *án*), *a*-rise (for *á*), *a*-do (for *at*), *a*-fford (for *ge*).
,, (Rom.): *a*-vert (for *a*), *a*-spect (for *ad*), *a*-mend (for *e*).
,, (Gr. *a*, not): *a*-pathy, *a*-theism, *a*-mnesty, etc.
(3) **-en** (Teut. *-en*): maid-*en* (dim.), vix-*en* (fem.), hav-*en* (agent), burd-*en* (pass. sense), ox-*en* (plur.), beat-*en* (pass. part.), wood-*en* (adj.), bright-*en* (Trans. verb).
,, (Rom.): ali-*en* (for *-enus*), kitch-*en* (for *-ina*), mizz-*en* (for *-anus*), kitt-*en* (for *-oun*, Fr. kit-*oun*).
(4) **-ther** (Teut.): mo-*ther* (agent, for *-der*), fur-*ther* (comp. *-ther*), hi-*ther* (adverbial *-der* or *-ther*).
(5) **-ish** (Teut. *-isc*): pal-*ish*, woman-*ish*, peev-*ish*, etc.
,, (Rom.): rad-*ish* (noun, for *-icem*), pun-*ish* (verb, for Lat. *-esc*, Fr. *-iss*).
(6) **-red** (Teut.): hat-*red* (for *rǽden*, rule), hund-*red* (for *rǽd*, rate).
(7) **-lock** (Teut.): wed-*lock* (for *lác*, sport), hem-*lock* (for *leác*, plant).
(8) **-ing** (Teut.): learn-*ing* (noun, for *-ung* or *-ing*), learn-*ing* (pres. part., for *-inde*).
(9) **-le** (Teut.): freck-*le* (dim.), bead-*le* (agent), britt-*le* (adj.), crumb-*le* (freq. verb).
,, (Rom.): catt-*le* (for *-alia*), cast-*le* (for *-ellum*), cand-*le* (for *-ela*), ais-*le* (for *-illa*), circ-*le* (for *-ulus*), humb-*le* (for *-ilis*).
(10) **-ling** (Teut.): seed-*ling* (double dim. for *-el* + *-ing*), dark-*ling* (adv. for *-linga*).
(11) **-er** (Teut.): timb-*er* (for *-er*, *-or*), rid-*er* (for *-ere*, agent), hott-*er* (comp. for *-er*, *-or*), bitt-*er* (positive for *-er*, *-or*), chatt-*er* (freq. verb).
,, (Rom.): arch-*er* (for *-arius*), lev-*er* (for *-ator*), tent-*er* (for *-ura*), attaind-*er* (for Fr. Inf. *-re*), rend-*er* (verb, for *-re*, Fr. Inf.).
(12) **-y** (Teut.): dadd-*y* (dim. for *-ig*), smith-*y* (for *-e*, place of action), might-*y* (adj., for *-ig*), ferr-*y* (verb, for the *i* in *-ian*, Inf. suffix).
,, (Rom.): deput-*y* (for *-atus*), jell-*y* (for *-ata*), enem-*y* (for *-icus*), famil-*y* (for *-ia*), stud-*y* (for *-ium*), progen-*y* (for *-ies*), joll-*y* (for *-ivus*, Fr. *-if*), sall-*y* (verb, for *i* in Fr. Inf. *-ir*).
,, (Greek): energ-*y* (for *-eia*).
(13) **-ure** (Rom.): capt-*ure* (for *-ura*), leis-*ure* (for Fr. Inf. *-ir*).
(14) **-ly** (Teut.): man-*ly* (adj. for *-líc*), fit-*ly* (adv., for *líc-e*).
(15) **-ate** (Rom.): cur-*ate* (for *-atus*), postul-*ate* (for *-atum*), prim-*ate* (for *-atem*), st-*ate* (for *-atus*, 4th declens.), agit-*ate* (verb, from *-atum*).

(16) **-ar** (Teut.): li-*ar* (for -*ere*, agent).
,, (Rom.): schol-*ar* (for -*aris*), vic-*ar* (for -*arius*), cell-*ar* (for -*arium*).
(17) **-ble** (Rom.): dou-*ble* (for -*plex*), fee-*ble* (for -*bilis*).
(18) **-or** (Teut.): sail-*or* (for -*ere*, agent).
,, (Rom.): chancell-*or* (for -*arius*, agent), act-*or* (-*or*, agent), emper-*or* (for -*ator*, agent), err-*or* (-*or*, abstract), mirr-*or* (for -*orium*, place), super-i-*or* (comp.).
(19) **-on** (Teut.): wag-*on* (borrowed from Dutch).
,, (Rom.): sext-*on* (for sacrist-*an*, Lat. -*anus*), pois-*on* (for -*ionem*, Lat. pot-*ionem*), li-*on* (for -*onem*), patr-*on* (for -*onus*), matr-*on* (for -*ona*).
,, (Greek): phenomen-*on* (for *ŏn*), surge-*on* (for *ōn*).

CHAPTER XIII.—BILINGUALISM, DOUBLETS, GRIMM'S LAW, VERNER'S LAW.

266. Bilingual Character of English.—One of the most notable peculiarities of English is the bilingual or double character of its vocabulary; § 23. Thus Romanic and Teutonic words of the same, or of almost the same, meaning frequently go in pairs; nouns of Teutonic origin are provided with adjectives of Romanic origin; or the same noun has two adjectives, one Teutonic and the other Romanic. A few examples will now be given in illustration of this point:—

(i) *Words in pairs.*

Teut.	*Rom.*	*Teut.*	*Rom.*
Abode	domicile	Brow	front
Answer	reply, respond	Build	construct
Ask	inquire	Building	edifice
Begin	commence	Burial	funeral
Belief	faith	Bury	inter
Bemoan	deplore	Buy	purchase
Bent	curved	Calling	vocation
Blunder	error	Clasp	embrace
Boldness	fortitude	Clothes	vestments
Bright	radiant	Cold	frigid

(ii) *Romanic Adjectives to Teutonic Nouns.*

Teut.	*Rom.*	*Lat. word.*	*Teut.*	*Rom.*	*Lat. word.*
Cat	feline	*felis*	Eye	ocular	*oculus*
Church (Gr.)	ecclesiastical	*ecclesia* (Gr.)	Foe	hostile	*hostis*
Cow	vaccine	*vacca*	Fox	vulpine	*vulpis*
Dog	canine	*canis*	Gospel	evangelical	*evangelium*
Ear	auricular	*auris*	Head	capital	*capit-is*
Egg	oval	*ovum*	Hearing	audible	*audi-o*

Teut.	*Rom.*	*Lat. word.*	*Teut.*	*Rom.*	*Lat. word.*
Horse	equine	*equus*	Sight	visible	*vis-um*
Husband	marital	*maritus*	Son	filial	*fili-us*
Island	insular	*insula*	Daughter		*fili-a*
Light	lucid	*luc-is*	Spring	vernal	*ver-is*
Lip	labial	*labium*	Stream	fluvial	*fluvi-us*
Mankind	human	*homo*	Sun	solar	*sol-is*
Moon	lunar	*luna*	Tongue	lingual	*lingua*
Mouth	oral	*or-is*	Tooth	dental	*dent-is*
Name	nominal	*nomin-is*	Tree	arboreal	*arbor-is*
Nose	nasal	*nas-us*	Wheel	rotatory	*rotat-um*
Ox	bovine	*bov-is*	Wife	conjugal	*conjug-is*
Sea	marine	*mar-e*	Husband		
Sheep	ovine	*ov-is*	Womb	uterine	*uter-us*
Side	lateral	*later-is*			

(iii) *Two Adjectives to the same Noun.*

Teut. noun.	*Teut. adj.*	*Rom. adj.*	*Lat. noun.*
Blood	bloody	sanguinary	*sanguin-is*
Body	bodily	corporeal	*corpor-is*
Brother	brotherly	fraternal	*frater*
Burden	burdensome	onerous	*oner-is*
Child	childish	puerile	*puer*
Cloud	cloudy	nebular	*nebula*
Day	daily	diurnal	*dies*
Earth	earthly	terrestrial	*terra*
Father	fatherly	paternal	*pater*
Fear	fearful	timorous	*timor*
Fire	fiery	igneous	*ignis*
Flesh	fleshly	carnal	*carn-is*
Friend	friendly	amicable	*amic-us*
Frost	frosty	glacial	*glacies*
God	godlike	divine	*div-us*
Hand	handy	manual	*man-us*
Heart	hearty	cordial	*cord-is*
Heaven	heavenly	celestial	*cæl-um*
Home	homely	domestic	*domus*
Kind	kindly	generic	*gener-is*
King	kingly	regal	*reg-is*
Knight	knightly	equestrian	*eques*
Life	lively	vital	*vita*
Milk	milky	lacteal	*lact-is*
Mother	motherly	maternal	*mater*
Night	nightly	nocturnal	*noct-is*
Room	roomy	spacious	*spatium*
Skin	skinny	cutaneous	*cutis*
War	warlike	bellicose	*bellum*
Water	watery	aqueous	*aqua*
Will	wilful	voluntary	*voluntas*
Woman	womanly womanish	feminine effeminate	*femina*
World	worldly	mundane	*mundus*

(iv) *Verbs in pairs.*

Back up (support) a claim.
Bear out (substantiate) a charge.
Beat off (repel) an attack.
Block up (obstruct) a passage.
Blot out (obliterate) a word.
Blow out (extinguish) a candle.
Break up (dissolve) a meeting.
Breathe out (exhale).
Bring under (reduce) a fever.
,, forth (produce) fruit.
,, out (elicit) facts.
,, out (publish) a book.
,, in (introduce) a custom.
,, to (resuscitate) a patient.
Bring on (cause) a debate.
,, up (educate) a child.
,, forward (produce) facts.
Buy back (redeem).
Call over (recite) the names.
,, off (divert) attention.
,, in (invite) a doctor.
,, up (recollect) a matter.
,, forth (evoke) applause.
Cast out (expel) from society.
,, down (dejected) with grief.
,, off (discarded) clothes.
,, aside (reject) facts.
Clothe (dress).

DOUBLETS.

267. Doublet defined. — Words derived from the same original elements, but differing in form and generally differing in meaning, are called *doublets.*

268. Origin of Doublets. — Doublets have arisen from various causes :—

(*a*) Our semi-vowel *w* was seldom sounded in French; so it was usually changed to a *g* or *gu* :—

Wile, guile; ward, guard; wise (manner), guise.

(*b*) Words of Romanic or Greek origin frequently appear in two different forms, one "Popular" and the other "Learned" (see § 42) :—

Abridge, abbreviate; aggrieve, aggravate; allow, allocate; amiable, amicable; antic, antique; appraise, appreciate; benison, benediction; chance, cadence; challenge, calumny, etc.

(*c*) Substitution of one letter for another (§ 59) :—

Fabric, forge; boss, botch; locust, lobster; deck, thatch; aptitude, attitude; cask, casque; prune, plum; servant, serjeant; ant, emmet; sect, sept; wrap, lap; porridge, pottage, etc.

(*d*) *Metathesis*, or change of place among consonants (§ 61):—

Granary, garner; wight, whit; scarp, scrap; task, tax; ask, ax (vulgar); thrill, thirl; gabble, jabber (here *r* is substituted for *l*).

(*e*) Palatalisation, or the substitution of a palatal consonant for a guttural (§ 63) :—

Bank, bench; dike, ditch; kirk, church; trickery, treachery; gaud, joy; gabble, jabber; gig, jig; lurk, lurch; disc, dish, desk, dais; etc.

(*f*) A change of inner vowel :—

Brown, bruin; shock, shake; these, those; dune, down; grove, groove ; hale, whole ; load, lade ; lust, list ; truth, troth ; cavalry, chivalry ; clause, close ; custom, costume ; one, an ; assay, essay.

(*g*) Excision of an initial letter or syllable :—

Adamant, diamond ; engine, gin ; defence, fence ; appeal, peal ; history, story ; affray, fray ; etiquette, ticket ; ensample, sample ; estrange, strange, etc.

(*h*) Interchange of words from cognate Aryan roots :—

Name, noun ; barb, beard ; beaker, pitcher ; knot, node ; foam, spume ; corn, horn ; eatable, edible ; brother, friar, etc.

Grimm's Law, Verner's Law.

269. Purport of Grimm's Law.—Grimm's Law does not belong to historical English grammar, but to comparative Aryan philology ; and therefore a very brief notice of it will be given in this book.[1] It is altogether beyond the reach of those who are unacquainted with Sanskrit, Latin, and Greek on the one side and High German on the other.

The purport of this law is to show (1) the shiftings of Mute consonants (see § 55) from the classical languages (Sanskrit, Greek, Latin) to the Low German, of which English is one ; and (2) from the Low German to the High German. The second has no connection at all with the etymology of English words, but concerns only those students who have mastered High German and desire to trace its descent from English or Low German. Even the first does not give the etymology of English words, but merely shows how they are allied to kindred Aryan words that have sprung from some common Aryan root.

The law may be roughly shown in the following table : here Class. = Classical, L.G. = Low German, and H.G. = High German.

	Class.	L.G.	H.G.	Class.	L.G.	H.G.	Class.	L.G.	H.G.
1. Dental . .	d >	t >	th	t >	th >	d	th >	d >	t
2. Labial . .	b >	p >	ph	p >	ph >	b	ph >	b >	p
3. Guttural . .	g >	k >	kh	k >	kh >	g	kh >	g >	k
Mnemonic letters.	S	H	A	H	A	S	A	S	H

[1] Mr. Sweet omits the subject altogether in his *Short Historical English Grammar*, and gives his reasons for so doing in the preface :—" Some

In stating this law its original author (Grimm) made two mistakes. He supposed (*a*) that the second shifting took place at the same time as the first, whereas in point of fact it was developed much later, since High German grew out of Low, and did not begin to exist till after the commencement of the eighth century; (*b*) that the second shifting was as perfectly carried out as the first, whereas in point of fact the second shifting was not complete even in the Dentals and Labials, and did not occur at all in the Gutturals.[1]

In the above scheme the symbol > means "becomes"; thus the Class. *d* becomes *t* in Low German; and the Low German *t* becomes (or rather is supposed to become) *th* in High German. S denotes the *Soft* (or voiced) consonants, H the *Hard* (or voiceless), A the Aspirated. Any one who has mastered the classification of consonants given in § 57, will easily remember Grimm's Law with the help of the three mnemonic words SHA, HAS, ASH. It will further help the student to understand and remember the Law, if he will pay attention to the fact that the only consonants to which it relates are the pairs of *Mutes* or *Stops* shown in § 55.

1. *Dental Series.*—SHA: Lat. **d***uo* > Eng. **t***wo* > High Germ. **z***wei*. (Observe that here the High Germ. letter is *z* = *ts*, which is substituted for *th*, *t* with a spirant (*s*) being used instead of the *t* with an aspirate; sometimes the Eng. **t** shifts to **ss**, as in Eng. *wa***t***er*, Germ. *wa***ss***er*.) || HAS: Lat. **t***res* > Eng. **th***ree* > High Germ. **d***rei*. (Another very simple example is Lat. **t***u*, Eng. **th***ou*, High Germ. **d***u*.) || ASH: Gr. **th***ugater*, Eng. **d***aughter*, High Germ. **t***ochter*.

Note 1.—In the combination *st* the classical *t* is not shifted to *th* in Teutonic: thus we have Lat. **st**-are, Gr. i-**st**-emi, Eng. **st**-and, Germ. **st**-ehen. The strong combination *st* has resisted change.

Note 2.—Sometimes a real shifting takes place, but is disguised; as in Lat. *sua*(**d**)-*vis*, Eng. *swee***t**, High Germ. *sü***ss**.

2. *Labial Series.*—SHA: Lat. (*s*)*lu***b***ricus*, Eng. *sli***p**, High Germ. *schlei***f***en*. || HAS: Lat. **p***edem*, Eng. **f***oot*, High Germ.

---

still plead for the retention of Grimm's Law on the ground of its being so interesting and having such a stimulating effect on pupils. The answer to this is, By all means teach it then, but teach it as an extra, not as a part of English grammar, any more than you would include French, Latin, or Greek etymology in English grammar."

[1] Skeat's *Primer of English Etymology*, p. 83. It occurred only in Old High German forms that are no longer in use; as in O.H.G. *chinni*, Mod. Germ. *kinn* (chin).

fuss. (Observe, the Low Germ. *ph* or *f* does not really shift to a High Germ. *b*, neither does the *t* of *foot* shift to High Germ. *th*, but to *ss.*) || ASH: Lat. f*rater*, Eng. b*rother*, Old High Germ. p*ruoder* (which in Mod. High Germ. appears as b*ruder*, in spite of Grimm's Law): Lat. f*lo*, Eng. b*low*, High Germ. b*lüh-an.*

3. *Guttural Series.*—(In this series, there is no shifting from Low Germ. to High, but only from Class. to Low Germ.) SHA: Lat. g*enu*, Eng. k*nee.* || HAS: Lat. c*entum* (for k*entum*), Eng. h*undred.* (Here observe the real shifting is from *k* to *h*, and not from *k* to *kh.*) || ASH: Gr. ch*olē*, Eng. g*all.*

Note.—In all instances the Teutonic *h* is found in lieu of the *kh* which seems to be suggested by Grimm's Law; cf. *cornu*, horn; *cord-is*, heart; *cent-um*, hundred, etc. Owing to difficulty of pronunciation the Teutonic languages discarded *kh.*

270. Verner's Law.—This law is intended to supplement Grimm's Law, by accounting for the apparent exceptions to it. It shows that Classical *t, p, k*, when preceded by an *originally unaccented* vowel, shifted one step further than is explained by Grimm. Thus the *t* in Lat. *ci*t*ra* did not stop at *th*, but shifted a step further to *d*, as in A.S. *hi*d*er* (to this place). Similarly the *t* in *pa*t*er* did not stop at *th*, when it passed into Low German, but shifted a step further to *d*, as in A.S. *fæ*d*er* (not *fæðer*, though in Mod. Eng. *d* has again become *th*). In strict accordance with Grimm's Law, owing to the stress thrown on the first vowel, *t* shifted regularly to *th* in Lat. *fra*t*er*, Eng. *bro*th*er.*

Note.—In the word *mother* there seems to be an exception to Grimm's Law, which Verner's Law fully explains: Lat. *mater*, A.S. *mó*d*or.*[1] But in Mod. Eng. the *d* appears as *th*. Perhaps the *d* was changed to *th* on the analogy of *brother*. Or it may have been due to dialectal influence.

The same law explains how the voiceless *s*, after being voiced to *z*, passed into *r*. Thus from the root *as* (to be) we get *are* instead of *ase* for the Third person Plural, and from the root *wes* we get *were* instead of *wese.* Another example is *rear*,

---

[1] The student must understand that the mark ′ placed over the *o* in A.S. *módor* does not denote that this vowel is pronounced with an accent or stress, but merely that the sound of the vowel is prolonged. The accent was originally on the last syllable *dor*, and the *mó*, though prolonged, was unaccented. Moreover, the accent was shifted back on to the former syllable before A.S. was committed to writing. Verner's Law only refers to a primitive accent, in very early times.

a Causal verb formed from the base *rīs-an*, to rise. From this base we have the Sc. *reis-a*, to raise (in which the *s* remains), and the A.S. *rǽr-an* (for *rǽs-an*), to rear.

In Lat. *gena*, A.S. *cinn* (sounded as *kin*), the shifting is in accordance with Grimm's Law; but A.S. *cinn* has become *chin* by palatalisation. Similarly in Gr. *phḗg-os*, Lat. *fāg-us*, A.S. *bóc*, the shifting is in accordance with the Law; but in Mod. Eng. we have not only *book*, but also a mutated form *beech*, in which the *ch* is due to palatalisation.

APPENDIX I.—NOTE BY PROFESSOR SKEAT.

NAMES OF VOCALIC SOUNDS IN MODERN ENGLISH.

THE difficulty of understanding and explaining the vocalic sounds in Modern English is chiefly due to the unfortunate names by which we denote the symbols *a*, *e*, *i*, *o*, and *u*.

For example, the symbol *ā* (long *a*) was used in Latin, and in all languages (including A.S.) which employed the Latin alphabet, to denote the sound of the *a* in *path* or *father;* and nearly all foreign languages still employ this symbol for the same purpose; and the *name* which they give to the symbol is still pronounced in such languages as it always has been; *i.e.* the name is sounded like the modern English *ah* (*a* in *path*, *al* in *calm*, and even (in many parts of Southern England) as *ar* in *cart*).

But the change in the vocalic sounds of Modern English, as compared with those of Middle English, is so great, that none of the present vowel-names are at all suitable for the symbols used to represent them. The names of the symbols *a*, *e*, *i*, *o*, *u* can only, at the best, be intelligently employed to denote the *long* vowels or diphthongs, and it is remarkable that only one out of the whole set still represents a pure long vowel, viz. *e* (*ee*). The names of the remaining symbols, viz. *a*, *i*, *o*, *u*, are all so pronounced as to form diphthongs. Even the name of the vowel *e* is misleading; for it denotes a sound which in Latin, and in a large number of languages which employ the Latin symbols, is denoted by (long) *i*. Indeed, we actually employ the symbol *i* ourselves, in order to represent the sound to which we now give the name of *e;* viz. in words derived from modern French, such as *unique*, *machine*, *glacis*, *quinine*, *pique*, and several others.

It follows, from the above explanation, that the vowel-names are wholly inappropriate for the symbols. The convenience of having names which are really appropriate for them is so obvious, that it is worth while for every English child to *know* them, in order that he may be able to distinguish what sounds are being discussed. All philologists are agreed that the only *appropriate* names for the symbols *a*, *e*, *i*, *o*, *u* (all supposed long) are the names which the

Romans themselves gave them.[1] These names are represented, respectively, by the following sounds:—

1. The symbol *a* was called *ah*; *i.e.* it had the sound of E. *a* in *father*, or of *al* in *calm*.

2. The symbol *e* was called *eh*; *i.e.* it had the sound of the *e* in *vein*; for it must be particularly noted that the *ei* in *vein* is a diphthong, composed of long *e* (*eh*) followed by a slight glide (denoted by *i*) such as is heard at the end of the word *they*, in which it is denoted by the final *y*. Or we may say that the *e* was sounded like Fr. *é* in *été*.

3. The symbol *i* was called *ee*; *i.e.* it had the sound of E. *ee* in *seem*, or of E. *i* in *unique*.

4. The symbol *o* was called *o*, the *o* being purely pronounced, as in the German word *so*. The E. *o* in *so* is not the same sound, being in fact impure; for it not only expresses the German *o*, but is followed by a slight after-sound, like a faint utterance of the Eng. *u* in *full*. This after-sound is expressed by *w* in the case of the word *know*, pronounced as (nou).[2] The Englishman who pronounces the German *so* as if it were spelt *zo* in English, can immediately be detected as being no German; his *z* for *s* is right enough, but the sound which he gives to the *o* is peculiarly and unmistakably his very own.

5. The symbol *u* was called *u*, as in E. *rule*, a sound which English usually represents by *oo*, as in *doom*, *loose*, *cool*, *soon*.

If the reader who has mastered the above facts will now reconsider the names of the English so-called "long vowels," he will begin to realise what the English vowel-names really imply.

1. The English symbol *a* is *now* called by a name resembling the very sound of *a* in the word *name*. This sound is precisely that of the *ei* in *vein*; *i.e.* the E. *a* in *name* is really a diphthong, such as in French is composed of the Latin *e*, followed by a glide which may be represented by a short *i*. Hence, in phonetic writing, the sound is represented by (ei).

2. The English symbol *e* is now called by a name which is pronounced like E. *ee* in *seem*, or E. (and Fr. and foreign) *i* in *unique*. It is a pure vowel, and was denoted in Latin by *i*, which is often written *ī* by grammarians in order to express its length. Hence, in phonetic writing, the sound may be represented by (ii), the *i* being repeated to indicate length.[3]

3. The English symbol *i* is now called by a name which is pronounced somewhat like the *ai* in Is*ai*ah, but with the former element a little shorter and less distinct. It may approximately be

---

[1] The Roman names for their letters of the alphabet are given in Postgate's *New Latin Primer* as follows:—Ah, Beh, Keh (*i.e.* C), Deh, Eh, ef, Geh, Hah, ee, Kah, el, em, en, Oh, Peh, Coo (Q), er, ess, Teh, oo (U, V), ix (X), ypsīlon, Zēta.

[2] All pronunciations which are denoted by true phonetic symbols are enclosed, as here, between brackets.

[3] The latter element is apt to pass into a glide; hence some write (ij), where the (j) represents the German *j* as in *ja*, or E. *y*. The glide is well heard in a word like *seeing* (sijing).

denoted by (ai), though the symbol (əi) is perhaps better. The meaning of the symbol (ə) is given below.

4. The English symbol *o* is now called by a name which is pronounced like E. *ou* in *soul* or *ow* in *know*. It really consists of a German long *o*, followed by a slight (u), where (u) denotes the *u* in *full*. Hence its phonetic symbol is (ou); though this is only approximate, unless we remember that the *o* is stressed, and the *u* is slight.

5. The English symbol *u* is now called by a name which is pronounced like the word *yew*, or the *u* in *duke*. The former element is the glide or semi-vowel which we usually denote by *y*, denoted in phonetics by (j); *i.e.* the German *j* in *ja*, or by (i). The latter element is the sound of long *u* in *rule*. Hence the phonetic symbol is (juu) or (iuu); where the repetition of (u) denotes that the latter element is long.

Recapitulating the above results, we see that, when we utter the names of the symbols *a*, *e*, *i*, *o*, *u*, we really utter sounds which, in older English, in Latin, and in most Continental languages, would rather be expressed by such symbols as (ei), (ii), (ai), (ou), and (iuu) or (iū). The accent falls on the former element in the case of the diphthongs which we denote by *a*, *i*, *o*; and on the latter element in the case of the diphthong which we denote by *u*. Only one of the symbols, viz. *e*, denotes a pure vowel; and even here, the sound meant is that of the *i* in *unique*.

When we apply their usual names to the short vowels, *i.e.* to the symbols *a*, *e*, *i*, *o*, *u*, as in the words *cat*, *bed*, *it*, *not*, *full*, it is obvious that, here again, the mere names are utterly inapplicable to the sounds intended. It follows that the English vowel-names are altogether useless for denoting sounds, unless in every case an example is given of the way in which the sound is written; and for this purpose the example given must be an entire word, having an invariable pronunciation. It would, obviously, be a great help to have a *true* name for every one of the *sounds* of the English vowels and diphthongs; and the following list may be taken as giving a *sufficient* approximation to the desired result.[1] The twenty vocalic sounds of the English language are these:—

A. Four sounds frequently denoted by the symbol *a*; one short and three long.

(1) Short: a sound between French *a* and French *e*. Name: short *æ*, pronounced "short *æ*," where by *æ* is meant the sound of *a* in *cat*, as heard in the South of England. In order to produce this sound, think of *cat*, and then sound the vowel *only*, omitting *c* and *t*. Phonetic symbol (æ). Sound: that of *a* in *cat* (kæt).

(2) Long. Name: long *æ*, pronounced "long *æ*." Phonetic symbol (ae). Sound: that of *a* in *Mary* (maeri). This vowel occurs by itself

---

[1] In other words, we can only speak clearly, so as to be always understood, if we give *foreign* names to the symbols. Unless this be done, it is impossible to emerge from chaos. And it must be remembered, that the pronunciation here spoken of is that of Southern and Midland English, that of the higher classes in London. In the North, the *a* of *cat* is often sounded as the Italian *a* in *matto*, and the *u* of *but* as the Southern English *u* in *full*.

only before a trilled *r* (*i.e.* an *r* followed by a vowel in the same or the next word). With an untrilled *r*, as in *care*, *bare*, it helps to form a diphthong, being followed by the sound numbered 18. That is, *care*, *bare* (before a consonant) are pronounced as (kaeə, baeə).

(3) Long. Name: diphthongal *ei*, pronounced "diphthongal *eh-ee*." Phonetic symbol (ei). Sound: that of *a* in *mate* (meit).

(4) Long. Name: long *aa*, pronounced "long *ah*." Phonetic symbol (aa). Sound: that of *a* in *path* (paath), *father* (faadhə). (There is no "short *ah*." The vowel formerly so pronounced has passed into the sound numbered 18.)

E. Two sounds commonly denoted by the symbol *e*; one short and one long.

(5) Short. Name: short *eh*, pronounced "short *eh*." Phonetic symbol (e). Sound: that of *e* in *bed* (bed).

(6) Long. Name: long *e*, pronounced "long *ee*." Phonetic symbol (ii). Sound: that of *i* in *unique*, or of *e* in *mete* (miit).

I. Two sounds commonly denoted by *i*; one short and one long.

(7) Short. Name: short *e*, pronounced "short *ee*." Phonetic symbol (i). Sound: that of *i* in *bit* (bit).

(8) Long. Name: diphthongal *ai*, pronounced "diphthongal *ah-ee*." Phonetic symbol (ai). Sound: that of *i* in *bite* (bait). Also written (bəit), meaning that the (a) is indistinct.

O. Three sounds commonly denoted by *o*, with which may be associated the sound of *aw* in *hawk*, seldom written with *o*, except in a few words, such as *off*, *soft*, *frost*.

(9) Short. Name: short *au*, pronounced "short *au*." Phonetic symbol (o). Sound: that of *o* in *not* (not).

(10) The unaccented *o* in *omit* (o'mit·), the phonetic symbol for which is written as (o') by Miss Soames, to indicate that the *o*, if not sounded as No. 18, is nearly pure, the element (u) being scarcely noticeable. It is, of course, quite different from the (o) in *not*, being a close *o* instead of an open one. Name: the unaccented *o*.

(11) Long. Name: long *au*, pronounced "long *au*." Phonetic symbol (ao). Sound: that of *aw* in *hawk* (haok), or *au* in *naught* (naot), or of *o* in *frost* (fraost).

(12) Long. Name: diphthongal *o*, pronounced "diphthongal *oa*." Phonetic symbol (ou). Sound: that of *oa* in *boat*, or *o* in *note* (bout, nout); also written (ow), as (bowt, nowt). The (u) is more distinct at the end of a word.

OO. Two sounds commonly denoted by *oo*; one short and one long.

(13) Short. Name: short *oo*; pronounced "short *oo*." Phonetic symbol (u). Sound: that of *oo* in *book* (buk), or *u* in *full* (ful).

(14) Long. Name: long *oo*; pronounced "long *oo*." Phonetic symbol (uu). Sound: that of *oo* in *boot* (buut).

(15) **U.** The diphthongal sound to which we give the name of *u*. Phonetic symbol (iuu) or (juu); as in *duke* (djuuk) or (diuuk).

(16) The diphthong *oi*; pronounced *oi*; composed of Nos. 11 and 7. Phonetic symbol (oi); as in *toil* (toil).

(17) The diphthong *ow*; pronounced as *ow* in *now*; composed of Nos. 4 and 13. Symbol (au); as in *now* (nau).

Three obscure vowel-sounds, the first of which only occurs in *unaccented* syllables.

(18) Name: the unaccented obscure vowel. Phonetic symbol (ə); called "turned *eh*," or (colloquially) "turned *ee*." Example: the final *a* in *China* (chainə).

(19) Name: the long obscure vowel. Similar to the preceding in sound, but long, and only occurring in accented syllables. Phonetic symbol (əə); called "double turned *eh*." Example: the *ur* in *turn* (təən).

(20) Name: the unrounded *u*. Phonetic symbol (ɐ), called "turned *ah*." Example: the *u* in *cut* (kɐt).

Hence there are eight short vowels (æ, e, i, o, o', u, ə, ɐ); six long vowels (aa, ae, ii, ao, uu, əə); and six diphthongs (ei, ai, ou, iuu, oi, au).

Note.—As "turned *ah*" is rather troublesome to print, there is no *great* objection to using the same symbol as in No. 18. For though the sounds are not quite the same, the fact that No. 20 only occurs in *accented* syllables always distinguishes it, *in practice*, from No. 18, which only occurs in *unaccented* syllables. Hence we may write *cut* as (kət). Miss Soames uses the symbol (œ), but it is liable to confusion with (æ).

It has already been said that the name *a* (ei) is very inappropriate, inasmuch as the symbol *a* originally meant the sound of *ah*. It is worth notice, on the other hand, that the sound of the *a* in *name* is so far from being always represented by the symbol *a*, that it can be represented in *twenty* different ways. Examples are: *fate, pain, pay, dahlia, vein, they, great, eh, gaol, gauge, champagne, campaign, straight, feign, eight, played, obeyed, weighed, trait, halfpenny.*

APPENDIX II.—LIST OF DOUBLETS.

1. Of Teutonic Origin.

Ant, emmet.
Bank, bench.
Blare, blaze.
Bold, bawd.
Boss, botch.
Bower, byre.
Box, bush.
Briar, furze.
Brown, bruin.
Chuck, shock, shake.
Clod, clot.
Clough, cleft.
Corn, churn.
Cot, coat, cote.
Crop, croup, group.
Crumple, crimple.
Cud, quid.
Dace, dart.
Deck, thatch.
Dell, dale.
Dent, dint.
Dike, ditch.
Dimple, dingle.
Dole, deal.
Draw, drag.
Dray, dredge.
Drill, thrill, thirl.
Dune, down.
Eft, newt (for *an ewt*).
Either, or.
Evil, ill.
Fat, vat.
Fetch, vetch.
Fife, pipe.
Finch, spink.
Flake, flag, flaw.
From, fro.
Fur, fodder.
Gabble, jabber.
Gad, goad.
Gage, wage (payment).
Game, gammon.
Gay, jay.
Gear, garb.
Gig, jig.
Girdle, girth.
Goal, wale, weal.
Gris-ly, grue-some.
Grove, groove.
Guard, ward.
Guardian, warden.
Guile, wile.
Guise, wise (manner).
Hack, hash.
Hale, whole.
Harangue, ring.
Heap, hope.
Heathen, hoyden.
Hoop, whoop.
Hump, hunch.

Hurtle, hurl.
Jeer, shear.
Kith, kit.
Knoll, knuckle.
Label, lapel.
Lair, leaguer, layer.
Lap, wrap.
Load, lade.
Lobby, lodge.
Lone, alone.
Lump, lunch.
Lurk, lurch.
Lust, list (desire).
Mar, moor.
March, mark, marque.
Marish, marsh.
Mash, mess.
Milk, milt.
Morn, morrow.
Mould, mulled.
Naught, nought, not.
Neither, nor.
Of, off.
Outer, utter.
Paddle, patter.
Paddock, park.
Peer, pry.
Porridge, pottage.
Pound, pond.
Pound (bruise), pun.
Queen, quean.
Rack, ratch.
Raid, road.
Raise, rear.
Rake, reach.
Ramp, romp.
Rank, range.
Reave, rob.
Reward, regard.
Ring, rink.
Road, rod.
Root, wart, ort.
Rover, robber.
Saw, saga.
Scale, shale.
Scar, share.
Scarf, scrip, scrap.
Scatter, shatter.
Scot-(free), shot.
Scratch, grate.
Screech, shriek.
Screw, shrew.
Shamble, scamper.
Shed, shade.
Shirt, skirt.
Shoot, scud.
Shuffle, scuffle.
Skewer, shiver.
Skiff, ship.
Skirmish, scrimmage.
Slobber, slaver.
Smoulder, smother.
Sniff, snuff.
Snivel, sniffle.
Snub, snuff.
Sop, soup, sup.
Spray, sprig.
Sprout, spout.
Spry, spark.
Squall, squeal.
Squander, scatter.
Stave, staff.
Stint, stunt.
Stove, stew.
Stumble, stammer.
Sweep, swoop.
Tease, touse.
These, those.
Thread, thrid.
Through, thorough.
Tight, taut.
Tinkle, tingle.
Tithe, tenth.
To, too.
Track, trick.
Treachery, trickery.
Troth, truth.
Trust, tryst.
Tuck, tug, tow.
Two, twain.
Wain, wagon.
Wattle, wallet.
Whirl, warble.
Wight, whit.
Wold, weald.
Wrack, wreck, rack.
Yelp, yap.

2. Of Romanic Origin.

N.B.—The asterisk marks the distinction between Popular and Learned; see § 42.

*Abbreviate, abridge.
Achievement, hatchment.
*Aggravate, aggrieve.
Affray, fray.
Alarm, alarum.
*Allocate, allow.
*Amicable, amiable.
Ancient, ensign.
*Antique, antic.
Appeal, peal.
Appear, peer.
*Appreciate, appraise.
Apprentice, prentice.
Aptitude, attitude.
Arc, arch.
Army, armada.
Assess, assize, excise.
*Assimilate, assemble.
Attach, attack.
Baton, batten.
Beldam, belladonna.
*Benediction, benison.
Brief, breve.
*Cadence, chance.
Caldron, chaldron.
*Calumny, challenge.
*Camera, chamber.
Campaign, champaign.
*Canal, channel, kennel.
*Cancer, canker.
*Cant, chant.
*Capital, chattel.
Captain, chieftain.
*Captive, caitiff.
Cart, chariot.
Case, cash.
Cask, casque.
*Castigate, chasten.
*Castle, chateau.
Catch, chase.
Cavalier, chevalier.
Cavalry, chivalry.

*Cave, cage.
Chair, chaise.
Cipher, zero.
Clause, close.
Coin, coign, quoin.
*Collect, coil, cull.
*Collocate, couch.
*Commend, command.
Committee, county.
*Complacent, complaisant.
*Complete, comply.
Composite, compost.
*Comprehend, comprise.
*Compute, count.
*Conception, conceit.
*Conduct, conduit.
Confound, confuse.
Construe, construct.
Convey, convoy.
Copulate, couple.
Corps, corpse.
Costume, custom.
Crate, grate.
Crevice, crevasse.
Crimson, carmine.
Crisp, crape.
Cue, queue.
Curriculum, curricle.
Dame, dam, donna, duenna.
Defend, fend.
*Deposit, depot.
*Describe, descry.
*Desiderate, desire.
Despite, spite.
Dictum, ditto.
Die, dado.
*Dignity, dainty.
*Dilate, delay.
*Direct, dress.
Display, deploy, splay.
Disport, sport.
*Dissimulate, dissemble.
Distain, stain.
*Diurnal, journal.
*Dominion, dungeon.
Duke, doge.
Eclat, slate.
Endue, endow.
Engine, gin.
*Errant, arrant.
Escape, scape.
Etiquette, ticket.
*Example, ensample, sample.
*Extraneous, strange.
*Fabric, forge.
*Fact, feat.
*Faction, fashion.
Faculty, facility.
Feeble, foible.
Feud, fief.
Fiddle, viol, violin.
*Fidelity, fealty.
Finite, fine.
Flower, flour.
Flush, flux.
Flute, flue.
Font, fount.
*Fragile, frail.
Furl, fardel.
Fusil, fusee.
Gaol, jail.
*Gaud, joy.
Genteel, gentle, gentile.
*Granary, garner.
Granite, garnet.
Guarantee, warranty, warrant.
Gullet, gully.
Gust, gusto.
Gypsy, Egyptian.
*Hospital, spital or spittle, hostel, hotel.
*Human, humane.
*Illumine, limn.
Imbrue, imbue.
*Implicate, employ, imply.
Inapt, inept.
*Indict, indite.
Influence, influenza.
Innocuous, innoxious.
*Integer, entire.
*Invidious, envious.
*Invite, vie.
Isolate, insulate.
*Juncture, jointure.
Junta, junto.
Jut, jet.
Lace, lasso.
Lamprey, limpet.
Lance, launch.
*Lecture, lesson.
*Legal, loyal, leal.
Levy, levee.
Limb, limbo.
Lineal, linear.
*Liquor, liqueur.
*Locus, lieu.
*Locust, lobster.
Madam, madonna.
*Major, mayor.
*Malediction, malison.
Mallow, mauve.
Manœuvre, manure.
*Masculine, male.
Master, mister.
Maximum, maxim.
Mean, mizen.
*Memory, memoir.
Minimum, minion.
*Mobile, mob, moveable.
*Mode, mood.
*Momentum, moment, movement.
Mosquito, musket.
*Monster, muster.
*Native, naive.
*Nucleus, newel.
*Obedience, obeisance.
*Onion, union.
*Oration, orison.
Ordinance, ordnance.
Ossifrage, osprey.
*Ounce, inch.
*Paganism, paynim.
Pain, pine.
Palatine, paladin.
*Pale, pole.
Pallet, palette.
*Pallid, pale.
Pane, pawn, vane.
*Par, pair, peer.
*Pass, pace.
Pastil, pastille.
Paten, pan.
*Patron, pattern.
*Pauper, poor.

Pelisse, pilch.
Pen, pin, fin.
*Penitence, penance.
*Peregrine, pilgrim.
Periwig, peruke.
Person, parson.
Picket, piquet.
*Piety, pity.
Pigment, pimento.
Pistil, pestle.
Pistol, pistole.
Plaintive, plaintiff.
Plait, pleat.
Plane, plan, plain.
*Pomatum, pomade.
*Portico, porch.
*Potent, puissant.
*Potion, poison.
Poult, pullet.
Pounce, punch.
Praise, price.
*Predicate, preach.
*Private, privy.
*Probe, prove, proof.
*Procurator, proctor.
*Prolong, purloin.
*Propose, purpose.
*Prosecute, pursue.
*Provide, purvey.
Provident, prudent.
*Prune, plum.
*Pungent, poignant.
Puny, puisne.
Purl (edging on lace), profile.
*Quiet, quit, quite, coy.
*Raceme, raisin.
Radish, race.
*Radius, ray.
Rail, rally.
*Rapine, raven, ravine.
*Ratio, ration, reason.
Recognisance, reconnaisance.
*Redemption, ransom.
*Regal, royal.
*Regulate, rule.
*Renegade, runagate.
*Renovate, renew.
*Reprove, reprieve.
*Residuum, residue.
*Respect, respite.
Rondeau, rondel.
*Rote, route, rout, rut.
*Rotund, round.
Sacristan, sexton.
Scabby, shabby.
Scutcheon, escutcheon.
Scuttle, skillet.
Sect, sept.
*Secure, sure.
*Senior, sir, sire.
*Separate, sever.
Servant, serjeant.
Settle, saddle.
Soil, sole.
Souse, sauce.
Sovereign, soprano.
*Special, especial.
*Species, spice.
*Spirit, sprite, spright.
Spy, espy.
Squire, esquire.
Stablish, establish.
*Status, state, estate.
Strap, strop.
*Strict, strait, straight.
Suit, suite.
*Superficies, surface.
*Supersede, surcease.
*Supplicant, suppliant.
Taint, tint.
Task, tax.
Temper, tamper.
Tempt, taunt.
Tend, tender.
Ton, tun.
Tone, tune.
Tour, turn.
*Tract, trait.
*Tradition, treason.
Travel, travail.
Treachery, trickery.
Triple, treble.
*Triumph, trump.
Unguent, ointment.
Unity, unit.
Valet, varlet.
*Van, fan.
*Vast, waste.
Veneer, furnish.
*Verb, word.
Vertex, vortex.
*Vocal, vowel.

3. Of Greek Origin.

N.B.—The asterisk marks the distinction between Popular and Learned; see § 42.

*Adamant, diamond.
*Antiphon, anthem.
Assay, essay.
*Balsam, balm.
*Basis, base.
Beaker, pitcher.
*Blaspheme, blame.
*Canon, cannon.
Canvas, canvass.
*Chart, carte, card.
Chicory, succory.
*Chirurgeon, surgeon.
Choler, cholera.
*Chord, cord.
*Chorus, choir.
Church, kirk.
Cithern, guitar.
*Climate, clime.
Coffin, coffer.
*Crypt, grotto.
Diaper, jasper.
*Disc, disk, dish, desk, dais.
*Dolphin, dauphin.
*Eremite, hermit.
*Fantasy or phantasy, fancy.
*Hemi, semi.
*Hemorrhoids, emerods.
*History, story.
*Hyacinth, jacinth.
*Hydra, otter.
*Iota, jot.
Mentor, monitor.
*Metal, mettle.

*Monastery, minster.	Pause, pose.	Pope, papa.
*Papyrus, paper.	*Phantasm, phantom.	*Presbyter, priest.
*Parabola, parable, palaver, parley, parole.	*Phlegm, flame.	*Scandal, slander.
Paradise, parvis.	*Plate, place, pate, piazza.	*School, shoal.
*Paralysis, palsy.	Plateau, platter.	Sponge, fungus.
	*Pomp, pump.	*Tripod, trivet.
		*Zealous, jealous.

4. Of Mixed Origin.

N.B.—*C.* stands for Celtic, *A.* for Arabic, *P.* for Persian.

Attar (*A.*), otto (*A.*).	Crook (*T.*), cross (*R.*).	Perk (*C.*), pert (*C.*).
Barb (*R.*), beard (*T.*).	Eatable (*T.*), edible (*R.*).	Poke (*C.*), pouch (*C.*).
Block (*C.*), plug (*C.*).	Foam (*T.*), spume (*R.*).	Pottage (*C.*), porridge (*C.*).
Bound (*C.*), bourn (*C.*).	Guest (*T.*), host (*R.*).	Ribbon (*C.*), riband (*C.*).
Brother (*T.*), friar (*R.*).	Knot (*T.*), node (*R.*).	Sherbet (*A.*), syrup (*A.*).
Bug (*C.*), puck (*C.*), pug (*C.*).	Lake (*R.*), loch (*C.*), lough (*C.*).	Tabour (*A.*), tambour (*A.*).
Bump (*C.*), bunch (*C.*).	Moslem (*A.*), Mussulman (*P.*).	Tack (*C.*), tache (*C.*).
Cell (*R.*), hall (*T.*).	Name (*T.*), noun (*R.*).	Turban (*P.*), tulip (*P.*).
Cole (*R.*), kale (*C.*).	Paddle (*T.*), spatula (*R.*).	
Cone (*Gr.*), hone (*T.*).	Peak (*C.*), peck (*C.*), beak (*C.*).	
Cool (*T.*), gelid (*R.*).		
Corn (*R.*), horn (*T.*).		

QUESTIONS ON HISTORICAL ENGLISH AND DERIVATION.

Collected in the order of their occurrence from London Matriculation Papers set since June 1880 up to Jan. 1898,—18 years. The month and year are noted against each question :—

1. Explain the following terms applied to the structure of words :—*root*, *stem*, *primary derivative*, *secondary derivative*, *compound word*.

Apply your explanation to the words *song*, *bait*, *batch*, *suds*, *thicket*, *spider*, *farthing*, *landscape*, *knowledge*, *wedlock*, *hemlock*, *eyry*, *along*, *gossip*, *waylay*, *walking-stick*. (June 1880.)

2. At what different periods has a French element been introduced into our language? Give examples of French words introduced in the several periods mentioned. (Jan. 1881.)

3. What is meant by *runes*? Tell whatever you know concerning any runic letters admitted into the English alphabet. (Jan. 1881.)

4. What is meant by *English roots*? What letter-changes from the English root have occurred in the following words :—*each*, *thunder*, *speak*, *crumb*? (Jan. 1881.)

5. Define the term "Grammatical gender." What was the original force of the suffix in *hunter* and *maltster*? Give other examples. Account for the gender now ascribed to Sun and Moon, and what were their genders in Old English? (Jan. 1881.)

6. Mention any English nouns that form their plurals by processes generally obsolete, and describe the processes. Which of the following are genuine plurals, and how do you account for the forms that are not such :—*alms, summons, banns, sessions, costs, eaves, weeds, riches, dice*? (Jan. 1881.)

7. What is the original meaning of the term *case*, and what does it now mean in English Grammar? Of what *lost* case-endings are the traces still discernible in our language? (Jan. 1881.)

8. Discuss the words italicised in the following :—

> Long *ago* we were *wont* to let plain *living* accompany high *thinking*.
>
> *Methinks* you *might* have spoken, but you *durst* not.

(Jan. 1881.)

9. Explain the forms *worse, next, first, farthest, furthest.* (June 1881.)

10. Explain the origin and the present use of the words *what, which, whether.* (June 1881.)

11. We write *he thinks;* why do we not write *he musts*? Illustrate your answer by reference to some other verbs. (June 1881.)

12. Define a *root*, and an *English root.* What are *hybrids*? Mention any hybrids that are generally recognised as good English. (Jan. 1882.)

13. What vowel-sounds were the letters *a, e, i, o, u* originally intended to represent? Point out the letter changes that have taken place in the following words :—*gossip, number, tyrant, fee.* (Jan. 1882.)

14. What is the real power of the Genitive case? Explain the following forms :—*their, golden,* for Christ *his* sake. (Jan. 1882.)

15. Derive *score, dozen, hundred, eleven.* How are distributive numerals expressed in English? Give the first three ordinal English adverbs. (Jan. 1882.)

16. What pronouns were originally used, where Relatives are now employed in our language? Explain the forms—*yours truly; to-morrow;* I and the lad will go *yonder; the* more, *the* merrier. Define Reflexive pronouns. (Jan. 1882.)

17. Give examples of a prepositional and a pronominal adverb,—of an adverb formed by the Genitive Singular of a substantive, and of a preposition formed by the past participle of a verb. Why are interjections not to be reckoned as parts of speech? Derive *well-a-day, alas.* (Jan. 1882.)

18. What is meant by *Diminutives* and *Augmentatives*? Enumerate, and illustrate by examples, the suffixes most commonly used in English in the formation of such words, and of patronymics. (Jan. 1882.)

19. How many vowel-sounds are used in spoken English? What are they? How many diphthongs are used in written English? What are they? (June 1882.)

20. Use the words *book, but, thou, be, who, why, enough, feet, ought, knew, best,* as examples of some means of distinguishing words in modern English, that belonged to the language in its earliest Teutonic form. (June 1882.)

21. Explain the formation of the words—*dean, sexton, vinegar, biscuit, tile, orchard, livelihood, allow, isle, island,* and add a few comments on the phonetic changes illustrated by their history. (June 1882.)

22. Tell the history of the Possessive case in English, and define the present limits of its use. (June 1882.)

23. Tell what you know of the origin and structure of the English alphabet. (Jan. 1883.)

24. Account for the suffix or inflexion in each of the following words:—*chicken*, *oxen*, *vixen*, *beeves*, *pennies*, *pence*, *spinster*, *widower*, *gander*, *drake*. (Jan. 1883.)

25. Explain as fully as you can the superlative forms *inmost*, *next*, *best*, *least*, *last*, *first*, and the comparative forms *nearer* and *worse*. (Jan. 1883.)

26. "You *ought* him a thousand pound." Explain this use of the word *ought*; show how we came by the two forms *own* and *owe*; account also for the forms *durst*, *quoth*, *methinks*. (Jan. 1883.)

27. Show that the following words were originally compound nouns:—*barn*, *orchard*, *stirrup*. Tell what you know of the Teutonic suffixes used in the forming of abstract nouns. (Jan. 1883.)

28. With what languages of Europe is English in its origin most closely connected? What exactly is its relation to Latin? What to French? (June 1883.)

29. Explain the term *Anglo-Saxon*. What objections are there to it? What terms have been proposed in its stead? Give reasons for its retention. (June 1883.)

30. Mention any words that have been added to our language in the nineteenth century. (June 1883.)

31. Discuss the plural form *children*. Write down some nouns that have no special form to express plurality, and account for them. Is it correct to speak of *a two-foot rule*? (June 1883.)

32. Examine the forms—*lesser*, *worse*, *foremost*, *elder*, *farther*. Derive *next*, *last*, *best*, *further*, *rather*. (June 1883.)

33. Mention some verbs that, being originally preterites, have come to be used as presents. Can you account for such a usage? (June 1883.)

34. Tell what you know of the origin of each of the following words, with comment upon any fact in the history of English that it might serve to illustrate:—*Avon*, *Chester*, *Grimsby*, *cloister*, *minster*, *cherry*, *beef*, *nuisance*, *cousin*, *potion*, *poison*. (Jan. 1884.)

35. Discuss each of these plural forms—*leaves*, *oxen*, *kine*, *men*, *brethren*; also the forms—*news*, *means*, *pains*, *riches*, *eaves*, *summons*. (Jan. 1884.)

36. Which form do you prefer to use—"He *dare* not," or "He *dares* not"? What is to be said on behalf of each form? Explain the forms *willy-nilly*, *won't*, *to wit*. (Jan. 1884.)

37. Explain with reference to their origin the use of the words *own* and *owe* in "I *own* a pound," "I *owe* a pound," "I *own* I *owe* a pound." Explain the verbs in the question "How *do* you *do*?" (Jan. 1884.)

38. What various sounds has the letter *a* in Mod. English? How does it come to have so many? Which of them is the oldest? (June 1884.)

39. Show as definitely as you can the influence of Norman-French on our grammar. (June 1884.)

40. Explain how it is that we have such forms as *Sunday* and *Monday* alongside of such forms as *Wednesday* and *Thursday*. Also how it is we say *Lady-day* and not *Lady's-day*. (June 1884.)

41. Derive the words *lady*, *madam*, *sir*, *husband*, *woman*, *bachelor*, *lass*, *cousin*, *uncle*, *archbishop*. (June 1884.)

42. Name the main sources which have contributed to form *modern* English, and state the period at which the influence of each has been chiefly felt. (Jan. 1885.)

43. Explain the origin of the suffixes in the following words:—*shadow*, *hillock*, *holy*, *busy*, *farthing*, *darling*, *worship*, *favour*, *burgess*, *ceremony*, *enemy*, *homage*, *terrace*. (Jan. 1885.)

44. What is the etymology of the following words:—*under*, *over*, *every*, *eleven*, *twenty*, *least*, *near*? (Jan. 1885.)

45. What traces are there in English of a Perfect formed by reduplication? Can you show by what process reduplication has disappeared? (Jan. 1885.)

46. Give the etymology of the following pronouns, and show how their use has varied:—*this*, *that*, *what*, *which*, *whose*. (Jan. 1885.)

47. What explanation has been given of the suffixes which mark the past tense in Weak verbs? (Jan. 1885.)

48. Distinguish between the terms *cognate* and *derived* as applied to words. Mention some words cognate with *bear* (the verb), and some derived from it. (June 1885.)

49. What is meant by a *letter*? Give some account of the letter *c* and its uses. What various sounds are represented in English by the letter *u*? (June 1885.)

50. Discuss the forms—*brethren*, *seamstress*, *indices*, *fisherman*, *cherry*, *kind*, *swine*, *cherubim*, *riches*, *uttermost*. (June 1885.)

51. Mention some usages in which *am* as an auxiliary has been ousted by *have*. (June 1885.)

52. Show clearly that English in its origin and basis is a Teutonic language. Also say by what other Teutonic languages it has been affected and influenced since its coming into this island. (Jan. 1886.)

53. Mention the various times and ways in which Latin has increased our vocabulary through the medium of the Romance languages. (Jan. 1886.)

54. What is meant by *organs of speech*? How would you define a *vowel*? how a *diphthong*? How many more vowel-sounds has English than vowels? (Jan. 1886.)

55. In what various ways are the letter *g* and the combination *gh* pronounced in English? How do there come to be various ways? (Jan. 1886.)

56. Can you explain the italicised letters in the following words?—child*r*en, wou*l*d, cou*l*d, again*st*, gen*d*er, vi*c*tuals, frontisp*ie*ce, crayfis*h*, m*ic*e. (Jan. 1886.)

57. Give half a dozen instances of words of which the present spelling obscures the etymology. How did such spelling come into fashion? (Jan. 1886.)

58. State the force or forces of the suffixes *-ster*, *-ism*, *-let*, *-some*, *-ard*, *-ish*. (June 1886.)

59. What is the origin of the *d* in the preterite of *love*? What of the *d* in its past participle? Explain the forms—*had*, *made*, *left*, *built*, *clad*, *methinks*. (June 1886.)

60. When is *dare* inflected in the 3rd Sing. Pres. Indicative? Can you cast any light on the forms *durst*, *wist*, *wrought*, *sold*, *sought*, *ago*? (June 1886.)

61. Mention some cognates of *better*, *nether*, *among*, *noun*. (June 1886.)

62. Give examples of all the various sounds of *a* in our language; also those of *ough* and of *ch*. (Jan. 1887.)

63. Is the difference in usage between *each* and *every* justified by their etymology? Why should you not say, "Neither of the ten suited me"? What alternative form of expression is there to "That is mine and nobody else's"? Which do you think is to be preferred? (Jan. 1887.)

64. Explain and illustrate the terms *synthetic* and *analytic* as applied to languages. By which would you describe the English language as it now is? (June 1887.)

65. Distinguish between the Teutonic and the Romance elements of the English vocabulary; and write two short sentences, one containing no words of Romance origin, the other none of Teutonic. Which is the easier sentence to write, and why? (June 1887.)

66. Classify the consonantal letters. What is meant by Grimm's Law, and to which group does it apply? How would you class the letter *h*? (June 1887.)

67. State some differences as regards verbal forms, case-endings, and suffixes, between the English of the fourteenth century and that of the present day? (June 1888.)

68. Illustrate the influence which the classical element has had upon modern English directly, and through the medium of the Romance languages. (June 1888.)

69. Several words are found to be common to the dialect of Scott and Chaucer. Can you account for this? (June 1888.)

70. Account for the formation of the following auxiliary verbs:—*may, am, will, could, ought, might, hast, must.* (June 1888.)

71. Chaucer has been called "the well of English undefiled." Discuss this with reference to the growth of English in Chaucer's time. (June 1888.)

72. Give the derivation of the following words:—*alive, dead, many, alert, entail, result, heresy, ideal, knife, key, bury, rather, king, lady.* (June 1888.)

73. Explain the suffixes of the following words:—*kingdom, every, seemly, business, farthing, hardship, piecemeal, nostril, gospel, orchard, namesake.* (June 1888.)

74. Discuss the use and abuse of technical terms. Whence do we chiefly obtain them? (June 1888.)

75. Give a complete list of English possessive pronouns, stating in regard to each its origin and the period when it first came to be used. (Jan. 1889.)

76. State the different forms that have been employed for marking comparison in adjectives, and explain the origin and exact import of the most usual forms. (Jan. 1889.)

77. What traces of reduplication can you adduce in the tense formations of verbs in English (Old and Modern). (Jan. 1889.)

78. Show the different usages of the following words, and account for these by their derivations:—*alight, burden, broil, wind, blow, race.* (Jan. 1889.)

79. Give the original and the derivative meaning of each of the following words:—*cynical, puny, trivial, agony, pagan, villain, heathen, economy, tally.* (Jan. 1889.)

80. Give, as concisely as you can, equivalents of Saxon origin for the

following words :—*frustrate, eliminate, elucidate, desiderate, prevaricate, identical, eradicate, corroborate, reciprocal, internecine.* (Jan. 1889.)

81. Explain exactly the following, commenting upon anything which is archaic in usage :

(*a*) Truly and indifferently to minister justice.
(*b*) Let him pursue his course without let or hindrance.
(*c*) Prevent us in all our doings.
(*d*) In good sooth.
(*e*) Vouchsafe us thy help. (Jan. 1889.)

82. From what sources do we principally obtain our naval, agricultural, and political terms? Illustrate your answer by instances. (Jan. 1889.)

83. What languages have existed, or do still exist, in the British Isles? (June 1889.)

84. Tell all you know of the development of the English language down to the Norman Conquest, and show how the Norman Conquest affected it. (June 1889.)

85. Tell all you know of *my* and *mine*, of *me* and *thee*, and of *his, hers, its.* (June 1889.)

86. What is meant by the Laws of Speech? Mention any of the ways in which they have affected our language. (June 1889.)

87. From what other sources besides Latin and the Romance languages have we borrowed words? Show that our vocabulary is constantly being enlarged? (Jan. 1890.)

88. Discuss these phrases :—*Next Lady-day, for conscience sake, a friend of mine, the Emperor of Germany's accession, the Queen's rebels, for John his sake.* (Jan. 1890.)

89. What adjectives have we to the nouns *parish, cat, horse, alms, church, bishop?* (Jan. 1890.)

90. Discuss the etymology of the following words :—*also, axe, could, only, songstress, such, testator, twain, vixen, whichever.* (June 1890.)

91. Show the marks of distinction between Weak and Strong verbs in Old and Modern English. (June 1890.)

92. Show how frequently in English the pronunciation of a word does not correspond with its orthography. How would you account for such discrepancies? (Jan. 1891.)

93. How many sounds has the symbol *a* in English? Also in what other ways can the sound it has in *hate* be expressed? (Jan. 1891.)

94. From what other parts of speech are Adverbs formed, and what is the function of Adverbs? Can you cast any light on the forms *darkling, whilom, piecemeal, afterwards?* (Jan. 1891.)

95. Show how the languages of the Celts and the Danes have at different times affected the English tongue? (June 1891.)

96. Show how at different times foreign words have become a part of the English tongue? What is meant by an acclimatised foreign word in English? (June 1891.)

97. Discuss the forms—*less, lesser; worse, worser; inmost, innermost.* (June 1891.)

98. Discuss the etymology of *our* and *ours, their* and *theirs, who* and *what, why* and *which.* (June 1891.)

99. Show how in word-building Prefixes alter the meanings of words,

and Suffixes their functions. Cite six derived words with English, six with Latin, six with Greek, and six with French Suffixes. (June 1891.)

100. What languages had already been talked in this island, or were being talked in it, when the Anglo-Saxon Conquest took place? Were they in any way akin to the dialects spoken by the Angles and Saxons? (Jan. 1892.)

101. Why is the speech of the peasants in Yorkshire so different from that of the peasants in Devonshire? and why are they both so different from the English of Literature? (Jan. 1892.)

102. Explain the terms *letter*, *vowel*, *accent*, *guttural*, *sibilant*. What two different pronunciations has the combination *th*? How many has the combination *ough*? (Jan. 1892.)

103. Give ten instances in which distinction of sex is denoted by words of quite separate origin, and explain in some at least of them why it is so? (Jan. 1892.)

104. Parse and annotate the italicised words in—

(a) He *must* go.
(b) He *ought* to have gone.
(c) He *ought* to go.
(d) He *need* not go.
(e) He *dare* not go.

And discuss: *Methinks; I wis; quoth he; so mote it be; this will never do.* (Jan. 1892.)

105. What are the adverbs answering to the adjectives *shy*, *far*, *fast*, *kindly*, *lowly*? Explain the forms *betimes*, *whilom*, *erewhile*, *piecemeal*, *ashore.* (Jan. 1892.)

106. Give as large a list as you can of Classical words which found their way into our language before the Norman Conquest, and point out how they were probably introduced. (June 1892.)

107. Mention ten words that have come to us from Italian, five from Dutch, five from Hebrew, and ten from modern French. (June 1892.)

108. Discuss the etymology and usage of the masculine possessive *his*, and the neuter possessive *its*. (June 1892.)

109. What are *doublets*? Show with illustrations in what various ways they have arisen in English. (Jan. 1893.)

110. State what you know of the history of every word in the present question, noting any peculiarities in the form or significance of each. (Jan. 1893.)

111. Trace the origin of the words—*priest*, *curate*, *bard*, *minstrel*, *soldier*, *fellow*, showing what light each throws upon the character of the intercourse to which its adoption in English was due. (Jan. 1893.)

112. State with illustrations anything you know about the effects of accent in English. (Jan. 1893.)

113. Mention as many as you can of the derivatives or cognates of *two*. (Jan. 1893.)

114. Write a short history of the 2nd personal pronouns (Singular and Plural) with regard to changes both in form and usage. (Jan. 1893.)

115. Give a concise account of the formation of Adverbs. Is there anything anomalous in the words *godly* and *goodly*? (Jan. 1893.)

116. Distinguish derivatives and compounds, and comment on the formation of the following:—*witticism*, *oddity*, *non-plussed*, *wondrous*, *bridal*, *lawyer*. (Jan. 1893.)

117. How do we find names for the new things that from time to time

have to be expressed in words, *e.g.* for new games, new inventions, new political or social ideas? Give instances. (June 1893.)

118. Explain why the pronunciation and even the language of the peasantry, in various parts of the country, are so distinctly different, giving a few specimens. (June 1893.)

119. What other permissible spellings are current of the following words —*inflection*, *programme*, *rhyme*, *era*, *mediæval*, *apothegm*? What is to be said for or against them? (June 1893.)

120. Show carefully how Grimm's Law, or any apparent exception to it, is illustrated by the following words:—*stand*, *father*, *third*, *sweet*. (Jan. 1894.)

121. State briefly what you know of the origin and history of each word in the following sentence:—"Meanwhile the great rhetorical fabric gradually arose. He revised, erased, strengthened, emphasised, with indefatigable industry." (Jan. 1894.)

122. What phases of English are illustrated by the plurals—*men*, *shoes*, *these presents*, *sheep*, *mathematics*? (Jan. 1894.)

123. Illustrate, from the names for the different parts or contents of a house, the characteristic differences between the Roman and the English element in the vocabulary. (Jan. 1894.)

124. Describe the principal sources of apparent irregularity in the conjugation of Strong verbs in modern English. Comment on the forms "I have *struck*," "the sun has *shone*," "I *shot*." (Jan. 1894.)

125. Illustrate the formation of Adverbs from cases of nouns and adjectives. (Jan. 1894.)

126. Distinguish between Compounds and Derivatives, and illustrate your distinction from the words—*orchard*, *flood*, *nest*, *bridal*. (Jan. 1894.)

127. Under what circumstances do words go out of use? (Jan. 1894.)

128. Give examples (not more than three under each head)—(1) of writers who have contributed to fix the literary language; (2) of writers who, since its establishment, have written in dialects. (Jan. 1894.)

129. What exactly do you understand by the statement that two languages are "related"? How would you describe the relationship of modern English to French, Greek, Welsh, Danish, and the English spoken by King Alfred respectively? (June 1894.)

130. In what various ways, besides borrowing from foreign languages, may the vocabulary of a language be increased? Give examples. (June 1894.)

131. Give an account of the vowel-sounds now used in educated English (using some phonetic notations, if possible, but illustrating your symbols by words in which the corresponding sounds occur.) (June 1894.)

132. Point out the inflexions in *then*, *than*, *win*, *there*, *whence*, *why*, *seldom*, and show how far their force is traceable in the present meaning of these words. (June 1894.)

133. Comment on the marks of comparison in the following, and point out which of them are, in modern usage, true comparatives: *worser*, *former*, *nearer*, *latter*, *inferior*, *elder*, *other*. (June 1894.)

134. Explain the forms of the first *four* ordinal numbers. (June 1894.)

135. From what sources have we the suffix *-y*? Explain its occurrence in the words—*duchy, flowery, body, jelly, jolly.* (June 1894.)

136. Mention other English words cognate with *cadence, hospital, tradition, quiet, potion, pauper*, stating what you know of the origin of each. (June 1894.)

137. Enumerate and account for the chief anomalies of modern English spelling. (Jan. 1895.)

138. Write etymological notes on the following words: *forlorn, alms, thunder, livelihood, went, pagan, alchemy, bask, Monday, island.* (Jan. 1895.)

139. What is meant by *gender* in grammar? Enumerate the various ways of indicating *gender* in English. Comment on *gander, tapster, vixen, bridegroom, songstress.* (Jan. 1895.)

140. Classify English adjectives according to (i.) their functions, and (ii.) their terminations. From what sources have we the suffix *-ous*? Explain its occurrence in *conscious, glorious, wondrous, courteous, righteous.* (Jan. 1895.)

141. Trace, as fully as you can, the history of the inflexions of the 3rd pers. Pronoun, Singular and Plural. (Jan. 1895.)

142. Discuss the origin of the Relative Pronouns, and distinguish their use in modern English. What equivalents are there in English for the Relative? Give illustrative sentences. (Jan. 1895.)

143. Account for the following forms:—*told, sought, caught, could, must, wot, are, went, ought, hight.* (Jan. 1895.)

144. Tabulate the Pronominal Adverbs, and explain their formation. (Jan. 1895.)

145. State what you know of the history of any *six* words in the following sentence:—"No man hardly is so savage, in whom the receiving kindnesses doth not beget a kindly sense." (June 1895.)

146. Give some account of the Scandinavian element in English. (June 1895.)

147. Classify the vocalic *sounds* (not letters) in English, denoting each by means of some word in which it occurs. (June 1895.)

148. Distinguish *accent* and *emphasis*, and illustrate the part played by the first in the history of English words. (June 1895.)

149. Illustrate the influence of the social and political institutions of the Normans on the English vocabulary. (June 1895.)

150. Account clearly for the differences between a *compound* and (1) a *derivative*, (2) two words in syntactical connection, with instances. (June 1895.)

151. Analyse each of the following expressions with its component parts, and explain how its syntactical function arose:—*lest, therefore, therefor, nevertheless, besides, anent.* (June 1895.)

152. Explain the terms—*auxiliary, past-present, strong-weak*, as applied to certain classes of verbs. (June 1895.)

153. Give a short account of the origin of adverbs. (June 1895.)

154. State the source or sources of the suffixes *-ate, -ish, -ling, -y*, with instances of each. How far do they serve to distinguish different parts of speech? (June 1895.)

155. Comment on the spelling of the following words:—*broad, once, doubt, could, whose, right.* (June 1895.)

156. Illustrate the chief varieties of Doublets. (June 1895.)

157. Explain carefully what is meant by calling English a Teutonic language. (Jan. 1896.)

158. Give some account of the influence of Christianity on the English vocabulary. (Jan. 1896.)

159. Write etymological notes on the following words:—(i.) *anthem;* (ii.) *chicken;* (iii.) *eleven;* (iv.) *fairy;* (v.) *gossip;* (vi.) *island;* (vii.) *rhyme;* (viii.) *righteous;* (ix.) *songstress;* (x.) *wanton.* (Jan. 1896.)

160. Write a short history of *-s* as the sign of the plural in English. (Jan. 1896.)

161. (i.) Enumerate and illustrate the chief methods of forming compound nouns; (ii.) Give three instances of monosyllabic words which are in reality compounds. (Jan. 1896.)

162. Discuss the inflexions in the following:—*him, their, hers, why, once, whilom;* give another example in each case. (Jan. 1896.)

163. Illustrate and explain the different uses of (i.) the Infinitive, and (ii.) the various verbal forms in *-ing*. Tell the history of *-ing* as the ending of the present participle. (Jan. 1896.)

164. Account for the decay of Strong verbs in English. Give one instance of the Strong past participle used merely as an adjective, and one instance of its use as an adverb. Explain these forms—*fell, brought, sold, taught, wert, wrought.* (Jan. 1896.)

165. How many tenses are there in an English verb? What is meant by saying that there is no future tense in the English language? (Jan. 1896.)

166. From what sources have we the prefix *a-*, and the suffix *-y?* (Jan. 1896.)

167. Classify prepositions according to their origin. Explain *but, between, except.* (Jan. 1896.)

168. What is meant by the distinction between "learned" and "popular" *borrowed words?* Under what circumstances have Latin words (not French) at various times been borrowed in English? Refer in answer to the above distinction. (June 1896.)

169. Show, if possible with a table, what vocalic sounds are used in ordinary spoken English. (June 1896.)

170. Write down (i.) *six* illustrations of Grimm's Law; (ii.) *six* apparent exceptions to it, commenting upon the latter. (June 1896.)

171. Give the force of the suffixes which occur in the following words, commenting upon any anomaly in the form or meaning of each:—*witness, childhood, girdle, lawyer, gosling, rookery.* (June 1896.)

172. Show accurately how the following cognate words are distinguished, and also how they are connected in meaning:—*corps, corpse; gage, wage; diamond, adamant; cage, cave; dish, desk, disc, dais; priest, presbyter.* (June 1896.)

173. Give two examples each of (i.) Strong verbs which have become weak; (ii.) Weak that have become Strong; (iii.) Strong participles that have been assimilated to the preterite (past tense); (iv.) Strong preterites that have been assimilated to the participle. (June 1896.)

174. Explain and illustrate the laws or principles involved in the formation of the following words:—*causeway, book-learned, hindmost, thirteen, piecemeal, darkling.* (June 1896.)

175. Show summarily in what various ways adverbs have been formed in English. (June 1896.)

176. Give a summary of the various ways in which the vocabulary of a language may be enlarged, with illustrations from English. (June 1896.)

177. Give a brief account of the process of inflexional levelling in English. (Jan. 1897.)

178. Trace the history of the 3rd Personal Pronoun, singular and plural. (Jan. 1897.)

179. Differentiate the following both as regards usage and origin:—*further*, *farther*; *later*, *latter*; *older*, *elder*; *outer*, *utter*; *foremost*, *first*. (Jan. 1897.)

180. Account clearly for the present and past tense forms of the chief Auxiliary verbs. Explain the modern use of *shall* and *will*. (Jan. 1897.)

181. Classify the Weak verbs, and explain the following forms:—*taught*, *sold*, *sought*, *fed*, *felt*. (Jan. 1897.)

182. Annotate the following statement:—Words, originally other parts of speech, are sometimes used as conjunctions. (Jan. 1897.)

183. Explain the force and origin of the following suffixes:— *-ship*, *-en*, *-ly*, *-ness*, *-y*. Give instances. (Jan. 1897.)

184. Explain carefully what is meant by (i.) Anglo-Saxon; (ii.) Anglo-French; (iii.) Hybrids. (Jan. 1897.)

185. Enumerate the principal Indo-European languages, and indicate, by description or diagram, how English is related to Italian, Sanskrit, Dutch, Erse. (June 1897.)

186. At what periods have Latin words been largely borrowed? Give six examples from living English of words so borrowed at each period, and show what class of the vocabulary was at each period chiefly affected by such borrowing. (June 1897.)

187. Illustrate the borrowing of words either from Celtic or from Scandinavian sources into English. (June 1897.)

188. Give a short account of existing case-forms in English, and also of some which no longer survive as cases. (June 1897.)

189. Explain the italicised letters in the following words:—a*d*vantage, s*c*ent, de*b*t, frontispi*e*ce, cou*l*d, ancien*t*. (June 1897.)

190. What peculiarities, of form or meaning, in the expression of relations of number, are illustrated by the following?—*score*, *triple*, *hundred*, *first*, *second*, *million*. (June 1897.)

191. Trace the origin of *who*, *which*, and *that*, as relative pronouns, and define their usage in modern English. (June 1897.)

192. Distinguish the origin of the suffix *y* in the following words:—*jury*, *body*, *jolly*, *army*, *wordy*, *jelly*. (June 1897.)

193. Explain carefully what is meant by the past-present or strong-weak verbs, giving the reason for each name. (June 1897.)

194. Explain the structure and meaning of the following:—*each*, *every*, *any*, *about*, *either*, *or*. (June 1897.)

195. In what different ways are adverbs formed in English? (June 1897.)

196. Show briefly that the English language is of Teutonic origin, and also that during the last thousand years it has been influenced by certain other Teutonic languages. (Jan. 1898.)

197. How has it happened that we have borrowed so largely from foreign languages instead of building words for ourselves? What home-spun terms might we have had for "astronomy," "arithmetic," "autumn," "agriculture," "library"? (Jan. 1898.)

198. Mention some of our earliest borrowings from the Latin, and prove by a few examples that we have gone on incessantly borrowing from it. (Jan. 1898.)

199. Illustrate the influence of Norman-French on our spelling and our pronunciation. Write down some words that we owe to other Romance languages. (Jan. 1898.)

200. What traces are there in our present grammar of more than one declension of nouns? Discuss the apostrophe in such forms as "stone's," "church's," "St. James'." (Jan. 1898.)

201. Mention some verbs now of the weak conjugation that once were of the strong, and *vice versâ*. Mention also some verbs of mixed conjugation; show that *tell* is not so. About how many strong verbs are there extant? (Jan. 1898.)

202. Mention some verbs that have no change of form in the preterite and in the past participle; also some that are defective; also some that are irregular. (Jan. 1898.)

203. Give some account of the etymology of adverbs. Comment on the forms *rather, piecemeal, too, very, farther.* (Jan. 1898.)

204. Explain the *a* in *aboard, amend, ado, arise, adown, along, alas, apace, aware, avert.* (Jan. 1898.)

205. Derive these words — *lone, street, king, church, engine, month, university, degree, college, matriculation.* (Jan. 1898.)

206. Describe any English dialect with which you are acquainted, and state what you know of its origin. (Jan. 1898.)

I. INDEX OF SUBJECTS.

The references are to pages.

II. INDEX OF SELECTED WORDS AND PHRASES

The references are to pages.

THE END